AMERICAN PHILOSOPHY
TODAY AND TOMORROW

AMERICAN PHILOSOPHY TODAY AND TOMORROW

EDITED BY
HORACE M. KALLEN
AND SIDNEY HOOK

Essay Index Reprint Series

The King's Library

BOOKS FOR LIBRARIES PRESS
FREEPORT, NEW YORK

First Published 1935
Reprinted 1968

LIBRARY OF CONGRESS CATALOG CARD NUMBER:

68-8474

PRINTED IN THE UNITED STATES OF AMERICA

FOREWORD

This book presents the views of twenty-five representative American thinkers on the problems with which the times confront the American as philosopher, and the solutions which Americans must find for tomorrow. The contributors are men living and working in all the diverse areas of the American scene—in Texas, in California, in the Middle West, in New England, in the Atlantic States. Few live where they were born and grew up; many follow vocations for which they were not trained and perhaps did not intend to seek. All but one or two have passed through the formal discipline in philosophy of the schools; they are "doctors of philosophy"; and most of them earn their livings by teaching philosophy or psychology in one or another of the institutions of higher learning of the land. But some have employed their philosophic training in the service of disciplines not strictly philosophic, such as education or economics; others have turned their training to non-pedagogical uses, such as literature, public service, the law, the labor movement, religion, politics, and racial betterment; several have combined academic teaching with these non-academic interests. Thus the volume derives directly not alone from the intrinsic interests of the philosophical discipline as such, but equally direct experience with major preoccupations of the national life also enters into the making of whatever message it conveys.

This message may or may not have been uttered before; but the younger generation of American philosophers who figure most numerously in the pages of this book have not elsewhere made public their philosophic *credos*.[1]

[1] Exigencies of space have compelled the editors to restrict the contributors only to those who have not published philosophic self-portraits before. For an account of the "pre-depression philosophy" of those who

What each author presents here, he presents newly, and he presents it independently, as his personal vision of today's philosophic problem and tomorrow's philosophic solution. Each has written down his own heart and mind, without any meeting with his fellow-contributors, without consultation, without discussion. Thus the book is automatically a representative cross-section of American philosophy in the making; within the limits of its size and scope it provides a true sample of the disposition of *living* philosophy in the United States. These twenty-five essays come from the pens of twenty-five men of twenty-five different temperaments, origins, backgrounds, interests and avocations. They tell in as many personal idioms why and how they come to believe as they do. From reading them there may arise a sense that an identical issue holds the attention of the various philosophers, with their different preoccupations and interests; that in spite of the independence of their essays from one another, they manifest a consensus regarding the principles and methods of settling the issue. Or the reader may come to feel that no common view emerges; he may hear only separate and contradictory voices, each crying alone in its wilderness. Or he may find them separating into little groups and parties and sects, arrayed against one another and irreconcilable. Whichever of these three patterns the reader finds, he may be assured that he has a faithful picture of the struggle of ideas and ideals in American life upon the plane of philosophy.

To give this picture an indispensable point of reference, the editors have suggested that each contributor write a brief account of himself with which to preface his essay. These, the editors believe, will be found not only to frame the picture, but to point it up.

HORACE M. KALLEN
SIDNEY HOOK

may be called the elder statesmen of American philosophy, cf. *Contemporary American Philosophy*, edited by Adams and Montague, 2 vols., New York, 1930.

CONTENTS

PAGE

FOREWORD   v

Aronson, Moses J.
THE HUMANIZATION OF PHILOSOPHY   3

Ayres, Clarence Edwin
THE GOSPEL OF TECHNOLOGY   25

Bates, Ernest Sutherland
TOWARD A SOCIAL PHILOSOPHY   45

Bode, Boyd H.
"THE GREAT AMERICAN DREAM"   65

Cohen, Felix S.
THE SOCIALIZATION OF MORALITY   83

Costello, Harry Todd
A PHILOSOPHER AMONG THE METAPHYSICIANS   101

Durant, Will
AN AMATEUR'S PHILOSOPHY   117

Edman, Irwin
THE NATURALISTIC TEMPER   139

Flewelling, Ralph Tyler
THE NEW TASK OF PHILOSOPHY   155

Holt, Edwin Bissell
THE WHIMSICAL CONDITION OF SOCIAL PSYCHOLOGY, AND OF
    MANKIND   171

Hook, Sidney
EXPERIMENTAL NATURALISM   205

Irving, John Allan
TOWARD RADICAL EMPIRICISM IN ETHICS   229

Kallen, Horace Meyer
PHILOSOPHY TODAY AND TOMORROW   251

vii

viii CONTENTS

PAGE

Koffka, K.
THE ONTOLOGICAL STATUS OF VALUE 275

Locke, Alain
VALUES AND IMPERATIVES 313

Morgan, Arthur E.
AN AMATEUR'S SEARCH FOR SIGNIFICANCE 337

Murphy, Arthur E.
A PROGRAM FOR A PHILOSOPHY 357

Nagel, Ernest
TOWARD A NATURALISTIC CONCEPTION OF LOGIC 377

Overstreet, Harry Allen
THE PLIGHT OF PHILOSOPHY 395

Randall, John Herman, Jr.
HISTORICAL NATURALISM 411

Schneider, Herbert W.
POLITICAL MORALITY 435

Sheldon, Wilmon H.
THE TASK OF PRESENT-DAY METAPHYSICS 449

Smith, T. V.
TRUTH BEYOND IMAGINATION 465

Weiss, Paul
A MEMORANDUM FOR A SYSTEM OF PHILOSOPHY 489

Williams, Michael
A CATHOLIC'S VIEW 501

AMERICAN PHILOSOPHY
TODAY AND TOMORROW

THE HUMANIZATION

OF PHILOSOPHY

MOSES J. ARONSON

MOSES J. ARONSON was born in New York City in 1902, but spent his early youth in California. Entering the University at Berkeley in 1919, he devoted his undergraduate years there, when not engaged in swimming or roaming over the foothills, to a study of philosophy and economics. Upon graduation in 1923, seized by the wanderlust, he went to Europe where he spent some time traveling through Germany and France, but finally settled down at the Sorbonne where he obtained the degree of Docteur de l'Université de Paris, with the distinction of "mention très honorable," in 1927. The following year he was appointed Lecturer at the University of Paris. From 1923 till 1929, during his sojourn in Europe, Dr. Aronson devoted himself mainly to a study of the writings of sociological theorists like Tarde, Durkheim, Simmel, Oppenheimer, Pareto, Lévy-Bruhl, Bouglé, Fauconnet, Davy, Duguit. While not a disciple of Durkheim, he has been deeply influenced nevertheless by the French sociological current of thought especially through attending the courses given in Paris by Lévy-Bruhl, Bouglé, Fauconnet, Mauss. Dr. Aronson is the author of a book entitled: La Philosophie Morale de Josiah Royce; Essai sur l'idéalisme social aux Etats-Unis, as well as of essays and book reviews in the field of social philosophy. He is Managing Editor of the Journal of Social Philosophy, and is now engaged in the writing of a history of Social Theories in Contemporary France. Formerly an Instructor in Sociology at Syracuse University, he has been connected since 1930 with the Department of Philosophy at the College of the City of New York.

THE HUMANIZATION OF PHILOSOPHY

Moses J. Aronson

Humanism and the climate of opinion. Every historical epoch has its own distinctive climate of opinion, its own *Zeitgeist* which seems to differentiate it from all other periods. The Middle Ages, for example, are commonly recognized to have been supernaturalistic in temper, morbidly preoccupied with the quest for otherworldly salvation. This medieval nostalgia for the supermundane colors the whole life of the period, and expresses itself most consciously in the philosophy of the times. It is not surprising that St. Thomas Aquinas should reflect, in his writings, the dominant passions and the regnant opinions of medieval Christendom. In fact many scholars have insisted that apart from its cultural milieu no philosophy can adequately be understood. Philosophy, it is claimed, is itself a cultural product which mirrors the tendencies, the interests, the values, the beliefs, and the ideals of a given civilization at a given time. It is significant that so traditional a thinker as Josiah Royce could subscribe to this viewpoint by saying that "as man is social, as no man lives alone, as your temperament is simply the sum total of your social 'reflex actions,' is just your typical bearing towards your fellows, the great philosopher, in reflecting on his own deepest instincts and faiths, inevitably describes in terms of his system the characteristic attitude of his age and people."

Applying this theory of "cultural determinism" as a working hypothesis to our own contemporary American civilization, we may be justified in affirming that the trend is toward a more and more self-conscious form of humanism in the realm of opinions and ideals. The history of America since the turn of the century supplies abundant evidence in support of this conjecture, that the prevailing climate of opinion is decidedly | humanistic. The past three decades have witnessed the progressive humanization of field after field of intellectual and practical enterprise. Even religion, that stronghold of supernaturalism, is yielding more and more to the spirit of the times by humanizing its doctrines and dogmas so as to make them acceptable to the children of the twentieth century. The contrast between the indifference with which Guyau's *Non-Religion of the Future* was received by the public of the end of the nineteenth century, and the popular enthusiasm which made such similar works as Potter's *Story of Religion* a best seller in the third decade of the twentieth century eloquently points to the way in which the wind is blowing. And economics, that dismal science, is also unmistakably evolving in the same general direction of an ever-increasing emphasis upon the humanistic significance of its researches. The general tendency among economists today is to substitute for the abstract and cruel fiction of an *homo oeconomicus* the more concrete notion of a human personality in quest for biological and psychological satisfactions. The center of gravity in economic theory is being shifted from problems of production to those of distribution and consumption. The profit-motive is being assailed on all sides, and "socialism," the doctrine which believes in the humanization of industry—heresy that it was barely a generation ago,—is now rapidly taking on the form of a new and universal orthodoxy.

From religion to economics, from the sublimest spiritual to the crassest material, all along the line the same general tendency toward humanization seems to be discernible. If any single pervasive characteristic may be attributed to the twentieth century, it would seem that that outstanding trait is its humanism, its recognition of the supreme importance of human values, its tendency to subordinate all else to the gratification of human needs, desires, and ideals. Just as supernaturalism characterized the Middle Ages, so humanism distinguishes the times current.

It was no mere accident, in the light of our culturalistic hypothesis, that various pragmatic philosophies should emerge simultaneously at the beginning of the present century, and continue to flourish with deepening influence as the decades roll by. For the very corner-stone of this type of philosophy is the doctrine that all knowledge is significant, in the final analysis, only to the extent that it enables mankind to control its environment and its own destiny according to the dictates of human values. F. C. S. Schiller, in my estimation, caught the full constructive implication of all Pragmatism when he christened his own private doctrine with the name of Humanism. He thereby seemed to admit that the originality of Pragmatism lay not so much in its emphasis upon the need for applicable ideas —a sufficiently important contention, to be sure—as in its novel and frankly humanistic *Weltanschauung*. Pragmatism is, of course, an instrumentalism, but it is a humanistic instrumentalism.

Instrumentalism or activism taken by itself would not suffice, after all, to differentiate the spirit of one epoch from that of another. For the solitary Yogi contemplating his navel, or the monk telling his beads, or the fisherman praying to his Madonna, differs in no essential way so far as the desire for efficient control is concerned, from the politician buying votes, or the revolutionary hoarding machine guns, or the physician injecting a serum. What seems to many of us as mere passive contemplation is looked upon by the contemplator as the most efficacious instrument for the attainment of his salvation. For one who craves the experience of enjoying a symphony, it would be just as unpragmatic to go to a golf-course as it would be for a golfer to attend a concert. Pragmatism's greatest contribution does not consist' merely in the significant reminder that one cannot attain certain ends by ignoring the proper means thereto, since even the drum-beating shaman, the star-gazing astrologer, the swooning mystic, the Jew-baiting Nazi, the scholar-exterminating Sovietist, would unhesitatingly retort that he was using the instruments most likely to enable him to attain the desiderated goal. If the modern man rejects as inefficacious the methods employed by preceding generations, the reason for that rejection, it seems to me, resides in the difference of the ends or values which constrain his behavior. Pragmatism is a humanistic instrumentalism.

What differentiates one civilization from another, one era from another, is its scale of values, its scheme of salvation. The twentieth century, we have reason to believe, is distinguished by its humanistic way of life. And if Pragmatism, in one form or another, has succeeded in permeating, consciously or unconsciously, all branches of contemporary philosophy, the reason for that universal, albeit perhaps silent, infiltration can only be that Pragmatism renders articulate the spontaneous yearnings, interests and ideals characteristic of the present age. Herein resides, as F. C. S. Schiller recognized, the deeper meaning of pragmatic philosophy, and the secret of its increasing vogue. When one considers that even Josiah Royce pronounced himself to be an "absolute pragmatist," and that Bertrand Russell has for the past two decades been devoting himself almost entirely to reflection upon problems of human welfare, it will perhaps not sound too rash to affirm that "we are all Pragmatists now." Historically envisaged, Pragmatism is seen to constitute the self-conscious ideology of contemporary civilization, the philosophic rationalization of the humanistic *Zeitgeist*. In the philosophy of Pragmatism, the twentieth century is beginning to come of age.

Humanism and the social sciences. Philosophy has been defined, in no disparaging sense, as the systematic rationalization of a given cultural epoch. From a historical point of view philosophy is perceived to be the expression of a specific civilization becoming self-conscious of itself as just that kind of a civilization. If Pragmatism or philosophic Humanism has dominated the thought of the last three decades, it is because the last three decades were characterized, in all regions, by a prevailingly humanistic climate of opinion.

The culturalistic hypothesis, however, is not the only one available to explain the triumphant development of philosophic Humanism. The same problem may be approached, not so much from the broad perspective of general social evolution, as from the more specific angle of scientific development. This line of attack, of course, is reminiscent of August Comte's suggestive Law of the Three Stages. Philosophy, according to this hypothesis, is found to reflect the state of the sciences. In primitive times, before the emergence of even rudimentary sciences, philosophy perforce had to be animistic, mythological, and theological. Philosophy, if we may call it such, then rationalized the prevailing climate of opinion with the help of the only tools at its disposal, namely, emotion, poetic imagination, and pure logic which, after all, is a variant of the poetic imagination.

As the sciences, beginning with mathematics, began to develop, philosophy, in turn, commenced to undergo a similar modification. It is no accident, from this point of view, that the Platonic theory is a mixture of poetry and mathematics. What else, given the times, could it possibly have been? Nor is Democritus in a category different from Plato. Both were united, in their divergencies, by the common mathematical spirit of the period. In their very differences they both paid homage to an identical source of inspiration, just as in our own days Idealists and Naturalists, in their sharpest discrepancies, equally testify to the hegemony of the physical sciences.

Philosophy had to wait for the development of the physical sciences before it could elaborate a genuinely naturalistic worldview. And in proportion as the sciences of nature extended their scope, philosophy received the impress of their growing prestige. Spinozism is as inconceivable before the seventeenth century as Platonism among the Hottentots. And the same reasoning serves to explain why Naturalism did not attain its full stature of philosophic maturity till well beyond the middle of the nineteenth century. That biology might attain its majority, and thereby close the circle of the physical sciences required the work of Darwin. Herbert Spencer and Bergson who, in my opinion, supplement one another and mark the culmination of the naturalistic tradition, could not possibly formulate their vast syntheses before the final incorporation of biology within the network of the physical sciences. By the end of the nineteenth century, however, Naturalism, rooted in the physical sciences, was in a position to attain its philosophic apogee.

Meanwhile, toward the end of last century, as the sciences of nature were maturing, and serving as the foundation for a naturalistic philosophy, a new set of sciences devoted to an empirical study of human phenomena were first beginning to be born. Psychology, ethnography, anthropology, linguistics, anthropo-geography, sociology, all these had their feeble beginnings during the latter part of the nineteenth century, rearing their inchoate forms in the shadow of the already full-grown sciences of physical nature. And just as Naturalism depended for its existence upon the physical sciences, so the philosophy of Humanism could not receive explicit statement till these social or human sciences had sufficiently developed. This development, as we know, dates from the last quarter of the nineteenth century, and the sciences have grown with increasing vigor into the twentieth century up to our own days. Pragmatism, or Humanism, as I prefer to call it, found voice in the twentieth century because only then, thanks to the growth of the social disciplines, did the scientific foundation first become available to serve as the necessary substructure for a humanistic philosophy.

Our two hypotheses, the culturalistic and the "scientific," appear to dovetail, and conspire to uphold the belief that Humanism is the philosophic expression of contemporary civilization. The culturalistic hypothesis led us to expect that if the present age were characterized by a humanistic climate of opinion, then its philosophy should reflect the dominant spirit of the epoch.

That such is actually the case has been verified by discerning in Pragmatism the philosophic rationalization of the humanistic temper. The "scientific" hypothesis, on the other hand, anticipated that if Humanism is indeed the proper philosophy of the twentieth century, then there must be something in the state of the sciences to render necessary that connection. This indeed was found to be the case when, in tracing the evolution of the sciences, it became apparent that the social sciences, foundation of Humanism, were uniquely characteristic of the contemporary period.

It is perhaps not too bold to believe that the truth has probably been struck when two hypotheses converge and mutually support each other in defense of the contention that Humanism is the philosophy which most adequately expresses the needs and the aspirations of contemporary civilization.

The sociological revision of philosophy. The advent of the social sciences together with the occurrence of certain profound changes in the general pattern of contemporary life seem to have caused some far-reaching disturbances within the domain of traditional philosophy, and to have rendered imperative its reconstruction along humanistic lines. Such disturbances, although disagreeable to those whose established way of thinking is challenged, should not be surprising, however, when it is considered that neither social phenomena escape the general flux and that changes in the sciences have always been accompanied by concomitant modifications in the realm of philosophy. One cannot help recalling, in this connection, the potent effect which the publication of Darwin's *Origin of Species* had upon the whole course of subsequent philosophy. Because of it, the preceding doctrines had to be reformulated in terms of dynamism, growth, adaptation, perfectibility. The social sciences, it seems to me, have already begun to determine, and are bound to continue a revision of philosophy from the humanistic point of view analogous to the reorganization which the biological sciences brought in their wake. And just as no single aspect of the classic philosophy escaped the influence of biology, so, it may be ventured to suppose, all branches of the older philosophy will be deeply affected by what may be called the sociological revolution in philosophy whose faint rumblings are already to be heard in the various doctrines of Pragmatism. Before Humanism can become the full-fledged and authoritative philosophic expression which contemporary civilization demands of it, cosmology, epistemology, ethics, esthetics—all these branches of philosophy—need to be reformulated in the light of the social sciences, and purged of their extraneous naturalistic as well as supernaturalistic ingredients.

The remainder of this paper will be devoted to an attempt to set forth tentatively, and in outline, the general contours of what, in the eyes of one contemporary, at least, would constitute a thoroughgoing system of Humanism.

The humanization of cosmology. Few students of philosophy probably ever forget the feelings of mingled rage and despair which marked their first encounter with the theories of Berkeley. Such reactions are psychologically intelligible, for nothing seems to fly in the face of common sense more absurdly than a doctrine which undertakes to question the reality of the external world. It is almost instinctively self-evident that somehow the subject of thought, the human individual, is surrounded by an objectively existing universe whose caprices, and habits, and meaning are recorded, with greater or less precision, in the different systems of cosmology or metaphysics. For what else is cosmology if not that branch of philosophy whose function it is to explain the nature of the universe as it exists in reality? A reconciliation with Berkeley's subjectivism is usually achieved when it is finally recognized that, after all, the good bishop was merely leading up to the doctrine that the universe did really exist as we experienced it, but only as a spiritual entity in the mind of God.

Naturalistic cosmologies as well as Idealistic metaphysics share in common the view which consists in envisaging the universe as an objective, material or spiritual, reality. Doctrines of transcendentalism differ not at all from theories of immanence so far as concerns the fundamental belief that somehow the external world of nature is an entity, *sui generis* or dependent upon a greater Power, friendly or alien to man, whose objective characteristics are definable in spiritual or material but, at any rate, non-human terms. And to this extent Plato and Hegel agree with Spencer and Russell in appealing to the common sense of the race.

To be sure, many take their stand on Kant's *Critique of Pure Reason*. No one can tell how far in the direction of Humanism his line of thought would have led had he not suffered a failure of nerve causing him partially to neutralize the first by his second *Critique*. But even Kant, at his boldest, never seemed to doubt that the world of nature was free from human ingredients. Cosmology, at least, would seem to defy humanization.

Contrary, however, to the cumulative philosophic tradition which, in this respect, upholds the popular conviction, the vast amount of data garnered in recent years by ethnographers and sociologists permit one to hazard a culturalistic theory of nature, and thereby to incorporate cosmology within a systematic philosophy of civilization. Writers such as Durkheim, Francis Cornford, Lévy-Bruhl, Jane Harrison, Masson-Oursel, and Znaniecki have from various angles attempted to draw the implications of sociology for cosmology, and have arrived at an hypothesis which challenges the common-sense attitude toward the external world. Their discussions, based on observations in the field, seem to bring out clearly that the various cosmologies with which we are familiar really constitute so many ways in which diverse cultures envisage the universe in terms of their own traditions and values. According to these scholars, therefore, cosmologies reflect, not so much the postulated objective external world, as the scale of values and the pattern of life which characterize the cultures wherein they are formulated.

This sociomorphic hypothesis appears so bold, if not rash,

that it would require a more adequate elaboration than this short essay permits. But several reasons may here be indicated for believing that the external world of nature can only be understood, not in isolation, but rather as a part of its contemporary culture. Hardly anyone will refuse to grant that by the time even the most primitive people began to speculate about the universe, humanity had already existed for countless ages. Now these long periods which preceded the origin of cosmic speculations were spent by mankind in transforming the primeval environment to meet its own needs. Consequently by the time the Unknown First Philosopher began to formulate his cosmology, it would not be exaggerating to say that nature everywhere already bore the impress of human values, and that it was already then too late to discover what primeval, non-humanized nature really was. It is reasonable to believe that even at the dawn of history it was already futile to speculate as to the state of nature apart from the civilization whose thoroughly transformed environment it constituted. A corollary of this would be that every civilization has its own "nature" which, technically speaking, is not the same for any other civilization. According to this viewpoint, traditional Naturalism seems to be somewhat optimistic when it believes itself in possession of a knowledge of nature which applies to all times and to all places; for this knowledge is of civilization all compact, and consequently undergoes the vicissitudes of social evolution.

That nature everywhere bears the mark of civilization to such an extent that it is no longer possible to dissociate one from the other is an assertion which may be challenged by pointing to the stars. The nature of the celestial bodies, it may be claimed, has not been transformed by man; such as they were at the time of Adam they are now. How indeed, it may be asked, can the evolution of culture have any bearing on astronomy? The answer is that, paradoxical though it may seem to common sense, astronomy, like mathematics and the other sciences, is no exception to the general rule of social determinism.

A vast amount of anthropological and sociological evidence has accumulated to support the opinion that the sciences are essentially similar to the industrial arts, having their origins in given civilizations whose needs and values they articulate. It is no longer possible to ignore the practical and social roots of sciences even so apparently abstract as mathematics and astronomy. In the demarcation of land, in the classification of objects, in the notions of property, in the rhythm of religious ceremonies and rituals, in the navigation over desert and sea, these sciences find their historical explanation. They grew, to be sure, with the centuries, but in all their successive modifications and differentiations, each in turn socially determined, they perforce continued to retain the deposit of the cultural traits in which they began. Differentiation means change but not utter discontinuity; growth involves the development of germs which themselves are never completely eradicated. Of course the astronomy of today differs vastly from the astronomy of the ancient Chaldeans, but the difference resides in the traditions and customs which, willy-nilly, color the astronomer's thinking and define the goal as well as the method of his researches. Consequently, while we cannot know with certainty whether the stars have changed or not, since in order to know that we must be in a position to compare our own observations with those of now extinct civilizations, we are, however, in a position to feel quite confident that our present science of astronomy is deeply tinged with concepts whose explanation lies much more in the tradition of science, which is a cultural tradition, than in the actual objective state of the stars.

Those portions of the universe which apparently have not been humanized by actual transformation still fall within the orbit of culture through the very nature of science which itself is shot through with social categories, with values of ends and means whose origin and function are purely human.

The humanization of epistemology. The suggestion that science is permeated with cultural influences brings up certain familiar problems of epistemology concerning the origin of knowledge and the criterion of truth. The rationalistic theories which maintain that knowledge is generated within the mind of the individual are seen to develop finally into doctrines of intuitionism. Spinoza and Hegel agree with Plato, after all, in making of knowledge a miraculous flash of insight. Miracles are explanations, however, which we may be willing to accept in the last extremity, but if something more empirical can be offered we should much prefer it.

Naturalistic epistemologies attempt to show how knowledge originates in a purely empirical fashion. Mind is no miracle, according to this view, but rather the consequence of a long series of bodily adjustments to the environment. Many Naturalists do not look upon it even as a special organ of knowledge, inclining to consider it, with H. G. Wells, as "essentially a food-seeking system, and no more essentially a truth-finding apparatus than the snout of a pig." In a word, according to the naturalistic explanation, knowledge is to be understood in biological terms as one of the products of the struggle for existence which endows upon the human being a survival-value.

From the humanistic or culturalistic point of view, this naturalistic theory, although obviously more tenable than intuitionism, nevertheless seems to stand in need of supplementation. Without in the least denying that man is undoubtedly a biological creature, the humanistic doctrine would maintain, however, that human knowledge requires for its fruition a cultural superstructure in addition to a biological foundation. Human beings are everywhere born into civilizations which already possess traditions and opinions, in a word, knowledge. This knowledge is cumulative, as we know, and transmitted by education from generation to generation. Consequently, it may be affirmed, the human individual, in the knowing process, does not enter directly into contact with primeval nature, but finds always interposed between him and the universe a veil of culture which can never completely be withdrawn. Considerations of this kind must have been uppermost in the mind of the ethnologist Bastian when he wrote: *"Ich denke nicht, sondern es denkt in mir."* As an anthropologist he was particularly impressed by the fact, which seems to be the consensus of opinion among social scientists, that self-consciousness is a cultural phenomenon, a product specifically of imitation, conflict, and education.

It is certainly not denied that the individual as an organism does undergo direct experiences with its environment; it is recalled merely that, in the first place, these experiences, through customs, habits, and education, are already strongly tinctured by social conditioning, and secondly, these biologic experiences taken in themselves can hardly be said to constitute genuine knowledge till they are incorporated into the whole body of previously existing traditions and opinions which the pattern of culture supplies. The difference between the infant's empty stare at an electric bulb, for example, and the mature person's comprehension of the same object would seem to reside, from the culturalistic viewpoint, not so much in the biologic development which separates the child from the adult, as in the richer system of socially acquired habits and opinions which differentiate maturity from infancy. Knowledge in the sense of specifically human understanding seems to have its origin within the cultural milieu.

It is to be surmised that a doctrine committed to the social origin of knowledge will also attempt to uphold the view that the distinction between truth and error is rooted in a cultural criterion. The traditional standard of systematic coherence cannot, of course, be accepted by a humanistic epistemology because it involves, to begin with, an absolutism which flatly contradicts the fundamental cultural relativism disclosed by the social sciences. Furthermore, coherence is itself a value dependent upon the civilization which honors it. From the humanistic point of view, science is not true because coherent; rather it is coherent because the culture which includes the scientific ideal within its pattern of organization, for reasons which the sociologists try to discover, happens to believe in the beauty or value of logical consistency. There have been civilizations, as Lévy-Bruhl attempts to show empirically, where the value of formal consistency which most of us so highly prize was appreciated by the aborigines even less than a formal tail-coat.

The doctrine which places the criterion of truth in empirical correspondence enjoys the advantage of appealing to common sense as well as to science. From the culturalistic point of view, however, it stands in need of modification and completion. Scientific verification, as Royce in his final work demonstrated, is not a purely individual enterprise, but a highly integrated co-operative social process involving the existence of a "community of interpretation." The criterion of scientific truth, it would seem to follow, is not correspondence so much as the consensus of qualified opinion which reflects, while reacting upon, the more public, social opinion of which it is the refined and self-conscious expression. The formula that ideas become true would be interpreted from the culturalistic standpoint to mean that ideas become truer and truer to the degree that they infiltrate more and more deeply into the public consciousness. No idea, in the final analysis, may be called a truth till it is accepted as such by any given civilization, and biding that eventuality ideas can only be said to struggle with fluctuating success for status in the realm of opinion. The history of civilization chronicles the vicissitudes of this battle of opinions in tracing the genesis, the development, the decline, and often the resurrection, of ideas. The ultimate criterion of truth seems to be the seal of acceptance which any culture places upon the hypotheses which offer themselves to it for selection. And to set up the contingent standards of one's own special civilization or group as the universal arbiter of all truth for all time would strike the culturalistic Humanist as nothing less than a case of flagrant epistemological imperialism.

The humanization of ethics. It would be natural to expect ethics to constitute the most humanized branch of philosophy, since it concerns itself primarily with the problem of human conduct. Strangely enough, the moral doctrines of the classical tradition which are still taught in many of our schools are intimately bound up with supernaturalistic metaphysics and otherworldly presuppositions. Even Plato, as we know, found some way of, so to speak, locating his earthly Republic in celestial regions; and Hegel, it is common knowledge, felt no compunctions in demonstrating that the Prussian way of life was an earthly adumbration of the Absolute's transcendental routine.

The quest for absolute and immutable principles of the Highest Good would seem, from the humanistic standpoint, to render futile the classic ethical doctrines. The *summum bonum*, practically envisaged, perforce remains irrelevant to moral behavior as humanly experienced. It constitutes, rather, a compensatory flight from the conflicts of actual life whose exigencies define the specific problems of morality. The great compilations of Hobhouse, of Westermarck, and of Briffault fail to reveal the existence, in reality, of a Highest Good, but disclose rather a panorama of shifting ideals and values as turbulent as the passions, as capricious as the desires which motivate human behavior. And as for the so-called ethical conscience, it is by now quite universally recognized that conscience, far from being the origin and seat of moral insight, is itself rather the conditioned product and expression of the prevailing cultural milieu. There are as many different types of ethical conscience as there are different kinds of civilizations.

The naturalistic or evolutionary doctrines of ethics, contrary to those of the classic tradition, cannot be accused of irrelevance, since they are frankly based on a study of human nature as it presents itself empirically. Moral codes, from this point of view, are looked upon as the expression of accumulated wisdom in the art of successful living which involves adequate adjustment to the environment. Ethical ideals are defined consequently as "the expedient in the way of our behaving," and are judged in terms of their survival-value.

Without in any sense derogating the significance of the naturalistic attempt to construct an ethics based upon the recognition that man is a biological organism rather than a pure spirit, the Humanist would be inclined to think, however, that the biological categories are not sufficient to explain the ethical aspect of human behavior. Here again it would be recalled that in the realm of moral values even less perhaps than in the field of knowledge, the human individual never enters directly into contact with primeval nature. Human conduct, it would appear, is much more a purely social relationship between man and man on the cultural level, than a commerce between an organism and its non-human environment. While it may be difficult to conceive of any moral values which would be deliberately anti-biological since, to destroy life is also to destroy morality, it does not follow that biological categories are sufficient to draw out the entire meaning of human values. Even the forms of courtship, for example, and of marital decorum, while obviously not opposed to the survival of the species, would seem to involve certain biologically irrelevant elements whose explanation would appear to reside mainly in the "superorganic" level of culture. When Aldous Huxley, who is a Naturalist, speaks of love as the "sweating of palm against palm," he is really calling attention not so much to a biological as to a sociological phenomenon, for it is significant to suppose that had he been the product of another civilization whose records are extant, he would have defined love then as the sweating of "nose against nose." It is no foregone conclusion, from a purely biological point of view, that the palm is endowed with greater survival-value than the nose; nor would it require excessive sophistication to imagine other more expedient ways of perpetuating the race.

The mores, the folkways, the traditions and customs, the whole network of values which together fashion the cultural pattern of a given civilization, from the humanistic viewpoint, constitute the specific foundation upon which to rear the superstructure of ethics. And a moral philosophy, based upon cultural-istic premises, would seek to disengage and render self-con-scious, within any given civilization, the ideals of conduct which are there striving toward explicit articulation and public acknowl-edgment. In the eyes of the Humanist, too, philosophy is a midwife whose function it is to ease the birth-pangs of a civili-zation in travail with new opinions and ideals.

The humanization of esthetics. Esthetics, judging by its neglect, gives the impression of being the black sheep of the philosophic household. The reason for this relative failure on the part of philosophers to reflect upon the artistic activities of man may be found to reside, perhaps, in the influence of the Christian tradition which looked rather scornfully upon the quest for beauty as a frivolous and pagan diversion from the more important matters of otherworldly salvation. It is not surprising, therefore, that in the great metaphysical systems which, after all, rationalized the Christian tradition, esthetics was treated as an abstract problem in the locus of value in general rather than as a specific philosophy of art. Beauty was treated as a transcendental, eternal and immutable concept which, in the final analysis, could only be apprehended by an act of intuition. But intuition, as was already pointed out, is incapable of explaining any problems, since it really amounts to an appeal to the miraculous. But the miraculous is no help in explanation. A more serviceable substitute, in the eyes of many, is the genetic biological hypothesis.

The naturalistic interpretation of art bases its reasoning on data drawn from biology and psychology, and attempts to ex-plain beauty in functional terms. The artistic creations of man-kind, from this point of view, are considered to be the spon-taneous expression of man as a purely natural organism. Dar-win's theory of sexual selection, for example, is based on data which led him to believe that beauty in the design and color-ing of feather and fur, in the pitch and melody of the voice, in the form and structure of the body, has its natural origin in the biological needs of the race. The play instinct, too, as Karl Groos pointed out, is a spontaneous expression of healthy animals, and lies at the root of what ultimately develops into art. In a word, from the naturalistic standpoint, art is envisaged as the product of the spontaneous self-expression of man as an organic being. Because human beings are the affective, emotional, organic creatures they happen to be, endowed in their very physiological natures with certain proclivities toward rhythm and harmony, they project these tendencies into the external world, and the result is what we call art. Such appears to be the essence of the naturalistic theory of beauty.

From the culturalistic perspective, however, it would seem impossible satisfactorily to explain in purely biological terms the specifically human characteristics of art. That art, like all other human enterprises, depends to some extent on certain biological conditions will certainly not be denied by anyone who recognizes man as a natural organism. But the Humanist is impressed by the thought that if man is indeed an animal, he is no longer the same animal he was at the origin of his species; man today is a biological animal who has been transformed under the accumulating influences of perhaps hundreds of thousands of years of his own culture into a new kind of creature. And this transforming influence may be ignored only at the cost of dealing with a biological-fiction rather than with a cultural-man. To establish a connection between the abstracted biological nature of man and the production of art is, in the Humanist's estimation, to overlook that very element in art which renders it specifically artistic; and that element is culture, the specifically human medium, the proper habitat of that neo-organic variant called Man.

Art, from the humanistic point of view, can be understood only as a function of civilization. Standards of beauty vary with different cultures and reflect the dominant needs and ideals of those cultures. Horace M. Kallen formulates the humanistic doctrine of esthetics when he affirms that "greatness, whether in painting or in music or in architecture, is a reflection of a public interest, not the projection of a private power. It consists of uttering the inward feeling or outward achievement—or failure—of a time or a civilization in moving and unmistakable symbols, symbols that reveal its own meaning to a people's heart; symbols that by expressing, clarify its purposes and define its ideals."

In esthetics, as in epistemology and ethics, the culturalistic Humanist is committed to the belief that values are socially determined, that they are relative to any given civilization at a specific time, that their function is to enhance man's life in ways which extend beyond the purely biological and that the business of philosophy is to contribute toward an understanding of these values which differentiate man from the other animals; to distinguish between values which are living and those which are already dead so as to arouse in mankind a reflexive consciousness of its deepest needs and highest aspirations and thus help it to achieve increasing control over its own destiny.

THE GOSPEL
OF TECHNOLOGY

CLARENCE EDWIN AYRES

CLARENCE EDWIN AYRES was born and reared in Massachusetts. As an undergraduate at Brown University he was attracted into philosophy and persuaded into economics by Alexander Meiklejohn, and these two interests have been combined, or rather merged, in his studies, teaching, and writing ever since. They served as major and minor for an M.A. at Brown in 1914 and a Ph.D. at Chicago in 1917. A year's instructorship in philosophy and social science at Meiklejohn's Amherst in 1915-16 brought him under the spell of Institutional Economics in the person of Walton Hamilton, and Chicago found him a ready convert to Instrumentalism. Ever since this time his vocabulary has consisted largely of the jargons of Veblen and Dewey. After three years of teaching at Chicago, he resigned to return to Amherst, where he remained until the fall of the Meiklejohn administration. Rebounding from one educational experiment to another he taught social philosophy at Reed College, but resigned at the end of a year when the death of President Scholz brought the college a reversal of policy. After an eighteen months' apprenticeship as a scribe on the staff of the New Republic he retired to the wilderness and produced the two books on which he makes retrospective comment in this article. During this time he spent one winter at the Wisconsin Experimental College. He returned to the academic fold in 1930 as a rather philosophic economist, first at Washington Square College of New York University and since then at the University of Texas. He is also the author of a biography of Thomas Huxley.

THE GOSPEL OF TECHNOLOGY

Clarence Edwin Ayres

Every student of the social sciences as he approaches the definition of his problem must encounter certain inevitable limitations. He is, in a sense, both physician and patient. To the question: "What is man that thou art mindful of him?" there is only one answer: "I am a man." In some degree this is true of all scientists. The astronomer who studies the larger phenomena of space and time, light and heat, is himself a creature of space and time, light and heat. Physicists are composed of electrons and chemists of molecules, and biologists are notoriously organic. Each of us is engaged in studying himself in some sense or other. But this is peculiarly true of students of the social sciences. Neither stars nor electrons, so far as we know, care what we think of them. They are not engaged in a conspiracy to shape our thoughts, whereas civilization is. In a sense civilization is thought and vice versa, and therefore the primary concern of social scientists, as distinct from physical scientists, is to detach themselves somehow from themselves.

This is not easy. Indeed we are only beginning to appreciate how difficult it is. To detach oneself from the taboos and sanctities of a foreign culture is easy enough. People have always done that, and quite recently with our facilities for travel and investigation we have done it on a tremendous scale. The mass of information we have accumulated about the "barbarians" of other climes and ages exceeds on a tremendous scale all similar researches by the amateur Plinys and Herodotuses of earlier times. This has presented us with a problem far exceeding theirs. In the face of all this comparative data can we continue to regard our civilization quite simply as "better" and "truer" and "higher" than all the rest? Can we even continue to cherish a conception of civilization which allows such questions to be asked? Hitherto we have continued in the main to do so. To be sure we have lost most of the dogmatism that was natural to Pliny and Herodotus. We are not as sure as they were of the unchallengeable superiority of our culture. How can we be, in view of the completeness of our knowledge of what other people think of us? But we still persist in regarding this as a temporary set-back, a momentary loss of confidence, from which we will emerge more dogmatic than ever and prepared to give the world an example at long last of a truly superior culture.

In my opinion this is an illusion. If we were not ourselves encumbered with the harness of our own civilization, we should see that the conception of civilization in terms of which all such judgments must be made is itself prejudiced and false. It is, indeed, the ultimate chauvinism. The point at which civilization imposes upon us still, as it has always done, the "idols of the tribe" is in the belief that somewhere—in the womb of the future, perhaps—there are idols which are real, and somehow, by research if not by prayer, we shall see them plain and make them ours. It is my settled conviction that this belief is fatuous and superstitious. In the sense in which beliefs and standards differ from one culture to another there is no such thing as "true" culture. Civilization itself, in that sense, is idolatrous and false. We believe in it—we accept it at its own valuation as the most precious thing in life—only because it imposes its valuation upon us now, as it has always done. Such, I think, is the plain evidence of our research, and such, therefore, is the issue which every student of the social sciences is obliged to face. Shall he credit the research—that is to say, science—or shall he adopt as his major premise the idol of the tribe?

This aspect of civilization I shall call "institutional." The word is admirably suited to such use. Its derivation and its various connotations all suggest the arbitrary, the artificial, the fiat of social usage. But I should like to suggest further that what is so regulated is human relationships: the scheme of subordination and authority which in its parts we commonly call "institutions." I refrain intentionally from using such a word as "tradition" because there are traditions of another sort. The arts and crafts exist and grow by virtue of traditions of a sort, but their lore is of a different character altogether. It came into being by discovery or invention, by cumulative dexterity, rather than by institution. Its function is to direct the hand, not to bow the neck. I should call this aspect of civilization "technology," and I regard it as the source of all progress and the focus of all that is valid and valuable in civilization.

This view of the matter seems to me implicit in the whole tremendous movement of modern civilization. In that movement, obviously, technological factors have been paramount. From this fact alone, I think, the influence of science on the modern mind derives. My own ideas have been chiefly formed, so far as I can judge, by reflection upon the work of John Dewey and Thorstein Veblen; but the importance of such men derives not from personal authority nor even from any notable originality, but rather from the clarity with which they have served as mouthpieces for the culture they express. What they have voiced is important, it seems to me, because it is obvious and mandatory. Thus I regard Dewey's "instrumental" philosophy and the "institutional" economics which derives from Veblen (though he did not christen it) as almost identical expressions of an almost inevitable trend: the trend of technology and science. Neither Dewey's philosophy nor Veblen's economics was derived by the usual process of textual modification and correction from the prevailing traditions of the pundits in these fields. Both men were more profoundly influenced by the repercussions of organic evolution than by any "established doctrine" of philosophy or economics. This is not only obvious to the modern student of their works; both men said so, clearly and repeatedly. I regard this circumstance as one of the most profound significance. What it means is that both considered that they were developing not the "logical" deductions of received doctrine, but the technological implications of current scientific discovery. For both the essential problem was to view human activity, thought, and even civilization as the performances of a strangely ingenious species of super-ape. Their philosophy begins by assuming that man is an animal possessing no faculty, mental, spiritual, or otherwise, not fully conditioned by his organic structure and therefore shared to some degree by other animals.

If it be objected that this is not a philosophy at all, since it provides no answer to the question: "What is the meaning of life?" I assent instantly and fully. I regard the question as nonsense and all possible answers to it as nonsense too—often pernicious nonsense—and if philosophy wishes to assert its claim to a monopoly of all such nonsense, I should not dispute the claim but simply find another word to designate a body of ideas. "Life" has no intelligible "meaning" for men which is not equally applicable to other animals. If simply to be alive spells success for them, I am prepared to accept the same standard. It is the only standard by which organic activities can be measured. I should say that the sole measure of the success of a society is the number of men alive in that society with no reservation but that of good sense or sincerity. If some one objects that China supports more life than the United States, I am not disturbed. In one sense this does actually indicate one very real superiority of Chinese civilization over our own: *viz.*, its age. If, after an equal lapse of time, this continent were still largely uninhabited, I should be disposed to regard that as clear evidence of the superiority of Chinese civilization. In the meantime, however, I should ask my interlocutor to bear in mind that the population of this continent has reached its present saturation more rapidly than any equivalent development in Asiatic history and promises to go very much farther. Therefore I consider that we have some ground for supposing that industrial society, as it has developed hitherto, is the most successful expedient known to history.

This is, of course, a "biological standard." I have heard economists urge it against Veblen as a criticism that he has none but a biological standard of value, as though this were a dreadful defect. If it is, I am prepared to throw in my lot with the biologists and the other scientists who are subject to similar defects and abandon economics, along with philosophy, to the shamans and medicine men for whom facts are not enough. What disturbs many people when the biological theme is sounded is the sincere conviction under which they labor that the application of biological standards to man necessarily means confining man's activities to those of the pig or dog—"mere eating and drinking," and so forth. Of course it means nothing of the sort. Not even the activities of pigs are confined to eating and drinking. Such a notion is a gross libel on the pig and an even grosser one on man. Human activity is not limited to breathing because breathing is an essential human activity. Neither China nor the United States is reduced to mere "animality" by the mention of the number of live organisms residing in each country.

But, the issue may be put, do people carry on all the manifold cultural activities of a great civilization merely that a hundred million bodies may organically function, or do these organisms function to some higher end—the ends, that is, of civilization? Obviously this is a philosophic question in the "higher" sense: that is, nonsense. To what "end" men live and civilization exists, I do not know or care. I must confess that it seems to me more sensible to say that men who are alive incidentally paint pictures than to say that men who paint pictures incidentally are alive, but the difference is largely one of expression since one can hardly paint without being alive or be alive without in some sense painting. I believe very strongly that we should refuse to agitate ourselves over the fine arts and other "triumphs of civilization." If these things are so very desirable, surely men (if men exist) will engage in them. They always have.

Moreover, all this solicitude for the "higher things" which demand a higher-than-biological standard is conceived in the interest not of artists but of owners. Everything "spiritual" eventually turns out to be sinister. We are told that "life" has a "higher meaning"—but by whom? Always such truths are vouchsafed us by some established theocracy or other; they are found to be infinitely precious to the anointed members of the community; it is the great unwashed for whose better understanding the select ones are so solicitous. The same is true of the "triumphs" of civilization. These triumphs, it always appears, are the precious possession of the elect. The working painter, for example, is "an honest old fellow who paints in the sticks for amusement, turning out clumsy pieces, badly built, but never anything that one could call a picture." It is only after such canvases have been acquired by the great that they become "works of sublime genius." [1] The moral is sufficiently evident. The spiritual grace which is the "end" of civilization is either authentic or it is worthless. In short, the "spiritual" end and aim of civilization is authority.

If I am crowding forward to the rebuttal in an argument the opening thesis of which as yet has scarcely been stated, that is because I believe that rebuttal is all that counts. The sole obstacle to the general diffusion of these ideas is not their obscur-

---

[1] I have often been violently opposed on the esthetic issue by friends who have challenged me to produce one single competent professional art critic whose views lent support to mine, and who have seemed to derive a singular pleasure from my inability to respond except with a shrug of the shoulders. I shall therefore take a proportionate pleasure now in referring my readers to the work of a thoroughly learned and professional English painter-critic, Mr. R. H. Wilenski, whose esthetic analysis seems to me fully to substantiate the social philosophy indicated here. See especially his *The Modern Movement in Art*, London, 1927. The description of the working painter quoted above is quoted by Wilenski in *French Painting*, London, 1931, from a French review of 1905, and refers to Cézanne.

ity but our resistance. Perhaps I am naïve, but I confess that I am perpetually astonished at the powers of resistance which civilization has built up—at the capacity of my contemporaries to cherish notions for which not one scintilla of evidence exists or ever existed in the face of overwhelming evidence to the contrary, and all this not because of a clear conviction of the necessity of sustaining the deceptions which are essential to society but rather from a vague, shuddering, superstitious fear of some un-named and awful eventuality should they ever quite release their hold on the ancient rites of their aboriginal ancestors. To give an instance, I am naïvely astonished that a man like Sir James Frazer, after tracing the natural history of superstition so as to show the clear, unbroken threads by which the practises of our own day weave back to the most extreme "beastliness" of the ultimate aborigines, can then actually propose to regard this not as an utter condemnation of our own civilization (the obvious inference, it seems to me!) but as a defense of superstition—since, for all its beastliness, it has produced our own sublimely enlightened selves. This seems to me utterly perverse, but it is the prevailing attitude. Scarcely anybody ventures to attack the superstitions on the basis of which, obviously, all our churches do business, without protesting that he does so in devout consecration to the interests of "true" religion; and the same is true of the domestic sacraments, the national establishment, the machinery of politics, and even the price system. We criticize, expose, "debunk"; but in the end we make our peace with the devil by coming out staunchly for "true" nationalism, "true" domesticity, or "true" cost accounting.

To my mind this is all nonsense. There is no such thing as true superstition. If our own civilization still harbors the beliefs and practises the rites of savages, so much the worse for our civilization. There is no such thing as true religion, true morality, true matrimony, true nationalism, true democracy, or true cost accounting any more than there is true tyranny or snobbery.

The whole scheme of power-relationships which we call institutions and usually mistake for civilization is savage in origin, depraved in character, and false in thought.

I am aware and have already remarked repeatedly that most people think otherwise. This does not disturb me. I know that their minds are veiled in superstition, and I feel quite free to say so because this judgment is not mine and it reflects no credit upon me. The contrast is not between one man and another but between science and superstition, and this opposition is absolute. Tolerance can exist between superstitions or between sciences but not between science and superstition. Thus "broad-minded" people often say that all religions "worship the same God," and see nothing outrageous in the celebration of the birth of the Christian Messiah with Gothic *tannenbaum* and Druid mistletoe. But they do not say that God created "pretty much" all of the world. For the same reason physics does not say that "nearly" every action has its equal and opposite reaction, nor chemistry that "most" substances are reduceable to elements, nor biology that "most" species have evolved from lower organisms. If one proposes to think in scientific terms, no other terms whatever are admissible. The logic of science is inexorable or it is meaningless.

Moreover, this logic can be applied to man and all his activities with the greatest simplicity and ease—can be and has been. The opposite supposition is a myth. To be sure, the myth is widely prevalent, but that is the nature of myths. Science is inexorable, but superstition is prevalent. I grew up nourished upon this myth, of course, as everybody does; and when as a university student I first learned of the existence of a school of thought which proposed to "account for the mind" in terms of neurones and language mechanisms, I scouted the notion as "ridiculous." I had already learned from the study of the philosophers that I was in "direct" communion with my mind and therefore needed no other evidence of its existence as a "mental" reality than this, and it never occurred to me (for the philosophers took good care not to suggest such a thing) that this was just what I had always been told about my "soul" and my "conscience," not to mention the saving grace of the Holy Spirit and all the other stock in trade of Sunday-school teachers with whom I had long since lost touch. As I look back upon all this, however, I am convinced that the sole difficulty which prevented my seizing upon "behaviorism" at once as both the simplest and the most obvious explanation of human thought, experience, and life was that it seemed to go against the grain. It did in fact go against the grain, not of my mind but of my ingrained superstitions. Therefore it was "ridiculous."

I use the word "behaviorism" with quotation marks because it has been claimed as the trade name of a certain firm of psychologists. In the wider sense, however, behaviorism represents the whole trend of modern psychology, which has been without any important exception toward the correlation of behavior mechanisms with the organic structures on one side and the culture traits of civilization on the other. This synthesis is the core of the whole intellectual position which I am calling (after Dewey) instrumentalism and of the institutionalist economics.[2] Economists trained in an older tradition have sometimes been genuinely bewildered by the insistence of some "institutionalists" that sound economics must begin with "behaviorist" psychology and of others that sound economics must begin with anthropology. The reason for such insistence, however, is not that the institutionalist wishes to correct some particular psychological assumption of classical economics with respect to "the profit motive" or "marginal utility," or that he wishes to view the price system against a background of primitive economics. This urgent intellectual necessity to think in terms of behavior mechanisms and culture traits begins farther back.

[2] Strangely enough, this point has never been more clearly stated than by Professor Suranyi-Unger in the American edition of his *Economics in the Twentieth Century*.

What the institutionalist means by it is that one's very notion of what is an economic problem will vary according as one thinks in terms of creative forces and mystic potencies or in terms of behavior mechanisms and culture traits, and this is of course true.

How important this synthesis is we can easily demonstrate by an experimental dissociation. If we imagine the study of all the organic functions of the human body to have been brought to its present pitch or higher by men totally ignorant of civilization's past and even present, it is obvious that they would be quite unable to account for human behavior mechanisms; and if we imagine a very full and complete stock of anthropological lore to have been accumulated by men wholly uninformed in anatomy and physiology, it is equally obvious that they would be at a complete loss to account for the continuity of the behavior patterns so completely recorded by their data. Both man and civilization are intelligible only when the two are regarded as obverse and reverse of the same phenomenon. This is why some people are able to maintain the pose of intellectual sophistication while at the same time persisting in the delusion that "the human soul" is inexplicable in natural terms. Their intellectual pose is sustained by some show of knowledge in one of these fields, while their obscurantism is made possible by resolutely closing their eyes to the other. No one who sees both need complain any longer that "man is a mystery."

As is well known, this synthesis germinated in the latter part of the nineteenth century. Thomas Huxley contributed substantially to it, and by the eighteen nineties it was in the air and men like Dewey and Veblen, whose minds were sensitive to such things, inevitably absorbed it. For each of them the resulting philosophy had clearly marked positive and negative phases. In Dewey's case the positive phase was "instrumentalism," while the negative is best indicated, I think, by his deeply ironic phrase, "the quest for certainty." As a logician Dewey showed how words are used by man as instruments by which he achieves

his purposes and that what we call truth can be usefully defined only in terms of such instruments and such purposes. As
an educator he was even more explicitly instrumental, insisting
upon the making-and-doing activities as the most important for
human evolution and therefore for the education of the young.
These, I think, have been his most constructive contributions.
Meantime, however, he was engaged in destructive criticism.
By profession a philosopher, he undertook to lay the great
conundrums of philosophy with answers such as had never been
given before since they were never possible before. The reason,
he said in effect, why these conundrums have never been satisfactorily solved is because they are insoluble, and the reason
they are insoluble is because they are meaningless. They are
strings of words put together, not for the purpose of stating a
specific difficulty but with the intent to confuse; and the artificial effect which they thus seek to produce is intended to delude
the mind with a falsely glimmering hope of mystic resolutions
and so to distract it from very real institutional confusions
for which otherwise less suave solutions might be sought.
Through the ages man has engaged in a quest for certainty—
for a "higher" certainty that is in the end meaningless; and he
has done so because of the uncertainties to which his life has
been wantonly exposed by the stupid cruelties of institution and
tradition.

In Veblen's philosophy the distinction between these positive and negative phases was clearly articulated. Its most important expression, I think, was in his antithesis of business and
industry, "pecuniary employments" and machine technology.
But the same distinction lies behind the antithesis between his
celebrated "instinct of workmanship" and the "instinct of sportsmanship" of which *The Theory of the Leisure Class* is the fullest exposition. When this book appeared Lester F. Ward remarked in a long and warmly appreciative review (which he
declared at the end of his life to have been the best review he

ever wrote) that Veblen had chosen to write of the instinct of sportsmanship but that it was to be presumed that he could have written just as incisively of the instinct of workmanship. More than a decade later, as everyone knows, he did so.

Thus it was Veblen's major thesis that civilization itself exhibits two contrasting aspects. One is technological and relates to work, and to this we owe all the material comforts, all the intellectual and artistic achievements, and all the progress we have attained. The other is institutional and relates to exploitation and enslavement—theocratic, military, political and pecuniary—to which civilization has somehow fallen heir. To this side of the picture he applied all the opprobrious epithets which an amazingly ingenious pen was able to devise. This is why I cannot help thinking it a singularly ironic turn of fate that the economic "school" of which he is the "master" should term itself "institutional." In his dealing with the traditional "principles" of economic thought Veblen was correspondingly caustic. Like Dewey, he criticised accepted economic theories, not as incomplete or even wrong in specific detail but as utterly false and deluded from beginning to end. Like Dewey he clearly implied that we should be much better off if we were to dispense with the whole fabric of question-begging rubrics "with no other verdict than 'good riddance.' "

Throughout the foregoing discussion I have treated the work of Dewey and Veblen, the philosophy known as "instrumentalism" and the economics known as "institutionalism," as a single body of thought. I have even gone so far as to represent this body of thought as the working out in various directions of the implications of a single idea or intellectual principle: the distinction of the technological from the institutional aspects of human behavior and culture. In doing so I have of course no warrant but my own. Neither Dewey nor Veblen ever announced himself as the promulgator of any such "system" or even indicated my dichotomy as the ruling principle in his own

mind, and certainly no consensus of opinion to this effect has
yet developed among their avowed "followers." On the contrary, both Dewey and Veblen have usually been reproached
with having produced no "system" and their followers with
having no ruling principle—only a rather vague state of mind.
But this criticism seems to me sadly mistaken. The work of
Dewey and Veblen seems inchoate, I believe, only because it
was frontier work. As time passes I think we shall be forced
by the whole trend of subsequent discussion to realize that a
very clear and definite principle does underlie the work of both
men and that from it derives the very real cohesion of the
intellectual movement which has followed them. This principle
may and doubtless will be stated very differently from the
fashion in which I have been trying to state it here, but that
it will be recognized and stated in a fashion not altogether different I have no doubt whatever.

The reason for my certainty (which may strike some of my
contemporaries as singularly egotistical) is that I do not regard
this intellectual "movement" as a personal phenomenon at all.
It does not derive from the personal genius or influence of any
man; its direction has not been determined by any man and
will not be; and the principle or axiom in terms of which we
shall represent it is not an expression of any man's individual
acumen but a projection in words of a cultural actuality. Our
civilization is itself passing through a process of transition and
approaching a crisis the magnitude of which it is impossible to
overestimate. The existence in the world of such a thing as modern science is a portent of what is happening. I have already
alluded to my own naïve astonishment at the persistence in
modern civilization of so much that is patently barbaric, but
probably it is even more naïve to regard modern science—that
prodigious cultural anomaly!—as a matter of course. Science is
far from being a matter of course. On the contrary, we have yet
to realize fully what it is and what it is going to do with us.

But one thing is clear: it is going to go a great deal farther than it has gone hitherto and it is going to do a great deal more than it has done hitherto. The movement of which I have been speaking and in which I have been trying to orient Dewey and Veblen and so myself is a part of the process. The philosopher Kant expected a revolution in our conception of man and culture comparable in magnitude and significance to the Copernican revolution. This revolution is indeed occurring, though it is taking a form scarcely hinted at in the work of Kant, and may prove so important for the future of civilization as to dwarf the significance of the Copernican cosmogony. For after all, the importance of the Copernican revolution is not that of an abstract planetary formula but rather that of a cultural transformation. To a certain degree at that point astronomy transformed civilization. But the transformation which is still to occur is vastly greater.

In this transformation what we call science is a dynamic force not because of "the power of the idea" but because what we call science is one aspect of a much greater and more potent social force: technology. The reason we have always found it so difficult to define science satisfactorily is that we have taken it cut of its cultural setting, made it an academic abstraction, and tried to describe the essence of what was in fact a fragment. Science is an activity: the activity of handling materials with instruments. No line can be made to lie between scientific and other materials except whether or not they can be handled instrumentally; and no line can be made to lie between scientific instruments and any other kind of machine or tool or workmanlike device except whether or not the tool or instrument is used to work materials. Science can of course be described as a state of mind, but only as the state of mind of that activity: the material state of mind; the instrumental state of mind. This state of mind has become frightfully (I use the word in its just sense) important in our civilization as the activity of which it is the state of mind has become also frightfully important; and it is correspondingly important that we appreciate the fact.[3] Science does not "lead to" materialism. Science is materialism. The only way the "social sciences" can be truly scientific is by assuming this, the only scientific state of mind, and regarding civilization as the series of physical activities of material beings. Since that is precisely what the philosophy of Dewey and Veblen proposes to do, I see no reason why we should hesitate to declare that it is preëminently scientific, the inevitable further consequence of the transformation of western culture which in a sense began with the Copernican revolution.

The progress of this scientific (or, as I prefer to say, using the broader term, technological) revolution has of course involved the destruction of illusions. It is impossible to cherish creation myths after accepting Copernican astronomy: hence the importance of astronomy. But it is equally impossible to cherish the Ten Commandments after accepting the results of modern archeological research. The whole effect of modern anthropology and sociology has of course been to bring established morality into the same disrepute which a little earlier overtook revealed theology. The effect of this is a complete moral relativism. The limitation of every taboo and every standard of value whatsoever to the pronouncements of the particular set of mores of the community which sets up the taboo or standard of value is now a commonplace among students of the social

[3] That is why I have so often and so violently challenged the smug piety with which certain scientists (of whom Professor Compton has provided the latest instance) attach the prestige of their laboratory triumphs to such nonsense as that "Science can have no quarrel with a religion which postulates a God to whom men are as his children." *Science: The False Messiah* (1927) was originally projected as an interpretation of instrumentalism in terms of the impact of technology upon modern culture, to be published under some such title as *Transition*. But the attack on spurious messiahship ran away with the book, though the larger theme is still present in the background and, I think, clearly perceptible to any reader curious enough to look for it.

sciences.[4] Thus comparative judgments upon different civilizations and even the conception of progress itself have been given up as insubstantial by many students who would therefore be correspondingly shocked by such sweeping judgments of approval and disapproval as I have set down here and even imputed to better men than I. And yet these judgments are the inevitable next step in the argument.

If the archeologist's spade has turned up convincing evidence that every people has claimed to be the "chosen people" and every ruffians' code the "law of God," the obvious presumption is that such claims and codes are all false and vicious; and if we accept the evidence of the spade against the claims of the theocrats on the ground that the spade represents science, that means accepting a material standard of judgment against all institutional standards whatsoever. I have denounced institutional standards *in toto* as superstitious and debased and have advanced instead the materialist-instrumentalist standard because the two are absolutely opposed. It is the essential character of the institutional scheme to claim sole credit for all that is high and fine in civilization. Present excellence and past progress are conceived as wholly institutional: a matter of individualism, or democracy, or nationalism, or monogamy, or Christianity. Such are the agencies, we are told, which alone have "made material progress possible." Examination with a

---

[4] This exaggerates somewhat, not the commonplace but the resolution with which social scientists stick to the doctrines they affect. I regret to say that most of them, while loudly affirming the doctrine of the mores, actually cherish most of the moral convictions of the communities in which they labor. It was to press the doctrine to its logical conclusion—the candid declaration that all established morality is nonsense of the creation-myth type—that I wrote *Holier Than Thou* (1929). So far as I know, the book has never made me any friends. The prevailing idea seems to be that although we all know about the mores, it is better not to think about the matter too much and very injudicious indeed to talk about it. A parallel to this state of mind can be found in the early history of Copernican astronomy, when people who knew what it meant nevertheless preferred to let the matter ride.

spade exhibits the utter falseness of all such claims. If, therefore, we credit the spade at all—if we credit science at all—we
are bound eventually to be forced to adopt it as our sole standard of truth and criterion of value and to dismiss institutional
claims altogether as false and base.

It is of course a moral dismissal which I am advocating. I
do not propose to act as though the institutional scheme did not
exist, nor to recommend that anyone else do so, for the simple
reason that it does exist. Nothing can alter the fact that I was
born an American and a Christian any more than it can alter
the fact that I was also born white, and I do not see that the
world would be notably improved by my pretended secession.
For effective secession is impossible. There is only one way by
which I can cease to be an American or even, in the only important sense, a Christian, and that is by becoming a citizen
and a communicant of another nation and religion, and that is
scarcely an escape from institutions. As I said at the outset, people who eagerly exchange one social order for another are not
escaping: they are simply swapping horses. This is an exercise
for which I can muster no enthusiasm. The only immediate and
practical consequence of the gospel of technology, it seems to
me, is an attitude of cynical indifference to the prevailing institutional weather, and I should like to point out that such an
attitude is neither rare nor disreputable. On the contrary, most
of the men whose statesmanlike skill in playing the institutional
game have won them the accolade of genius have been cynics
and "opportunists"; they have had no illusions about their
countries or their parties or their corporations, but have merely
bargained with fate. Mr. Alfred Smith has recently denounced
the frankly experimental policy of President Roosevelt as "opportunism." So it is. But that is no very serious defect. Opportunism has doubtless been the policy of many men who have
played the game by instinct rather than as the expression of an
articulately experimental philosophy, but it amounts to the
same thing. The intent to experiment which President Roose-

velt avows is doubtless better than the instinct to play the game which Mr. Smith imputes to him. But even instinctive experimentalism is better than delusion. The world has suffered less from its cynical opportunists than it has from its demoniac fanatics.

Moreover, to accept facts is not a counsel of defeat. According to the gospel of technology, indeed, there is no such thing as defeat or victory: there is only work. And the work which immediately requires to be done is the intellectual work of the post-Copernican revolution. Can civilization proceed without the doubtful benefit of institutions? We do not know. It never has. Perhaps that is the denouement toward which technological progress—mechanical and intellectual—is carrying us. But whether this is so or not, our great task is to find out. It is a tremendous task. As yet we scarcely know the meaning of industry. We need to do so. We need to know what up to the present we have only dimly and most reluctantly and falteringly recognized: how complete the contrast is between all the ideological traditions we have inherited from our institutional past and the new instruments we have been forging in our shops. We need to expose the nonsense of our institutionalized culture as it has never been exposed, and we need to set ourselves resolutely to the task of reconstructing the long, slow process by which, in spite of all the nonsense and all the waste of tyranny and corruption, we have somehow managed to survive and carry on. The progress of civilization has been very real and very great. But if it is to continue, we must now understand it. We must understand it as the survival of a species of social animals—survival and vast multiplication. We must understand this peculiar organism and his unique ways and means of life. To do so is the only true social science.

TOWARD A
SOCIAL PHILOSOPHY

ERNEST SUTHERLAND BATES

I was born on October 14, 1879, at Gambier, Ohio, in the shadow of Kenyon College. My ancestry was English, Highland Scottish, and German. My father, of New England extraction, was born on a farm in the Western Reserve, served in the Northern armies during the Civil War until severely wounded at the battle of Chicamauga; after his recovery, he became a lawyer for five years and then left the profession because of what he considered its inherent dishonesty, going into the Episcopal ministry and at the time of my birth also acting as professor of philosophy, a combination then more popular than now. My mother was the daughter of a Methodist minister. So the clerical influence was very strong on both sides of the family.

My secondary education was received at the University School, Cleveland, a private school of experimental tendencies. From there I went to the University of Michigan, specializing during my college course in history, philosophy, and literature, three subjects that have always had an almost equal interest for me. Graduating in 1902, with the degree of A.B., and receiving the A.M. degree in 1903, I taught English literature for two years and then went to Columbia for further graduate study where I obtained the degree of Ph.D. in 1908, with a dissertation on Shelley's *Cenci*. There followed seven years at the University of Arizona as head of the English department, and ten at the University of Oregon, first as professor of American literature and later as professor of philosophy.

Being by that time disheartened with American education in the colleges and universities, I gave up teaching to enter upon a precarious career as a literary free lance, a course which, with the exception of three years as literary editor of the Dictionary of American Biography, 1907-10, I have pursued ever since, and with no regrets. Besides numerous articles—they seem to me innumerable—in the magazines, and a good deal of inevitable hack work, I have managed to get out three books, *The Gospel according to Judas* (1928), *This Land of Liberty* (1930) and *Mary Baker Eddy: the Truth and the Tradition* (1932), written in conjunction with John V. Dittemore, and since 1932 I have been on the staff of *The Modern Monthly*, the only important independent radical magazine in the country. Although I became a theoretical socialist at college, my active radicalism had its birth in my disgust with the American reaction during the World War, and even then it remained merely an ineffective and really individualistic rebellion for many years. It is only, to my shame be it said,—though a shame shared with most of my American contemporaries—since about 1930 that I have begun to work out what seems to me a satisfactory social philosophy. In this, as in all the rest of my career, I have been a fairly typical product of a transition era.

TOWARD A SOCIAL PHILOSOPHY

Ernest Sutherland Bates

I. THE REALISTIC VICTORY

The various meanings of the term "meaning" have furnished a theme for innumerable treatises. Neglecting minor variations, there are at least three of these meanings which must be clearly discriminated before philosophy can get far with its proper task.

The "meaning" of a word is understood when one knows what idea is symbolized by the word, and the "meaning" of a concept is understood when one knows the objects, events, or relations to which the concept is applicable. Thus, the word "Jabberwock" has literary meaning when we know that it expressed Lewis Carroll's idea of a mythical animal with "eyes of flame" that comes "whiffling" and "burbling" through the "tulgey wood," but the class concept, "Jabberwock," would have no meaning outside of myth and logistic because no such animal is believed to exist and he would be a madman who should set out in search of it. "Meaning," in this first sense, is attained when a symbol is properly referred to whatever is intended to be symbolized. It is concerned with the tools used by the philosopher, and other men, in thinking, and has nothing to do directly with truth or error. The distinction here between the meaningful and the meaningless is simply the distinction between sense and nonsense, and a great part of the efforts of philosophy in the past has been devoted merely to making sure, not always successfully, that the philosopher has not been talking nonsense.

A second meaning of the term is found when it refers directly to objects or events: as we may ask, for example, what was the meaning of the World War? Here we can answer the question when we can indicate the causes and consequences of the event, or, if one insists, we could answer the question if we could indicate all the relations involved in the event. "Meaning," in this case, means intelligible relationship. And in this instance, unlike the former, "meaning" is capable of indefinite enlargement according to the number and importance of the relationships discovered. We are now dealing, not with a question of subjective clarity but of objective truth.

Finally, there is the more inclusive sense in which "meaning" is equivalent to "value," an identification early made in philosophy and almost universal in common parlance. Such is the sense in which the term is used by Mr. Theodore Dreiser, for instance, when he declares that life is meaningless. Mr. Dreiser, or the man in the street who echoes his sentiment, does not mean that life cannot be understood in terms of its physical setting and relationships; in fact, Mr. Dreiser and those who revel in a similar pessimism believe that life can be fully explained by chemistry and physics; but the more complete and adequate this explanation the greater their pessimism. To be meaningful, in their sense, life would have to belong to a block universe embodying, not only intelligible relationships but also moral purpose and esthetic value.

The detailed conception of just such a block universe was, of course, the achievement of Greek metaphysics. In the classical tradition which set the pattern for later philosophy, the final object of philosophic study was supposed to be a metaphysical reality that possessed meaning in all three of the senses indicated above: it corresponded to its concept, it was in principle entirely intelligible, and it was morally and esthetically perfect. Philosophy, being concerned with an ultimate reality of this highly satisfactory character, became a kind of recondite and esoteric religion. The essential truths presented by religion in a popular form with much reliance on emotional faith and verbal authority were reinstated by philosophy, after prolonged critical examination, as universal principles, more chastening, indeed, to individual desires and hopes than were the dogmas of popular religion but in the last analysis corroborative of religious insight.

That the Reality supposed to be intellectually contemplated by philosophy or emotionally apprehended by religion was radically different from the inferior reality encountered by human beings in their daily lives is fairly obvious and was never denied by the classical tradition. Less obvious, but apparent on reflection, is the fact that this metaphysical reality owed its alleged superiority to its being a highly preferential selection from human experience of those elements in the latter which possessed intelligibility or other value. These elements, abstracted from the non-human setting of conscious experience, were then given independent status, their scope was imaginatively enlarged, and they were finally asserted to be the cause of the human experience of which they had originally been a part.

After John Dewey's masterly *Reconstruction in Philosophy* it is unnecessary to point out how the actual dualism of Greco-Roman society was reflected in the philosophical dualism between metaphysical and empirical reality or to stress the degree to which Aristotelianism was, in our modern phrase, a "rationalization" of the aims of that society. Nor is it needful to show how the revision of Aristotelianism by Aquinas accentuated the hierarchical character of metaphysical reality itself, thus bringing it into conformity with the feudal and Catholic needs of his period. Similarly, the connections between modern psychological idealism and the individualistic tendencies of the Reformation, the Romantic yearning for the infinite, and the rise of the national state have been too often pointed out to need reiteration. From Plato to Hegel the fundamental procedure of metaphysics was the same: the reification of those elements of human experience which at the time were deemed particularly desirable, while the characteristics of metaphysical Reality shifted according to the social—and sometimes even the personal —bias of the metaphysician, this last extreme of irresponsible individualism appearing most clearly of all precisely in those divergent philosophers of the Absolute—Fichte, Schelling, Schopenhauer, and Hegel.

Bishop Berkeley, the founder of psychological idealism, frankly avowed the religious motivation of his philosophy, thinking quite rightly so far as the immediate philosophic future was concerned that his discovery of the ego-centric predicament would cut the ground from under materialism and atheistic disbelief. The transcendental leap later made from subjective to objective idealism and the towering structures of thought reared upon the latter basis supplied intellectual justification for whatever could be retained of the by now attenuated dogmas of Christianity, and proved the superiority of philosophy to every other form of human endeavor. Possessing the sole key to the inner nature of Reality, philosophers could afford to look down with contempt upon the piddling efforts of scientists and men of affairs busied with detailed facts, the meaning of which they could not understand. Even toward their less intelligent and adroit allies, the priests, philosophers were tempted to adopt an attitude of half-scornful condescension. In a word, the philosopher was in the happy position of being able to despise all things except himself, for, though his "empirical self" was subject to time and circumstance, its alter-ego, the "transcendental self," was one with God.

Meanwhile, science went on piling fact upon fact, achieving relative truths that actually worked in our relative world, quietly leaving the philosopher to his union with an Absolute Truth that emphatically did not work or even pretend to work on the "lower level" of sense experience. With unprecedented rapidity, the principles of science applied in industry remade the surface of the world and fundamentally altered the conditions of living for all men, including the philosopher.

By the end of the nineteenth century the disparity between

the impotent boasts of philosophy and the actual achievements of science had become intolerable even to philosophers themselves. The débâcle of idealism that ensued was much more than a technical or logical defeat. It meant that the traditional philosophy was so definitely out of harmony with the accepted principles by which men lived that it was necessary to abandon its entire metaphysical basis. Bereft, through the decline of religion of emotional support from that quarter, the metaphysical basis, when subjected to rigorous scrutiny, turned out to be just as hypothetical as any other, while its assumptions, being unlike those of science unprovable by further experience, altogether lacked the pragmatic value of the latter.

After almost a century of prestige, idealism went down like a house of cards in a decade of attack upon it. By revealing the incapacity of idealism to deal with error, by demonstrating the necessary priority of being to knowledge, by proving that even mathematical truth—the logical core of idealism—has only relative validity, by showing that the ego-centric predicament involves nothing more than a methodological skepticism, by exposing the incorrect character of the idealistic notion of consciousness as substance instead of function, and by establishing the instrumental nature of actual thinking—by these combined frontal attacks the realists succeeded in razing the foundations of idealism to the ground.

The result was nothing more and nothing less than the abandonment by philosophy of its pretended access to a different kind of knowledge than that achieved by science. This belated attainment of modesty may seem a slender reward for all the expenditure of effort required to reach so humble a goal. Yet the giving over of mistaken aims implies in itself a substitution of other aims, and the relinquishment of the ancient quest for unattainable and useless certainty is a necessary preparation for the active pursuit of such limited but imperative knowledge as may and must be won by mortal men if they are to attain any of their desires assuredly and purposefully instead of transiently and by accident.

It may be argued and indeed has been often argued that philosophy without metaphysics is not philosophy at all but a mere general matrix for the as yet undeveloped social sciences, and it is assumed that this is or would be a great tragedy. But the important thing is surely that the work which is needed should be accomplished; whether those who accomplish it should bear the name of philosophers or scientists would seem to be a somewhat minor matter. Furthermore, the positive achievements of philosophy in the past, as contrasted with the unfulfilled promises of metaphysics, have mainly consisted in the very fact that philosophy has served as a matrix for the development of the successive sciences which, when definitely established, have then followed their separate careers, the last of them, psychology, winning its independence from philosophy barely within our own day. If philosophy should eventually disappear as a separate discipline, this would mean that the various departments of knowledge had been able to develop such a completely harmonious set of premises and conclusions that a coördinating agency among them was no longer needed. Such a happy culmination is not so imminent that one needs to devote a great deal of time to its consideration. As far as we can see into the probable future, the increasing establishment of separate sciences will render the existence of a separate discipline devoted to the unity of human experience more, not less, necessary.

II. CONTEMPORARY PESSIMISM

It is here, in its central task, that contemporary philosophy has failed most signally. Left in possession of the field of battle by the defeat of idealism, the realists have not known what to do with the spoils of victory. Since that victory was won by epistemological arguments, they have continued, like tiresome bridge-players, to go over and over the same conflict, still squeezing the dry orange of epistemology after they had already extracted most of its juice. Some of the leaders, such as Dewey, Santayana, Whitehead, Perry, and Sellars, have moved on to further battle-fields, but the movement as a whole has lost vitality. Indeed, a certain nostalgia for the old assurances of idealism is not unevident, as if indolence in the pursuit of new truths justified a return to past errors.

In large sections of the reading public, technically non-philosophic but sufficiently aware that science has replaced religion and metaphysics as the highest court of appeal, a similar nostalgia for the past is still more manifest. The bad habit continued during many centuries of first reading human values into the universe and then recovering them for human life with an added transcendental lustre about them had behind it a vastly pathetic and permanent realization of mortal weakness. Man in his insignificance can hardly believe that any experiences of his, even his most cherished ones, can be "really" valuable unless they are shared by mightier forms of life.

Nothing could be more natural to man than this basic inferiority complex. All animals seem to have an instinctive sense of their own relative prowess and weakness: the cat does not need personal experience to follow the fleeing mouse or shun the pursuing dog, the panther pounces, the lion stalks its prey, the rabbit scurries to its hole, their behavior admirably expressing the actualities of the competitive world in which they find themselves. Man, on his first appearance, was no exception. One of the least impressive denizens of earth, inferior to most of his rivals in strength and speed, ill equipped for either fight or flight, he easily recognized his own unimportant place in the sun. Out of this aboriginal sense of inferiority were born the many forms of animal worship in which primitive man expressed his obeisance to beings more powerful than himself. Only very gradually, as his apparently slight advantages of hand and tongue and a more complex nervous system enabled him to improve his lot, did his animal gods take on human form and develop first into anthropomorphic deities and eventually into universal metaphysical principles.

Always, as has been earlier indicated, these objects of worship embodied values that man had found in his own experience —where else could they have come from?—but had found so intermittently and precariously that the very love of them impelled him to deny their human origin, thereby, of course, denying any intrinsic value in himself. Hence the unpleasant grovelling spirit that infects much religious ritual; hence the recurrent willingness even of philosophers to contemplate the damnation of actual men to the glory of a hypothetical god. On the other hand, the equally unpleasant arrogance of metaphysicians may be taken quite literally as over-compensation for a sense of organic inferiority.

So the paradoxical situation has now arisen that at the very moment when science has put into men's hands the technical means for securing far greater happiness and self-realization than ever before in human history, there is also perhaps more general pessimism and despair than ever before or at least more frequent expression of such pessimism and despair. "If there is no value in the universe as a whole," men cry, "how can there possibly be any value in my own insignificant life?" Could they but realize that we do not know and never have known anything about "the universe as a whole" and that it is doubtful whether the expression even has meaning, while human values remain precisely as they were before, they might be willing to use more effort to eliminate the actual evils of war, poverty, disease, and tragic social injustice.

The pessimism of the hour is accentuated by the evident fact that the greatest scientific success has been won in mathematics and the physical sciences, including biology, which eliminate from their consideration every kind of meaning except that of rational explanation, the half-born social sciences that have endeavored rather feebly to deal with non-intellectual values lagging far behind. From this has arisen a widespread conviction that moral values, not being found in the facts recognized by the physical sciences, cannot be facts at all. This supposedly tough-minded conviction, pre-pragmatic but lingering on in the face of pragmatism, has never been better expressed than it was by William B. Sumner, who stated it with the utmost degree of clarity permitted by the essential confusion of thought behind it.

"Every ideal is a phantasm; it is formed by giving up one's hold on reality and taking flight into the realm of fiction. When an ideal has been formed in the imagination the attempt is made to spring and reach it as a mode of realizing it. The whole process seems to me open to question; it is unreal and unscientific; it is the same process as that by which Utopias are formed in regard to social states, and contains the same fallacies; it is not a legitimate mental exercise. There is never any correct process by which we can realize an ideal. The fashion of forming ideals corrupts the mind and injures the character. What we need to practise, on the contrary, is to know, with the greatest exactitude, what is, and then plan to deal with the case as it is by the most approved means."

It is cruelly easy to point out that in his final phrase Sumner gave away his whole argument. The "most approved means" must be a means to something, and that something is manifestly the previously rejected ideal value which "the case as it is" does not realize, as otherwise there would be no occasion to "deal" with it at all. Logically, on the Sumnerian view, "what we need to practise" would be simply to refrain from practice other than "to know, with the greatest exactitude, what is."

The passage would not have been worth quoting did it not express a moral skepticism which is much more prevalent today than when Sumner voiced it forty years ago, a moral skepticism all the more dangerous because of its half-hearted and pseudo-scientific character. The notion that we can "plan" without knowing what we are planning for, combined with a rejection of all ultimate aims as "Utopian," is the very bedrock of our recent policies of social and political reform.

It is important to note the exact point at which Sumner's argument—the argument, be it remembered, of one of our leading nineteenth century social scientists—ceased to be scientific. For Sumner was, of course, quite right in recognizing that the trustworthiness of science depends upon the rigorous elimination from its methodology of all aims other than the aim to know the object as it really is. The demonstration of the possibility of such knowledge is the first objective of a realistic philosophy, the assumption of this possibility is the necessary (though too often unacknowledged) presupposition of all serious thinking. This assuredly means that all knowledge is knowledge of facts, and that the answer to every "Why" is to be found in the answer to a previous "What." But it tells us absolutely nothing about the character of the facts to be discovered further than that this character, whatever it may be (atomic, organic, teleological, or accidental) exists independently of its own subsequent discovery. The indifference of mathematics and the physical sciences to moral and esthetic qualities is not due to any primordial prejudice against these qualities; on the contrary, mathematics in the beginning had its "sacred numbers" and the Ptolemaic cosmology was long defended on the score of its beauty and moral economy. Through long experience these sciences learned that in the formal and physical relationships that were the object of their study, evidence of any constitutive moral or esthetic purpose was simply not discernible. (The recent efforts of a few religious-minded physicists, in their off-hours, to derive moral consolation from the "indeterminism" of the quantum theory may be dismissed, first because indeterminism or chance is the direct opposite of moral purpose, and second because such moral considerations are entirely irrelevant to their practice as physicists).

When one turns, on the other hand, to the social sciences, which study human activity, then ideals, purposes, and plans are among the most important of the facts to be considered. The notion that they must be ruled out beforehand and the study conducted solely in terms of physical causation is simply the obverse of the idealistic fallacy; as the latter misreads physical nature by the importation of mental qualities so the latter misreads human nature by denying that it possesses any mental qualities. Admittedly, human behavior is a form of animal behavior, but to stop there and fail to recognize the distinctive characteristics of the human animal is to stop at the beginning. The fact that we are not gods does not condemn us to be subhuman.

III. Social Reconstruction

Contrary to a widely accepted view today, investigation of the origins and results of the individual and group activities of human beings may, in principle, be carried on just as objectively as the investigation of any other facts. In practice, it is much more difficult to obtain assured results for three reasons: the phenomena considered are much more varied, often to the point of seeming contradiction; human beings, gifted with speech, in reporting their activities have contracted a habit of lying not open to electrons, stones, trees, and inferior animals; the personal equation, the bane of all science, is more likely to be unconsciously reënforced by group and class interests. Difficulties, however,—even great difficulties—do not constitute impossibility. Varied phenomena simply require a more varied technique of approach. Lying is merely one of the social phenomena to be studied. Deliberate surrender to personal or class bias, so popular today, is logically inconsistent with the recognition of it as a bias.

The instance of the work of Karl Marx may well be cited as a test case, since the "frank" acceptance of class bias is so often considered to be a Marxist position. Through his study of history and economics, Marx was able to establish scientifically, as he believed, certain fundamental conclusions—that the course of history, in its main outlines, and cultural development, in its fundamental aspects, have been directed by changes in the form and control of economic production; that these changes have been correlative with the development of social classes and an implied or overt class warfare; that the modern capitalistic form of production is, for a number of reasons, essentially unstable, and tends necessarily to accentuate class warfare to a point where the capitalistic system will break down and the proletariat will assume economic and political control. Now it is quite possible, however unlikely, that one might accept all of these conclusions pessimistically, admitting the facts to be as Marx asserted them to be, admitting the logic of his inferences, yet deploring the whole spectacle and particularly its conclusion. Had Marx been under the influence of a "cultural compulsive" —which in his case would surely have been a bourgeois compulsive since his upbringing, early environment, and personal tastes were all distinctly bourgeois—he still might have produced *Das Kapital* though it would probably have been written in an elegiac or sardonically Spenglerian tone. As a matter of fact, of course, having observed the human waste and misery incident to the capitalist system he not only prophesied its destruction with enthusiasm but devoted a great deal of energy to an attempt to organize the working class so that it might fulfill its "historic rôle" more adequately. Without doubt his revolutionary zeal actually motivated both his economic studies and his endeavor to apply their results in practice, but just because it intensified his search for information and sharpened his logic the result was not mere propaganda or rationalization of desire but objective science.

It is hardly doubtful, in the light of all the evidence, that the majority of men are governed in their so-called thinking by their wishes rather than by either facts or logic, but this principle cannot be universalized to include all men without becoming self-destructive, since then the formulation of the proposition would itself necessarily be an instance of wishful thinking and would have no objective value.

The prejudice that a proposition cannot be "really" or scientifically true unless it can be universalized—a prejudice which is a legacy from the older philosophical tradition—appears in extreme form in the insistence that no science is worthy of the name unless its results can be reduced to mathematical statement. This is only a modification, often not realized to be a modification, of the old demand for absolute truth. But in the first place, modern mathematics itself disclaims absoluteness, recognizing its relativity to its own assumptions and permitting alternative geometries with different assumptions, and in the second place mathematical statement is not the same thing as mathematics. As soon as one departs from the formal entities of mathematics and introduces real objects in their place, as in the Newtonian law of gravitation, these objects become subject to the evidence accumulated by observation or experiment, and their hypothetical relations, no matter how mathematically formulated, are subject to limitation or change. Because the entities considered by physics and chemistry are extremely simple and uniform in comparison with those considered by biology and the human sciences they lend themselves to mathematical formulation as the latter do not. This does not mean, however, that such formulation is necessarily any "truer" in either the pragmatic or correspondence sense of the term than is a non-mathematical statement of more complex relationships. The Darwinian doctrine of the mutability of species is just as true as the Newtonian doctrine of gravitation and is apparently less subject to exception.

It must be admitted, of course, that mathematics and the physical sciences, because of their generality, are basic to all the later sciences. Electrons and protons go their way unaffected by our hopes and fears and purposes, but our hopes and fears and purposes are not unaffected by the behavior of protons and electrons. A man, as Santayana somewhere says, should not imagine that he contradicts the laws of physics every time he wags his tongue.

On the other hand, the wagging of a man's tongue, if he happens to be a Mussolini or a Hitler, may affect, to the point of life or death, the careers of many millions of human beings. Its wagging, and to what purpose it shall wag, or whether it be permitted to wag at all, are matters that seemingly are more amenable to human control than are the laws of physics. We cannot set the stars in geometric patterns or hasten or delay the death of suns, but we might, it would seem, achieve a more rational human society, since we could hardly with any amount of effort achieve a less rational one than we have. The attempt, at least, is open to us.

In other words, as we descend, or ascend, the scale from mathematical physics through biology to the sciences of human society, passing from the general to the particular, what we lose in exactitude of knowledge is compensated by the direct relevance to our lives of the knowledge that we have or at least might have if we willed.

Were there no intrinsic values in human experience, there could be neither affirmation nor denial on our part of values anywhere because the very idea of value would never have arisen. The notion that mere extension or continuance could in themselves confer value, as in the old argument that human life would be valueless without immortality, is patently absurd. It is only because our lives have their transitory moments of high value that we cherish the fancy of an endless continuation of them even though a more exacting psychology shows that their transitoriness actually enhances their value. The spectacle of the eternal sufferings of the damned was said by medieval theologians and poets to increase the joy of the heavenly saints by contrast with their own bliss, and the idea of Hell had value as warning to dwellers on earth, but for the damned themselves their immortality of pain was the most complete negation of value that the medieval fancy could conceive.

Can anything be a value if no one values it? If the question had not been so often asked, and sometimes with an affirmative answer, it would be seen to be as grammatically meaningless as any other attempt to separate a transitive verb from its object, as if one should ask whether an object of knowledge can be an object of knowledge if there is no knowledge. If anything is known it is, *ipso facto*, knowable, and in the same way if anything is valued, it is, *ipso facto*, valuable.

Men show by their behavior that they find intrinsic value in the free exercise of their capacities, both individual and collective, as seen in artistic creation, the pursuit of knowledge, sport, travel, friendship, love, and the enjoyment of sense pleasures. That the values here are intrinsic is proved by the fact that such activities are carried on for their own sake irrespective of further rewards—not, indeed, all of them by all men, but some of them by all men, and all of them by some men. The many possible varieties of "the good life," meaning the life that is worth while both to its possessor and to society, will be compounded of these different activities in divergent measure according to the special aptitudes of the individual. To increase the number of such good lives, in this latitudinarian sense, would be the main aim of a rational society.

Unfortunately, the bulk of human activity has never been of this character but has been servile, concerned with the mere maintenance of life and possessing only imputed value as the necessary means for the attainment of actual values. Finally, a large amount of human activity has taken such anti-social forms as exploitation, crime, and war in which whatever individual values may be achieved are purchased at the expense of greater disvalues. Manifestly, a rational society would seek to reduce to a minimum the necessary servile activities—the progress of technology having now made a very low minimum possible— and would seek to eliminate the anti-social activities entirely exactly as it would seek to eliminate disease.

The great service of pragmatism was to break down the absolute separation between theoretical knowledge and other modes of human activity. Without underestimating the factor of disinterested curiosity, one must admit that its gratification is only one among many values and, for most men, not the most important one. It must be admitted, further, that theoretical knowledge usually, if not always, arises out of practical needs and remains psychologically incomplete until it is practically applied. Nothing is less satisfactory than a picture of rational society so excessively rational that it can never be approached in practice. The philosopher's task is not done until he has shown, not only the end but the means by which the end may be at least progressively attained.

From this point of view, Karl Marx was much more truly a philosopher than most of those who go by the name. Hampered though he was by contradictory elements in his own thought—on the one hand by his almost exclusive reliance on economic factors to the neglect of the psychological, and on the other hand by his inheritance of Hegelian dialectic, itself ultimately derived from the psychological, so that his system could easily be misinterpreted as a crushing of the individual instead of as a freeing of the individual—he nevertheless understood the necessity of integrating the ideal with the actual and of developing a technique for the transformation of society.

Marxism will probably long continue to be resisted in America even by personally disinterested critics because it so largely runs counter to our main social tradition. The latter, however distorted in practice, recognized positive elements of value in the individual which Marx failed to safeguard sufficiently. For this reason, the coming social philosophy in America to be at all effective must achieve a new synthesis of economics and psychology more valid, at least for America, than Marxism. It will recognize as definitely as did Marx the anarchic character of capitalism under which community prosperity is inherently impossible, the prosperity of one group (manufacturers, farmers, white collar workers, or labor) being always balanced by the losses of some other group; it will understand more fully than was possible for him the effects of technological development upon the social set-up; and it will be more concerned than he was with the corrupting effect of "the profit motive" upon individual character, with its tendency under stress toward infantile regression to a fascist psychology as hostile to the achieved gains of the past as to the potential gains of the future: the net results of these inquiries probably entailing a very considerable reconstruction of the Marxist technique of reconstruction.

All this is to say that what we need is a twentieth century American Karl Marx. At the moment, the chances of his appearance do not seem particularly bright, yet, out of the present conflict between pigmy Marxists and non-Marxists, giants may eventually be born even in our unphilosophic land.

It seems somewhat unlikely that they will arise out of the class of professional academic philosophers. This may, perhaps, be regrettable, but the loss will be not to philosophy but to the academicians. Philosophy, the science of meanings, will be carried on by others in the endless effort to make life more meaningful even if those who take its name in vain are content that their own lives continue meaningless.

BOYD H. BODE

Born Oct. 4, 1873 at Ridott, Illinois. Degrees: A.B., University of Michigan, 1897; Ph.D., Cornell University, 1900; LL.D., University of Michigan, 1932. Taught philosophy from 1900 to 1909, as assistant, instructor, and assistant professor at the University of Wisconsin, and as professor of philosophy from 1909 to 1921 at the University of Illinois. Professor of education since 1921 at the Ohio State University.

Books: *An Outline of Logic, Fundamentals of Education, Modern Educational Theories,* and *Conflicting Psychologies of Learning;* also joint author of *Creative Intelligence, Ourselves and the World,* and *The Educational Frontier.* Contributor to various philosophical, psychological, and educational journals. Chiefly interested in the significance of education as an instrumentality for social and cultural progress. Have found the Depression a great help in promoting the idea that education must assume a direct responsibility for the character or quality of social change and the reinterpretation of the idea of democracy.

"THE GREAT AMERICAN DREAM"

Boyd H. Bode

A recent writer on American civilization makes the remark that our history, unlike the history of the great powers of the Old World, begins with marked abruptness. Our record does not trace back continuously to a Golden Age, when the gods walked the earth with men; it does not transmit to us, from the twilight zone of myth and legend, the shadowy forms of rulers endowed with the qualities of supermen and with despotic power; it has no period when knighthood was in flower, with a background of serfs and peasants to serve as props in the play. The story begins only four short centuries ago. It unfolds itself in the full light of our modern day. Its central interest lies, not in the activities of a small group of glorified heroes and leaders but in the fortunes of the common man. According to the writer just alluded to, its special significance lies in the emergence and development of what he calls the "American dream of a better, richer, and happier life for all our citizens of every rank;" a dream which, in his judgment, constitutes "the greatest contribution we have as yet made to the thought and the welfare of the world."

This "American dream" is inwoven in the whole structure of our national life. Although the span of our history is so brief, it has proved to be sufficiently long to produce a distinctive mental pattern, a unique outlook or spiritual attitude, a sustaining national tradition. This tradition is commonly known among us as equality of opportunity. To understand this tradition it is necessary, as our historians are agreed, to take special account of the molding influence of our American frontier.

This influence naturally required time to make itself felt. The first colonists did not at once become Americans. They were not filled with a consuming desire to achieve equality of opportunity. On the contrary, they were merely transplanted Europeans, who tried to live according to the ideas which they had brought with them from the Old World. They struggled manfully to make America look as much as possible like Europe. The new social order which they brought into being had an upper, ruling class and a disfranchised lower class: it determined the rank of students in Harvard College, for example, by social position; it cultivated distinctions of dress and manners; it maintained in the South a landed gentry through the system of primogeniture; it dealt harshly with persons who departed from the standards of the prevailing religion and social custom; it developed a culture that was thoroughly European in spirit. These early colonists kept to the old ways, so far as circumstances would permit.

In the long run, however, these new circumstances proved to be too powerful. When the flood of population finally broke through the barrier of the Appalachian mountains and spread itself over the Mississippi Valley, Europe was gradually left behind. In the great open spaces of the Middle West distinctions in social rank had little meaning. One man was as good as another. The frontier set its own standards, which were based largely on the law of the survival of the fittest. On the frontier it was much more important that a man should be courageous, self-reliant, resourceful and persistent than that he should have a grandmother who had been presented to the queen. In fact, there was no apparent reason why he should have a grandmother at all. Writers like Mark Twain took special pleasure in ridiculing such weakness for grandmothers and similar evidences of attachment to the social distinctions of the Old World.

A new era had begun. The common man was coming into his heritage. The frontier was a magic solvent of all the social distinctions and stratifications that had piled up during centuries of

European history. The common man gloried in his common-
ness. To the aspiring politician it was far more of an asset to
have sprung from a log cabin, or even from the sidewalks of
New York, than from landed estates and a line of belted knights.
Politically, a distinguished ancestry might easily prove to be a
handicap. One might almost say that the lack of a razor or of a
change of new underwear became a guarantee of all the manly
virtues. Even when communities became more settled and
affluent, the spirit of the frontier continued to make itself felt.
As long as men could go West and grow up with the country,
there was little chance of developing the social stratifications of
the Old World. The line of the frontier might continue to
recede across the interminable stretches of the great West, but
from decade to decade it persisted as a major factor in shaping
the life of the nation, until the spirit of the frontier had become
embedded in the national tradition. It became a tradition of
faith in the common man, a tradition of faith in the supreme and
ultimate value of personality, a tradition which required every
man, as a solemn right and duty, to stand on his own feet and to
exercise independence in thought and action.

This, then, is the tradition which has been called the "American dream of a better, richer, and happier life for all our
citizens of every rank." Back of this dream lay an implicit faith
in the inherent worth of the common man, in the untutored
wisdom of the plain people. Equality of opportunity was guaranteed, not by the social order, but by the frontier. The resources
of the continent were at the disposal of all comers. Government
was viewed with distrust. According to Jefferson, an occasional
rebellion is a necessity, in order to keep government in check.
"God forbid," he says, "we should ever be twenty years without
such a rebellion." We may remind ourselves that the period of
frontier development was closely related in time to the period
when a world-weary civilization loved to talk, through spokesmen like Rousseau and the Romanticists, about a state of nature
in which men could be themselves, unhampered by social and

governmental restrictions, and develop in accordance with the divine image in which they were created. Poets writing from the security of their own firesides spoke feelingly of the "noble savage" and claimed, with Pope, that "the state of nature is the state of God."

This general feeling of distrust of government was shared by the men of the frontier. While they were under no delusions with respect to the noble savage, they were naturally sympathetic to the notion that the great dream required freedom from the mass of social conventions and governmental restrictions which they had left behind. Such freedom, plus the opportunities offered by the frontier, was considered sufficient to make a democracy. In other words, the frontier not only gave impetus to the dream of a better, richer, and happier life for everybody, but it was also supposed to provide the conditions for its realization.

This conception of democracy has an attractive simplicity. Unfortunately, it underestimates the importance of social organization in the development of the individual. The frontier undoubtedly developed certain admirable qualities. But owing to the lack of social relationships the range of these qualities was sharply limited. Esthetic appreciation naturally found little encouragement in the desperate struggle with an unfriendly environment. Sustained social coöperation had little place in the affairs of the thinly populated settlements. Intellectual stimulation extended only a short way beyond the exigencies of everyday life. Hardship, privation, and an appalling loneliness were the common lot of the pioneer family. Education, even under favorable conditions, was confined to the rudiments. Ability and character had almost no avenue of expression except in the accumulation of property. Narrowness and superstition were the inevitable products of such conditions, unsoftened by the amenities that spring from more intimate social intercourse. Only a misguided sentimentalism can see in such conditions the ideal setting for personal development, even though we may not care to say with Tennyson: "Better fifty years of Europe than a cycle of Cathay."

One would naturally suppose that these limitations would be most evident to the frontiersmen themselves. But this appears not to have been the case. Perhaps the frontier could not afford to admit its shortcomings candidly, without destroying its morale. At any rate, those traits for which there was no adequate opportunity of expression on the frontier were severely discounted. Esthetic appreciation was looked down upon as effeminate and effete. The need of companionship and social intercourse was regarded as the mark of the tenderfoot. Scholarship was dismissed contemptuously as "book-learning." On the other hand, the qualities that were useful in frontier life were exalted, and the fearful drudgery which this life involved was made endurable by being invested with moral and religious sanctions.

This idealization of the frontier presently met with powerful support from the outside. Even before the frontier ceased to exist as a physical fact, it passed over into the realm of literary romance, so that, like John Brown's soul, it still went marching on. Our writers of Wild West stories, from Bret Harte down, have labored industriously to create for us a Golden Age of our own, a Golden Age that was just around the corner in the immediate past, an Age in which the great American dream had already come true. They made it an age of men reared on the bosom of nature and grown to astounding proportions of heroism, nobility of spirit and refinement of sentiment. The grammar and the table manners of these dashing figures might, indeed, fail to meet the requirements of polite society, but underneath those rude shirts were hearts of purest gold. By the standards of the artificial social order in which they were born these men were perhaps outcasts and criminals, but in these new surroundings, where men were men, they rose to a new stature and became the true Americans. Thus the American dream was transformed into a daydream, a bed-time story. It became a

lingering recollection of something that never happened, of a
fulfilment that never took place, of a West that never was on
land or sea.

What we call our American faith in the common man appears
to have been tinged throughout with this romantic notion of an
inherent nobility in every individual, which, if given the chance,
will express itself as the result of an inner development, in much
the same way as a chicken is hatched from an egg. From this
standpoint the chief function of government is to protect the
individual against outside interference. Government must have
very limited functions and must, so far as possible, be local in
character. This conception of government very soon became an
issue in our political life. At the very outset of our career as a
nation, Thomas Jefferson appeared as the spokesman of the
common man, but it is significant that the common man in whom
he placed his faith was not the man with a job in town, but the
small farmer out in the country. On the other hand, the realistic
Hamilton was utterly incapable of recognizing the voice of the
farmer as the voice of God, and so he advocated the traditional
doctrine of government by a special and privileged class. Jefferson's advocacy of the common man has linked his name for all
time with the American dream; but the emphasis in Jefferson's
thinking was on the protection of the individual against the
encroachment of government, and not on the function of government to provide equality of opportunity through industrial
and economic organization. The strength of Hamilton's position
lay in his deeper perception of the meaning of social organization in the development of character and capacity. His weakness
consisted in his insensitiveness to the great dream, which kept
him from dealing with social organization as simply an instrumentality for the development of spiritual values in all the
members of the community. To put the contrast in extreme
form, Jefferson discounted social organization to the point of
making the development of personality independent of it;

whereas Hamilton emphasized social organization to the point of making the individual subordinate to it.

In the main our tradition to this day has been Jeffersonian rather than Hamiltonian. The area of governmental functions has been extended enormously, but we still cling to the fiction that these functions are being employed merely for the purpose of giving every individual plenty of elbow-room, as in the days of the frontier. We talk about maintaining the American way of life, but we make this a cover for subordinating the interests of the many to the interests of the few. As a result we have an astonishing gap between theory and practice in our American life. In theory we hold to equality of opportunity; in practice we have surrendered political and economic control to the great corporate units that shape our destinies. In theory we hold to the inalienable right and duty of each individual to develop his God-given powers; in practice we measure success in terms of possessions and income. In theory we protect independence of thought and action; in practice we insist on conformity, in the name of Americanism. In theory we endorse liberty of conscience; in practice our requirements for citizenship, as determined by recent court decisions, make it very doubtful whether Christ himself, if he were to return to this earth, could meet these requirements. As a historian has recently said, we talk like Jefferson but we act like Hamilton.

The influence of the frontier in identifying equality of opportunity with economic opportunity and with the notion of unrestrained competition is a fairly familiar fact. That this same influence also created a general demand for "likemindedness" is less well known, but is of perhaps equal importance. The Middle West, as Dewey points out, "has never had an interest in ideas as ideas, nor in science and art for what they may do in liberating and elevating the human spirit." [1] It was hardly to be expected that an interest in ideas as ideas would find congenial soil in an environment which considered its simple scheme of life

[1] John Dewey, *Characters and Events*, vol. II, p. 448.

essentially adequate and which was absorbed in the task of developing its material resources. Moreover, under the primitive conditions of the frontier the church naturally became the center of social life and intercourse and the guardian of moral and "spiritual" standards. It was hospitable to the spirit of kindliness and fair dealing, but by no means equally hospitable to the spirit of free inquiry. It thus set a pattern that became tremendously powerful. Not to belong to a church was ground for suspicion, as politicians have known for a long time; in fact, to entertain ideas of any kind that were out of line with those prevailing in the community was pretty sure to gain for an individual the reputation of being "queer" and to cause him to be regarded as, to that extent, a less desirable member of the community.

When we call to mind the nature of the task that confronted these young communities this development is not hard to understand. The restraints that operate in older communities were largely absent. Respect for law and order, to say nothing of the ordinary decencies and refinements of life, together with neighborliness and coöperativeness had to be invested with social sanction and authority. This sanction and authority, as exercised by the church, naturally tended toward placing a premium on like-mindedness, and toward fostering a corresponding disposition to frown upon all departures from types. "As the frontier ceased to be a menace to orderly life, it persisted as a limit beyond which it was dangerous and unrespectable for thought to travel." [2]

The tendency to achieve and maintain group solidarity is no new thing. In the present case this tendency was operating under special conditions so as to produce a conception of "Americanism" that was a betrayal of democracy. The disposition to judge Americanism by the standards of the Ku Klux Klan and to compute it in terms of percentages is the logical product of this development. In brief, it led to an exact repetition of what was

[2] Dewey, *Op. Cit.*, p. 450.

done in other forms of society which made no pretense of being democracies. It set up specific beliefs and practices which were not open to criticism, and it insisted that those beliefs and practices must be the basis for determining the meaning of Americanism and Democracy.

The result, in brief, has been that our American democracy has developed an orthodoxy of its own, differing in content but not greatly in spirit from the orthodoxies of the past. It is one of the ironies of history that this development has tended to provide special privileges and immunities for exactly the same vested interests as those which dominated the older non-democratic communities. In our schools theological doctrines were protected by public sentiment and even by legislative enactment; the power of our invisible government was sheltered by the cultivation of an ignorant reverence for the Constitution and a fatuous belief in the significance of voting; the dominance of economic privilege was strengthened by the perpetuation of frontier notions with respect to rugged individualism and equality of opportunity. Unconventional ideas were strangled at birth by being labelled socialism, communism, atheism, and the like. Meanwhile our pedagogues, with a singular lack of a sense of humor, even for pedagogues, were devoting themselves to measuring things that bore no relation to the only problem which really mattered or to preaching a purely sentimental doctrine of respect for personality, of regard for individual differences, of the need for independent thinking and creativeness and social sensitiveness. They were all for critical and independent thinking, but with the tacit understanding that in teaching our young hopefuls to swim we must not permit them to go near the water.

For a considerable period the operations of the forces which were transforming us from a rural to an industrial and highly integrated nation were not apparent to the average citizen. We managed to cling to the pleasant delusion that the basic principles of democracy had been solved, once and for all, with the adoption of the Constitution. But when the wrath of God fell upon us in the autumn of 1929 our nakedness became progressively revealed. When we took stock of our financial and industrial situation, our cherished economic individualism was stripped of its halo. When we looked to the church to bolster up the morale of the people, we found that in its preoccupation with personal salvation it had permitted initiative and leadership in matters of social welfare to pass into other hands. People generally, and particularly younger people, had formed the habit, not of opposing the church but of forgetting all about the church, leading one of its prominent spokesmen to declare that "judged by its hold upon men and measured in terms of what it professes to desire to see accomplished, the church at present must be ranked among the least effective of the agencies by which man is seeking to better his lot." [3] When we looked to Europe, whence we had recently returned from the war to end war, and to the Orient, with its great commercial possibilities, we found that while we were engrossed in watching the stock market, we had become cordially hated and that the stage was being set for another world war. In business, in religion, and in government our leadership had failed us. And to cap the climax, the reward for the faithful services rendered to the vested interests by our educational system was the decision that education consisted mostly of fads and frills and should be cut to the bone.

For education the present state of affairs has a peculiar significance. The historic lament of Cardinal Wolsey to the effect that if he had served his God as he had served his king he would not have got into his ultimate predicament is something that education can afford to take to heart. If we had a truly democratic system of education, then the bearing of education on continuous readjustment to changing conditions would be evident; and the moral to be drawn from a calamity like the present depression would be the need of more education of the

[3] Stanley High, "The Revolt Against God," *Harpers Magazine*, May, 1933, p. 654.

same kind. But in so far as education shares in the responsibility for the present situation it has little ground for complaint if its program is curtailed. A famous baseball manager is said to have remarked, when his club finished at the bottom of the list, that he intended to sell his best players because he could win last place with a much cheaper team.

Education in America is at the cross-roads. Historically our schools have been pledged to the task of perpetuating our democracy. It is an undeniable fact, however, that we have usually contrived to keep the much lauded spirit of the frontier out of our schools. On the frontier itself this exclusion was readily understandable. The schools on the frontier confined themselves, in the main, to the inculcation of "tool" subjects. Qualities like creativeness and independence in thought and action were quite properly considered out of place in subjects such as spelling and addition. As our school system developed, the notion that our social order was essentially perfect from the start made the cultivation of the frontier spirit seem superfluous. So we were content to praise this spirit, as a kind of ancestor worship and with no thought of permitting the matter to go any further. If the social structure which we have inherited is regarded as fundamentally complete and final, it follows logically that the chief business of the schools is to acquaint the pupils with this structure and to cultivate a type of citizenship that identifies patriotism with loyalty to the beliefs and customs of the past.

Stated in terms of our present discussion, the problem confronting American education at the present time is the problem of developing in our schools the spirit of the frontier. A blind loyalty to the accidental customs of the past means disloyalty to the ideal of equality of opportunity. New occasions teach new duties. Time was when it seemed quite feasible to determine beforehand the skills, the information, and the beliefs or attitudes which an individual would need so as to fit into the social order with a minimum of friction. It was possible, so to speak, to plot his curve in advance. That time is past. The schools now have a unique responsibility for enabling the American people to make an intelligent judgment regarding the meaning of equality of opportunity under present conditions, and to decide independently whether they are willing to pay the price.

From the standpoint of pedagogic comfort it is a misfortune to live in a period of accelerated change. Things will no longer stay put, even during the brief span of an average lifetime. We have only recently become industrialized, which means that we must reconsider our philosophy of industry. We have witnessed the breakdown of old ways of living, which means that we must reconsider standards of conduct. Through improved means of transportation and communication we have become a next-door neighbor to the rest of the world, which means that we must reconsider our foreign policy. Through science and corporate modes of behavior our outlook on life has been changed, which means that we must reconsider the tenets of traditional religion. We find ourselves thrust into a new world with an equipment of old habits, old loyalties, old attitudes. The task of securing flexibility in our basic forms of thinking is, in a sense, a new obligation for education. There is reason to think that the chief cause of the maladjustments which are appearing in all the major areas of life is to be sought, not in lack of intelligence, nor in lack of goodwill, nor even in the sinister power of vested interests, but in the tyranny of old habits of thinking and of conduct.

The spirit in which education should undertake its task is indicated by our tradition. When education becomes an instrumentality, either for maintaining the *status quo* or for promoting a predetermined set of beliefs, it ceases to be democratic. The proper function of education in a democracy is to make provision for the continuous reconstruction of basic beliefs and attitudes, but according to no predetermined pattern. Its attitude must be genuinely experimental, its method must be the method of intelligence, and its final test of value for all institutions, from industry to religion, must be the development of personality in a continuously changing social order.

Everyone admits now that in countless instances individual lives are being warped, that injustice has entrenched itself in our social institutions, that national rivalries are endangering the very structure of our civilization. Yet these things persist, because our loyalties are misdirected. If the spirit of democracy is to survive, we cannot hope to provide a remedy either by inculcating prescribed loyalties or by placing an unenlightened emphasis on the development of individual capacity and on the cultivation of social sensitiveness and the spirit of coöperation. Nothing short of a direct attack on the discrepancies and contradictions that lie at the heart of our cultural heritage will provide the perspective which is demanded by modern conditions.

An approach of this kind, it should be noted, is not merely a proposal to organize our educational program around the current "problems of civilization." It carries the much more radical implication that we are to make a conscious effort to set into sharp contrast those conflicts among our beliefs and ideals which are responsible for the maladjustments that have appeared in each of the main areas of life. For this afflicted generation the areas of special stress and strain lie in the fields of economics and industry, religion, government, and the like. In each of these fields the situation is typically the same. We bring into them certain beliefs or ideals which we have inherited from the past, but we also give allegiance to beliefs or ideals which were developed under the pressure of more recent conditions and which do not harmonize with the rest. The average person is at best only vaguely aware of these discrepancies. He does not see the situation with sufficient clearness to reconstruct his total outlook or attitude, and so he becomes confused. He loses his sense of direction; his beliefs are not backed by depth of conviction. In brief, he tends to become, except where his immediate interests are concerned, a bystander rather than a participant in the process of reshaping the social order.

It seems reasonable to insist that education must assume responsibility for making people intelligent with respect to this situation. In American history, for example, it should be made clear that the ideal of democracy, as developed under the conditions of the frontier is very different from the ideal of democracy which has been growing up under subsequent conditions— an ideal which requires subordination of the profit motive and which calls for extensive modification of the present industrial and economic order. Unless this contrast is clearly seen, intelligence is frustrated, and our loyalties either operate blindly or they become paralyzed. It is not the business of education to lay down the pattern for a new synthesis, but it is emphatically its business to create the insight that a new synthesis is needed and to provide favorable conditions for a critical and independent reconstruction of these conflicting beliefs or dispositions into a unified outlook or attitude.

A similar procedure is obviously possible in other parts of the social science field. In the natural sciences we encounter a general conception of the universe, of truth, of man, and of the basis for moral values, that is at odds with those traditional views which antedate the development of modern science. In literature and the arts we have the material for clothing these disembodied ideas with the flesh and blood of human emotion and aspiration. In all these areas special care is needed in order to bring these contrasts and their implications to the surface as a basis for a new integration of beliefs and also as a point of reference for the cultivation of an interest in ideas as ideas or for the cultivation of interests of a more practical nature.

It remains to point out in conclusion that an educational program of this general character would not, even if successful, guarantee a new lease of life to the ideal of equality of opportunity. Guarantees of this kind are incompatible with the spirit of democratic institutions. What is contended for here is, first of all, that a democracy must continuously reëxamine and reinterpret the meaning of its institutions and practices if it is to endure as a democracy. For this reason a democracy requires an educational system that is distinctive from all others. It must cultivate a realizing sense that its Golden Age is not in the past but in the future; that its spiritual heritage is not a finished product but a dream, which in many essential respects is still a dream; that equality of opportunity must be provided, not by nature but by the social order. It is undeniably possible that as the American people gain a wider view of all that is involved, they will prefer to retain the familiar beliefs and values and bid good-by to the dream. Education cannot make its appeal to intelligence and then refuse to abide by the test. Its task is to keep the frontier always open, in the faith that as the meaning of equality of opportunity continues to grow the American people will rise correspondingly to new levels of achievement and to new perspectives on their historic past and on the future.

THE SOCIALIZATION
OF MORALITY

FELIX S. COHEN

Born 1907 in New York City. Graduated College of the City of New York (A.B. 1926); Harvard University (M.A. 1927, Ph.D. 1929); Columbia University Law School (LL.B. 1931). Member of the New York bar. Author, *Ethical Systems and Legal Ideals* (1933); "What is a Question?" (1929) 39 *Monist* 350; "The Ethical Basis of Legal Criticism" (1931) 41 *Yale Law Journal* 201; "The Subject Matter of Ethical Science" (1932) 42 *International Journal of Ethics* 397; "The Blessing of Unemployment" (1933) 2 *The American Scholar* 203; and other articles in legal and philosophical periodicals. Contributor to the Encyclopaedia of the Social Sciences. Lecturer at the New School for Social Research, 1932-1933.

THE SOCIALIZATION OF MORALITY

Felix S. Cohen

I. The Poverty of Desocialized Morality

It was the peculiar fate of my generation to be born into a world of collapsing faiths. The years of the War and the years after played havoc with the dreams of many centuries. Hopes which had fulfilled the lives of intelligent men and women became heaps of dust. The vision of Progress through Science came to reek with the stench of gunpowder and poison gas. Men's faith in the permanent values of philosophy and religion could not survive undimmed the spectacle of philosophers and chaplains cursing each other across the lines of battle. Hopes of securing a better world through trade union organization, woman suffrage, or political reform, hopes which had informed many useful lives, were silently abandoned and won few new champions. Traditional American faiths in Temperance, in Democracy, and even in Personal Success, never took hold of the hearts that were molded in the years of the War. Even the ideal of patriotism came to seem a hollow sham in a war fought by conscript armies and financed by Big Business on a basis of three and one-half per cent interest compounded quarterly.

This is not to say that the War actually destroyed vital growths of the human spirit. Rather it probed ideals and movements that had been long afflicted with internal decay. It revealed the hollowness of the moral ideals of past centuries, and it left all contemporary faiths weaker,—so that an acute critic of literature could say, a few years ago, that tragedy was no longer possible in our age because we had lost all belief in ultimate values.[1]

Loss of faith in traditional moral values found varied expression. A widely professed belief in "tolerance" or "freedom," centering in this country about the natural right to get drunk, proceeded from the premise, "There are no certain moral principles," to the conclusion, "It is wrong for us to impose standards upon other individuals,"—and thus attempted to derive a moral code from the fact of moral ignorance. Popular exploitations of anthropology, psychology, and psychoanalysis offered cumulative reassurance to those who felt it necessary to regard moral standards as products of superstition, conspiracy, indigestion, or sexual aberration, and even Einstein's theory of relativity came to be popularly regarded as mathematical evidence for the proposition that every moral belief is as good as any other moral belief. Our pervasive distrust of our own lingering beliefs produced the peculiar educational dogma that teachers (other than teachers of education) should not teach facts or doctrines but should rather permit students to develop "from within" and to think "independently." Above all, the loss of faith in traditional moral values led to intensified revolt against any assertion of moral or social responsibility, in every craft and art of modern life from the writing of poetry to the manufacture of munitions.

None of these tendencies of the post-war years was new. Each is readily traced back a century or more. But each has reached a point of new intensity in the last two decades.

Here is the problem, here the setting, of a new philosophy of values, a new morality, to be molded in the two or three decades before us. For one thing is certain, that no civilization can endure which distrusts its moral foundations as profoundly as we have come to distrust the ideals that order our social existence. No society can long exist in which the disintegrating forces of class interests and class rivalries, economic, racial, and national, find no other court of appeal than the field of violent

[1] Krutch, *The Modern Temper*, 1929, chap. 5.

struggle. It is true, no doubt, as the communists urge, that the bitterness of national and racial hatred may be overcome by an intensification of the class struggle, leading to the international consolidation of opposing forces of labor and capital. It is equally true, as the fascists have shown, that economic and political conflicts within a nation may be silenced by an intensification of national and racial hatred. But the substitution of one hatred for another offers no permanent basis of peace in an interdependent world. The suicide of our civilization can be prevented only by the discovery of a new pattern upon which its life can be integrated, a new synthesis of conflicting human desires.

One hesitates to assign this vital task to the province of ethics or morality. For recent centuries of philosophical discussion have endowed the words "ethical" and "moral" with a milk-and-watery flavor and an odor of Sunday School sanctity. To speak of a "moral" man, a "good" woman, or an "ethical" druggist is to say very little about human values. Preoccupation with "moral" problems is commonly regarded as psychopathic in adults. Economists, judges, and artists, alike, are quick to resent the suggestion that moral questions exist in their several fields of endeavor. Yet the critique of a society's ideals and standards is inevitably a moral problem, a problem reaching to the ultimate values of human life, and one cannot even outline the task of transvaluation without in some measure appraising the strength and weakness of traditional moral theory.

If the substance of traditional moral theory offers only faltering or irrelevant answers to the problems of conduct that the modern world poses, this is not because problems of social existence have become unmoral, but rather because moralists have become unsocial.

Moral theory in the western world of the last two or three centuries has been dominated by the tradition of individualism, largely drawn from the precepts of the New Testament and the economic and political ethics of Protestantism, spiced with the worldly observation of men like Machiavelli and Mandeville, and attaining its purest philosophical formulation and reductio ad absurdum in the Kantian doctrine which denies the existence of moral problems in the sensible world, and reduces morality to a logical postulate devoid of social content.[2]

The morality of the individualist tradition is a morality of peculiar narrowness, being addressed almost entirely to the moral problems of persons who have nothing important to do. For children and slaves, the only significant questions of conduct arise in situations of intimate personal relationship, and it is in this restricted context that the problems of temptation, sin, sex, love, manners, proprietary and intellectual honesty, selfishness and discipline are treated by moral philosophers. Moral philosophers have had little to say about such matters as peace and war, the distribution and the use of economic power and political force, the functions of scientific thought, of education, and of artistic endeavor, the changing substance of cultures, and the physical conditions of existence.[3] These are matters which, although they do not present problems of conduct to children or slaves, do present problems of conduct to legislators, voters, artists, scientists, business men, workers, philosophers, teachers, revolutionists, judges, and other individuals who exercise power over human lives. And the patterns of life even of children and slaves are very profoundly affected by the answers that are given to such problems.

The poverty of modern moral theory is apparent if we contrast with the content of contemporary morality such moral codes as are embodied in the writings of the Pentateuch, in the

[2] I do not mean to suggest that Kant was a consistent Kantian. I have elsewhere indicated some of the empirical social assumptions that characterize his legal philosophy. See *Ethical Systems and Legal Ideals*, 1933, pp. 107-108.

[3] It is hardly necessary to mention that such philosophers as Perry, Dewey, Parker, and Laird have, in recent years, launched a forthright attack upon the provincialism of traditional moral theory.

dialogues of Plato, or in the scholastic summas. Each of these historic codes makes a resolute and straightforward attempt to deal with all the basic problems of human conduct that a given civilization proposes. Each of these codes seeks to define the place and function of the artist, the property-owner, the teacher, and the ruler. In none of these codes is an attempt made to justify modes of conduct fraught with human joy or suffering, after the manner of modern moralists, by assigning the subject to a "non-moral" realm of art, science, industry, or statesmanship and refusing to discuss it.

It would seem that modern moralists have suffered a loss of nerve. A monarch fearful of revolt may secure absolute obedience by commanding his subjects to do as they please. Modern ethics asserts its sovereignty by issuing to the owners of property the unbreakable commandment, *Laissez faire*. Nor is the morality of *laissez faire* restricted to economic realms. So weak is the empire of contemporary ethical theory that it must needs grant autonomy or near-autonomy not only to the business man, but as well to the artist, the scientist, the educator, and the statesman in fashioning ideals of right and wrong within the various provinces of human activity. Ideals thus fashioned are class ideals, reflecting the narrow interests of professional groups. The ideals of modern art reflect primarily the artist's appreciation of the technical difficulties presented by certain materials and of the skill exhibited in their conquest, rather than a concern with the significance and value of human experiences evoked by the artistic creation. The success of economic enterprise is measured by the standard of entrepreneur's profit (even when, as in the case of certain public enterprises, the entrepreneur is trying not to make a profit), rather than by an appraisal of the cost of human energy and sacrifice that the enterprise demands and the value of the human interests it serves. Law finds in its own hallowed past and in the aesthetic harmonies of the legal system itself the touchstones of criticism which a comprehensive social morality once provided.[4] And each profession in modern society has its own code of ethics which is primarily designed to lend respectability to the vested interests of the profession and to protect its members from the just claims of society.

The gradual abandonment by moral theory of its significant social content has roots deep in the material and intellectual foundations of our civilization. Chief among the factors which have contributed to the desocialization of morality must be listed the growing complexity of industrial civilization, the accelerated rate of social change, and the submergence of human personalities before the impersonal institutional forces of modern society.

The complexity of the moral scene. It is natural that the vast complexity of modern life should lead men to believe that the vision of an integrated social morality is an anachronism in contemporary civilization. Such, at least, is the belief of those moralists who have remained loyal to the philosophical ideal of wholeness, and in this loyalty have retreated, step by step, from the realms of human conduct that bear most deeply the imprints of our complex social structure. Such, too, is the belief of those who have been faithful to the moral realities of new and complex social situations and in this faith have abandoned the philosophical effort to systematize specific prescriptions for specific social ills.

The complexity of a social system, which engenders intellectual difficulties for the moral philosopher, operates more directly upon the springs of moral feeling. The complexity of urban life is revealed in increasingly minute specialization of human activities. The moral significance of the self-supporting farmer's task is clear, the moral values of success and failure are vivid, and the personal relationships to which the task gives rise are simple

---

[4] I have elsewhere attempted to analyze the logical difficulties which this narrow conception of ethics imposes upon law and the social sciences. See *Ethical Systems and Legal Ideals*, 1933. The major thesis of this volume is restated, in words of one and two syllables, in *Modern Ethics and the Law*, 1934, 4 Brooklyn Law Review 33.

and direct. So with the task of the petty artisan or the family physician. The moral overtones of action are less clear to the mill-worker, the seed salesman, the stockholder of an industrial corporation, the nose and throat specialist, or the uniformed orderly of a great hospital.

Increasing division of labor, which marks the growth of civilization, destroys not only the traditional moral patterns of individuals' working lives but as well the communities of experience out of which moral attitudes grow. Morality is a function of uniformity. Envy and contempt, rivalry and emulation, sympathy and antipathy, praise and blame, presuppose a community of interest and experience. Those whose lives are spent in unrelated occupations meet in a meager community, and the shrinking of morality to rules of sportsmanship and good manners, in certain social groups, testifies to this meagerness. Increasingly the standards which demand men's effective allegiance are standards reflecting the special interests of small homogeneous occupational groups rather than the interests of a whole society.

Morality and the tempo of industrialism. If morality is, in general, dependent upon uniformity, it is peculiarly dependent upon temporal uniformity. Just as uniformity of social position or occupation leads to the compulsive attraction of the "normal" or "natural," so uniformity in time lends the force of tradition, reverence, and loyalty to moral beliefs. This is not simply a consequence of superstition and inertia. Time is required for the analysis and verification of moral beliefs.

The morality of any age, then, is likely to be most firmly fixed in those realms of life which are least affected by social change.

The simple, enduring problems of personal relationship maintain moral grandeur while changing historical conditions seem to make questions of economic, political, or cultural policy ephemeral. The prestige of a historic tradition can attach only to those beliefs that we share with a remote past. Unfortunately the scale of moral problems and the required range of moral vision have been comparatively narrow in the simpler societies from which we derive our moral traditions. Jesus will bring back to life a poor unfortunate whose death has come to his attention, but it would be entirely inconsistent with the biblical Jesus to expect him to bring back to life a large number of people who have died in a village he has not visited, or to prevent the death of a large number of children by teaching people how to pasteurize milk. To the extent that modern ethics is affected by the tradition of Jesus, therefore, it tends to consider larger social problems as unimportant and unreal, and to focus moral criticism upon the personal behavior of individuals rather than upon social institutions. Moral aspects of the economic order are dismissed as Jesus dismisses the indignant protests of his disciples when a woman anoints his head with a costly perfume. To the objection that for the price of the perfume a multitude of the poor might have been fed, Jesus gives the characteristic individualist answer: "ye have the poor always with you, and whensoever ye will ye can do them good; but me ye have not always" (Mark:14:7).

Morality and slavery. Most people, no doubt, are uninterested in broad social questions because they have no voice in the decision of such questions. Interest would be misplaced energy. A slave class will not develop an ethics relevant to the problems of social policy which its masters face.

Instructive is the appeal which the morality of primitive Christianity made to a people without political power. Distinguished from the earlier Jewish morality, with its detailed analysis of social and economic relationships, primitive Christianity made a virtue of the necessity under which its audience labored to take no thought for the morrow, and to render unto Cæsar that which was Cæsar's. To the extent that people today feel impotent in the realm of social affairs they are ready to accept the narrow limitations of a moral code that ignores the fundamental problems of government, economics, and culture.

And this feeling of impotence is almost universal in contemporary society, not only in the ranks of the oppressed, but even among the rulers of society, who are themselves the puppets of collective forces they cannot understand. Increasingly the significant questions of modern life seem to be decided not by human beings but by machines and institutions and impersonal economic laws that wreak their will upon an enslaved human race.

II. The Task of Moral Philosophy

The task of modern ethics would be hopeless indeed did not the very forces which have destroyed the morality of individualism provide the basis of a new integration of human interests. Neither the complexity of modern civilization, nor the rapidity of its material transformations, nor the shifting of significant human choices from a personal sphere to a collective sphere, obstructs the way to a socialized morality. Rather each of these factors in the disintegration of traditional morality presents itself as a material element in the reconstruction of moral theory.

The simplification of a social order. The belief that a universal morality can arise only out of a simpler society than our own is a half truth. What makes a society simple is a moral theory. The complexity of modern society is not an objective fact. Complexity is always relative to the starting point of analysis. The description of planetary movements was an extremely complex affair when the earth was used as the point of reference, and became increasingly complex as observations became more accurate, but the complexity vanished with the substitution of the sun as a point of reference. Modern civilization is oppressive in its complexity if we conceive its movements in terms of individual liberties, individual duties, and individual personalities. It may come to seem a rather simple affair when analyzed in terms of social functions.

The complex specialization of human activities ceases to be a divisive force in the social structure when specialized functions are coördinated in a great social effort. Politicians, artists, and steel workers may have little of importance to say to each other in the nations of the West. That is not true in Soviet Russia. The coördination of diverse social functions in an integrated moral order informs each vocation of civilized life with a social ideal and a clarified moral task. Specialization ceases to be an escape from the domain of morality; it may become a condition of social usefulness. In a collective morality there is more room for specialization, for variation from common norms, for the development of rare human potentialities, than there can be within an individualistic morality, just as there is greater scope for diverse talents in the collectivity of a baseball team than in a field of nine runners.

Nothing, then, could be further from the truth than the spectre of men emerging into standardized robots under a socialist order of society. Social harmony no more requires that each individual play a simple tune, much less the same tune, than does orchestral harmony. The robot today is the product of an individualist morality that impoverishes the human spirit by denying it participation in the vital collective forces of modern civilization. Genius is achieved not by Robinson Crusoes fired with the individualistic passion for self-sufficiency, but by men who can rely upon their fellows to perform tasks for which they are not fitted and are thus freed and helped to fashion rare gifts. Heretofore such social coöperation as genius demands has been assured only by the natural communism of a harmonious family life or by the fortuitous favor of society's rulers. A socialist society makes universal the material security which the flowering of the human spirit requires as a condition of existence. It destroys the adventure of men's uncertain search for food, and destroys as well the individual initiative that finds expression in the course of self-aggrandizement, but it destroys these things to make room for a higher adventure and a wider initiative.

Moral sanctions in a changing society. The shadow of transi-

toriness which changing material conditions cast over the
established traditions of morality is as subjective as is the appearance of complexity in our social order. Indeed, change is no more
than complexity along the dimension of time.

Change is disconcerting only where there is no goal. The loss
of moral moorings which early capitalist industrialism brought
to the nations of the West, exemplified in such movements of
despair as the machine-wrecking of the Luddites and the more
sophisticated glorification of the escape to the primitive, stands
in sharp contrast to the purposeful industrialization of Russia
under Soviet rule. Material change, far from being a disruptive
force, may itself become the stable axis of a morality oriented to
the dynamic forces of industrial civilization. If revolutionary
changes in the material bases of life make the moral traditions
of the past irrelevant to the contemporary world, these changes,
come to consciousness, create a revolutionary morality that is not
dependent upon the sanctions of precedent and inertia, that finds
adventure, hope, and faith in every essential break with an out-
worn past.

Morality and power. Finally, the increased range and scope
of moral problems in the modern world, which seems to rob the
individual of power and responsibility, itself creates the basis of
a new integration of human values. The apparent impersonality
of the forces that mold contemporary civilization reflects only
the meagerness of personalities integrated by an individualistic
formula. This poverty of personality is itself overcome by a more
comprehensive social morality. Such a morality substitutes for
the individualistic defense of man against society the Aristotelean
thesis that man finds the completion of his personality in society.
Only in so far as man consciously identifies his powers with
wider social forces, and participates in the responsibilities, the
purposes, and the achievements of society, does he lay valid
claim to the values of civilization.

The sense of moral impotence in the presence of overwhelming social problems derives from the attempt to attack these problems with the weapons of a narrow personal morality. Personal kindliness, however adequate to adjust the relations between a master and a domestic slave, is pathetically inadequate in the relationship between an industrial corporation and its employees. To that relationship morality can be relevant only if morality incorporates the social organization of knowledge, which is science, and the social organization of human powers and purposes, which is politics.

Socialism, as the fulfillment of democracy, offers all men the power out of which moral responsibility is born. It lifts this power and this responsibility from fields which become increasingly trivial, to the heights of self-conscious control over society's destinies. It shifts the focus of moral values from traditional problems of retail charity and retail murder, courtesy and sexual decency, personal thrift and prudence, to the long-range government, the growth of science and culture, and the material conditions of human existence. Redefining the moral virtues and vices, it replaces the heroes, saints, and gods of the past with new exemplars of the good life, as in Russia, for instance, the figure of Christ, who deals with all things in an intimate and personal way, has been replaced by the figure of Lenin, the exponent of statistical morality. Creating new moral forces to govern the institutions of industrial civilization, socialism sublimates the passion of personal envy to the passion for social justice, turns human pride from the vision of personal success to the vision of collective achievement, and endows the ideal of universal brotherhood with the warmth of personal friendship. Out of the pettiness of personal fear there may be distilled hatred of the forces of despotism, love of liberty, and courage for battle. The triviality of human effort is man's fate only in a planless world. In the collective integrations of socialist society, and in the struggle for a socialist society, human power and human dignity are reborn.

III. The Metaphysical Basis of Socialist Morality

Analytically the distinction between individualist and socialist morality lies in the unit of integration applied to conflicts of human interests. Individualism assumes the task of integrating the conflicting desires of a person into a harmonious pattern of satisfactory living, through the disciplined subordination of momentary impulses to more permanent purposes, through the enlightenment of selfishness, and through the cultivation of a concern for one's future that eliminates the occasions of regret for one's past. The terms of this integration,—remorse, temptation, conscience, sincerity, self-respect,—do not stretch beyond the individual life. Traditional morality assumes that a life so integrated is necessarily socially valuable, and it is on the basis of this assumption that individualism ignores or minimizes the rôle of social control and the scope of social responsibility and sanctifies selfishness if only it is "enlightened." This assumption may be roughly true within a social structure in which an individual's conduct is comparatively unimportant to his fellows or in which human equality and the simplicity of human relations make the Golden Rule a dictate of practical prudence. But as the material conditions of life lend increased importance to the influences of individual conduct upon other individuals and cast these influences in forms that do not permit of payment in kind, it ceases to be a matter of practical prudence to act as one would have others act. Indeed in a society of specialized functions this ceases even to be a meaningful possibility. It becomes increasingly obvious in the contemporary world that the individualist moral values of consistency, prudence, courage, and enlightened selfishness do not guarantee a life of social value. Self-mastery attained through these traditional virtues may turn a life that is inspired by class or racial hatreds into a tragic catastrophe for the human race. The moral significance of human conduct comes increasingly to demand social standards of measurement.

Traditional individualism denies not only the need of a social integration of human interests but the possibility of such an integration. It assumes that the calculus of prudence is not only a major part of virtue but an eternal and objective fact. This assumption can scarcely withstand the analysis of psychological and anthropological science. Enlightened selfishness, far from being a matter of instinct, is instilled in human beings only through an arduous process of education dominated by the moral imperatives of individualism. The untrained child, no less than the martyr, the soldier, or the animal defending its young, may sacrifice its own future advantage to another's urgent need. Calculating selfishness is a product of individualistic morality. In a socialized morality which submerges individual purposes in more comprehensive social ideals, the significance of the whole concept of selfishness vanishes.

The traditional philosophy of individualism defends the immutability of human selfishness by a metaphysical dogma rather than by any convincing scientific evidence. The dogma that the individual is an ultimate unity and society an ultimate plurality predetermines that all the adjustments, balances, and compromises which are the substance of morality must take place within an individual life, that, for instance, the socially ordained sacrifice of one man's life or property for the benefit of others is unjust, though the individually ordained sacrifice of today's pleasure for tomorrow's, within a single life, may be commendable.

To this metaphysical dogma, the philosophy of socialism opposes a wider perspective, which reveals something of the unity of the individual in society itself and something of the plurality of society in the individual life.

Every human life may be viewed as a society of moments, each moment with its distinctive focus of interests, each with capacities for hating, loving, or disregarding other moments interconnected by physical relationships that do not guarantee a harmonious integration of interests, and attaining that integration only through adherence to norms of personal conduct that are the fruit of hard-won human wisdom. Loyalty to an ideal or pattern of life distinguishes an individual, a character, from a temporal succession of human activities related only by the fact that they occur in a single biological organism. The possibility of a social integration of conflicting interests is substantiated by the integration of conflicting interests in an individual life.

The power of an individual, that is to say his ability to retain his integrity under pressure and to exert pressure in turn to mold other lives, depends upon the effectiveness of the moral integration which subordinates successive immediate interests or desires to long-range purposes. It is equally true that the strength of a society derives from the moral integration of the diverse interests of many individuals, and it is becoming increasingly clear that a social order which does not secure such internal harmony must sooner or later give way to a more complete, stable, and effective integration of human desires.

The development of a socialized morality is therefore more than an ethical desideratum. It is a practical postulate of the continuance of modern civilization. The needs of civilization impose upon contemporary moral philosophy the task of integrating the life of society as traditional morality has integrated the lives of individuals. Ultimately a universal or social morality can rest only on a classless culture and a socialized conscience. The task of laughing down the provincialities of contemporary class culture, of breaking the control of art by monopolistic groups, of liberating taste and enjoyment from the slavery of pecuniary and competitive canons, of exposing the provincial ethical assumptions that bar the road to useful thought in the fields of economics, jurisprudence, and sociology, of liberating human imaginations so that men may see through complex economic and political structures to the joy or suffering they create, of dramatizing the institutions of society so that they evoke the forces of love and hate which have been traditionally directed towards personalities, of widening human loyalties to the point where one may look to his own future impersonally and find in a social ideal inspiring patterns of life, these are not tasks for the Sunday School moralists of the individualist tradition. In these tasks every realm of human culture must make its revolutionary contribution.

To speak thus of socialization in terms of the human soul is not to deny the physical actualities of technological evolution and class struggle, but only to deny the claim that irrational forces monopolize reality. It seems to me more useful and more nearly true to view the socialization of institutions and the socialization of the human soul as parallel aspects of a single task. For in the last analysis the human soul is neither the master nor the slave of its environment. The human soul *is* its environment, seen from within.

A PHILOSOPHER AMONG
THE METAPHYSICIANS

HARRY TODD COSTELLO

HARRY TODD COSTELLO, Brownell Professor of Philosophy, Trinity College, Hartford, Conn., was born in Richmond, Indiana, on November 1st, 1885, of Irish and Scotch-Covenanter stock. Attended the public schools and Earlham College. At Harvard, in graduate work, he was a favorite of Professor Josiah Royce. Harvard sent him to Paris, where Bergson was at his zenith. But Costello was more interested in scientific methods.

He lectured on logic at Harvard, and assisted Bertrand Russell in a course on the foundations of mathematics. His salary growing smaller rather than larger, he resigned to take a temporary post at Yale, and thence to Columbia, where he did not fit. No one was then interested in mathematical logic, or in Husserl, Meyerson, or Whitehead, whom he tried to introduce to American students. He studied political and economic theory on the side, and by desperate grinding endeavored to learn to write passable English.

After five years, he was finally offered, in 1920, an *ad interim* appointment to the professorship at Trinity. This post had a modest salary attached, the first which enabled him to meet expenses. Though on the verge of nervous breakdown, he made such a success in devising ingenious methods for enabling lazy undergraduates to learn without effort to themselves, that his job was made permanent. He tried to avoid waste in choice of reading, and wrote a pamphlet to help others in this respect ("Books for a College Student's Reading," Ed. 2, 1928).

A PHILOSOPHER AMONG THE META-PHYSICIANS

Harry Todd Costello

There are occasions when some average American citizen is led to inquire of me what it is I do for a living. I reply that I am a college professor of philosophy. Whereupon he says "Oh!" and turns to a more discreet topic, like the weather. To be a professor at all, in the United States, is to dwell under a cloud. In the South, a negro lawyer or physician is sometimes called "Professor," as a compromise, to avoid calling him "Mister." A professor is supposed to have an "academic outlook," whatever that may mean. The American defense reaction against "brain trusters" is immediate: they are intellect on the loose, without that balance of practicality which is supposed to come when one has "faced a payroll." We may admit that no reasonable person would want to turn the country over to the professors. Certainly no one would want it who had ever been present at a faculty meeting, one of those meetings in which, as Rollo Walter Brown puts it, "everyone who speaks subtracts from the sum of human intelligence." But outside of faculty meetings, professors are very various in character. Some are even surprisingly intelligent. The practical man feels the constraint of dealing face to face with people, and scorns the airy intangibleness of ideas. The fact is, however, that the people melt away, while the ideas stubbornly move on. The primary objection to the professor in politics is that he has, or ought to have, a job elsewhere in which he is more nearly indispensable.

But are not professors of philosophy among the dispensables? On the contrary, it is well for some of us that the country as a whole does not realize the tremendous potential importance of philosophy, and even of teachers of philosophy. Otherwise it would insist on such radical reconstruction, that some of us would be suffering from "technological unemployment." I am not denying that the group of men who now teach philosophy in this country stand above the average of professorial ability. We used to say of our fellow students who failed in their graduate work in philosophy, "He is all right; he will go over to psychology or something, and become a great experimental scientist." But the trouble is, that to be a philosopher nowadays, one needs to start with an I. Q. that flirts with the 200 mark, and add thereto a couple of centuries of close application to acquire the preliminary rudiments. The best are rare; and if you are not among the best, there is less reason for your being at all, than in most occupations.

If the system of education, as it now is, could have made a philosopher, I should myself have been a tolerably good specimen. I was one of the last products of that supreme philosophic Faculty at Harvard in the age before Lowell, about which people still speak in awed tones: "There were giants in those days." Perhaps I should be described as its "last straw." Even now there echoes through my memory the regretfulness in the voice of Professor Santayana, as he completed his examination of me for the doctorate. "I have no doubt, Mr. Costello," he said, "but that you will get your degree." He resigned a few months later. I know I was not educated when I took my degree; and I am not educated now. Henry Adams never knew the half of it, when it comes to uneducatedness, though he did dabble a bit in philosophy. We ought somehow to reconstruct our universities, as regards training philosophers. For a few philosophers, really equipped, would be a great thing for the world.

I

Somewhat at random, the space allotted me being brief, I pick on a topic that I have lectured about. Let us consider the relations of science to philosophy. A strange world it is, which physical science now reveals to us, and even the philosopher must feel a bit disconcerted there. Perhaps at this moment, as I write, in some subatomic region on the tip of my pen, some ultra-minute Aristotle is peering across the lonely spaces that stretch out toward the neighboring atoms, and considering whether his own orb is really the center of the physical world. We ourselves, earth and sun and neighboring planets, are nothing more than a mote whirling down the corridors of the universe—as Jeans puts it, in size we are as a grain of dust blown along Fifth Avenue to the size of the whole city of New York. And as Anatole France has said, our whole star city, our universe of island universes, with its billions of flaming suns and its millions of Milky Ways, may be itself only a drop of lymph in the body of some insect in a world of dimensions unimaginably great. Do not blame this sort of thing on the philosopher. It is merely the scientist doing a little measuring. The appalling thing is that it is based on scientific fact.

Of course, the scientist, dealing with this universe of electrons and stars, has recently come to be more conscious of philosophy than he ever was before. It must not be supposed that philosophy is the dark region out beyond the light of present scientific knowledge, which science will in due time absorb and illuminate. Rather does philosophy deal with those questions to which a scientist gives, by implication or presupposition, some sort of tentative and even rash answer whenever he says anything. You can no more think and escape the field of philosophy than your body can escape the field of gravitation. The scientist merely becomes conscious, or fails to become conscious, of the philosophical background of his own thought. There is not any break between science and philosophy.

This interlinkage between science and philosophy became evident to scientists recently with the Einstein theory, or evident enough to make many of them very uncomfortable. I doubt if any fairly well-trained philosophical thinker was quite so much upset. The philosopher was already familiar with the possibilities of non-Euclidean geometry, which few experimental scientists had taken seriously. Not that the present form of the theory of relativity is altogether satisfying to the philosopher. Some of the popular arguments for relativity have a queer way of refuting their own premises. But the more serious difficulty is that relativity presents itself at first as a mere convenient way of describing the world. Yet the philosopher is soon wondering whether it must not be something more. The theory of relativity presents itself as something artificial, like lines of longitude on the earth's surface. For instance, it is hard to settle whether two events remote from one another are simultaneous. But just in the same way, it is hard to tell whether two chips, floating side by side around the bend of a curving river, are really exactly abreast of one another, or one is a little ahead. You settle it by a definition and a convention. Yet the fact that you can use your convention does seem to indicate something about the nature of the world.

For example, you say, with your general theory of relativity, that just for the purpose of calculation you are going to treat time as a fourth dimension of space. This, you add, must not be taken to mean too great a change in the ordinary notion of time. It is merely for convenience. Maybe, indeed, you have not intended to change much in the ordinary notion of time— though perhaps you have—but if you do not watch out, you will make a startling metaphysical change in the notion you must hold of space. Consider the addition of an ordinary space dimension. Suppose that I, having been confined to a north-south line through Chicago, am then set free to travel east-west, say to Cleveland. I am not merely able to add east-west places to my visiting list, but also an enormous number of new north-south places, as for instance those north and south of Cleveland. If I make time a new dimension of space, I add an enormous number of new spaces. The earth moves around the sun in an ellipse—only it does not! The earth is not swinging in an ellipse,

acted on in Newtonian fashion by an existent force of gravitation pulling it toward the sun, and counterbalanced by the equal
and opposite non-existent centrifugal force. No, says relativity,
it is not acted on by forces; it is merely going in the straightest
line it can follow on the road from here to next year. It never
returns to the old place again, for after a year it comes to a
different but similar place in another space, the space of a year
from now. This is not supposed to be metaphysical, like Newtonian forces. But can you escape the metaphysical implications
of what you are saying? You may say you are only in fun. You
remember that is what little Ernest said when he had swallowed
the buttons—but "mother knew that the buttons were in Ernest."

It is commonly said that all the special theory of relativity
does is first to postulate the constancy of the speed of light, for
all possible ways of measuring, and then work out the consequences. Unfortunately, it not merely says that the speed is to
be taken as constant, but also that this velocity must be treated
as if it were infinite. It is the "as if" which troubles the philosopher. How seriously is it to be taken? Does the light of a star
flash instantly to me, with a real causally zero interval, but
only seem, from an outside point of view, to linger centuries
on the road? Or suppose I came riding past you on a ray of
starlight, a disembodied intelligence. Would I think I lived
in a solid world, and that your body, flattened pancake-wise
to nothing, was a ray of light passing me? One grows nervous
in face of such possibilities.

No wonder there are scientists who grow irritated, and would
suppress the "speculative mind" which flits off thus wildly into
"metaphysics." "Let us have done with metaphysics," they say,
"and admit into science only what is verifiable fact—tangible,
visible, observable datum." Unfortunately this is itself an old,
old metaphysical theory, and one which has the most uncomfortable, not to say devastating, consequences. Already one begins to glimpse the rapids ahead when such a scientist suggests

that, though the light leaves the sun eight minutes and more before it reaches us, we must not even ask where it was in the meantime, for that is unverifiable, and therefore completely meaningless. He who lives up to this standard of the meaningless will live in a queer world. The hither side of the moon is made of what look like rocks; but the other side, being unobservable, is nothing but meaningless metaphysics. What a fantastic moon! If I say that there is something in my room which looks like a chair when I look at it, that is science; but if I assert it is still there when I look the other way, that is mere speculation. Let us remember, also, that it is going beyond observation to assert there is *not* an elephant in the room, for I cannot observe what is not. It is going beyond observation to assert the truth of any universal statement, any law of nature, for that also is negative, denying that something or other is to be found anywhere, and no sum of observations of what is seen can insure that you have seen all. It is going beyond observation by the senses to believe in the minds of our fellow men. Even the "facts" are not equivalent to what I may observe, for a fact is something that imposes itself on us with necessity, and I cannot see necessity—I can only think it.

The philosopher sometimes annoys the scientist when he points these things out. But the philosopher does not want to be "metaphysical" in any bad sense. He does not want to be captious, or skeptical, or even agnostic. He is keenly aware, however, of the amount of assumption and ignorance mixed up with the best of our knowledge. He is painfully aware that nobody has a good theory of what happens when I see a color. No one has even a reasonable hypothesis concerning exactly what happens when I decide to write a letter, and then sit down and write it. Some of the earliest Mohammedan philosophers said that the world is made of qualities, and the world is made of atoms, and God only knows how and why the two go together. After more than a thousand years, with an immensely greater detailed knowledge, we still find that the world is made of

qualities and atoms: of hard, brown objects I observe and call
a table, and of unseen, whirling clouds of minute specks or quiv-
ers in a vacuum of space. As yet Allah alone knows the secret
of how these two can be one.

II

"Forget metaphysics," you say to me, "and tell what you, as
a philosopher, have to say about the world of practical affairs.
Talk to us in our own language." I fear you ask me something
hard. How shall I avoid metaphysics, and yet talk to you in
your own language? I suppose it was what you call metaphysics,
when the medieval theologian built up a whole structure of
world-theory out of a single verse of the third chapter of the
book of Exodus. But did you ever observe a modern constitutional lawyer conjuring forth what the United States Constitution of 1787 had to say about railroads or about radio? There
may be metaphysics in notions of Substance and Essence and
Platonic Idea. But do you find none in the notions of National
Honor or National Interest, for which men still fight and die?
What is a Nation, except that which is created in the thinking
of it? I often hear some sarcastic reference to those medieval
Scholastics who debated how many angels could dance on the
point of a needle. I really think that was a nice point of debate,
what constitutes individuality: could things the same in place,
time, and character still be different? But suppose one of those
old debaters were now awakened from his sleep, and faced with
the facts and the evidence and asked to decide, "Just what
makes a Republican a Republican, and a Democrat a Democrat?"
Would he not beg to be returned to the Middle Ages, where
they used to discuss questions that had a meaning and an answer?
I like to talk to students about social ethics. But I wonder if I
am giving them what they need, to live and talk the language
in this world of today? Mr. Bertrand Russell has spoken with
deserved praise of old-fashioned formal logic, as being an ex-

cellent "training in those habits of solemn humbug which ar so great a help in later life." But I wonder is there anything else in our philosophical curriculum which is really of like practical use?

Saint Thomas Aquinas took great interest in the ways and variations of those disembodied personalities, the angels. Perhaps if he were back among us, he might be persuaded to write a book on corporations. These also are disembodied personalities, though some of them have fallen like a star in recent years. The corporations take shelter in the crannies of our law, in the refuge prepared for those other aliens among us, the negroes. The state, like Frankenstein, bade them be, but scarcely dare exorcise them away again. Yet they are rather ill treated among us. If an ordinary man's debts double, we do not say, "Look, how prosperous he has become!" But a corporation's stock is a debt against the corporation, and a queer debt, for which the corporation very probably never got much of anything in the first place. Yet let it jump from 50 to 100 on the market, and all the friends of the corporation gather round and chant for joy. These friends who own this stock even claim to own the corporation, and property is a great thing, as we all know, for he who owns property takes care of it. But let the poor corporation get into trouble, and these caretakers dump their stock on the market and hastily disappear. An owner is supposed to manage. But there are kind people who take this burden off the stockholders' hands, being assisted by a higher order of angels, the holding companies. These are spiritual beings of such power, like Archimedes' lever, that if a man had a long enough chain and hierarchy of them, and ten dollars in cash, he could run the country. That is, provided nothing slips. Of course, if something does slip, one may have to take hasty refuge in the eastern Mediterranean. It seems like a far-away day when John Stuart Mill said that capital originates in abstinence. For corporation capital originates by rubbing the Aladdin's lamp of optimism. He whose corporation has this year made an extra hundred thousand capitalizes it for a million, and trades the million and some promises against the hard-earned savings of the abstinence of the poor. If you sell bad stock, you take some money out of your victim's pocket and put it into yours, a simple process and wicked. But if it is good stock that you sell, you mortgage the future of some corporation. You put a permanent burden on industry and take the proceeds away for yourself—and this is supposed to be good. On the whole, I think Aquinas was happier with his angels.

It is easy to joke about these metaphysical absurdities of the practical world, but the joke is a bitter one when people are suffering. Let us try to be more constructive, and take up one illustrative problem. What is the best arrangement for the social control of corporations engaged in industrial production? There are those who tell us the profit motive is essentially low and selfish, and impossible to combine with any rational scheme of social planning. But, after all, the profit motive is a motive and a drive and a social plan is not. It is foolish to sacrifice any source of power. Because the natural tendency of steam is to expand and dissipate without turning into mechanical motion, it does not follow that a steam engine is impossible. In the social and economic world we need analogous constructive inventions.

There is no great use in talking about construction unless we also have adequate diagnosis. At least twenty or twenty-five reasons must be discoverable why capitalism is a good arrangement, and no less number of reasons why it is not. And so it dismays the philosophic mind to encounter a book or an article by a leader in social thought, and discover that his whole argument is based on one or two such reasons. Perhaps we are then told that industry must be "socialized," which turns out to mean let us have the government take it over. Now one great danger to any social plan, as well as a danger to political democracy today, is the existence of small well-organized groups, very clear about their own immediate advantage. Government control of industry would merely shift the set-up of these group, and probably increase their power. Is this socializing industry Any effective government interference, moreover, even were it to put in practice some ideal social plan, is bound to wreck the life-work of thousands of estimable individuals whose modes of behavior are adjusted to the present imperfect arrangements. Social invention must consider transitions, and do something more than change the bosses. The mind that can think philosophically is, therefore, the only mind that can intelligently face our present problems of diagnosis and social invention, and reach that higher practicality which consists in taking all the factors into account without losing balance.

Perhaps it is rash of me, after such a characterization of our needs, to debate any specific difficulties in a paragraph or two. But I will try. The income of a country is what the country produces, in things material and immaterial, shoes and ships and sealing wax. Wages are paid out of things produced—out of things, not money. If there is less produced, there is less to divide. Unfortunately, however, it is always to the advantage of each producer to keep down the quantity on the market of what he is himself producing. It gives him an advantage in exchange. But the producers of other commodities must then follow suit. The government of the United States has recently been helping the farmers to play their part in this little game. But what is advantageous for each, if it could be done by each alone, is disastrous to all if done by all together. Raising prices and limiting production in order to pay better wages is, therefore, an intrinsically fallacious procedure. Of course I am not arguing that the largest possible production would be the best. Conceivably we might produce twice as many shoes as people can wear. Actually we do build shoe factories beyond all necessity. But we do not in practice run the factories thus built. The business men are shrewd enough to see to that. Over-production and under-production produce the same unhappy symptoms of industrial stagnation, but it is from the latter that we suffer most.

How this comes about is in part a result of our price system. Industrial management is enslaved by price. Profits and losses are a matter of margin of difference between sales prices and costs. It is almost a purely mathematical result of the arithmetic of differences that a very small change in price has a vastly greater effect on profits than even very large changes in volume. But a small increase in volume may mean a sharp break in price. If the reader will work out specific examples, he will find that often a cut of as much as one-half in volume, which brings, say, a ten percent increase in price, may actually increase profits considerably. Since most businesses are running fairly close to the edge which divides profit from loss, and few can run for long at a loss, the pressure on industrialists to watch prices and incidentally to keep production down is tremendous, even apart from any price agreements or monopolies. Yet of course this restriction of production, Veblen's "conscientious withdrawal of efficiency," means that men are unemployed and itself reacts to reduce sales and profits in a vicious circle.

This is the problem. The social invention or rearrangement that would solve it might require possibly some distinction between earned profits, due to more efficient methods and accompanied by a larger wage bill in a growing industry, from unearned profits, due to restriction. The latter might be taxed severely. Or industry might be compelled at all times to carry, in proportion to total income, the same percentage of wage load (or wage load plus unemployment tax), thus eliminating the profits gained at the expense of labor. If the government were intelligent, it would use the tariff as a weapon against restriction, for too high a tariff keeps prices so high that sales and wages are restricted. The government has a right to ask of those helped by a tariff that they show they are increasing internal production rather than reducing it.

It is the regrettable fact, however, that almost anything the government can do in this vital problem will not only be opposed by vigorous small groups, but will go so directly contrary to all the natural tendencies of thought of all business men that it will be widely and stubbornly resented. Any real effort to increase production and bring down price will be especially fatal to those small business men for whom Senator Borah has so kindly a regard. And it must be insisted that even if the government went to the extreme of taking over all industry, it cannot for long run all industry at a loss, so that the problem will break out again inside government management. The Russian experiment in no way refutes this. The social invention that we need must not be merely a change of bosses, even though the new bosses have hearts filled with benevolence.

The problem we have just been considering, like others we mentioned previously, is, of course, not in the strict sense a problem of philosophy. As a problem of what ought to be done it falls, indeed, within the wide range of the subject of social ethics. But in the present paper we have been considering, not philosophy, but the philosophical attitude toward problems in other fields. Such an attitude would involve, in the first place, constant suspicion toward all emotionally charged language, as for instance when we are asked to replace our "acquisitive society" by a "socialized industrial order." In the second place, we must insist on a diagnosis of the situation that does not forget the intricate complexity of social problems, and is immediately on its guard against what look like self-evident axioms. In the third place, there is endless scope for imagining new social inventions, but these must be such as will utilize the drives and motives which already actuate the majority of people. We must remember that regimentation, even under a national plan, is likely to be in the long run inimical to novelty and invention, as well as to ideas not consonant with the reigning orthodoxy. We shall not be deceived into thinking that a mere change of bosses is any substitute for real social invention. In the fourth place, we shall of course not let ourselves be deceived by simple panaceas, such as manipulations of the currency, some of which are analogous to increasing the wheat crop by decreasing the size of the bushel. Of the same sort are most schemes for putting buying power directly in the hands of consumers, as for example the Townsend Old Age Pension Plan. We ought to have wits enough to see at once that with our present price system the effect would be to boost prices and skyrocket profits, to the direct reverse of the effect intended. In conclusion may I add that while Comte considered the lawyers to be our leading verbal metaphysicians, Hegel was probably nearer right in extending that honorable title to "practical men" generally. They far easier fall victims of their own familiar language with its soothing formulas and slogans than does any student of speculative philosophy.

While I am optimistic enough to believe that there is always a constructive way out, if we could only have the wit to find it, in our present situation today with all its burden of maladjustments I regret to believe enough wit will not be forthcoming. But the efficiency of mechanical production is now so enormous that American industry may by sheer power, in the immediate future, stagger to its feet and plod on, still carrying on its back all its useless loads. In some ways we are not so badly situated. I am sorry to see labor and capital now fighting one another. But I should be still more fearful if they united in harmony in some of our key industries and combined against the public. We pay miserable wages for such a rich country. But almost every citizen has, within the last two or three years, become wage-and-hour conscious, as he never was before. Higher minimum wages, even higher median wages, are a matter of actual serious discussion. Here we are. There is confusion around us. We have built a high-speed machine and are running it with the brakes on. But let us not lose our perspective in judging it.

If we could go back, though only for a few hours, into the midst of a great European capital or small European town, of as little as two hundred years ago, into the midst of the ugliness of that time, the crudity, the brutality, and the smell, I think we might be glad to come back again to the spacious light and promise of present-day America.

AN AMATEUR'S PHILOSOPHY

WILL DURANT

WILL DURANT (WILLIAM JAMES DURANT) was born at North Adams, Mass., Nov. 5, 1885; was educated by Catholic nuns and priests in parochial schools and the Jesuit college of St. Peter's, Jersey City, N. J., where he received the degree of B.A. in 1907. He spent two years in a Catholic seminary at Seton Hall, South Orange, N. J.; left the seminary in 1909, continued for two years further at Seton Hall as professor of various languages, studied at Columbia 1913-17, took the degree of Ph.D. there in 1917, and taught philosophy there for half a year. In 1914 he began to lecture at Labor Temple, Fourteenth Street and Second Avenue, New York; he continued these lectures every Sunday and Wednesday for thirteen years, and founded there the Labor Temple School. He had abandoned all thought of writing books, until E. Haldeman-Julius, of Girard, Kan., dropped in by chance upon a lecture on Plato, and liking it, asked Mr. Durant to write it out as a "Little Blue Book." Out of this and subsequent lectures and essays grew *The Story of Philosophy* (1926). Mr. Durant followed this in 1927 with *Transition: a Mental Autobiography* (1927); *The Mansions of Philosophy* (1929); and *Adventures in Genius* (1931); but his main industry, since 1926, has been the preparation of the first volume of *The Story of Civilization.* He lives a secluded life at Great Neck, N. Y.

AN AMATEUR'S PHILOSOPHY

Will Durant

I. An Approach to Philosophy

Of the many happy days which I spent as a graduate student at Columbia University I remember one with especial vividness. I had passed two pleasant years in studying psychology, chiefly experimental, under Professor Woodworth and his aides, and had learned to love his genial and hesitating ways. Now I confessed to him, as he sat smoking his pipe contentedly in his office, that I was abandoning psychology for philosophy. He reproved me gently for this infidelity to science, and predicted remorse.

"Some day," he said, "you'll be sorry that you left empirical and experimental work. You'll grow tired of abstractions, and then you'll come back to science."

I knew more then than now, and was quite sure that I would not regret my choice. I had been lured by the great names in the Department of Philosophy; I was confident that there was an almost Spinozistic wisdom behind the magnificent forehead of Professor Woodbridge; and behind the mystical speech of John Dewey I thought I saw just that combination of realistic skepticism and idealistic aspiration which suited a young man who had jumped from a religious seminary to an anarchist school, and could not quite make up his mind whether to be a cynic or a saint. Day after day I sat enthralled as one of these great teachers read the Roll of Honor of human thought, and the other drew up tentatively, line by line, a charter of mental and moral freedom and reform. Everything they said was vague, but that was because they dealt with problems immeasurably more complex and difficult than those which had occupied me in the psychological and biological laboratories; Professor McGregor's dog-fish, Professor Calkins' protozoa, even Professor Morgan's banana-flies seemed to behave and beget in simple fashion compared to the unmanageable organisms whose "human affairs" formed the burden of Plato's thought, and whose problems of state agitated Confucius and Mencius, Bacon and Hobbes, Locke and Leibniz and Comte. I felt that I had passed from a small world to a vast one, from a successful study of isolated parts to a faltering perspective of the whole. I was glad that I had made the change. I looked with condescending indulgence upon the patient young men who had remained faithful to their graphs, their *Drosophila*, and their worms.

Youth is the age of Yes or No, of Absolutes and Certainties; and since youth may be defined as the period between physical puberty and mental maturity, it is a prerogative of which time does not inevitably deprive us. I am still too young to understand that the man who is doing things that have no interest for me may be as necessary as the statesman and the philosopher; that the analytical study of the part is just as valuable as the synthetic study of the whole, and has the advantage of being possible. For after all, philosophy in my definition of it —as total perspective—is a delusion of grandeur, an inflated idea of which only youth could be guilty. How could this imprisoned fragment called the mind ever understand, or glimpse, the whole? All that we can hope for is to see the parts of our experience in ever wider perspective, more and more *sub specie totius*—in the light of that Whole which will be forever a fancy and a goal.

That same impatience which leaped so eagerly from piety to radicalism, and from chromosomes and sigmas to cosmic perspectives and perfect states, flung itself savagely upon those quiet men who, knowing that the Whole is a mirage, devoted themselves to some part, or specific problem, of philosophy, and became experts in metaphysics, esthetics, or epistemology. I found it hard to dally with persons who took seriously the cautious obscurity of Hegel, or with graceful men who discoursed on the meaning of beauty without having ever created or captured it; or with those timid spirits who announced that they had produced the world by perceiving it, and that all things, even their wives (as Mme. de Staël suggested to Fichte), were constructs of their "transcendental unity of apperception." But in my second half-century I am forced to admit that there is something to be said for all these men. The world as we know it is, of course, endowed with a peculiar color and form, taste and odor, temperature and timbre, by those human senses through which we perceive it; and doubtless that same elusive eel, "objective reality," presents a very different face to the tentative tentacles and polygonal eyes of a crab, or to the browsing nose of my dog. The man who wishes to think things through to his human capacity must still tinker with metaphysics, and take his stand, however privately, with atheism or religion, mechanism or vitalism, determinism or free will. There is, in the puzzle of beauty, a fascination which can bring a vicarious exaltation to a Bosanquet, and provide a fitting matrix for the flashing gems of Santayana's prose. Even a *theory* of Aphrodite has a warm seductive charm.

Nevertheless, having made these obeisances and apologies, I remain obstinately addicted to what I should like to call the Platonic view of philosophy, as a discipline of integrated thinking which *begins* with logic and epistemology, passes on to metaphysics and religion, and *culminates* in the application of a widened mental background to human conduct and the state. Philosophy is not epistemology, but epistemology is a part of philosophy. Philosophy is not metaphysics, but metaphysics is a part of philosophy; it is the imaginative and hypothetical completion of cosmic perspectives unreached by scientific or verifiable knowledge. Philosophy is not ethics or politics, but ethics and politics are a part of philosophy; my prejudice lies in considering them the most important parts of philosophy, to which the others should serve as guides and preparation.

Philosophy is concerned with "facts" only in their widest significance and values; it is a study of the "real" in terms of the ideal, of the "true" in terms of the good and the beautiful. Logic studies real and ideal thinking; metaphysics, real and ideal being; esthetics, real and ideal form; ethics, real and ideal conduct; politics, real and ideal society. Any study which aims to discover facts belongs to science. Epistemology, as essentially an inquiry into the facts of sensation, perception and understanding, may soon be embraced within the science of psychology; it is now a part of philosophy only by an unscrutinized tradition, precisely as psychology itself was a part of philosophy in the nineteenth century, and as physics (or "natural philosophy") was a part of philosophy in the seventeenth century. When such factual studies are surrendered to science, philosophy is left with a clearer conception of its own purpose, and a sharper concentration of its energies upon its proper task of coördinating knowledge for the illumination of ideal goods.

Using imagination to complete knowledge, philosophy is as much akin to poetry as to science; relating the actual to the beautiful, it is to that extent an art. Perhaps that is why the great systems of philosophy, like the great religions, the great poems, the great plastic and structural masterpieces, can never be "refuted," and survive every critic but time. We know that the great systems are something more than beautiful, even when we suspect that they are something less than true.

II. IRRATIONAL SOURCES

Insofar as I have any philosophy today—any consistent interpretation and evaluation of experience and desire—it has been formed along this Platonic or Baconian approach, and by a strange composition of hostile forces external and internal, environmental and hereditary. The two basic factors in this personal equation were socialism and Catholicism.

The strongest was religion. Catholicism sank so deeply into my manner of feeling and thinking that not all the ninety-nine volumes of Voltaire have been able to eradicate it. Below the medulla I am still a Catholic; I am still moved by the incredibly beautiful story of Christ, almost as much as when, like another Aloysius, I mounted nervously to the altar every morning to partake of the body and blood, soul and divinity, of the young Saviour who, better than any other man, I think, has phrased for us our dream of what we might be. A certain tendency to sentimentality, to a self-indulgence in the ecstasy of feeling, came to me either with the chromosomes, or with this dramatic religion that has satisfied so well the thirst of the soul for poetry. Perhaps because of this constitutional Catholicism, I am physiologically incapable of materialism or mechanism, and still shudder a little at the word *atheism*. I find it difficult to think in terms of a new moral code adapted and natural to an industrial civilization, and tend spontaneously to apply to the younger generation, living in an urban environment, moral standards derived from an agricultural economy.

From this haven of conservatism I marched, with juvenile precipitation, into the most radical phases of the socialist movement. A certain skeptical strain, aided for a few years by a degree of prosperity shockingly unbecoming to a student, has always made me suspect in socialism a naïve fetichism of government. I distrust governments, and tend to think of them in terms of insatiable tax-gatherers with advanced views about morality; I incline by thoughtless individualism rather to Thoreau, Emerson and Whitman than to Marx and Stalin; I find myself irrevocably saddled with eighteenth-century ideals of freedom in the face of twentieth-century ideals of order that are obviously destined to victory. But I can never forget the day when for the first time I listened, with passionate resentment, to the story of industrial exploitation, political chicanery and slum destitution as told by a socialist orator in the public square of the town where I spent my youth. I went home aroused, and announced that I would never rest until capitalism was destroyed. I too became a street-corner Demosthenes, and so eloquently did I preach "Socialism the Hope of the World" (this was the title of my discourse) that I convinced myself; and to this day, despite my doubts, and my disappointment with the conditions which I found in Russia after fifteen years of socialism, I am still emotionally a socialist, hating exploitation, and almost ready to abandon liberty of work and thought if the sacrifice can bring economic security and justice to the masses of mankind. If I have fretted at the scholastic irrelevance of logic and epistemology to the major problems of modern life, and have exhorted philosophy to come out of the class-room into the world, it has been, I think, because socialism filled me with anger at our industrial chaos and brutality, and inclined me to feel that the highest purpose of thought was to remold this sorry scheme of things a little nearer to our hearts' desire. That is why I preferred the *Republic* to the *Nicomachean Ethics,* and admired Bacon for being both a philosopher and a statesman under the same hat.

These are the prejudices which have begotten my view of human life. If I proceed summarily to expound that view in terms of intellect and reason, the reader will not be deceived; he will see, beneath the forms of logic, the secret dictatorship of habit, interest and feeling.

III. About Pilate

To begin logically with logic, with the attempt to answer Pilate and define the truth: I find myself confusedly sympathetic with both the mysticism of Shankara and the rationalism of Voltaire. Perhaps the Hindus are right—the effort of the intellect to understand the world is a noble and amusing folly. All these tremendous tomes on the art of reasoning are, when

deflated, merely manuals of the art of explaining our prejudices
and justifying our desires; they are not ways of arriving at
"truth." Truth, as total perspective, could be possessed only
by God; if medieval theology was correct, this much may be
said for Pilate, that he asked his question of the only one who
could answer him. Since no answer was given, we must be content with such partial perspectives as can come to a drop of
water trying to understand the sea, or an atom charting the
Pleiades. There is no great likelihood that the human brain,
which aches at a little calculus and breaks under the Presidency,
will ever comprehend this careless immensity of which it is so
transitory a fragment. Philosophy is the study of a part in
terms of the whole; its first lesson is that the whole is vast,
and the part small; modesty is the beginning of wisdom. Reason
is a great boon, and has lifted us a bit above more horizontal
animals; it encourages us to weigh and clarify our impulses, and
to explain our purposes and beliefs; it maps the world in a
thousand hypothetical ways which have helped us to modify
and control our environment. But it is not a test of truth. A
million unreasonable, irrational things have happened in this
world, from the cure of Zadig's eye to the quantum leaps of
the electron; and when we have shown that a thing is contrary
to reason we may be sure that it will some day come true.

But if the Brahman, or M. Bergson, offers me intuition as
a guide to truth, all my rationalist youth rises to protest. If
intuition means direct perception, as in Spinoza, I accept it as
an ultimate guide, with reservations to be stated anon; if it
means a simple awareness of our consciousness, I accept it as
the most immediate and irrefutable perception in the world.
But if it means a mystical faculty of feeling the "Soul" of the
Universe, or even of the individual, it is a blind man's buff,
which, like a Delphic oracle, will give us whatever testimony
we may desire. When I obey the instructions of the mystic,
close my eyes, put Flents in my ears, try to shut out all external sensation, and look inward, I find nothing: this is a point

on which many critics are agreed. It is true that I have, in such introspection, a sense of empty "Being"; I feel then like the God who defined himself as "I am who am." But I am not sure that this vague sense of being is not (as William James suggested) merely a sum of sensations partly internal and chiefly visceral, partly external in the sense that some "sound" gets through the best-stuffed ears, and some visual sensation survives the most conservative shutting of the eyes. Even the visions of the anesthete are probably memories and internal sensations moving haphazard in a dance uncontrolled by perception or purpose. If I see God when I introspect it is only Shankara's Brahman—the flow of a waterless river, the tide of an immaterial ocean, an essence impersonal, neuter, qualityless, indescribable, and perhaps non-existent.

"Intuition" means either this formless introspection, or direct perception, or a reasoning process so swift that the reasoner is unconscious of the premises or the steps. I believe that direct perception is the only test we can have of the only truth we can find. But I would not encourage obscurity by calling it intuition, though I know that *intueri* means to perceive directly rather than mystically to feel; I would call it by the simple, matter-of-fact name of sensation. Under "sensation," however, I would include that complex of internal senses by which we become conscious of our internal organs, of our mental processes, and of our personal identity. Understanding the word in this double sense, I should say that sensation, rather than reason or intuition, is the least unreliable of our tests of truth. Certainly the senses may deceive us; but we find this out only by other senses, as when we perceive by our fingers that the half-immersed stick is not as crooked as it seemed; and we are never quite confident of anything until we feel it with—or within—our skins. The most distant stars are but images on our retinas, the most distant sounds are but vibrations in our bones; the airy castles of modern mathematics are merely possibilities of sensation. The most subtle reasoning is in the end nothing but a tentative prediction that under given circumstances certain sensations will be received. Science is the organization of sensory experience into formulas susceptible of sensory verification. Truth is permanently consistent sensation.

IV. THE LURE OF METAPHYSICS

I do not believe that Pilate would have been thrilled by this answer to his question; he would have looked upon it as sophomorically simple, and if he had been trained in the schools he would have considered it shamefully intelligible. He would have washed his hands of logic, and gone back to his study to confer with Lucretius and Cicero on the nature of things and the gods. For that is, of course, the point at which his inquiry was aimed; he wished to know what this universe is, how it came into being, by what laws it operates, and what are its purposes, its significance, and its destiny.

To these eternal queries of the metaphysical mind sensation has as yet no answer; and therefore every answer given is only a supposition or a prayer. When we define truth as consistent sensation we are disturbed to note how brief and fragmentary, proximate and limited, our truths are; they constitute a vacillating science and elude a philosophy that must ever grope beyond sensation; they tell us of things as they seem today, but their reports are subject to change without notice; they suggest to us a world impinging upon our eyes and ears, our nose and tongue and skin, but they bear no *tangible* testimony to a world unfelt, unheard and unseen; such a world remains for each of us a personal, unsharable secret. We are proud ratiocinative insects, logic-chopping animalcules, whose "total perspectives" are perhaps nearer to "reality" than the *Weltanschauung* of a fly pluming itself on its circumnavigation of an orange.

Nevertheless we shall not soon be content to live without metaphysics. That fine curiosity which arises out of the dangers inherent in everything strange and unknown, and which generates at last sciences that fling their formulas around Betelgeuse, cannot stop at protons and stars; it reaches over and under them to seek their ultimate cause, as if the transitory could ever find the ultimate; it burrows into the atom, and sniffs about the throne of God.

I try to get along with a minimum of metaphysics, for I am obsessed with the absurd grandeur of its enterprise. When I am asked to choose between atheism and religion, materialism and spiritualism, mechanism and vitalism, I first affirm my ignorance, and then, under life's compulsion, I indulge desire and hazard my choice. Taking my stand on direct sensation in what I trust (without much confidence) will not seem a secret surrender to mysticism, I find that I am the one thing, in all my experience, which I am privileged to observe both from within and from without; and I note that my behavior, which seems mechanical to a microscopical minority of my fellow men, appears to myself to be an operation occasionally infused with foresight and purpose; and this internal perception is so vigorous that I have never been able to take seriously the notion that an organism is a machine. What it is, I know not; but I believe that we shall have to find, for its description, terms vastly more complex and subtle than those with which our factories have intoxicated us.

For similar reasons—some of them probably unconscious—I have, for some twenty years past, rejected the determinism which so fascinated me in my youth. I see men being molded by environments, and environments being molded by men; I know some persons who seem to be slaves of heredity, and some who seem to have mastered it. I sense in others what I perceive in myself: that in addition to Bradlaugh's trinity of heredity, environment and circumstance, there is another factor that enters into human choice—the force of life itself. That force does not seem neutral; it is capable of growth, of ambition, of imagination, of artistic creation, and perhaps of weighting the scale, for a time, in favor of development. We often behave as puppets, but now and then we do not; only a straining of theory can picture as puppets young Shakespeare mouthing tragedies while holding horses, with "not a thought but turned on dignity," or Flaubert dying at his post after thirty years of struggling for the perfect phrase. Let us compromise: we shall apply determinism when we judge others, but shall never use it as a shield for ourselves.

Materialism engages more of my admiration for its monolithic simplicity. External sensation seems to vote in its favor overwhelmingly. My eyes and ears, tongue and nostrils, fingers and skin, tell me nothing of a spiritual world; Shakespeare is to me only a maze of ink-spots on a closely-printed page, or some noises in the theatre; and any Beatrice, to any Democritus, is but an undulation of rosy flesh in the unethereal ether. Why is it that most of us would agree with Dante about Beatrice, rather than with Democritus? Partly because our senses report to us not matter so much as energy, leaving matter unknown to us except as a sum of forces impinging upon our nerves. But chiefly because the most powerful of all the senses is the internal sense; and this internal sense, revealing an airy nothingness, apparently spaceless and atomless, as the inner center of ourselves, leads us to conclude that within these educated monkeys that surround us there are "souls" like our beloved own, though seldom so subtle and sensitive. If I had to choose between materialism and spiritualism I should cast my lot with spiritualism; for there is nothing so real and immediate to me as this internal sense, which persistently reports to me a situation indescribable in terms of molecules and space.

But if I take the combined testimony of all my senses, external and internal, I get a picture characteristically hypothetical, and as full of a suspicious duplicity as experience itself. I see myself then as a "material body" inhabited by a "spiritual soul." But I see these two aspects of me in continual union and interaction; my thoughts seem to lead to actions, and my actions generate thoughts; my ideas are merely the first stages of actions, and my actions are merely unimpeded ideas. I note that a little change in temperature, or in the degree of oxygen in the air I breathe, or in the regularity with which the blood flows to my brain, can destroy, to all appearances, that strange reality, my "soul," and that inner sense which testifies to it. I perceive that in other animals—even in that most faithful and tolerant of my philosophical comrades, my dog—the "soul" and the "body" are apparently two sides of the same complicated phenomenon; and so far as my senses can see, the two sides begin and end, are born and die, together. I find that there is no essential difference between myself and my dog, or between my dog and his fleas (if I may so traduce him); we are all, God help us, in the same boat of merciless mortality. Probably —though I know nothing about it—there is no essential difference between an animal and a plant, or between a plant and a rod of iron; perhaps some day all of them will be better understood and studied in terms of organism than in terms of machinery. But the organism seems to be a unit, neither matter in the sense of "body," nor mind in the sense of "soul"; each organism, and presumably each cell of each organism—perhaps each "atom" of each thing—is a "psycho-physical" complex, at once and in every part "material" and "spiritual." Who knows what the atom would look like if we could see it, as we see ourselves, from the "inside"?

As to religion, I have everything of it except the creed. I like its drama, its sentiment, and—in Latin countries—its elevating but lenient morality. I look upon it as a poem which endeavors to give consolation to the defeated and the bereaved, a lasting significance to the individual life, and a steady income to the clergy. I accept Spinoza's God, as the law and structure of the world; I accept Bergson's God, as the growth and vitality of the world; but I doubt if this fusion of a static and an activating deity would satisfy the theologians. I feel a certain poetic divinity in Nature, and have learned to enjoy almost all her moods. Now and then, walking through a peaceful rain, or crunching the packed snow underfoot, or watching the moon steal over quiet waters, or the sun melt icicles from the trees in a January thaw, a certain animal content envelops me, unifies me almost mystically with the earth and every form of life, and fills me with a vague but intense gratitude to some being whom I cannot name. In such moments I feel how slight and frail all the enlightenment of intellect is beside the silent forces of Nature around me and within me. I turn contentedly away then from everything that I have learned in my books, and it seems to me that all the things that this Nature does are justified; that, as the old Stoics thought, wisdom can be found best by yielding to her fully, and accepting her as our guide. Then the woman who has made fine children appears to me infinitely superior to the man who has written many books; the simplest *proletaire*, harassed and secretly pleased by his children, takes on a dignity lost by those who, in escaping Nature, have only fallen from the tree of life; then birth and death become parts of a natural rhythm in which both find harmonious place, and can be borne peaceably, with understanding.

But I know, with my partial self, that all this poetry is mere animism; that this Nature which has given me all pleasures will take them all away; that she has made my life depend upon a willingness to struggle, fight, and kill; that she is interested in me only as a biological experiment, and as the host, perhaps, of a few billion sperms; that a few years hence she will look on placidly as her busy bacteria turn me into fertilizer for weeds and grass, and a luxury for worms. The world presents, in my small experience, a neutral scene of suffering and happiness, order and disorder, beneficence and cruelty; these are, of course, mere human viewpoints, with which the impersonal Soul of the World shows no active sympathy; Nature has no prejudices as between geniuses and fleas. Perhaps there is a design in this confusion, as far above my fragmentary understanding as a Five-Year-Plan would be to an army mule. Sometimes I think I sense that Oversoul when I sink into my dumb being introspectively; perhaps this universe, so material and mechanical to my outer sense, harbors an inner spirit as imperceptible to me as mine must be to the mosquito that exploits the natural resources of my flesh. But even that Oversoul seems indifferent to me, and to my absurd longing for some lasting significance. Another century, probably more, must elapse before humanity completes again its periodic task—anew undertaken when Copernicus put an end to the Middle Ages—of reconceiving God.

V. BIOLOGY AND ETHICS

The decadence of religion is probably the basic phenomenon of our time. It is, I believe, far more important than any change from individualism to socialism, and will be recalled long after our economic experiments have failed or succeeded, or been in either case forgotten. Historians today write great volumes and deadly monographs on the decay of paganism and the rise of Christianity in the classic world; but comparatively few of them—though we are all Marxians now in interpreting history—bother to study the economic revolts and changes that accompanied or prepared for Christianity. I believe that the most crucial experiment going on in our age is not Russian communism but Russian atheism. The sight of 160,000,000 people trying to live without supernatural religion is to my mind more interesting than the picture of 160,000,000 people exchanging private exploiters for the State. The results of this experiment in religion must have a profound and lasting influence upon the behavior and history of mankind.

Changes in the forms of political or economic organization are never quite fundamental, since under every form the biological sources of human conduct will probably issue in the exploitation and government of the weak and simple by the clever and strong. Indeed, it is just this biological background of life that repeatedly frustrates the earthly realization of social ideals, and perpetuates the demand for the consolations of religion. The founders of our Republic neglected to take God into their confidence when they conspired to make an egalitarian state; and the obstinacy of Nature in continuing to make some men strong and other men weak has upset a hundred ideal constitutions.

Ideals, when they are not material interests phraseologically disguised as moral aspirations, are usually memories of our childhood security in the family; as we plunge into the competition and warfare of life we recall with longing the coöperation and protection of our childhood home, and vision wistfully a world in which "all men are brothers," and a loving "Father" watches over us from the sky. To that degree social idealism has a biological basis; it is rooted in the family, and consists in the desire and effort to extend the mutual aid and tenderness of the family to ever wider realms—to the village, to the religious or economic community, to the city, to the state, at last to all mankind. It is against this background that we form our ethical concepts; morality, except in a Nietzsche here and there, means for us actually the coöperation of the part with the whole, of the individual with his group; and ideally it means coöperation with the largest group: in Christianity with all men, in Buddhism with all life.

The great moral conflict which constitutes the basic drama of human affairs is between the coöperation which we learn in the family, and the competition which we learn in later life. Biology is cold to our ideals, for it recognizes no way to development except through struggle and elimination, selection and survival. It smiles when a gentle anarchist expounds "Mutual Aid as a Factor in Evolution"; it knows that coöperation exists only as a means to larger and more effective competition. We form groups in order to compete with other groups in the unavoidable war of life; we unite only under the stimulus of a common danger or a common need, and tend to divide and resume individual competition as soon as the danger is past. All men will be brothers only when all the earth is attacked in that interplanetary war which invention is preparing for the delectation of the future.

It is this inescapable competition that lurks under all forms of coöperation, this "strife," as Heraclitus put it, that "makes some of us gods and some of us men," and so "is the father of all things." In this strife the weaker individual or group will sooner or later be mastered and used by the stronger individual or group. Already a master aristocracy has formed in Russia; and already all the coöperation in Russia must gather itself into competition and struggle against Japan. Suffering cannot be legislated out of the world, though its form and incidence can be changed, and it may conceivably be diminished on the physical plane as fast as it grows, through developing sensitivity in species and individuals, on the mental and moral plane. For some time to come there will be discontent, bitterness, bereavement, pain; and death will continue to generate consoling religions and philosophies. Against the biological background of human life, in which nothing is certain except decay, only the sophomoric soul will expect an end of religion, or be anxious to offer to the unhappy a Copernicus and a Darwin in exchange for a Dionysus and a Christ.

This is not to say that ideals are unattainable; on the contrary, their realization is made possible by that same struggle which dictates their limitation. For within this limitation—that mutual aid is essentially a factor in competition—there are wider realms in which coöperation is practicable, and necessary, than any in which it has operated before. Most of those economic and political ideals of coöperation which we vaguely designate as socialism are clearly in the *Zeitgeist*, and seem destined to increasing fulfillment. As invention proceeds, requiring ever larger units of production and exchange, ever faster modes of communication and transport, ever increasing interdependence of individual with individual, of group with group, of nation with nation, coöperation becomes the first necessity of successful competition. The individual cannot "go it alone"; the sect cannot survive without merging with other sects; the state must combine with other states to preserve itself in trade and war. Even at the height of the nationalistic curve France and American, which agree only in hating Bolshevism, undertake to coöperate with Russia against common foes. Coöperation becomes a biological asset, and morality, which is coöperation, finds for itself a wider base, and is permitted to rise to a larger loyalty. Soon it may be less than treasonable to think in international terms; perhaps—who knows?—the time may come when it will be possible for a man to preach universal love without weakening the state, as Buddha weakened India and Christ weakened Rome.

VI. Philosophy and Despair

The last problem in philosophy is philosophy itself. Of what worth is it to individuals and societies; what good and evil can it do? At times it appears as the noblest of all human enterprises, this reckless attempt to understand the world and man purely for the joy of understanding; at other times it seems only to undermine faith, hope and charity, and to confirm the terrible warning of Ecclesiastes, that he that increaseth knowledge increaseth sorrow. Our growing knowledge is in one aspect merely a growing ignorance; at each further step into the telescopically vast or the microscopically minute we come upon unsuspected worlds, whose operations laugh at those "natural laws" which are our precarious formulation of an ever fragmentary experience. Consider how science has added to our ignorance since the Middle Ages, when every *villein* knew just who had created man and the world, just when, by what means, and for what purpose and destiny. Would that we knew as much as the man in the street! Or as little. *Felix qui non tentavit cognoscere causas;* fortunate the man who can sink himself into the immediate and the particular, never pondering the purpose and beneficence of the whole. Perhaps that "total perspective" which philosophy craves would be a suicidal end to human happiness, even to human existence; as old Babylonian and Hebrew myths expressed it, no man can see God and live.

In short, the progress of science has increased what H. G. Wells, forty years ago, called our "skepticism of the instrument." We are not so exalted over knowledge and intellect as were those magnificent Enlighteners who made the eighteenth century bright—at last red—with "the indefinite perfectibility of mankind." Perhaps the Goddess of Reason was in truth a harlot, and has left a paralyzing curse upon those who courted her too intimately. We see ourselves shockingly foreshortened in a new perspective of fragmentary brevity; we cannot strut the earth, on our short leave of absence from nonentity, with that grandiose confidence which helps men to accomplish the miracles of history. The more we learn, the less we hope; we perceive the strength, even the necessity, of tradition and instinct, and how narrow are the limits within which they will tolerate permanent and salutary change. We lose the supernatural basis of our moral code, and tend toward an Epicurean riot delightful to the individual and enfeebling to the race. Thought liberates action from morality, and the citizen from the state; calculus replaces conscience, and individualism first stimulates, and then destroys, the society in which it is uncontrolled; and emancipated souls follow their whims into chaos. Finally, thought frees the individual from the species; it teaches him birth-control, separates sex from parentage, rescues woman from mechanical motherhood, frustrates the Schopenhauerian "snare" of love, brings sterility to the intelligent, and leaves the ignorant to continue—and dominate—the race. Perhaps the man who invented thought was an enemy of mankind.

We seem driven back to an old and challenging aphorism— that religion stands at the cradle of civilizations, and philosophy at their end; a nation begins with poetry and ends with prose. It may be so; it may be that without a myth we die, and that a poem is the first necessity of a people. Let us comfort ourselves, then; myth still enthralls most of us, and its devotees have a high birth-rate; there is a good chance that these dour philosophers will be beaten again, if only because they can fill volumes more readily than cradles. We must not exaggerate the influence of thought; the people are not profoundly touched by our syllogisms, and take from science only those marvels which create wealth and generate faith; consider the recent fertility of astronomers and physicists in religious inspiration. Humanity will build a new religion, celestial or Utopian, to console or to inspire it; or it will accept and survive all our skepticism, and enter upon another humanist and earthly Renaissance.

Our time may not know the issue, but it will witness the struggle and the spectacle. The twentieth century becomes, under our eyes, a battleground on which, over the corpse of the past, issues as vast and heroic as any in history are being fought out for the control of the future. Democracy fighting for its life against dictatorship, Protestantism fighting for its life against Catholicism and occultism; religion fighting for its life against atheism; capitalism fighting for its life against communism; Europe fighting to hold its own against a resurrected East: these are some of the actors in the magnificent drama of the twentieth century. Life will be worth living, if only as an esthetic spectacle, as a scene crowded with beauty and terror, tragedy and comedy, suffering and nobility. But the wisest of our children will not be those who will merely enjoy the spectacle. It will be those who will climb out of the pit upon the stage, and lose themselves in the action.

THE NATURALISTIC TEMPER

IRWIN EDMAN

Born November 28, 1896, in New York City. Went to school at Townsend Harris Hall and Columbia College from which I was graduated
in 1917. Began to teach at Columbia in 1918 and received my doctor's
degree in 1920. Published in 1920 a book entitled *Human Traits*, which
was used for many years as a text for the psychological and philosophical
phases of the orientation course at Columbia known as Contemporary
Civilization. In 1925 published a volume of poems and an imaginary
portrait of a young American intellectual entitled *Richard Kane Looks
at Life*. In 1929 published a small volume on aesthetics called *The
World, the Arts, and the Artist*, as well as a volume of essays; in 1932
a study called *The Contemporary and his Soul*. I have contributed frequently, both poetry and prose, to various journals and expect to publish
this spring a volume called *The Mind of Paul*, which I gave as the
Schermerhorn lectures at Columbia two years ago. My chief course at
Columbia is The Philosophy of Art, and it is around that theme and out
of the materials of the arts, especially poetry and music, that most of my
philosophical interests revolve. I am one of the Book Editors of the
Journal of Philosophy.

THE NATURALISTIC TEMPER

Irwin Edman

It is very difficult for a philosopher, especially one at all familiar with the career of philosophical ideas, to commit himself, as it were in midstream, to a single point of view, to call or even to regard that point of view as ultimate, and to say, "Behold, here is my philosophy." It is particularly difficult when one conceives, as does the present writer, the history of philosophy itself as a phase of the history of the human imagination and the enterprise of philosophy to whatever discipline it is and should be subjected, as an essentially imaginative undertaking, a cousin on one side to poetry in the flight of its hypotheses, and to religion in the seriousness of the issues it raises and the seriousness with which it regards those issues. It is difficult also when one has even a modest acquaintance with the methods and net results of current psychological and biological inquiry to be able to treat in isolation the current professional issues, to convert logical distinctions into metaphysical principles, to be hypnotized by a methodology abstracted from all subject matter. All "problems" in philosophy, however subtle and exact the analysis they involve, seem to observation unprejudiced by professional interest, to originate in skepticisms and paradoxes familiar to all honest human reflection. The issues traversed by epistemology, logic, metaphysics, cosmology, ethics and aesthetics are attempts with a certain scrupulousness to resolve human issues and straighten out human perplexities. These disciplines may come to require treatment by experts and to be both the career and the delight of a small professional class. But it seems to me to misconceive the origin and the function of philosophical thought in its larger human context to forget how these issues arose historically, how they arise repeatedly in the individual psyche, what clarification they bring to the understanding peace of the individual and to the society of which his individuality is a function.

Such an approach may err in the direction of turning or seeming to turn speculation into a more abstract form of belles lettres or an intellectualized economic history, ignored by the literary public and reviled by the logicians. But to treat philosophy humanely does not necessarily mean to treat it loosely. To be humane is not necessarily to be incoherent. I cannot help thinking that a sense of proportion—no harm even in a philosopher —would require on the part of a thinker today a recapitulation in his own mind of the origins of philosophical thinking in history and in human nature, and the consequences of it in both. It is such a recapitulation that I propose briefly to make, and from that recapitulation to draw certain morals for philosophy, at least for my own.

I would begin by reminding the reader that philosophical thinking is only one form, though a highly sophisticated one, of human thinking. It originates in those indecisions and perplexities which provoke the mind and the imagination when the gross and immediate practical demands of life and society permit a little space and a little leisure. It develops when to the reflective mind the convention of habit and tradition does not account for the facts of experience or gives an adequate rationale to the accepted ways of living. The origins of philosophy are then largely (as has so often been pointed out) in skepticisms moral and poetic. Questioning of accepted standards generates the problem of morals, and in the search for new standards more satisfying to rational inquiry the conception of the Good Life emerges. The reader educated in the general tradition of European culture hardly needs to be reminded that European moral philosophy may be said to have begun with the skepticisms of the Sophists, and the attempts of Socrates and Plato.

recognizing the solid grounds of skepticism, to build more solid standards to replace the shattered tablets of a brilliant society recognizably in a state of decay.

Or again the reader needs only to be reminded of another source of philosophy, namely the equivocations in which the mind finds itself when it begins to reflect upon itself and upon its knowledge. I refer to those moments in the individual psyche when for some reason the senses themselves and the hitherto so tangible objects of their revelation both seem to be suspect. The stick looks broken in water; one cannot even see one's self. There come, too, those deeper and more disturbing ambiguities of reason when reason questions its own competence or is bemused by the paradoxes reason itself has contrived or discovered. Zeno's name is a memorial to such perplexities, for it was he who left to Plato and to all philosophers the heritage of the conceit that motion is impossible because it turns out in reflection to be a succession of rests, as it was Parmenides who befuddled philosophers into thinking that clearly analyzed Being could not even be said to be. These puzzles have provided both entertainment and challenge to philosophers. But they are after all refinements upon natural uncertainties; out of felt, not trumped up ambiguities, theories of knowledge and theories of logic arise. Or again the birth of speculation may be studied in those curious discoveries, familiar to the layman and certainly to the poet, when the line between appearance and reality, between shadow and substance, between dream and waking seems very fine and very indeterminate. Such moments direct the mind to looking beyond the changing, the precarious and the therefore essentially unintelligible to and for something changeless, intelligible, ultimate—the real. A sensibility to time and illusion, a hunger for the eternal and the authentic, when nurtured carefully together, come to generate a metaphysics, a consideration of, an inquiry into the nature of being itself.

Obviously neither an account of the psycho-genesis nor of the historical genesis of speculation is speculation, but it is well for philosophers to remind themselves how their problems arise out of the natural skepticisms of the human mind and the native uneasiness of the human heart among time and change and things. Such a self reminder will prevent them from treating their "problems" in a dialectical vacuum or from indulging in the petty and perverse luxury of technicalities for their own sake. It will prevent them from taking fantastic and irrelevant verbal structures for the dialectical garments of facts. It will help them to remember that philosophers are after all nothing but men thinking, and that, however responsibly that thinking be carried on, it derives from genuine human issues, has as its materials humanly discoverable facts, and to be thinking rather than verbal sleepwalking, must have as its subject matter the common world of sun and stars, of birth and death, of war and peace, of hope and fear and love and hate.

But to say this is not to deny that the enterprise of thinking straight about problems generated by the friction of a perplexed creature in an uncertain world involves a scupulous exploring of those contradictions and difficulties in which any thinking on major issues involves the human spirit. There is, as Morris Cohen (and Hegel before him) has pointed out, an inevitable antinomy in thinking, a polarity involved in any consideration of any issue. Any thesis involves any antithesis and the mind is impelled to frame some new synthesis in which these opposites are reconciled.

Change involves the unchanging, time implies timelessness and beginnings end. Sustained thinking on the major issues of nature and life, if it is to be more than vague soothsaying, must subject its vision to discipline, observe the meaning of what it thinks and the consequences logically involved in its proposed avenue to the truth. A philosophy must be something more than a vision, however noble, of the world. It must in itself be an illustration of that careful and logically fastidious procedure, that self-critical reflection which has marked the classic philosophers. To that extent method is of the very essence of philosophy and logical issues are at the very center of its problems. Logical analysis of method itself, a pre-occupation with method have their rights in philosophy. Logic is the asepsis of philosophical thinking. But there is a "Critique of Pure Logic" to be written and the first step would seem to be that of reminding those who wish to substitute method in the abstract for a critical reflection upon experience of what they are perniciously doing. Aristotle classified experience, he did not impose some one else's categories upon it. The pre-occupation with theories of knowledge and with an abstracted methodology seems to be a hint of decadence in philosophy, especially when theories of knowledge and of logic are offered as world views in themselves. Critical reflection is an instrument of philosophy, and like other instruments may be a joy to the virtuoso or to the connoisseur when played, but it is only an instrument in the larger service of philosophical reflection, which is that of experience become critically circumspect of itself, "life understanding its own conditions."

It is easy to see how a critique of method becomes an obsession by it, and how method arrogantly or innocently translates itself into a metaphysics. The movement of dialectic is that of internal cogency and self-enclosed consistencies. A philosophy compact of pure logic may start with any assumptions and arrive unchecked by brute experience at the most implausible and fantastic conclusions. There are rationalistic philosophies no less pure reverie and pure dream for all the consecutiveness of their internal dialectic and the march of their demonstrations. The seduction of idealistic systems seems at least to one not an idealist in philosophy to lie precisely in the ease with which the purity and consecutiveness of their thinking is identified with the ultimate nature of things. Reality is proved to be more perspicuous and clear than experience ever or always shows itself to be.

For the end of philosophy and its beginning is in the desire (provoked by doubt) to understand. The philosopher is born into a world of things and events, illusions and disillusions, facts obdurate and auspicious, including the gleams and glimmerings of those ideal fulfillments which facts provocatively suggest. He seeks to frame a theory of nature, that is, a generalized version of experience, in which phenomena become intelligible. By intelligibility I do not mean that miscellany of facts and relations in experience are to be forced into a single formula which is imposed upon them and is held to constitute the Meaning of All things, summarily called the Absolute. I mean rather that a philosopher can try reasonably to express in generalized form the impact of experience, render clear to himself the context of things with each other and himself with things, and provide himself with an instrument at once for contemplation and control. He is privileged to seek a theory of Nature, but he will never forget that it is Nature of which his theory is the theory or formulation. Nature, moving and intransigent, does not wait upon his theories; his theory is at best a considered statement of Nature. Intelligibility in the universe is to be found by following the lead of one's subject matter, and one's subject matter, as was remarked above, is the common world which philosophers share with other and less reflective human beings.

The point of view here suggested may be called roughly Naturalism. The characteristic naturalistic theories, whatever be the detailed version of nature that any of them gives, is the assumption, practical and biological in essence, that there is an order, that the appearance and disappearance of objects and the movements of events do connect systematically, the terms of which need not be referred to anything beyond that system or order itself. It goes without saying that such an insistence on the self-sufficiency of nature sets itself up in opposition to "supernaturalism," for the conception of a supernatural universe does nothing but double the natural one with a ghost-like and capricious imitation of the latter. The point of view here suggested seeks "explanation" in some form of elements in some

regularity of motion, a regularity not dependent on any precision or intention of any being beyond the system. The elements are what they are, the regularities likewise; all are given,
ultimate and accountable. They are referred to no explanation
beyond themselves and they constitute all the explanation that
may be given of any object or event. Such assumed regularity
(and it seems to me clear that such an assumption is inevitably
made, even if only implicitly, by all human animals including
idealists in philosophy) removes caprice and isolation from objects and events. The objects cohere and events connect. The
naturalistic assumption changes the world from an apparent
phantasmagoria, from an evanescence of appearances to a per-
manence of ultimate elements whose combinations and permu-
tations constitute at once the being and the explanation of
apparent and changing things. Such a conception of the universe
yielded to the Greeks (it yields to a modern) numerous satis-
factions not necessarily allied to one another, nor any of them
dependent on sentimental idealizations of nature or any provincial current theory about it. Order and recurrence are accounted for without resort to providential purpose or causal
miracle. The universe becomes intelligible rather than puzzling,
and out of the mist of appearance arises a predictable and intelligible daylight world.

But the reader needs to be reminded that a materialistic
mechanism, though the most characteristic and familiar form
of naturalism, is not the only form of it. A naturalism in philosophy is not dependent on one or on any theory of physics. The
assumption that it does is held by many educated people and by
the popular imagination. This is largely due to the fact that
Newtonian science and Cartesian philosophy managed to make
formulation, mathematical, mechanical, material, so effective a
principle of explanation and so effective a principle of practical
control. But a naturalistic temper does not depend on an alliance
with any particular formulation of simple billiard ball materialism or modern mathematical physics. For it is a temper, more

than a cosmology, it is the assumption of a regular order which it identifies with or as nature, a nature of which the thinker regards himself and his thinking as a consequence and a part. To be a naturalist one needs to pay no more devotion to Democritus or Lucretius than to Spinoza. The naturalist will not confound structures with which he operates for the substance of nature itself. Structure is a function of events, matter is the character of events with respect to regularity and stability, their causal sequence, the mind the order of their meanings in their logical connections and dependencies. But this sequential order and this order of meanings are not two separate realms; they are two ways of operation of what is fundamentally and ultimately an irrational and inexplicable flux, a surd fertile with possibility of control and of understanding. Reason for the naturalist is the name for a considered and deliberate exploration and direction of what is at its core an irrational momentum, an impulsion and a tendency which within reason emerges as a more or less effective way of behavior. But the connections made through discovery or through logical elaboration are translations into effective symbols of the tendencies or habits of the flux which no scheme of rational analysis could predict or impose in advance.

The naturalistic temper derives, I think, fundamentally not from any theory of physics, though some theories of physics may seem to it happy articulations of what it feels instinctively to be the hang of the world. When it becomes a cosmology, that cosmology is a generalized formulation of recognized experience, rather than an attempt to ground experience on a theory of the world. "I think," said Descartes, "therefore I am." It seems a more candid and a more honest recognition of the facts, to say, "I am; therefore, I think." For thinking is the function (a late and fortunate turn in animal evolution) of an animal that finds itself living. In living, it finds itself doing many other things besides thinking, and thinking about a world which can be thought about and which lends itself to manipulation and control as the consequence of the thinking process, to contemplation of nature and living (a part of nature) and thought (a part of living).

I should go so far as to suggest that all men are naturalists by tacit and inevitable assent, whatever subtle or noisy or rebellious formulas they make about the nature of things. Their actions, their hopes and fears, their loves and hates, are better evidence of their genuine—and sound—philosophy than the proofs they talk themselves into about an alleged world which is contradicted by every casual encounter they have with a fact, with sun and rain, with a child or a parent, a flower or a friend.

The world which experience encounters may for purposes of understanding and control be reduced to elements and relations. But the nature that man thinks about he admits long before he has thought and in the intervals when he is not thinking. It is the nature in which acorns grow into oaks, boys into men, relations into communications. It is the nature in which the tongue utters speech and the body flowers into the entelechy of the soul. It is the nature wherein bodily life comes to a glow of realization in consciousness, blossoms into dreams, ideals and purposes. There is no contradiction between body and mind; between nature and spirit; the latter in each case is the realization of the possibilities of the former. Art, religion, thought, and imagination are functions of nature just as much as are breathing and digestion and the movements of molecules and stars. The opposition sometimes alleged to exist between the natural and the ideal depends usually on a conception of nature, restricted to purely mechanical terms. Ideals are as natural to matter as are flowers or fruit to the soil, and with respect to their origins, their conditions, their precariousness and their value they may very accurately be compared to them.

There is, it seems to me, extraordinary liberation in beginning with the obvious hypothesis that man is essentially a family member of however an imperfect world, in the recognition of nature as the matrix and source of all we can hope and believe and think and dream and do. The problems of philosophy become then primarily those of clarifying the issues that genuinely face a creature acting and dreaming in the midst of a half friendly, half hostile environment (the only one he has), of what may be the possibilities to be realized, the goods to be attained in such a world. The philosopher will reserve the privilege of detaching himself sufficiently to see himself and all nature as a spectacle. Nature allows him, through the familiar natural miracle of thought, this right. But he will consider, too, if he is not inhuman, the conditions under which detachment and contemplation may flourish. For the happiness of speculation is one of the goods of life, and a philosopher in the modern world has no need of theory (he has only to look around at the distressing fact) to see how much that flight into the infinity of thought is conditioned by the finitudes of social opportunity and economic circumstance. The good (which is to say, all goods) including such apparently private ones as soliloquy and speculation, are social in their origin and social in their consequences.

A philosopher, therefore, is willy nilly confronted with the question of what is commonly called a social and political philosophy, even when by taste, temperament and competence he would or should be occupied with other matters. He may emulate the ambition to become, along with Plato's ideal philosopher, a spectator of all time and all existence, but he knows very well that he is living here and now, and that is from the vantage or disadvantage point of contemporary circumstance that he is surveying the nature of things. Speculation may be, as Aristotle said it was, the highest good; it is certainly the noblest and chastest of the luxuries. But there are, as Aristotle spent the larger part of the Ethics in pointing out, other goods, and the good of thinking itself is conditioned by those. There are philosophers who pride themselves on having passed beyond good and evil, on having attained a Buddhistic Nirvana in which all values are equal or indifferent, the night in which, as

William James remarked of the absolute, all cows are black. But most philosophers cannot find it within conscience or reason to ignore social and moral issues or, regarding philosophy as a critical understanding of the conditions of the life in a natural world, absent themselves from the infelicity of reflection upon the problems of a decent or ordered Life. Such reflections they have learned, with a certain tang of bitterness of late, cannot be conducted in a social vacuum any more than general philosophical issues can be conducted in isolation from the biological and historical conditions of thought.

Values are relevant to the human nature in terms of which values are discriminated. Human nature is essentially social and gregarious in character and lives in and with respect to a social medium. The philosopher of today and probably even more so of tomorrow will find it increasingly difficult to think of a possible good life in a sick society, and his calendar of virtues will be increasingly framed with reference to that co-operative commonwealth in which alone individuality itself can be generously nurtured. His attention will be directed to those aspects of the current capitalist economy which promote unhealthy isolations and distortions and to a consideration of those social conditions which will promote wholeness of life and that genuine freedom in which alone the philosopher's pet good, thinking, can flourish. By temperament, perhaps, it is the very essence of philosophy to see both sides, to be detached from the struggle. But the philosopher may even come to see, as was recently said, that to be above the battle is to be beside the point. For the social, which is to say the moral values, which he after consideration regards as the most complete realization of human capacity, i.e., the Good Life, may be frustrated or defeated by elements and interests in our present-day society which in their private stupidities or cupidities or greeds are enemies, often unconsciously, of the good life. Government, the Machine, the complexities of international economic organization, the fanaticisms of resurgent nationalisms, these may not be the subject matter over which the philosopher's imagination loves to play. But if realization seem to him the measure of the good life, he will have critically to consider the obstacles and opportunities which these offer toward such realization. In the necessary preoccupation with such analysis, he will not forget that instruments, including that of analysis, are simply instruments. The realized life will be measured by him by standards which he finds best exemplified in the activity and enjoyment of art. For art as experience is the best instance of that organization of energies which is another and more specific way of defining the good. It is possibility turned into actuality, fact flowering into ideal, existence generating value. It is the illustration in scattered moments of appreciation or of creation in even a chaotic and routinated society of what an ordered society and a liberated life might be.

The domain of aesthetic creation and enjoyment is, I think, the context in which the question of value, so long a theme of controversy in philosophy, is to be understood. From the point of view of traditional idealistic philosophy, one of the chief stumbling blocks of a naturalistic approach is its apparent exclusion of values. There can be no values without a status beyond the empirical and existent. "What makes a value valuable?" the idealist asks, and answers that the value of a value is the dignity and warrant conferred upon it by its context in a word transcending time and change, and changing and temporal existences and preferences. There are no values in nature; value is derived from some inclusive system of comprehensive and intelligible good. Much of what is called a theory of value is the attempt to wrestle with the difficulties of accounting for the presence of values in existence, where they are present, and for their frequent absence from existence.

Existence is sometimes thought of as a declination from the good, a partial privation of that plenitude of Being in which value and existence are one. Or value is regarded as essentially illusory, as purely subjective and miraculous embroideries upon physical objects and events.

The insistence that existence cannot generate or sustain values on its own account, the denial of nature as the source and matrix of values, is in reality an echo of tradition that had a cosmological contempt for the natural world and a moral contempt for the human nature which from the point of view of a naturalist is one of the processes of natural existence. No good was a good that had no moral warrant, no certificate from a supernatural world. Nothing purely natural and purely human in its origin, purely human in its relevance, could be intrinsically or ultimately valuable. Nothing could give a meaning to existence, unless all goods, meanings and values were bound into a single and absolute system of good, meaning and value.

Values need no such certification. They are what they are. They are those aspects of natural processes, those junctures of events that are prized immediately. Idealists in philosophy talk as if a good must be proved to be good before it becomes good, proved in terms of a comprehensive interrelation of all goods, or sanctioned by something beyond the immediate good itself. Thinking on values is really comparison and estimation of diverse goods, a consideration of their causes and their consequences. But values and goods are what they are, what any given human energies and impulses find them to be. They are generated by natural processes and precariously sustained by them.

The activity of art is the activity in which goods are most explicitly and adequately realized and sustained, the enjoyment of art those aspects of existence in which values, goods, are immediately found. They are fulfillments either found in Nature or achieved through intelligent direction of natural energies toward foreseen possibilities that constitute the work and the opportunity of intelligence in a tractable world. The enterprise of art plays the same function for the naturalist that the realm of ends played for traditional idealistic philosophy.

Values are ends of processes immediately enjoyed. Art is the chief summary name for both those objects which exemplify realizations immediately enjoyable, and those processes which contrive (contrivance being itself a natural process) to create and sustain them.

It is, finally, perhaps in the domain of art, too, that anything like a naturalistic religion must be sought. Faith in the possibilities of experience intelligently to redirect itself, to find the materials for its ideals in nature consciously controlled, to make the objects of faith the objects of fulfillment and realization that creative and imaginative thinking may first discern out of the suggestions Nature itself generates—this is the temper of the only possible naturalistic faith. It is really a faith in what man, himself an incident in natural processes, may do to render his existence rich with meaning and possibility through generous imagination and ingenious contrivance. This is not a belief in God in any traditional sense; but is a belief in the possibilities that Nature itself opens to an investigation, modest in its adherence to discoverable possibilities, audacious in its imaginative use of them in the interests of rendering existence insofar as possible the exemplar and the incarnation of goods.

THE NEW TASK
OF PHILOSOPHY

RALPH TYLER FLEWELLING

Born DeWitt, Michigan. Educated in Public Schools of Michigan; Alma College, University of Michigan; Graduate Degrees: S.T.B., Ph.D., LL.D., Boston University; Graduate Research, University of Paris. Publications: *Christ and the Dramas of Doubt*; *Personalism and The Problems of Philosophy*; *Philosophy and The War*; *Bergson and Personal Realism*; *The Reason in Faith*; *Creative Personality*; *Basic Ideas of East and West*; Contributor to various symposia and encyclopedias. Founder and Editor of *The Personalist*. Director and Professor, School of Philosophy, University of Southern California. Visiting Professor, College of Chinese Studies, in Peiping, under California-in-China Foundation. Lecturer, 1934-35 in Yenching, Nanking, and other Chinese Universities. Honor Societies: Phi Beta Kappa, Phi Kappa Phi, Pi Epsilon Theta. Member, Eastern and Pacific Divisions, American Philosophical Association, American Member, Organizing Committee, International Congress of Philosophy.

THE NEW TASK OF PHILOSOPHY

Ralph Tyler Flewelling

For the first time in many decades the minds of scientific men are turning with interest and inquiry to learn the verdicts of philosophy. Unfortunately there is little promise of help from this direction, since the now dominant schools of philosophy have engaged in a mad race to outrival their scientific colleagues in devotion to a basic materialism under various names. Science has been the first from the midst of this mechanistically minded group to discover the fatuity of the naturalistic metaphysics. Personalistic philosophy of every description might now properly fill the air with "I-told-you-so's," but its period of humiliation and abnegation has been long and painful and has become at last habitual. Moreover, the hostile systems that surrounded it are as unconscious of their scientific decapitation as was Hajji Baba of the plight of his horse, whose rear had been cut off by the descending portcullis but which went along unnoticed until the animal was led to water. In fact, humanitarian motives would lead us into a serious condition respecting the future of materialism were it not for a lively sense of the capacity of that ilk of philosophers to cling still to the illogical and the disproved with the desperate dogmatism of a Fundamentalist theologian. To an onlooker the interesting fact in the present state of philosophy is the completeness with which science in her progress has betrayed that type of philosophy which was far more anxious to appear scientific than it was to be logical or consistent.

It is seldom in the history of thought that revolutionary changes are heralded abroad. They are as silent and unnoticed by the casual observer as a sea-change or a shift in barometric pressure. The masses of men go on grinding at the mill of commerce, or are occupied in the field of industry when some discovery is made, some fundamental change arrives in the mood of thought, and henceforth things can never be the same. Frequently even profound thinkers are beguiled by their obsessions and prejudices, or narrowed interests, away from the deeper significances that spring out of these discoveries. Nevertheless they involve the passing of an old order of thought and the arrival of a new. Such is the period through which we are moving, which in spite of the apparent triumph of materialism and the complete dominance of the mathematical method points to a future whose mood will be in striking contrast to that of yesterday. In fact, this change could have been wrought only by the complete victory of materialism. The very brilliance of its success was needed to disclose its inadequacy. Such an hour points out to philosophy its task, which is to revive the creative imagination, to suggest new combinations, and to propose new solutions where the old have broken down.

The beginnings and the progress of science up to the present have been inextricably bound up with mathematics. It was inevitable that it should be so, for mathematics was itself the earliest science. The fact that it dealt with quantity and number gave a practical and utilitarian interest. Thus it became not only the foundation for research into the problem of reality, but it provided likewise the method.

There is no doubt that nature is particularly amenable to the mathematical method. It would necessarily be so in a universe composed of individuals. In such a world, statistics are possible concerning as many subjects as can be imagined. Whether the statistics are apropos to the subject, and whether they represent any valuable meaning, is quite another question. Since mathematics deals primarily with quantitative measurement, we have then a quantitative science. From its original principle it sets out to view the complete world of experience from the quantitative standpoint. The reason it can discover no other reality is that it looks for no other—in fact, can from the vantage ground of mathematics recognize no other. This method has undoubtedly proved of great value so far as quantities are concerned, but of qualities it is unfitted to treat except as it can discover some sort of point-index parallelism and reduce to scale. In such a case its point-index may be meaningless for the essential quality. Applying, for instance, the quantitative method to the understanding of a painting by one of the old masters, we could weigh it, measure it in square inches, analyze its composition chemically, and determine the exact amount of alkali, carbon, lead, and other elements contained in its ash. Such scientific description would, however, tell us nothing about the important reality of the picture, namely, its quality. Any conglomeration of elements whether in or never in a picture would mean as much.

At last we have happened upon a day when the limitations of mathematical explanation have become apparent to the scientists themselves, and the loss of faith has left many in a confusion which seems at the moment to present inextricable difficulty. We are refusing any longer to see our world through the single eye of mathematics. We are going to use two eyes, and maybe many more.

In truth, mathematics has no way of dealing with living, moving, and changing experience without first reducing it to a dead and static fiction. It must have a fixed meaning, and in the living world there are no fixed meanings, except fixed academic meanings, and these are often far from any living reality, and subject to the vicissitudes of individual understanding. The inadequacy of mathematical explanation lies, therefore, in its incapacity to deal with any but fixed meaning. Its world must stand suddenly still while it geometrizes about what ceases to exist the moment any cross-section is taken of it. There is no provision in mathematical and static explanation for disclosing the meaning of movement, growth, and life. These facts yield themselves only to a direct, intuitional understanding for which mathematical explanation is only a jotting down of certain well-nigh meaningless points or figures to indicate to the mind a pictorial progress. These figures bear to life and reality only a pictorial and point-index character in an attempt to recover dead facts and revive dead meanings. They no more express realities than the figures in the chess-score represent the brain operations of the players.

A mathematically minded science has suddenly discovered the static and inadequate nature of its explanation just at the moment that it is most aware that highest reality consists of living relations, a world that is throbbing with activity, infilled with force and, mayhap, with the purposive energy of supreme and directed intelligence.

One science after another has been forced to give up its absolutes, constants, or universals, which were its fundamental mathematical postulates, as has been so lucidly put by Robert A. Millikan in the closing pages of the little volume, *Time, Matter, and Value.* This remarkable scientific confession fairly represents that portion of the scientific group which is alive and self-conscious. It is enough that science has awakened from the long lethargy of an absolutism of which both theology and philosophy had already pretty much ridded themselves. Science now makes the discovery that it has no "absolutes" except as fictions of the understanding. This fictional device reduces a living world of changing relations to static in order to analyze it, much as we might stop the cinema to a "still" to recover features that were too swift for the eye. But when we stop the machine for a "still" we are no longer dealing with the mobile, nor even with the present (which means existing) facts. The single picture at rest is essentially different from the multiple relational picture of which it is now the unrelated fragment. This will seem an extreme statement, but facts can never be isolated from the moving world of relations without the destruction of their most salient features.

Out of the wreckage of Absolutist expectations the scientist had hoped to save at least one constant on which he could write some universal equation by which, as by the rope of an Indian magician, he could pull himself up once more to a sense of security and lie down again to his "dogmatic slumber." This slender thread of trust remained in his belief in the constant speed of light, but alas, this presumption too threatens collapse, as the latest researches seem to indicate that the speed of light is variable.

In science, philosophy, and religion, the one demand of our anthropomorphic imaginations is security. We are afraid of insecurities of every kind. We long for a universe in which there are no secrets, no skeletoned closets, no surprises, though that sort of a universe, if we had it, would be entirely devoid of interest or inspiration. So we call out against the Almighty for not making us such a universe, and we bend every effort to make it such ourselves. In philosophy we do this by attempting systematic explanation, the erection of a system in which there shall be no logical incongruities. In science the plan has been to admit nothing but such facts as those for which we could conceive working wooden models. Whatever facts we had were stretched upon these frames of explanation. Once this was done, we relapsed into a smug, know-it-all satisfaction. All of these efforts, in whatever field, had the common purpose of security. We must have dependables, and we have expected to add to the security of observed facts in a changing world by building about them systems of explanation that would make them appear reasonable. The difficulty with this method is that reason itself is not a set but a changing term. It depends on the activity of living, and sometimes of growing minds. Therefore in spite of our objections to anthropomorphism, and our violent denials of its influence, every systematic attempt at explanation, from theology to science, has anthropomorphism woven into both warp and woof of its texture. Even our facts, in spite of ourselves, must have meanings, and all meanings are mental interpretations, even though they be of direct experience afforded by the five senses.

But once our scheme has been widely approved, we begin to build upon it, first with the timid assurance with which earth-quake-evacuated homesteaders returned to their homes the fourth day after the quake, and then within a short time we are identifying the various guesses of our systematic ordering with the facts themselves. In these systems of ours we are careful to leave no room for contingency. In our Absolutist enthusiasm contingency is a blind spot. Our "either, or" philosophy demands no exceptions, and we insist on *perfect* security or declare we have *none*. But unfortunately, the world, being a living thing, does not proceed on the "either, or" basis. It has a frequent habit of being "both, and." This fact has been a scandal in theology, which has had great difficulty in separating always the sheep from the goats. It is to be charged with the acrimonies that afflict philosophy, and it has reduced a proud and haughty science, just at the moment it promised to take over and supersede both theology and philosophy, to the pitiful confession that in the last limits of objective matter there is nothing more certain than the Principle of Uncertainty. Forces are no longer to be conceived as continuous, but as discontinuous. Instead of a meticulously dependable continuity, we have quanta. If only quanta would in themselves be good enough to act in some metrical or even predictable rhythm, though without rhyme or reason, we could still fool ourselves by talking about the necessary "laws" of their action—but they are, at least with respect to any specific atom, unpredictable. Viewed individually, they are as capricious in their decisions as our Aunt Fannie. It is only the fact that Aunt Fannie and her decisions are multiplied beyond the grasp of human comprehension that atomic activities are dependable at all. We ought to look carefully at the deflated coin that science has handed us, for it is no "universal" truth, but only a general one. "Absolute" has shrunk up in the wash like big brother's wool shirt into "general," which easily fits the baby.

What we actually have, then, is averages of activity which hold for atoms as for men. Only in the case of atoms, the cases are so innumerable and so fine that we overlook the exceptions. Nor should we be much dismayed or disturbed to discover contingency in the world-order, for, in all practical affairs, all successfully living people have had to compromise with their absolutes. If they could not have a whole cake they have in general learned to take a half-cake, or indeed whatever cake they could get. There is only now and then a "bitter-ender" so fanatical as the civil engineer that swore he would go naked if the tailor would not survey him with a transit instrument for a suit of clothes. We seem to be living in a world of which the best we can do is to obtain a good working knowledge.

If, then, we build our little scaffolding of security upon such fictional suppositions as we can gather, and the outcome shows any appreciable advance in moral insight, in understanding, in mastery of nature, this might in the end turn out the best we could do. Of course it does not accord with the grandiose pattern we had picked for ourselves of "know-all," "test-all," "be-all," but the result may be far better for ourselves and for the world at large.

When we stop to consider, it is amazing how large a place these necessary fictions take in practical affairs. It is always better for me to assume that my neighbor is a gentleman even though he may turn out a bandit. The practical result is better if one assumes that the woman one marries is the "only" and perfect one, for in that presumption lies one's only hope of becoming a perfect husband and being measurably happy. I must presume there is a God whose presence in it indicates the friendliness of the universe if I am to be saved to moral heroism and that unselfishness which alone can be the redemption of society. At any rate, here and there a failure, as in the case of marriage, does not seem to deter many of our leading people from the attempt. The few examples are more than balanced by those who keep on trying after many failures.

What I am trying to get at is the necessity of working hypotheses which in one sense are undemonstrable and their results unpredictable, but which are disclosed, in the result they produce in the generality of cases, to be the highest wisdom and the highest truth, highest in the sense of most valuable.

Science has now seemingly arrived at the point where it must recognize the fictional character of its postulates. In every case its Absolutes or universals have been disclosed as only relatively such—a mental supposition made necessary by the analytical functioning of the mind to provide a *pou sto* as a platform or frame of reference from which to work. Nor is this to be considered in any sense a scientific retreat or defeat. It is in the line of the greatest scientific advance ever known. In our efforts to frame water-tight systems of reason there has been no provision for advance, for discovery of new truth. When we have our system rationally arranged we have a tendency to be satisfied with it. We naturally oppose any discoveries that upset it, since we are put in the position of advocates. We doubt and deny all facts that appear against us, as witness the general chorus of disclaimers that arose in the scientific world against the Einsteinian theory of Relativity.

If science can arrive at the understanding of the tentative nature of its hypotheses, it can transfer from the ranks of the dogmatic to the ranks of the living, and it faces a whole new world of achievement of which it does not now dream. Nor is the outcome a wholly pragmatic one in its accomplishment, for from the actual tests of its theories may come a completer knowledge of the universals as tentative working hypotheses, and this truth holds with equal validity in the fields of theology and philosophy.

We have already hinted that the discovery of the Principle of Uncertainty, and the failure of the last constant, the speed of light, may not be the death-knell of science. On the contrary, we look upon this as the most hopeful discovery that science has made in two centuries. This is not to overlook the benefits accruing from the old systems of dogma or universals. Perhaps that was a necessary step toward the organization of scientific thought. However, ancient good shortly becomes uncouth, and it is now certain that the scientific swaddling clothes are outgrown. We fortunately observe a science of "brass tacks," having practically to accept contradictory hypotheses as a working basis. Logically, light either moves in waves, quanta, or in corpuscles, and the effect of the two is vastly different, so that it would seem necessary to discard one of these hypotheses. As a matter of fact, both have to be accepted as true, and science has not yet been able to frame a generalization that can embrace both sets of facts.

Far be it from me to gloat over this scandal in the scientific household, but the problem is exactly analogous to the one raised in the philosophic family between universal and particular, and at the theological fireside by the possible relation of its Absolute to the finite. It may appear that the solution of the deadlock may in no case be a formal and logical one, but may in all cases be practical and specific. That is to say, the logical solution may tarry indefinitely in the face of the practical solutions of life. The scientist assumes the wave theory with one set of light experiments, and the corpuscular for another. He would like to frame them into a universal pattern, but cannot. His living solution of this predicament, however, is vastly better for science and for his individual soul than the denial of one or the other theory because it seems illogical. Science has finally achieved its freedom from the dogma of reasonableness, and at last may begin to deal with a living universe with some prospect of success.

For reasonableness is not the fixed and absolute thing we have thought it. The enthronement of the Goddess of Reason by the Parisian revolutionaries was no advance in the history of progress. It was the acceptance of a false and betraying thing, as indeed the symbolizing person borne to the Notre Dame that day was picked from the brothel. What is absolutely reasonable one day is not the next. The untempered worship of reason has continually betrayed us. The automotive power of the steam engine was unreasonable before it was accomplished. The telegraph was equally absurd until that first message flashed by Morse. To the hard and fast scientist, Graham Bell was insane until he actually talked across the Charles River, and even then the "tough-minded" boldly declared that his discovery could never have any practical use. Science demonstrated by logic, in the very face of the examples of soaring birds, that a heavier than air mechanism could never fly, until the Wright brothers gave the logical demonstration the lie. This dependence upon the Goddess of Reason has proved her a harlot in her failure to keep faith, at least since the dawn of European history. Reasonableness kept the Pythagorean affirmation of planetary sphericity and heliocentricity from acceptance until the time of Copernicus. Logical reason and scientific dogma held up the development of the airplane from da Vinci to the twentieth century. Of course, the moment the unbelievable discovery is made it becomes reasonable, and we immediately embody it in the corpus of our dogma, fondly assuming it had always been there.

Were we to go by the law of reason alone, were we to confine ourselves to the logical order we so much respect, we should never make any discoveries or advances at all. It is the breaks with reason that set forward the achievements of civilization, as is clearly shown by the noble army of martyrs whose bodies have been burned in the market-place but whose tombs we decorate with garlands. When it comes to progress, life is ever lord of death, and the living is stronger than logic.

What becomes, then, of reason as the arbiter of all knowledge? For one thing, when it cuts across the living hopes of men, when it tends toward the ossification of society, when it hinders the progress of inquiry and its dogmas stand in the way of insight into the living world, it must take a place subordinate to the demands of life itself. But someone will say, what becomes of our security—security of thought, of life, of institutions? The answer is that living men should never *feel* secure, even as they can never *be* secure. The sense of security is never a friend but an enemy. The sense of insecurity is God-given, as was voiced by the poets and prophets from Aeschylus down. This fact possesses implications both for philosophy and theology. The prospect of error is the great inspirer of knowledge in philosophy and science, and the possibility of evil is the salt which keeps religion from corrupting. Instead of inveighing against the goodness of God because of the possibility of evil, we should thank that capacity for suffering which keeps us morally awake and provides the power for spiritual conquest which draws in its train the consciousness that spirit is supreme. Our academic difficulties in all these fields spring out of the fact that the world is alive and changing. It will not stop even for our investigation. Everywhere we must train a pilgrim mind to keep step with its movement by a living insight which cannot be mapped by a Euclidian-like geometry of reason, but which is in large part also intuitive, the direct apprehension of a living nature by a living mind that transcends all formal reasoning or logic.

Our search for reasons has led us into the too often blind alley of mathematical analysis, the search for some absolute and qualityless unit from which to construct a world, with the result that we know, like the boy left at home alone, all about the cogs and wheels and pinions of the family clock, but we do not know enough about it to put it together again. The statistics that we gather are often futile for real understanding. The amazing thing about our world is not the extent of it nor the statistical population of the galactic group. The amazing thing is the organization of it. Yet we have made comparatively no attempt to know, and very little to exploit, it as structure. This knowledge is not to be gained in any great degree by taking it still further apart. Here the single mathematical method of analysis is doomed to failure. For this larger insight we shall need to look within, we shall need to learn to understand ourselves, to conquer the inner relations, to discover how they apply in the social order, and in a Universe that is relative. This field of knowledge is all untilled because the dominating method has been that of despising the self as the most insignificant part of the universe. Nor has this sentiment been relieved by the universal practice of psychologists to study the exceptional, the pathological, and the morbid, as if the only object for wonder and understanding were not the normally functioning structure of mind but its occasional breakdown and failure. Compared with masses of dead, inertial, space-filling atoms which we now know exist only in materialistic fancy, the self may have seemed unimportant, but in the new world of thought opening before us, it will be well to shake off the false humility of our pretending self-abasement. For within our own spirits is the clue to the structural, functional, organizational aspect of the universe. Within ourselves we seize upon a knowledge of that power which is greater than all else because it is the power that moves the sun and all the stars.

If, now, science, philosophy, and theology can come to look on the world not from the sole standpoint of reason, which always deals with a dead and static past, and shall weave into its insights the organismic, the structural, even the revolutionary, and the irrational, we may be headed for a greater term of progress than mankind has ever known.

It has long been a scientific fancy to transfer the macrocosmic fact into the microcosmic dream. We have often been told that the atom is merely the microcosmic repetition of the larger universe. Atomic activity has been conceived as orbital. Do the planets move in their orbits? So, we are told, must we conceive of the internal activity within the atom of proton, electron, and neutron, to say nothing of photons and positrons. It is a fascinating imagery. Even in the Principle of Uncertainty so lately set forth we find the unpredictability imaged as a switch from inner to outer orbit without reason, continuity, cause, or spatial significance, something as the mind commands instantaneously the several portions of the brain. With the nebular theory of the atom we have no quarrel, since though it may be—strictly speaking—unverifiable, it may yet furnish a valuable assumption until a better can take its place. We may be pardoned our sense of humor, however, that so many minds can accept such an imagery without umbrage as thoroughly scientific, because mechanistic—minds which revolt at once at the suggestion that the appearance of intelligence in the one organ or system we have the best means of knowing implies its presence in the system as a whole. Yet in our capacity to know, this latter imagery rests on a far securer basis than the former. There are far more convincing reasons to conclude from the presence of intelligence and contingency in our own personal systems to their presence in the macrocosm, than to guess the orbital character of the atom from that of the solar and other systems.

From physics itself comes the proposition that for the future we must be less concerned with analysis and more concerned with nature as an organism. If this is true, and the truth is now borne in to us by the whole trend of recent science from the discovery of Relativity to the founding of the Principle of Uncertainty, the nearest clue we have to an autonomous organism is our own. "Know thyself" becomes more than the superstitious utterance of the ancient Sibyl, and its repetition by Socrates appears to have been in the line of the highest wisdom. If we find contingency in the atom, we are justified in believing that our own common sense did not belie us, even in the face of the Behavioristic hue and cry, when we believed in the contingency of our own free choices and wills.

It seems strange to be forced to the realization that here lies an all but virgin field for investigation. We assume to know much about the universe, and yet have treated as unimportant the sole vehicle by which that knowledge was made possible to us, and at the same time that crowning gift of mind and personality which has given us a certain superiority over all other facts and objects of the universe. If now we are going to attempt the understanding of our universe from the organismic standpoint, the closest and most significant object of study is the self. But it is obvious we shall have to get rid of our sophisticated horror of anthropomorphism and be willing to look at the facts even though they speak well of man. At any rate, what we have assumed as being the quintessence of scientific disinterestedness we discover to have been a preposterous pose, like the grimacing technique of ancient Chinese armies, assumed to frighten opponents from the field.

The new region of scientific and philosophic endeavor is full of promise. What are the forces that connect man with his world; what the intricate system of relations by which he knows, by which the world corresponds to his knowledge and his will; whence arises the creative imagination with its powers of manifold representation and insight, its capacity for leaps in the dark to new discoveries; can these powers be trained or increased; what is the nature of his deeper dreams and their cosmic significance? Much of this field has been left to the uncontrolled emotions of religion and avoided because of seeming religious implications. These and many more suggestions come trooping in their train as the proper and practical fields of a new understanding which shall attack life from the standpoint of the living.

THE WHIMSICAL CONDITION
OF SOCIAL PSYCHOLOGY,
AND OF MANKIND

EDWIN BISSELL HOLT

HOLT, EDWIN BISSELL, psychologist: visiting professor of psychology at Princeton University. Born Winchester, Massachusetts, August 21, 1873; A.B. Harvard 1896, Ph.D., 1901; A.M. Columbia, 1900; instructor psychology, 1901-05, assistant professor, 1905-18, Harvard. Author: *The Concept of Consciousness*, 1914; *The Freudian Wish*, 1915; *Animal Drive and the Learning Process*, 1931.

THE WHIMSICAL CONDITION OF SOCIAL PSYCHOLOGY, AND OF MANKIND

Edwin Bissell Holt

I

The field of human society affords many brilliant illustrations of what David Hume called "the whimsical condition of mankind." It is true, for instance, as Dr. F. C. S. Schiller has remarked,[1] that "all human institutions have a way of growing into perversions of their original purpose that block its attainment. . . . Those who run the institutions are allowed to acquire interests that conflict with the professed purpose of the institutions they serve." It is true that any very widely accepted opinion, if outside the range of immediate physical fact, will be found on examination to be not an observed truth but merely some fond chimæra that answers to the heart's desire. And it is true that "the strange infirmities of human understanding" are even more strange and more infirm than was to be imagined at the time when Hume wrote. Reason is not a light that guides us on to truth. "All it can do," as Professor Kallen has recently said,[2] "is to argue a foregone conclusion."

These and other whimsicalities of our common lot may be studied with profit by anyone so inclined, provided that he has a shrewd flair for discovering those excellent authors of whom the man in the street and the reviewer for the Sunday maga-

[1] *Logic for Use*, Harcourt, Brace, N. Y., 1930, p. 2.
[2] "Reason as Fact and as Fetich," *Journal of Philosophy*, 1932, vol. 29, p. 570.

zine have never heard. But on all such matters the hungry student will find practically nothing in the academic "science of social psychology." This fact is a further whimsicality that may itself solicit the student's attention. The academic "text-book" of social psychology, he will find, is a farrago of vague, pedantic, and utterly useless abstractions. The mental blindness of nearly every academic social psychologist for any observable fact of human nature is so unfailing and complete as almost to compel admiration. What can any intelligent parent think, for instance, when he reads: "We must . . . look upon the gang [the typical boys' gang] as nature's special training-school for the social virtues"? Again, it is taken as axiomatic that sex "license stimulates desire without limit, and ends in impotent agony," so that "regulation is imperatively called for"; notwithstanding that in the married state and among animals, the two cases where complete sex license is to be found, it produces the very opposite result. So far as any discovery of causes for societal phenomena goes, complete chaos prevails. The name of any phenomenon is regularly presented as its cause: thus it is the "herd instinct," which causes men, wolves, and some other animals to go in herds; cannibalism causes men to be cannibals; etc. In one author of repute we read that "language is a product of the need of coöperative understanding"; again on the same page, that "men's usage makes language" (*i.e.*, speaking makes speech); and on the following page that "language . . . is the result of belief in magic." The only fact conveyed by these silly statements is that the author is ignorant of what causation is. Then there is the ever popular fallacy, a main tenet of the Durkheim school, that "society" is something prior to and over and above individuals. It gives rise to such statements as the following: "Human nature is not something existing separately in the individual, but a *group-nature or primary phase of society,* a relatively simple and general condition of the social mind"; or again, "The moral sense has no significance from the point of view of the individual, but only from that of the larger association" (*i.e.*, society).[3] Both statements are, of course, false.

All this may seem whimsical enough, but a still more whimsical fact remains to be noted. This is that there is one fundamental fact which underlies all societal phenomena and which alone goes a long way toward explaining them all; and this all-important fact is either overlooked or, if mentioned, is denied with a unanimity which is certainly not accidental. This fact is that man, no less than every other living creature, is always and inevitably self-interested, ego-centric. The quality of self-interest is so conspicuous (in spite of dissimulation) in almost every human transaction, is written so large over human history, and is so invariably taken into account by every intelligent man of affairs, that one is dumbfounded to find that it figures practically not at all in academic social theory. The term self-interest, egotism or any synonym therefor is rarely to be found in the index of a work on social psychology or sociology.

Now this anomaly characterizes not merely the psychology of the present day. It will be remembered that those philosophers in the past who have ventured to assign due importance to human selfishness, such as Voltaire, Helvétius, Adam Smith and Jeremy Bentham, have been uproariously "refuted," derided, sometimes slandered, in every way belittled, and eventually ignored in a way that suggests conspiracy. And something more than mere indirection there certainly is. To cite but one instance, and that a modern one: the late Mark Twain wrote an altogether temperate essay on human self-interest which is entitled *What Is Man?* He worked at this, off and on, through some twenty-five years; and commonly referred to it as "my Gospel" or "my Bible." In February, 1883, he presented a tentative version of this essay before the Monday Evening Club. "They

---

[3] The above quotations are all from actual authors. I do not give their names, for that would be invidious. The authors quoted are no more incompetent than most other social psychologists.

scoffed and jeered at it; denounced it as a manifest falsity." [4]
In 1899 he wrote to W. D. Howells: "Since I wrote my Bible
(last year), which Mrs. Clemens loathes and shudders over
and will not listen to the last half nor allow me to print any
part of it," etc.[5] In his seventy-first year he wrote, regarding it,
to his friend the Rev. J. Twichell: "For seven years I have
suppressed a book which my conscience tells me I ought to publish. I hold it a duty to publish it. There are other difficult
duties which I am equal to, but I am not equal to that one."
Shortly after that (1906, some two years after the death of
Mrs. Clemens) he at last had *What Is Man?* printed—privately
and anonymously! [6] "It was not over-favorably received,"
writes Mr. Paine. Nor was it at first included in the Collected
Edition of Mark Twain's works; it was added later, in a supple-
mentary volume, with uniform binding. There is not one word
in this little work to which the slightest objection can be taken
on any ground save that human selfishness is a theme strictly
tabooed. And it would be interesting to know how many persons, even today, have ever heard of this essay, which is one of
Mark Twain's very few serious utterances.

Is it that the self-interest of mankind so little likes to look
at itself that all reflective thought on the subject is instinctively
tabooed? Or is it, perhaps, that the self-interest of some more
grossly self-interested portion of mankind has felt it to be advantageous, and found it to be possible, to place an effective
taboo on all open consideration of the subject? It is easier to
practice burglary where no one suspects the existence of such
a means of livelihood. And the power of observation, of actual
independent observation, is so rare (for the social psychologists
are not alone here) that the mass of mankind can safely be
trusted to know nothing except that which is bellowed at it

[4] A. B. Paine, *Mark Twain, a Biography*, Harper, N. Y., 1912, vol. 2,
pp. 743-4.
[5] *Ibid.*, vol. 2, p. 1080; see also vol. 3, p. 1321.
[6] Van W. Brooks, *The Ordeal of Mark Twain*, Dutton, N. Y., 1933,
p. 303.

through a loud-speaker. And how easy it is to shout through the loud-speaker that self-interest existeth not.

Now "self-interest" is itself a name, and although it is, in my opinion, the correct name for an observable feature of every transaction between two or more human beings, it will by no means advance us, at present, to pretend that self-interest is a *cause* of social phenomena; to say, that is, after the manner of most social psychologists, that self-interest makes men self-interested, that self-interest accounts for deceitfulness, or the like. We must go further, clearly: but to what?

Even a physicist is constantly tempted to say that a body falls "by gravitation." Is "gravitation," then, a cause? It is one instance of that action at a distance which is called the mutual attraction of masses, a "universal law." But "gravitation" no more makes bodies gravitate than "self-interest" makes men selfish. "Attraction" does not cause two masses to attract each other, nor are they "obeying" the "law" which describes, *i.e.*, narrates, the direction, rate, etc., of their respective movements. I fear that many physicists can be as justly criticized on this point as can the social psychologists. But the way out is rather more obvious, perhaps, in the field of physics than in that of psychology. Certainly Kirchhoff and Hertz were correct in declaring that explanation is only complete description; but that does not justify the mathematically minded physicist in assuming that one or more equations describing the movements of the masses (or, in other cases, "statistical laws") *are* a "complete description." Any description in terms of "action at a distance," one feels, is incomplete: there must be something more, something as yet unsuspected, behind a phenomenon so "inexplicable." A more complete description would surely leave the mind more satisfied; and satisfaction is what is primarily meant by "explanation." [7] But the real causes, and this is our present

[7] This aspect of *actio in distans* has been most interestingly discussed by É. Meyerson, *Identité et Réalité*, Alcan, Paris, 1926, pp. 76–86, 513–527.

point, will never be extracted from the actual masses as they move, and be put into the word "gravitation" or "attraction," or into any formulation of a "law": they will always remain in the masses and the field in which these masses move. Words and equations can only name, and direct our attention to, aspects of the real phenomena. Now gravitation or attraction is merely the name for a phenomenon which has not as yet been explained. The concrete bodies which exhibit mutual attraction must be studied further.

II

The concrete bodies which exhibit self-interest must be studied more analytically; and these bodies are living human beings. Now these living bodies are so complicated in structure and function that there is little hope of deciphering their plan, of picking out fundamental properties from superficial manifestations, unless we examine successive steps in the process of their construction. We must glance at the development of the human embryo.[8] Its very earliest movements are altogether random movements: it slowly writhes and twists, bends or unbends a limb, etc., but all with no vestige of purpose or coördination. The reason for such utter aimlessness has been revealed by the microscope. The embryonic nerve-muscle system, at this stage of development, consists of the following three sorts of elements: (1) sensory cells, many (not all) of which are mature enough to be susceptible to stimulation (by pressure, warmth, etc.), each provided with a nerve-fibril (neuron) that will conduct nervous impulses to the central nervous system; (2) a vast number of "connecting" neurons, both long and short, lying wholly within the central nervous system (brain and spinal cord); (3) motor neurons which start within the central nervous system and run out to all muscles. At this stage of the

---

[8] The present writer has given a more comprehensive account of this early "learning" process, citing the physiological evidence, in *Animal Drive*, vol. I, Holt, N. Y., 1931.

development the sensory neurons are not connected with the "connecting" neurons, nor are these connected with one another or with the motor neurons. Sensory impulses coming from sensory cells (sense-organs) to the central nervous system jump across from one neuron to another as best they can, and if they can; and if they succeed in reaching some motor nerve (and so, making some muscle contract), it is fortuitous which motor nerve is reached. Therefore the muscular contraction is fortuitous, random; and all movements are at this stage random.

For sake of clarity we can leave out of account many complicating details, consider only the fundamental facts of the central nervous system, and can speak somewhat metaphorically of the process of nerve-impulse conduction without falsifying the facts which we wish to understand. Any one of the connecting neurons may be considered as a more or less long fibre (axon) having a (cell-body and) tassel of short dendrites at one end. Nerve-impulses can enter such a neuron only through the dendrites of the tassel, from which they pass along the axon to its farther end. Where any such axon ends there are regularly found, lying in greater or less proximity, the dendrite tassels of other neurons; and the space intervening between the axon-end and these many dendrites is called a synapse; it is occupied by non-nervous tissue, which offers some resistance to the passage of nerve-impulses. But if the impulses are strong enough to push through the non-nervous tissue at the synapse, they may reach many dendrites and start nerve-impulses in more than one neuron. Thus at a synapse nerve-impulses arriving over one neuron may spread to several, or even many, neurons.[9] And such a spreading of impulses, from one neuron

[9] The strength of impulses from one neuron which have crossed a synaptic gap and set in action several other neurons may be as great on *each* of these latter as it was before crossing the synapse. For conduction on a nerve is in some respects like the conduction of fire along a miner's fuse: each fuse will burn as brightly even though fifty of them have been lighted from only one match.

to several, regularly occurs. Thus nerve-impulses set up by the stimulation of a sense-organ or a group of sensory cells will regularly, if they come closely enough on one another's heels (which is what the "strength" of a nerve-current amounts to) pass the synaptic resistances, traverse neuron after neuron, spreading at each synapse to a greater number of neurons, and will finally reach a considerable number of motor neurons and through these reach many different muscles. These muscles will contract if the current-density ("strength") on their motor neurons is sufficiently high. But this muscular activity will be fortuitous, random, purposeless. As Sherrington has said, the impulses from any sensory cell can pass through the central nervous system and come out to *any* muscle whatsoever.

Our problem now is to find how any purposeful muscular activity is ever brought about. It is here that "learning" begins, and this learning depends on a simple principle, the "reflex-circle," which has been described by the Dutch physiologist, Dr. S. T. Bok. Let us consider the hand of a human foetus a few weeks before birth. The foetus is curled up rather snugly, and the little hand is commonly held in a lightly clenched position, the fingers bent over on the palm. When at any time a random motor impulse contracts a flexor muscle in one of the fingers, that finger will necessarily touch or press against the little palm. But this at once stimulates two sensory surfaces, the tip of the finger and the palm, and sends two sets of nerve impulses back to the central nervous system so quickly that the flexor finger-muscle is *still* pressing the finger on to the palm. For the central nervous system, and this is the exactly crucial point, these two incoming currents, from two particular sensory surfaces, are the *instantaneous result* of an outflow of current on a particular motor path (to a flexor muscle of a certain finger).

The synapses on the way to this particular muscle are at the moment carrying impulses, they are active or, according to a conception of Sherrington's, electrically "charged"; and this means that for the time being they offer less resistance than do other, inactive synapses to the passage of further nerve-impulses. So that the two sets of sensory impulses which reach the central nervous system at just this moment encounter, in spreading, less resistance on the path to this particular finger muscle than they encounter in any other direction. Just these paths are at the moment "open," and they take more of the incoming currents than any other path takes. But this intensifies the flexor contraction, which in turn intensifies the finger and palm pressure and so intensifies the two incoming sensory impulses, which increase again the flexor contraction; and so on and on. This is the reflex-circle. It tends always not only to maintain but to intensify itself.

But those impulses from random sources which first opened the motor path to the flexor finger muscle may not and in general will not continue long. And without their support the reflex-circle may (at the outset) be unable to maintain itself; and then it weakens and fades out. For the synaptic charges unless maintained will soon subside.

As long as the reflex-circle is kept in action, however, another process is taking place. The dendrites at an active synapse are stimulated to grow, as C. U. Ariëns Kappers has shown, and they grow toward those axon endings from which they are receiving nerve-impulses. This growth is very slow; but it is permanent. It reduces the width and therefore the resistance of the synaptic gap. Therefore, each time a reflex-circle is set up, as described above, even for a short time, the slight growth of dendrites leaves a series of synapses of permanently lowered resistance along its course after all synaptic charges have subsided. The next time this same flexor muscle of the finger is the seat of a random contraction, the same reflex-circle will be set in action but this time more readily, for now at least some of the synapses along its route start with a lower resistance than they had at first. And the synaptic resistances along this path will now be still further reduced, and permanently. Thus in time a pathway of exceptionally low resistance will be established, which runs from two sensory (tactile) surfaces, a spot on the palm and one on the inner surface of the particular finger-tip, through the central nervous system and out to the particular flexor finger-muscle with which the process started, that is, whose random contraction first caused those same two sensory surfaces to press against each other. And now, whenever any light pressure is applied to either of these two sensory surfaces the flexor muscle will contract and bend the finger over on the palm.

We have considered only one flexor muscle of one finger. The four fingers have three joints each, and each joint has its flexor muscle. Random contraction of any one of these twelve flexor muscles will, in general, press the inner surface of one finger-tip against a corresponding spot on the palm, in precisely the same way as in the case already considered. A reflex-circle will be set up, and a pathway of permanently lowered resistance will be established from certain two sensory surfaces to that flexor muscle which, in contracting, brings just those two sensory surfaces into contact. After these twelve reflex-circles have been established ("learned"), all twelve can be set in action together by pressing some suitable object, such as a ruler, gently against either the palm or the palmar surfaces of the four finger-tips. All four fingers will bend on to the palm; that is, the hand will *grasp* the ruler.

Thus significant and "purposive" reflexes are developed ("learned") from purely random muscular contractions; or more exactly, from the sensory stimulations which, as we have seen, such random contractions directly effect. This grasping reflex is so far developed in any healthy baby at birth, that the two little hands will close round a cane tightly enough to support the baby's whole weight, hanging, for several minutes.

Let us consider random contractions of the extensor muscles

of the fingers. The contraction of an extensor muscle straightens or unbends its finger-joint, and will never bring the finger-tip to press against the palm. But it will often bring the outer (volar) side of the finger in contact with some external object; perhaps, in its confined position before birth, in contact with some other part of the infant's own body or, after birth, with bedclothes, pillows, etc. The reflex-circles which are developed by random contractions of extensor muscles of the fingers will necessarily involve sense-organs lying on the back or volar surfaces only of the fingers; and these latter will become connected through the central nervous system with those extensor finger-muscles whose contractions have brought just these volar surfaces into collision with outer objects, and so stimulated these surfaces. As a result, a gentle pressure on the outer or volar side of a baby's finger makes the finger unbend; and in so doing it presses back against the pressure applied to it.

Similarly, any random movement of a baby's arm or leg is liable to bring some surface of the limb into collision with an outer object, and so to effect a stimulation (pressure) of that surface. This surface will necessarily be the one which happens to be carried *foremost* in each particular random movement; the rear surface will never collide with anything. So that the reflex which is developed, whether the muscles involved are at the wrist, elbow, shoulder, ankle, knee or hip, will always be such that the surface stimulated moves foremost, just as it did during the learning, and presses toward the stimulating pressure. It returns the pressure. In this way the entire surface of the limbs becomes "educated," so that stimulation of any spot on the skin excites a reflex which makes the member return the pressure that stimulates it. Pressure on the soles of the feet, for instance, excites reflex extension (straightening) of the hip, knee, and ankle, the so-called "extensor thrust"; and our ability to stand and to walk is very largely due to this reflex.

Now this principle of reflex-circle is the basis of all early learning in the child.[10] It produces a vast substratum of reflexes, involving every sensory cell and every contractile (muscular) cell in the entire body, and countless pathways, of more or less lowered resistance, connecting the sensory with the motor elements. And this great substratum of reflexes, thus permanently established, determines the general characteristics of the individual's behavior through his entire life. As one physiologist, referring to the simpler reflexes, has expressed it: "Such is the groundwork on which the cerebral cortex, as on a piano, plays the most complicated melodies. . . ."[11] Thus, for instance, the grasping reflex and the extensor thrust of the legs are employed or "played upon" by the "higher centers" in almost every moment of waking life. And learning by the simple principle of reflex-circle extends to acquisitions which are more obviously related to the "mental" life than the illustrations so far adduced would suggest. For instance: a baby's breath comes in and goes out through a channel where it must pass several motile organs, such as the vocal cords, hard and soft palates, tongue, gums (teeth) and lips; and the muscles of these organs receive their quota of random innervations. So from time to time the baby's breath inevitably produces a sound; and it produces different sounds according to different random contractions taking place in these motile organs. If the baby's hearing is normal, each sound produced instantly stimulates the baby's own ears. And the sensory impulses so produced pass to the central nervous system and there find "open" the motor paths to precisely those muscles whose contraction has just forced the breath to produce this particular sound. A reflex-circle is started, and the sound just made will be made again; and again. This period in the baby's life is not an easy one for the mother,

[10] The writer has shown in *Animal Drive*, vol. I, as for that matter the reader will readily see for himself, that the reflex-circle is precisely the same thing, described in neuromuscular terms, which Pavlov has described in behavioristic terms as the "conditioned reflex."

[11] R. Magnus, *Körperstellung*, Springer, Berlin, 1924, p. 619.

who soon tires of the incessant "ma-ma-ma—"; "pa-pa-pa—"; "la-la-la—"; "goo-goo-goo—"; etc. But the mother is soon rewarded, for presently when she goes to the crib and says "Mamma's here," her precocious little darling actually and for the first time replies, calling her by name, "ma-ma—!" After its lalling and babbling exercises the infant has to repeat "mamma" whenever that sound stimulates its ears. It is now indifferent whether that sound proceeds from its own or its mother's throat. Such are the beginnings of speech.[12] And *deaf* babies do not learn to speak.

The reflex-circle determines the general character of the reactions of any of the higher organisms. And what that character is becomes evident from a consideration of the reflex-circle principle. In each case, as we have seen, learning is based on a random movement and on the resulting sensory stimulation which that movement causes to be impressed on the organism. If the random movement has no such result, there will be no significant learning. For it is precisely the stimulation that *results* from the random movement which acquires a pathway of lowered resistance through the central nervous system and out to the very muscles that have just made the random movement. This will produce the movement again, which will again (by collision or otherwise) bring about the same sensory stimulation. Thus after the circle has been permanently established (learned), pressure on the palm, for instance, makes the fingers bend over and put *more* pressure on the palm, pressure on the soles of the feet makes the legs straighten and receive *more* pressure on the soles of the feet, mild pressure on any dermal surface stimulates a reflex movement which carries the surface forward toward the pressure. Thus the spot pressed receives more pressure. So universal is this fact that the word "responsive" is seldom used of an avoidance reflex, which causes the organism

[12] This mechanism has been described in greater detail by Dr. I. Latif: "The Physiological Basis of Linguistic Development," *Psychological Review*, 1934, vol. 41.

(or some part of it) to shrink away from a stimulus; although strictly speaking, avoidance is a "response." Again, the child repeats the sound that stimulates its ears, that is, reacts so that it gets the *same* stimulus again. This is as true of drumming and thumping sounds as it is of lalling and babbling.

No reflex-circle can be learned which has not this property And how shall we name this property? One is at first tempted to call it *outgoing* or *outreaching*. But these terms will not quite do. Closing the fist is not exactly outgoing; nor is holding the lips, jaws, or legs pressed against each other (three definite reflex-circles) outgoing. Since there seemed to be no name in English for precisely the property in question, the late Professor H. C. Warren has suggested the term adience (*ad* + *eo*). Adience, then, is that property of all the early reflexes whereby the reflex gives or "inflicts" on the organism (reproduces, repeats, etc.) *more* of the very stimulus which touches off the reflex. So that "more" is bound to be more and more and more . . . And this adience is the basic characteristic of the activities of all the higher animals, including man.

Avoidance is the only apparent exception. Every moderate stimulus elicits adience, but if with "more and more and more" the stimulus becomes over-strong then each muscle which was engaged in the adient movement finds the impulses which activated it switched [13] over into the exactly antagonistic muscle; the adient movement is precisely reversed; and the sensory surface is withdrawn from the over-strong stimulus. Normally, only over-strong stimuli, as Sherrington has remarked, are avoided; and normally no avoidance reaction to the same stimulus at a moderate intensity is learned. Yet it can be: a child that has been severely burned will often exhibit avoidance on even seeing the object that caused the burn, and from a distance at which no warmth can be felt. The permanent fixation of a true

[13] By a fairly well understood mechanism (motor half-centres), which has been studied specially by J. von Uexküll and C. S. Sherrington; and by many others.

avoidance reflex, such as this, is unusual and unfortunate; and is commonly accounted a psychic trauma or wound. Apart from such cases, and from the normal reversal of reflexes under over-strong stimulation, all animal and human reflexes are adient, and pertinaciously adient. The so-called "higher processes," when they proceed to play upon the simpler reflexes as on a piano, have nothing but adience to play upon, to set in action. They are as sure to produce adience as a pianist is to produce sound. Moreover, that further learning which produces the "higher" processes is still entirely dependent, like the reflex-circle, on the growth of dendrites; and it appears in every way to confirm and to extend that same adience which is so infallibly a property of the great substratum of simpler reflexes. These "higher" processes often bring us to the necessity of choosing between two horns of a dilemma: we must select one thing and reject another. But such rejection is not avoidance; it is merely a lesser adience which has to yield to a stronger. If the preferred object is unobtainable, we at once find ourselves adient to the object which we have just rejected.

With this basic quality of adience once pointed out, it is easy to perceive the large adient element in human conduct at every phase, from infancy to old age. The cuddlesomeness and affec-tionate "responsiveness" of the infant lie in the fact that to any gentle, kindly stimulus the infant responds with a gentle adi-ence. We call the little one naïve and innocent because no other reflexes as yet exist to overlie and obscure (as ulterior motives) this simple and spontaneous adience. And in later life the word caress means only to solicit gently a responsive adience, like that of a child. When the infant is a little older, its clinging quality and its persistent reiteration of sounds and repetition of many of its movements are still pure adience. As the infant becomes a child, his eager grasp and impulsive pressures are more forcible; and not infrequently destructive. He shows a general forwardness, not yet tempered by caution. When the child becomes a youth, his adience takes the form of curiosity and acquisitiveness, enthusiasm for exploration and adventure. He collects postage-stamps, butterflies, etc.; and if he puts things together constructively, it is on an ever-expanding scale. He presses forward to an open road, pushing aside or overturning obstacles and thoughtlessly overriding the prerogatives of others.

All of these traits persist in the grown man, but in the man they take on a sterner coloring. Forwardness, curiosity, acquisitiveness, and enterprise are more determined than they were, and more resourceful. They now come to be called ambition, the lust for wealth and for power. If they are tempered by anything resembling a consideration for others, it is not by reason of any quality that is inherent in the organism, but by reason of an external factor of which we shall presently take account.

If now the reader will look squarely at this picture he will readily see that we possess a general term which accurately summarizes all these traits: and that general term is, precisely, egotism. I am not aware that there is any form of adience which is not self-interest, or any form of self-interest which is not directly traceable to adience. Adience, in short, is the physiological term, and egotism, selfishness, self-interest are the behavioristic and societal terms for one and the same thing. It may seem, on first thought, that scientific curiosity, for instance, is a very different thing from the lust for power; but it seems not so different to the animals that are mutilated and destroyed in research laboratories. They know only too well that scientific curiosity is an instance of the lust for power. And we, if we have had close contact with scientists, know that scientific ambition and prestige are commonly as grimly self-centered as the manœuvers of any highwayman.

This basic egotism is the fundamental property of all behavior, whether of animals or men. And we have it now not as the mere name of an unexplained phenomenon, but we have it as a fact explained. We know that when we speak of egotism we are speaking of reflex behavior which is determined by an antecedent growth of dendrites, under certain conditions which we also know. If we now seek to explain behavior in terms of self-interest we shall not be mouthing tautologies, for self-interest is the activity of neuromuscular pathways along which, under specified conditions, dendrites have been stimulated to grow. And if now the Monday Evening Club or all the Sunday morning clubs together scoff and jeer, we shall preserve our equanimity. This basic egotism is the one essential clue in the field of social psychology.

III

The unit in human society is the individual man or woman, and the simplest social relation is found when any two persons are in such proximity that each acts as a stimulus on the other and so excites in the other some response; at first an attitude, and then overt behavior, conduct. This mutual relation between individuals, two by two, must never be lost sight of. If three or more individuals are in proximity, each is stimulated by every one of the others, and stimulated usually to diverse attitudes and lines of action. What he does, his actual response, will be a resultant, an algebraic sum, of the impulses which the others as stimuli excite in him. And the same is true for every other member of the group. The upshot of what all the individuals do, each under this multiple stimulation, is called societal behavior. And history is about nothing except just such societal behavior. But let us return to the simple dual relation, the fundamental unit of societal dynamics.

Each of any two individuals is adient to the other, unless one of them is so much more formidable that he stimulates the other to avoidance. Adience means approach and then appropriation, and the varieties, degrees, and disguises of this appropriation are innumerable. But any individual will appropriate to himself the person, the labor, the possessions, and the life of any other individual if he can, and if he has use for them in any further adient enterprises of his own. Such is the plainest teaching of history; and history further teaches that this propensity knows no limit. If any man, other than the ever-voluble moron, seeks to darken counsel by denying this teaching, it is because he has projects of his own which he fears may come under scrutiny.

The aggression of one individual will arouse in the other avoidance, resistance, or counter-aggression, according to the strength and resourcefulness of the other individual. Aggression met by counter aggression is warfare in some degree, and the most unstable of social relations. But unless the aggression of one is met by resistance, and an adequate resistance, on the part of the other, some form of the master-slave relation will develop between them. This is likewise an unstable social relation; for the natural adiences of the under-dog are held down. And physiological adience is a living force; it is expansive and pushes for an open road. Whenever an obstacle is encountered, the result is pressure against the obstacle: to push it out of the way, to push through or round it, in some way to circumvent it. This pressure terminates only with the success or with the death of the exploited party. He will ceaselessly try, until he finds his own open road, or his grave. It is a situation of unrest. And this word is well employed in such expressions as "marital unrest," "industrial unrest," "social unrest."

No social equilibrium, no tolerable degree of stability, is to be found except where the opposing individuals, or the opposing parties or factions, are fairly well matched; so that each is able to resist effectively the adient (or the aggressive) propensities of the other. This situation is, of course, seldom realized. Yet it is not idle to point out that an approximate equality between the individuals who constitute a society, equality of physical and of mental power, is a necessary, though not a sufficient, condition for social stability. Perhaps no one has pointed this out more explicitly than the late Félix Le Dantec,[14] who calls

[14] *Égoïsme, base de toute société*, Flammarion, Paris, 1918.

:he power to resist aggression the "capacity to injure"; by which
1e does not at all mean an *intention* to injure, or any other
.ort of hatred. There is every difference between the stealthy
:ellow who plans to knife you, and the healthy strong man who
1as no such thought in his mind but who will strike you in-
:tantly if you strike him.

Le Dantec goes on to show that equal capacities to injure,
:he condition of social equilibrium, will not result in a social
deadlock. It possibly would so result if the mystical democratic
dogma, that all men are equal and alike, were true. But the
great number of forces operating on our planet brings it about
that not even any two of us are alike. We grow up with different interests and develop different aptitudes. One man likes to
hunt, another likes to fish, and another likes to cultivate a farm
or to build houses. Working with interest at his favorite game,
every healthy individual produces more than he can use of one
commodity, but nothing of many other commodities which he
wants: the term "want" meaning a physiological readiness to
seize and appropriate. So when men meet they exchange their
produce; they barter. And if the capacity to injure is fairly
equal among men, the mutual exchange will leave both parties
satisfied: both have gained by the transaction. Such a social
relation tends to be permanent; at least, unlike the master-slave
relation, it leads to no tension, contains within itself no factor
of disruption. It is a matter of daily observation that no friendship, marriage, business association, or other relation between
human beings is in equilibrium and gives promise of enduring
unless, first, each party is getting something (tangible or intangible) from the other, and unless, secondly, the commodities
or benefits thus mutually exchanged are approximately equal
in value. Man addresses himself to nature for what he can get,
and he addresses himself to his fellow men with precisely the
same intent, and *never* with any other. Man cannot but be
adient and self-seeking.

But does this fundamental fact about the social relation even begin to cover the field? It seems, at least, to be fairly swamped by other phenomena, and to lie hidden from men's minds. For as one approaches the social scene one encounters a most bewildering tumult and a veritable barrage of words, raucously shouted, so that one at first despairs of gaining any inkling of what is really taking place. Cries of divine guidance, tithes, disinterested leadership, taxes, bolshevism, confiscation, protective tariffs, industrialism, unemployment relief, capital levies, dictatorships, printing-press money, patriotism, repudiation of debts, uplift, depression, and so on fill the air. One recalls the Tower of Babel. But the Biblical story is partly untrue: words were made by mere men, and by mere men they are used. And to bandy words is to do not much. What else are these chattering humans doing beneath their distracting barrage?

Where such confusion threatens it is well to hold fast to physiology. This bewildering riot is the work of human beings endowed with adience, and we shall do well to cease to listen, for a time, and to watch what they are actually up to. Now the relation of mutual give and take is basic, and one of its earliest collective manifestations is the case of a group of sellers purveying to a larger and more scattered group of buyers; as where a commercial company, an organized group of producers and distributors, offers its wares to any and all who will buy. If buyer and seller have a like capacity to injure and if the commodity purveyed is strictly tangible, the buyer is able to know fairly well what he is getting, and that he is getting his money's worth. But if the commodity is intangible, the buyer knows far less and may in fact know nothing as to what he is getting; for the show-down in the case of an intangible is not easy, not positive, and it is seldom immediate. If you buy a dog-collar or a typewriter, you know that you are getting approximately your money's worth. But if at a more pretentious establishment you buy an Egyptian scarab warranted to be three thousand years old, or a picture guaranteed to be the work of Titian, you are running a great risk of being cheated. And if you send your son to college and buy him an education, neither you nor he will perhaps ever know whether he received an education in any real sense of the word, or whether indeed one was even offered to him. Wherever the commodity bought is intangible the buyer needs, as a part of his "capacity to injure," the capacity to see through deception, the discernment to detect what is being done to him. For either party to a transaction will invariably get all that he can from the other, and in every possible way.

Nowhere is this more true than in the case of those two collective transactions which are called the church and the state. The commodities purveyed by these two institutions, namely safe conduct through all eternity and the protection of a good government, are of all commodities quite the most intangible. And these two, or any other, institutions are, if we brush aside the verbal cobwebs and see the actual facts, as strictly commercial enterprises as is a lottery, a soap factory or a peanut stand. The great unorganized group of buyers (communicants of a church, citizens of a state) pay dearly enough, one would suppose, for these two institutions to detect their commercial and self-interested basis.

It is to be observed that by as much as the commodity purveyed becomes intangible, by so much some more or less elaborate ideology plays an essential part in the transaction: connoisseurship in the case of works of art; astrologic lore in the case of fortune-telling; theories, legal fictions and dialectical intricacies in the profession of law; therapeutic doctrines and professional systems or "schools" in medicine; theologies, creeds and rituals in religion; constitutions, enactments, regulations and ideologies without end in government. How much of any ideology is scientific and true, and how much of it is humbug, is the all-important thing to determine. The non-scientific part (which is not infrequently the whole) of an ideology is always a specimen of wish-thinking which argues and "reasons" toward some millennial condition, some merely subjective dream of bliss. And this millennial hope, that is, the verbal patter which

conjures up the delectable delusion, is that intangible com:nod-
ity which the profession or institution, for good hard cash and
other valuable considerations, purveys.

It is further to be observed that as the commodity sold becomes more intangible, the smaller and better organized group
of sellers takes on a different color. The sellers are no longer
manufacturers or producers; they are confidential advisers, professional counsellors, moulders of opinion, leaders of thought,
builders of empire, lords of destiny. In short, they are shamans.
They adorn themselves in prestigious raiment; they take to
themselves fantastic epithets (All-Highest, Serene Majesty,
Holiness, Lordship, Excellency, Highness, Honor, etc.); and,
lo, they come clothed in power. All this you can study, in minia-
ture and make-believe but down to the nicest detail, in the
Lodge of your secret fraternal order. The shamans distil the
millennial hope and exact in exchange not merely money but
also power. The profits are not inconsiderable.

The case of institutions and their intangible commodities perfectly exemplifies the dual scheme, outlined above, in which
two individuals, or groups of individuals, are adiently disposed
toward each other; and in this case the larger group, the herd,
seems seldom in the course of history to have possessed the
"capacity to injure," the ability to protect itself against the ag-
gressions and encroachments of the smaller but better organized
group of "leaders." And wherever the respective capacities of
these two parties to injure have not been tolerably well balanced, the stronger party has shown readiness to appropriate to
itself anything pertaining to the other party.

Under the auspices of religion, when religious leaders had
full sway, Christendom passed through a period known as the
Dark Ages. And the history of these Ages copiously illustrates
our thesis that adience unchecked soon becomes an aggressiveness that knows no limit. The church, or churches, are moribund
today; the State has usurped their pretensions and their prerogatives. Today the leaders, political leaders now, have prac-

tically full sway. We are well within the penumbra of a new Darkness. If reports are to be believed, the greater part of the countries that make up Western Civilization are working over-time to manufacture enough nitro-glycerine and poison-gas to exterminate their neighbors. This is at the direction of political leaders, but it is made possible by the mass-idiocy of the herds that, as often in the past, are everywhere actually begging to be led; "clamoring for a Caesar," as M. Gustave Le Bon has said. Western Civilization, Christendom, seems determined to destroy itself.

IV

The picture is not roseate. The shade of the late Mrs. Clem-ens "loathes and shudders over" it, no doubt, and deplores the mention of any part of it. Most Americans, especially those of the more leisured classes, are going blithely on with their child-ish amusements. Victims of the national comfort complex, they are as ignorant as the ostrich of what is in store for them. They will prefer to die so, at the gaming-tables or the races. Yet if there should be a single reader of these lines who feels that the present condition of society has for him more than a languid and academic interest, he will perhaps be willing to consider the subject for a few moments longer.

Three topics call for special study: ideologies, taken objec-tively, that is, as mental processes by which great masses of human beings are deluded; leadership, as an omnipresent human phenomenon; and the utter helplessness of the buyers, their lack of any "capacity to injure" the sellers. This last is the most concrete, the most difficult, and the most urgent question.

It is hard to hold ideologies off at arm's length and to study without being to some extent seduced by them; and specially when an ideology has become a national atmosphere, the fa-miliar mentality and language of one or more nations. As a per-tinent example, consider the slogan: "Dictatorship of the proletariat." As Prof. F. H. Giddings has remarked: [15] "The phrase is a falsehood." It is self-contradictory; for a dictator is one and only one, while a proletarian is each and every one of a vast multitude. Yet how admirable an opiate for the masses! Each poor artisan, as the leader vociferates: "Arise ye prisoners of starvation! Arise, ye wretched of the earth! The proletariat shall be dictator!" swells to bursting with long-deferred hope: "Ah, now I, I at last, shall be dictator"; and casts his vote. The leader eagerly gathers up the ballots. "Thank you, my friends. Yes, I will consent to be, in place of all of you, your dictator"; and hastens away to the executive palace, to contrive new taxes and perfect his schemes for the general servitude, in "five-year" doses until the proletarians and farmers are inured to the yoke. No more laughable and unblushing millennial hope was ever concocted than the final stage of Communism: when, after ample time to get a surgeon's hook inserted in every nerve and fiber of the body-politic, the dictator and his associates promise voluntarily to remove all hooks and gracefully efface themselves, stepping down and out to the novel experience of anonymity and honest toil. The executive palace must fairly rock with merriment.

A travesty of the events? No, the actual events are a travesty on this! Anyone who will look into Leon Trotsky's *History of the Russian Revolution* [16] will find that this Revolution, as of course every other revolution, was fought out by a few hundred delegates, *i.e.*, leaders, supposed to "represent" millions of proletarian "dictators" scattered over a vast domain. But the art of "representing" a constituency, viewed realistically, is the art of catching (and retaining) the votes of that constituency. Any other notion of political representation is a fiction; as perhaps the notion that there *is* any collective will or mind to be represented is a fiction. And the art of one who would be the supreme

[15] *The Mighty Medicine*, Macmillan, N. Y., 1929, p. 111.

[16] Translated from the Russian by Max Eastman, Simon and Schuster, N. Y., 1932, 3 vols. The quotations which follow are from vol. 3.

dictator is the art of catching the votes of the representing delegates. So far as leaders of an opposing faction go, Trotsky is alive to the facts: ". . . sick and tired of these bragging and narrow-minded leaders who fed them first with phrases and then with measures of repression" (p. 309); ". . . the millions of workers and peasants represented in this congress, whom they [delegates of the opposition] are ready now as always to turn over for a price to the mercies of the bourgeoisie . . ." (p. 311). But he views leadership of his own faction through other-colored glasses; as do all the rest of us mortals, always. In the speech last quoted from, he declares proudly: "We have tempered and hardened the revolutionary energy of the Petersburg workers and soldiers. We have openly forged the will of the masses to insurrection. . . ." Such is the "dictatorship" of the proletariat.

This was in the fateful first hours of the October Revolution and before the Congress of Soviets which opened on the 25th, in Smolny. On the second day, "The evening session of the Congress was to create a cabinet of ministers. M-i-n-i-s-t-e-r-s? What a sadly compromised word! It stinks of the high bureaucratic career, the crowning of some parliamentary ambition. It was decided to call the government the Soviet of Peoples Commissars: that at least had a fresher sound." (p. 322.) And it would better fool the dictator-proletariat into forgetting about all the high bureaucratic careers. "Lenin, whom the Congress has not yet seen," has returned from exile and hiding, and is now produced. This grand panjandrum of the occasion, impressive not by reason of jewels or insignia of rank but by reason of his audacity and fervor, is "apparently oblivious to the long-rolling ovation, which lasted several minutes. When it finished, he said simply, 'We shall now proceed to construct the socialist order? . . . The speaker began immediately by reading the draft of a declaration to be published by the government still to be elected. The text had not been distributed, technical equipment being still very weak. The Congress drank in every word of the document as pronounced." (pp. 323-4.) Some day the delegates will tell the "dictator" what they have decided to do to him, now that Lenin has graciously imparted his instructions to the delegates. So pleasing is the prospect that "The whole praesidium, with Lenin at its head, stood and sang with excited enraptured faces and shining eyes." (p. 328.) Presently, "Lenin is again in the tribune—this time with the little sheets of a decree on land. . . . The essence of the decree is . . .: 'The landlord's property in the land is annulled immediately and without any indemnity whatever. The landlord, appanage, monastery and church estates with all their goods and chattels are given in charge of . . . The confiscated property is placed as a national possession under the protection of the local soviets. The land of the rank-and-file peasants and rank-and-file Cossacks is protected against confiscation.'" (p. 330.) But this last not for long! At this very moment the life of the Congress and the lives of all participants were hanging by a thread. It would be madness to forfeit the votes of the rank-and-file peasants and Cossacks: these were delighted to see the feudal and ecclesiastical holdings "nationalized." But they must be for the present fooled into supposing that they themselves would remain undisturbed. "It still remained to determine in experience how the peasants themselves would understand the conversion of the land into 'the property of the whole people.'" (p. 332.) The proletarian power could preserve itself only by pretending for the moment to give the peasants their long-cherished "agrarian revolution." "The peasant had to be taken as the revolution found him. Only a new régime could re-educate him. . . . The decree together with the instructions meant that the dictatorship of the proletariat assumed an obligation not only to take an attentive attitude toward the interests of the land laborer, but also to be patient of his illusions as a petty proprietor. . . . The collated instructions were anything but the last word. They represented merely a starting-point which the workers agreed to occupy while helping the peasants to realize their progressive demands, and warning them against false steps. 'We must not ignore,' said Lenin in his speech, 'the resolutions of the lower [formidably numerous] ranks of the people, even though we are not in agreement with them.' . . . Opportunism? No, it was revolutionary realism." (pp. 332-3.) "Henceforth the agrarian revolution is legalized [*i.e.*, the peasants are tricked into supporting the Soviets], and therewith the revolution of the proletariat acquires a mighty basis." (p. 334.) Thus the Soviets craftily utilized the peasants' envy and hatred of the propertied classes in order to seize this property, and after that to pry the poor peasant himself off his own bit of earth. "Arise, ye wretched of the earth." Yes indeed, arise and be "educated," while we snatch even the earth out from under you.

This case is cited here to show that the political problem of how the many are to be one is not solved by employing a collective noun which seems to be in the singular number, because it lacks the letter "s," as a designation for the many; such nouns as proletariat, totalitarian state, party, class, nation, people, mankind, man. Such a verbal expedient serves only to delude the many: for a time! And this instance sufficiently illustrates the scope, the nature, and the purpose of ideologies.

The history of this tragic piece of nonsense, running back to Karl Marx and back still further to Babeuf and his associates in the French Revolution, has been most succinctly and luminously traced by M. Louis Rougier in two works,[17] both of which well repay study. For, as one is dismayed to discover, our own Declaration of Independence is traceable historically to the same source. M. Rougier, specially in the *Mystique démocratique*, rather nicely separates the wheat from the chaff; and one comes to realize that the democratic ideology was by no means born with Babeuf. The early Greek city-states were familiar with one or another variant of it, and occasionally put it into practice. And always the weakness of the democratic idea, the destruction

---

[17] *Les paralogismes du rationalisme*, Alcan, Paris, 1920, pp. 13-30, 36-53. *La mystique démocratique*, Flammarion, Paris, 1929, pp. 1-155.

of democracies, has been the incapacity of the citizens to prevent the usurpation of tyrannical power by a leader, or a small group of leaders.

The Greeks learned all that need be learned of the psychology of leadership, and have transmitted it to us. In Book V, Chap. XI of his *Politics*, Aristotle gives us "the ancient prescriptions for the preservation of a tyranny, in so far as this is possible; *viz.*, that the tyrant should lop off those who are too high; he must put to death men of spirit; he must not allow common meals, clubs, education, and the like; he must be upon his guard against anything which is likely to inspire either courage or confidence among his subjects; he must prohibit literary assemblies or other meetings for discussion, and he must take every means to prevent people from knowing one another (for acquaintance begets mutual confidence). . . . A tyrant should also endeavor to know what each of his subjects says or does, and should employ spies, . . .; for the fear of informers prevents people from speaking their minds, and if they do, they are more easily found out. Another art of the tyrant is to sow quarrels among the citizens; friends should be embroiled with friends, the people with the notables, and the rich with one another. Also he should impoverish his subjects; he thus provides money for the support of his guards, and the people, having to keep hard at work, are prevented from conspiring. The Pyramids of Egypt afford an excellent example of this policy; also . . . all these works were alike intended to occupy the people and keep them poor. Another practice of tyrants is to multiply taxes, after the manner of Dionysius of Syracuse, who contrived that within five years his subjects should bring into the treasury their whole property. The tyrant is also fond of making war in order that his subjects may have something to do and be always in want of a leader. . . ."

"Again, the evil practices of the last and worst form of democracy are all found in tyrannies. . . ."

"Such are the notes of the tyrant and the arts by which he

preserves his power; there is no wickedness too great for him. All that we have said may be summed up under three heads, which answer to the three aims of the tyrant. These are, (1) the humiliation of his subjects; he knows that a mean-spirited man will not conspire against anybody; (2) the creation of mistrust among them; for a tyrant is not overthrown until men begin to have confidence in one another; . . . (3) the tyrant desires that his subjects shall be incapable of action, for . . . they will not attempt to overthrow a tyranny if they are powerless. Under these three heads the whole policy of a tyrant may be summed up, and to one or other of them all his ideas may be referred: (1) he sows distrust among his subjects; (2) he takes away their power; (3) he humbles them." [18]

We further learn from Aristotle that the evils of leadership are found, as indeed we must already have suspected, not alone in democracies or tyrannies but also in any form of government whatsoever. The nature of kingly leadership is brought out, rather amusingly, in a small volume which is commonly attributed to Voltaire.[19] A monarch (the King of Prussia?) is supposed to be conversing informally with his nephew. "Of Politics. Since it is agreed among men that it is a contemptible and criminal act to impose upon one's fellow, it has been necessary to find some term to smooth the thing over: and the word *politics* has been chosen. Little by little this word has come to be used only of Sovereigns, because one cannot in decency call us scoundrels or knaves. Be that as it may, here are my views on politics.

"I understand, my dear Nephew, by the word politics, that one must always seek to dupe others. It is the way, not to gain the advantage but merely to come out even. For, be advised, all states on earth pursue the same course. Now, this principle once

[18] From the translation by B. Jowett. The excellent translation by W. Ellis is readily obtainable in Everyman's Library, No. 605, Dutton, N. Y. Books IV, V, and VI of the *Politics* are specially important.

[19] *Entretiens sur l'Art de Régner, divisés en cinq soirées* (1766). The author and place of publication are not indicated.

accepted, do not blush to contract alliances with a view to your own advantage exclusively. Do not make the stupid blunder of not repudiating them when you see that it will be to your interest to do so; and above all follow vigorously this maxim, *that to despoil our neighbours deprives them of the means to injure us.* Politics, to speak exactly, builds up and perpetuates Kingdoms. Therefore, my dear Nephew, you must understand it and work it on a large scale."

The leader, in short, is the man whose only thought is to dominate his fellows; his scheme of life is the "pecking-order," and his sole aim is to rise, by pecking others, as high as he can within this order. His only education lies in the art of buffeting and parrying the buffets of rival leaders and the art of hood-winking the masses whom he would lead. He is of the aggressive type, and exhibits physiological adience, selfishness, in its crudest and most unmitigated form. When his aggressiveness is not held within bounds by other men's "capacity to injure," his ambition becomes furious and insatiable: he is eager to appropriate the persons, the labors, the possessions, and the lives of his fellow men. Always with a pretended alibi, of course: it is for the glory of God, for the welfare of the State, for the aggrandizement of the party, the solidarity of his union, his college or his club; always impersonally and for "the good of the cause."

What, lastly, of this utter helplessness of the buyers, the masses, their lack of any "capacity to injure" the sellers? The ancient maxim, "Divide and rule," gives us the clue that perhaps the helplessness of the masses lies in their divisions, their lack of cohesion. And indeed it is notorious that wherever men live in amity, exchanging their labors and commodities honestly and equitably, there the professional leader can make no headway. A group of persons must lack cohesion, must be divided by mutual jealousies, distrusts, and hatreds, before any broad program of leadership can be feasibly undertaken. Otherwise it is held in abhorrence and derision. Hence the maxim:

you must divide before you can rule them, and also before you can sell them an ideology.

Now the elementary adience, as previously mentioned, develops into intelligence [20] as the individual grows and learns. And intelligence is no less self-interested than primitive adience, but it is more farsighted. It knows that bandying blows does not produce food and raiment. The growth of intelligence is merely the continuance of learning by the adient organism. And our problem comes down to this simple fact, that the human race has not yet learned what the essential mechanism of leadership is. When it learns that, if it ever does so, it will have passed a very critical point in its evolution. If one looks into the psychology of primitive magic,[21] one discovers that the primitive man consults his shaman from the same motive which impels us to resort to some leader. He feels helpless in some situation and instead of studying the situation empirically ("realistically") to learn what he shall best do, he languidly calls for someone else to tell him: he seeks professional advice. The someone else is not genuinely interested in solving his problem, but is of course delighted to take his money. The great modern superstition, our magic, is to turn at every juncture to some professional, some leader; and a thousand rationalizations are in the air to make such a course seem reasonable. Our modern civilization is at every point actually founded upon this superstition. It is this contemporary magic and the terrific cultural compulsives which surround it, that call for the closest study by anyone who realizes that the present situation is critical.[22]

[20] The course of this development is outlined in *Animal Drive*, vol. I.

[21] L. Lévy-Bruhl's *Le surnaturel et la nature dans la mentalité primitive*, Alcan, Paris, 1931, is one of the best works on this subject.

[22] This study should not be primarily in books. Yet books are helpful: for instance, G. Le Bon, *The Psychology of Socialism*, Macmillan, N. Y., 1899; R. Michels, *Political Parties*, translated by E. and C. Paul, Hearst's International Library Co., N. Y., 1915; A. Lipsky, *Man the Puppet*, Frank-Maurice, N. Y., 1925.

There is another way of life, remote from modern magic. This way has been finely sketched by Professor Kallen in his altogether penetrating and luminous study, *Individualism*.[23] But it cannot be quite adequately imparted in words. One must study earnestly the vile diabolism which underlies our modern magic, and then construct for oneself the picture of a society in which men should renounce this magic and pursue a wiser, more far-sighted self-interest.

[23] H. M. Kallen, *Individualism*, Liveright, N. Y., 1933. See also the same author's *A Free Society*, Ballou, N. Y., 1934.

EXPERIMENTAL NATURALISM

SIDNEY HOOK

I was born in New York City, December 20, 1902. Spent my early youth and boyhood in Williamsburg, Brooklyn. Graduated from P. S. No. 145, Jan. 1916; from Boys' High School June, 1919. B.S.S. from the College of the City of New York (Feb., 1923). Studied at Columbia University, while teaching in the New York City schools, with Professors Dewey, Montague and Woodbridge. University Scholar 1924-5: University Fellow in Philosophy 1926-7: M.A. 1926: Ph.D. 1927. Guggenheim Research Fellow in Philosophy 1928-9, studying at Berlin, Munich, and Moscow. Instructor of Philosophy at Washington Square College, New York University 1927-32. Assistant Professor 1932-33. Associate Professor and Chairman of the Department, 1933-. Lecturer at the New School for Social Research 1931-. Actively interested in the theory and practice of the working-class movement.

Partial Bibliography: *The Metaphysics of Pragmatism*, 1927; *Toward the Understanding of Karl Marx*, 1933; contributor *Essays in Honor of John Dewey*, 1929; *Columbia Studies in the History of Ideas*, Vol. 3; editor and contributor *The Meaning of Marx*, 1934; contributor to *Journal of Philosophy, Philosophical Review, Mind Monist, Erkenntnis, Encyclopedia of the Social Sciences, Nation, Modern Monthly, New Republic, Saturday Review of Literature.*

EXPERIMENTAL NATURALISM

Sidney Hook

Were the phrase not so encrusted with misleading associations, I should call my philosophy "dialectical materialism"; materialism, because its explanations make no appeal to entities or processes which are not empirically verifiable by scientific method or logically inferrible from experienced data; dialectical, because it holds (a) that there is an implied temporal reference in every description or generalization, (b) that the processes of discovery and interpretation—as distinct from the validity of their results—cannot be completely dissociated from the socio-historical culture of the age, and (c) that under certain conditions, human thinking, construed as meaningful selective behavior and not as a passive reflection or image of the external scene, plays a creative rôle in the world. The vested interests, however, of a political church, and factional sectarian controversy motivated by everything but a desire for the truth, have incurably ruined the phrase "dialectical materialism" as a clear-cut differentiating mark of one's philosophic allegiance. I prefer, therefore, for the sake of accuracy, to select a more neutral characterization.

Since I have elsewhere developed my philosophical position in more technical form, and encouraged by editorial prescriptions as well as by the presumable interests of a lay audience, I shall take the liberty of presenting my views in a kind of philosophical autobiography. In this way not only will the formal concatenations of my beliefs be made clear but their history, cultural context, and probable development.

I

My earliest interest in philosophy arose in the course of my reading when still a boy, and was strengthened soon thereafter by active participation in the socialist movement and the study of its literature.

I can still recall the day when a few snatches of amateur epistemological discussion in *Martin Eden*—used by Jack London to flavor a scene in an artist's crowded kitchen—fired my imagination and I set out to fathom the mysterious terminology which, I felt, must have, despite its tantalizing obscurity, worlds of meaning. When I finally learned to my astonishment that the existence of the external world was a problem, I resolved to save the foundations of the universe, and for a long time worried over the question of how to answer Berkeley. Unable to refute Berkeley I resolved that none of my friends should enjoy the luxury of unapprehensive dogmatism, and set about infecting them with the virus of doubt. I found that it was just as difficult to convert people to subjective idealism— even after their first contemptuous shrugs or flashes of indignation—as it was to unconvert them if, for any reason at all, they fled to this formally impregnable position. The sides taken did not seem to depend upon the strength of the arguments used to support them.

This was my first philosophical seizure but my last one with epistemology. Although I was always a realist, and with a great deal of moral fervor, it was not until I read Dewey and Woodbridge that I realized why the problem—how is knowledge of the external world possible—was insoluble in its own terms. Like every other process, once the process of knowing was dissociated from its specific beginnings and endings, from its relation to other activities and modes of experience, especially the need for acquiring reliable information and principles to settle concrete problems and fix belief, it was possible for a philosopher to raise more questions about it than a host of wise men could answer. Once the initial and final phases of any temporal process are split into isolated and independent states, how can they ever be coherently related, especially by a logical analysis which treats all terms as if they had no temporal character? The futility of this approach seems to me to be evident not only in epistemology but more particularly today in sociology where the social whole is first broken down into sharply separated factors and then "understood" in terms of a mechanical cause and effect relation between the parts. In the social realm such a technique is both muddled and dangerous, for it leads not only to sweeping dogmatisms when explanations are offered but to fanatical practice when social control is attempted by those who accept the explanations.

My social interest, although motivated by entirely different considerations, fed into my technical philosophical interest. Always a voracious reader, I devoured the literature of the socialist movement at an age when righteous passion at the indignities of the existence which surrounded me in the proletarian slums where my family lived, helped me to understand and to fix firmly in my mind the fundamental truths of the class-struggle. But there was more in the literature of the movement than a concern with economics and politics. Engels' *Anti-Dühring* and *Feuerbach*, the fragmentary discussions of philosophy scattered through the writings of Marx, the discussions of Labriola, Dietzgen and other critics and commentators, raised questions which seemed to be interesting on their own account and at first blush to have precious little to do with the theory and practice of social revolution. And as subsequent reflection convinced me, many of them actually did not. I could not see, for example, what social consequences one way or the other flowed from the hotly disputed question, "whether oats grow according to the Hegelian dialectic or not"; or what political effects were bound up with Engels' acceptance of the mistaken theory of infinitesimals as a foundation of the differential calculus. But although I was later to discover that considerable

portions of the so-called socialist philosophy were cultural sur-
vivals of the cosmic evolutionary optimism of the 19th century
and at best superfluous baggage for a movement which aimed
at revolutionary transformation of the social order, at the very
outset I recognized its fundamental premises as closer to the
position of naturalism—or scientific materialism—than any other
regnant doctrine. About its naturalism I was extremely keen.
An early revolt against supernaturalism and all organized religion, induced by a reading of Lecky, Lea and Draper, and
fortified by my own boyhood experience of religious discrimination and persecution, led me to appreciate the tremendous
secular and humanizing impact of a thoroughgoing naturalism
upon all phases of culture. That is one of the reasons, besides
its demonstrable falsity, why I could never share the position
of those who called themselves *orthodox* Marxists—people who
having given up the traditional religions still believed in a
church, *the* Party, and who, when challenged, fell back upon
a new religion based on the inevitability of socialism.

However, I could never see that the specifically philosophical
problems which faced the naturalistic outlook—the nature of
time, causality and logical implication—had any relevance to
concrete problems of political theory and practice. Yet it was
their pursuit which fascinated me most. And so, although I
found political activity with its jealous absorption of all one's
time and energy to be bad for one's philosophy, and any attempt
at philosophical clarification of fundamental ideas to be anath-
ema in politics, I could give up neither, which probably accounts
—kind friends have suggested—for certain difficulties in both.

I came to adolescence during the War and the post-War
period when the educational system of the country was in
the throes of a collective obsession. My high school teachers,
in those days a miscellaneous lot of men who had failed to get
into other professions, ranted against everything German. Without ever having read a line of Kant, Hegel or Nietzsche, they
bandied their names about as being indirectly responsible for

the War. (I couldn't say that I had read them either, but the *Nation* and G. H. Lewis' *Biographical History of Philosophy* supplied me with my ammunition for classroom war.) Every critical attitude in the social sciences was suspect as Bolshevism. Mathematics classes were occasions for fervent pleas to plant potatoes and to save peach pits, and in all other subjects every opportunity was seized to turn the recitation into a kind of psychic war-dance. Inside the schools, students were terrorized by teachers and student-patriots for discussing the merits of a capital tax over Liberty Bonds as a method of financing the War, for quoting the Declaration of Independence to speakers sent by the National Security League and the Daughters of the American Revolution, for pointing out that the canards about the leaders of the Russian Revolution, Lenin and Trotsky, solemnly taught as part of modern European history, were so contradictory that they could not all be true—in short, for trying to carry on the educational process which their teachers had funked. Things were not much better in the colleges. I still recall that during my first college year—a year after peace had been declared—I was stopped by a professor in the midst of a report in which I had claimed that Calhoun's logic was superior to Webster's, with the words: "When you are not preaching sedition, you are preaching secession." Outside of school, any peaceful meeting called to discuss or debate the issues of war and reconstruction was enough to bring down the Gegans and Scullys and Browns of Palmer-Lusk fame, whose unwelcome acquaintance on several occasions I was compelled to make. Perhaps I was young and foolishly impetuous, but I believe it would have been difficult for any inquiring student, on the basis of my experience during those years, to avoid the conclusion that most of his teachers were fools and the rest cowards.

It was during this period that I picked up a copy of Bertrand Russell's *Justice in War-Time,* and learning more about the fortitude with which he had sustained unpopularity and imprisonment, continued to read his more popular works. There was nothing he wrote on social subjects which I did not already believe; but what fascinated me beyond all else was the method by which he got at his conclusions and the simple shining clarity of the arguments with which he would eliminate opposing views. Fortunately for me, I soon afterwards began the study of philosophy with Professor Morris R. Cohen, himself a great admirer of Bertrand Russell but convinced, however, that Russell's philosophical power had declined in direct proportion to the growth of his civic zeal and social interest. My sense for method and evidence was strengthened by Professor Cohen's teaching and my enthusiasms, although disciplined, were not dampened. His was the first critical mind I had encountered in the educational wilderness and I revised my hasty judgments about the function of schools and teachers in society. From an educational point of view, his only philosophic infirmity was a tendency, bordering on genius, to distort the positions of eminent contemporary philosophers with whom he disagreed.

Logic for some years thereafter became my driving philosophic interest. Like all initiates into its easy mysteries, I made a perfect nuisance of myself by the indefatigable spirit with which I pointed out, classified and held up to public light the fallacies in the perfectly comprehensible speech of my friends. To their protests that I knew what they meant, I responded that I wasn't interested in what they meant but in what they said. But behind all this was the feeling that logic, and particularly the logic of scientific method, was the only method by which the raging fevers of stupid and cruel intolerance could be diminished. All the fanatics I knew, whether they were professional patriots or heresy-hunting Communists, were either completely impervious to logic or conspicuously lame in following an argument. When they talked themselves into glaring contradiction either they did not know it, or were completely unabashed, acting as if their inconsistency reflected a higher law of nature. The notion that fanatics are too logical and suffer from too great a desire for consistency rather than too little is a sheer superstition. Most of them are not even aware of the plainest implications of their statements. In the joy of my first discovery, I leaned over backward and tried to assimilate scientific method to formal logic rather than vice versa. In the murky atmosphere of a world in which there were so many different variables influencing each other, so much uncertainty and confusion, I had a hunger for something one could be sure about. One could be sure about logic even at the price of not saying much. And in those days, with the memory of the intellectual nightmare of the war and the post-war period still fresh in my mind, I was not as interested in saying things as in exposing the vicious nonsense which was being said. I knew that logic was no substitute for insight and vision, but I knew then, and still believe, that nothing significant could be accomplished in the world—even in the social world—by an open defiance of the implications of what we believe or do. Men may be controlled by blind passion but not the material things and situations upon which they ultimately depend.

As a Marxist, I knew that history is not to be understood in terms of the thoughts and passions which move men but in terms of the conflicting group pressures and interests which express themselves through them now in one way, now in another. But there is nothing incompatible with Marxism in realizing and emphasizing that *how* these interests express themselves makes a genuine difference. Whether the presumed interest is the same as the real interest, and whether the real interest can be furthered by one mode of activity rather than another, are questions which can be truly settled only when interests, so to speak, become self-conscious, when they are logically formulated, appraised and tested in action.

Whatever may be the relevance of logical thinking as an historical and social influence, there can be no question of the importance of its presence or absence in individual life, unless one is prepared to assert that a man's ideas are self-contained entities separated by non-osmotic tissues from the world in which he lives, enjoys and suffers. But if we take thoughts to be the motor cues of planned, executed or suppressed actions, then ideas are not feeble rays thrown off by a kind of phosphorus substance in the brain, but ways of living and acting. What is called character in a man's life—and no character is fixed—can either be read directly from the pattern of his activities, or since the pattern by itself tells us little about the future, from the integrating ideals which he professes, under suspicious scrutiny, to be carrying out. Without some integration of the conflicting desires which solicit him, no man can achieve the honesty of purpose that represents the whole of morality's demand. Without some ability to do logical sums and exercises, to weigh alternatives and see implications, the self-consciousness necessary to integration in a world suggesting many possible paths of development for a sensitive and complex organism to follow is impossible. Indeed, it is no paradox but a reliable generalization that the man incapable of thinking, of knowing what he wants and what he means, cannot be honest either to himself or others. No matter what its rôle in social life, in individual life a modicum of logic is necessary for integrity of intellect and character. Is it not true that by a man's logic we judge him? But, of course, not only by his logic.

Further interest in, and reflection upon, logic led me to metaphysics. And like most young students of philosophy who have read the early Russell and savored the flavor of logical propositions whose validity is independent of experience and true for all possible worlds, I became, for a while, a staunch Platonic realist. This is an interesting phase in the development of students of philosophy today and I have watched many of my own go through it. Platonic realism seems to be a necessary transitional stage in the attempt to achieve philosophical clarity. Whoever remains stuck in it, I have noticed, seems to be rendered intellectually sterile. It makes, however, a many-sided appeal. Not only does it deal with eternal certainties so dear to men in a social crisis, not only has it the prestige of the exact disciplines of mathematics and logic which philosophers neglected in the 19th century, but it gratifies the insistent demand of youth—and its greatest weakness—the demand for intellectual simplicity. According to Platonic realism, what is intelligible can be grasped by an immediate intellectual intuition, and is capable of being broken down upon analysis into ultimate logical truths. Existence is essentially unintelligible. Nothing can be said not to have Being which can be the subject of a sentence. If the being it has is not existent, it is subsistent. A particular wheel exists, but "roundness" subsists; so does "a wheel whose like has never been seen before." Round-squares, golden mountains, the integer between 2 and 3, subsist too. The existential context of meaning, communication, intent and history are dismissed as so much irrelevant psychological data and no problems are left to be solved—except all the important ones.

Another characteristic feature of Platonic realism—and this, I think, is a significant clue to its acceptance—is the generous contempt in which it holds most other philosophies. This comes about as follows. The problems which Platonic realism ignores (not to speak of those which its easy dualism creates) are the knottiest and most difficult problems of philosophy since they concern the relationship between form, content, process and time. So complicated are these problems that it is often difficult to tell whether those whose philosophy is based upon the assertion of their metaphysical union and primacy are really talking sense or not. It is not Bergson, it is not James, it is not Bradly, it is not Dewey who repel the logical realists—when they actually get to reading them—but the hosts of their hangers-on, who enunciate in the name of their alleged masters and with an air of making new discoveries, propositions which were already commonplace truths or falsehoods in antiquity. Who does not know the flock of dabblers in philosophy whose stock in trade consists of statements like: "Everything moves," "Truth is what any culture says it is," "The law of identity is false," "Reality is spirit, mind, this, that or something else"? I know that it was a great relief to have at hand the sharp instruments of logical realism with which to scalp all the non-professional prophets of the philosophy of gush and go. Logical realism will always make a call upon tough-minded students of philosophy until they learn that one can avoid uttering nonsense without thereby acquiring any great wisdom.

It was as a rather militant logical realist that I left college for graduate work at Columbia where for one year I constituted myself the official opposition to what I called "the psychology which was being passed off as philosophy." But a sad fate was in store for me. One day I sat down to write a definitive refutation of Professor Dewey's pragmatism. Of pragmatism I was a sworn enemy, having heard it refuted time out of hand by former teachers but never expounded. Nor did the reading of James or Schiller make me relent. James seemed to me to skirt all the difficulties, particularly those pressed against him by the philosophical formalists as well as those created by himself when any one of his books was compared with any other. Schiller's offer of pragmatism to the theologians as the best device for saving their religion scandalized me as such a piece of philosophical prostitution that I was blinded to the worth of his writings on the nature of hypotheses. Peirce, although brilliantly suggestive, never seemed to me a consistent thinker. Dewey, whom I could not answer, nonetheless could not convince me.

All of Dewey's contentions about the processes of thinking I was willing to grant, but I could not see how the formal characters of logic and the criteria of logical validity could be derived from empirical considerations. John Stuart Mill, I thought, was an illustration of the blind alley into which all empirical approaches to logic and mathematics led. Starting then from the fact that there were certain formally valid propositions, I raised the question as to the source and test of their validity. The question, however, of the validity of any set of formal, presumably non-existential, propositions turned into a question of their consistency. The only proof of the consistency of propositions with which I was acquainted introduced empirical considerations. How, then, establish their validity? The only recourse was to fall back upon inspection and immediate intuition. But immediate intuition smacked dangerously of the psychology I was trying to avoid. I was compelled to ask myself what a valid intuition was and how I recognized it as such. With this the question of "meaning" became focal and it began to grow upon me that without some ultimate denotative reference to events or processes, one could never tell whether propositional functions were nonsense syllables or not. The nonexistential logicians had gone from the unquestionably true statement that their meanings were independent of *any* particular exemplification to the highly dubious statement that they were independent of *all* possibility of exemplification. And with this, the game of Platonic realism was up and I found myself in the camp of my enemies. For if the meaning of a proposition necessarily involved the possibility of performing some operation to reveal its denotative range, the truth or falsity of a proposition could only be defined in terms of the predictive functions of meaningful statements, and determined by examining the consequences of the actions they pointed to.

It was not easy to surrender the paradise of subsistence and the comforts of truths necessary and universal in all possible worlds. I contested every inch of the way, but all my reading, arguing and consultation with my logical realist friends proved to be fruitless. I was converted to pragmatism in a very unpragmatic way. Dewey's writings took on a new significance as treatises on the theory of meaning, and the last vestiges of supernaturalism—for that is what Platonic realism is—disappeared from my thought.

The weakness of Platonic realism becomes most apparent when the questions of meaning, consistency and applicability are raised. For once challenge the assumption that terms can have meaning independently of the possibility of exemplification in some event, process or operation, then the inevitable retort that these are "mere" matters of psychology and history can be met by showing that the Platonic realists have a definite psychology based upon the dogma of immediate knowledge and a definite theory of time according to which only the present exists.

The naturalistic approach to logic regards logical principles either as the formal expressions of the structure *of* some subject matter in space and time and, therefore, in some sense historical, or as the leading principles of the methods and techniques of inquiry which have enabled men to solve specific problems or difficulties. This approach has its difficulties—difficulties, of course, which are not solved by pointing to the weaknesses of Platonic realism. For there seems to be a great many mathematical and logical principles which have no reference to existential subject matter even at many removes and do not function as principles of inquiry in solving specific problems. But the very claim to be dealing with a subject matter at no point infected with "the evil" of existence is at the source of many of the difficulties and paradoxes of contemporary foundational logic and mathematics. It is in this field that the experimental or operational theory of meaning permits not only a defense of the naturalist approach but, as the work of Dewey, Bridgman, Nagel, and the logical positivists shows, makes possible a beginning in clearing up some of the mysteries clustering around the concepts of infinity, zero, irrationals, and classes which contain themselves as members.

The question may be asked, why such concern with saving naturalism against all varieties of *a priorism* whether it be Platonic realism, Hegelian idealism, conventionalism or mechanistic materialism? Although it was the intrinsic inadequacy of these postions—and this was the only relevant philosophical ground—which led me to reject them, I must confess that here, too, there were at least two other non-philosophical motives which sharpened my critical zest. *A priorism* always seemed to me to be

associated with theology and social conservatism. The sharp separation between existence and validity, and the problem to
which this gave rise, of accounting for the ontological status
and truth of universal and necessary propositions, made it particularly easy to postulate a cosmic consciousness—in short, the
mind of God—as their locus and guarantee of validity. Descartes' dualism led him to base the necessity of the truths of
arithmetic upon God's mind and God's goodness. That absolute
idealism was an implicit theology did not have to be argued in
view of the admissions of Schelling, Hegel and their followers.
Nor can any view which holds that every segment of the world,
past, present and future, is part of one great machine of inter-
locking mechanisms escape the plausible, even if logically unjustified, analogy to the existence of a supreme machine-maker.
By different routes, then, all *a prioristic* philosophies seem to
converge on God.

The social uses of *a priorism* have been clear, I think, from
the days of antiquity when Plato deduced the aristocratic rule
of philosophers from the idea of true knowledge, and Aristotle
provided eternal justification for slavery on the basis of disparity in human talents. My Marxism had taught me to be
suspicious of absolutisms of every kind, and although I could
not find any Marxist who could give even a remotely plausible
historical interpretation of the specific varieties of *a priorism*,
their general function as rationalizations for entrenched conservatism was clear. Indeed, one did not have to be a Marxist to
see this. There is a passage in John Stuart Mill's *Autobiography*
which has always seemed to me not only to explain a great deal
about Mill's philosophy but to state effectively the point I am
making:

*"The notion that truths external to the mind may be known
by intuition or consciousness, independently of observation or
experience, is, I am persuaded, in these times, the great intellectual support of false doctrines and bad institutions. By the aid
of this theory, every inveterate belief and every intense feeling,*

of which the origin is not remembered, is enabled to dispense with the obligation of justifying itself by reason, and is erected into its own all sufficient voucher and justification. There never was such an instrument devised for consecrating all deep-seated prejudices. And the chief strength of this false philosophy in morals, politics and religion, lies in the appeal which it is accustomed to make to the evidence of mathematics and of the cognate branches of physical science."

II

I had now to come to grips with the different varieties of naturalism, to set them in their historical context, to work out their fundamental motivation and relate them to the conflicting group values, which struggled for domination in the social scene. Under Professor Woodbridge I got still further away from the baubles of essence doctrine. His method of analysis always took as its point of departure some concrete situation and his insistence upon control by subject matter was the best antidote to that lingering fever of philosophical adolescence which might very well be called "dialectic flutter." Universals and essences were naturalized as the structural principles of the concrete. Logical order could be discovered in nature; there was no need to look for it elsewhere. This emphasis upon structure was in line with the rationalistic naturalism of Professor Cohen, for whom logical principles represented the most general metaphysical invariants of all being, out of time because they held for time, and necessarily true because they could not be confronted with a significant alternative.

Again it was the influence of Professor Dewey which led me away from the modified Aristotelianism of Woodbridge and the ambiguous rationalism of Cohen to a further development of my naturalism. The analysis of the concepts of invariance—in use in any fruitful inquiry—convinced me that it was unnecessary to attribute an absolutely fixed ontological status to them.

In nature there was warrant only for relative invariants. To isolate them from their knowledge-getting context and set them up as a kind of grammar of eternity seemed to me to be playing God to creation. *Relative* invariants, I could see as the indisputable necessary condition for prediction and control in all fields of nature and society. Emphasis upon them was justified in view of the uncritical tendencies toward a free and easy temporalism which exalted novelty, discontinuity and chance to a point where the recurrent connections, patterns and organization of events—upon which all intelligible explanation depends—disappeared. And for purposes of calculation, invariants could be abstracted from the existential complex in which they were found and considered by themselves. But when it was forgotten that these abstractions were the working rules of various formal and material branches of knowledge, and converted into imperatives of all thought and practice in all fields for all time, it prepared the way for that metaphysical isolation and hypostasis of the criteria of logical validity, upon which traditional dualisms have fed. It was this hypostasis which seemed to me to be behind the periodic resurgence of scholasticism, the easy flights to eternity on the borrowed wings of Spinozism, and the revival of neo-Platonic mysticism even among mathematical physicists—in short, the most important currents of what goes by the name of the classic tradition in philosophy.

What can an "invariant" be from the point of view of the experimental theory of meaning? It is either a resolution to handle particular situations in a certain determinate way or it is some structural or functional fact discovered whenever certain relevant operations are performed. The most general invariants—logical invariants—are those that always turn up whatever the technique of inquiry might be. Experimentally, the concept "always" has meaning only because of its reference to a temporal process or operation, necessarily incomplete. Let us not mistake this experimentalism for arbitrary relativism. Against all species of conventionalism and "pure" dialectical method, which deny all objectivity to truth, accept all starting-points as equally valid because they are all undebatable axioms, and which are therefore, prepared to sell any picture of the world modeled to any heart's desire, the experimental philosophy in its sober materialism contends that resolutions to treat things in a certain way can only succeed when they yield to the structural features of the subject matter treated. But the materialism of experimentalism is historical and evolutionary. For the structural features of any subject matter in this world is of a subject matter which is itself a segment of space-time, considered not as substance but as process. Consequently, unless it is proved that the temporal non-formal aspects of subject matter can never affect the formal, logical aspects, allegedly eternal, no absolute invariants can be established.

Until I could emancipate myself from the fear of verbalisms which gave the appearance of self-contradiction, I could not assert this position. Translated into the language of orthodox nontemporalism, I knew it did not make sense. For, after all, how could one speak about an invariant changing, or a law having a history, except in terms of a more inclusive invariant or law? And how could logical principles have temporal coefficients when no significant alternatives to them could be formulated? But this was letting language impose upon me and forgetting that the appearance of verbal contradiction only reflected the attempt to catch up, so to speak, with the character of time. To put descriptions into fixed symbols and then, not merely to disregard their temporal contexts but to deny their existence, was equivalent to treating time as if it had no temporal qualities at all, as if it were something which was all run out, a series of befores, heres, and afters with no pasts, presents and futures. Of course, the opposite of a logical proposition cannot in the nature of the case make sense. For that would demand finding a case to which it did not apply and it has been so formulated as to assume that all the cases are in. But the nonsense which now results from negativing a logical proposition is no guarantee that the original proposition will "always" make sense, *i.e.*, operationally speaking, that it will always enable us to organize our experiences. However, there is a shorter way out of the difficulty. No claim should be made to the title of absolute invariants for the widest structural relations of experience. Our task is to analyze and organize them into a hierarchy of levels of generality. Each level would be relatively invariant to the one above it.

The fundamental issues between rationalistic and experimental naturalism, I now believe, can be traced to differences in emphasis which are motivated more by cultural and personal considerations than by strictly logical ones. Both admit that there is a legitimate distinction between the unique, specific, irreducible, on the one hand, and the repetitive, general, typical on the other; between propositions whose opposite is unintelligible and those whose opposite is meaningful. Both accept the dialectic polarity (in the sense of Hegel's doctrine of Essence) of the fundamental metaphysical categories: term-relation, continuity-discontinuity, particular-universal, concrete-abstract, so that any discussion of one involves necessary reference to the other. But in the face of concrete problems it is not enough to recognize that polar categories are necessarily involved in order to solve them. The necessities of action compel the acceptance of one series of categories rather than another; and contemplation, the favorite activity of philosophers, since it has definite consequences, is one form of action. Depending upon the *purposes* of action, so manifestly conditioned by the culture, country and class in which we live and by the personalities we are, one set of decisions rather than another will result. Reflection upon decisions already taken and to be taken, determines the selection of, or rather the emphasis upon, one cluster of categories instead of the other. It is this accenting of the categories of movement over those of stability, of the freshly occurrent over the old recurrent, or vice versa, which is the foundation stone of a man's metaphysics. And although the difference in emphasis may in the beginning be slight, when the structure of thought is completed that difference makes all the difference in the world to the kind of life and the kind of society we know.

What kind of philosophers—really what kind of men—lay their foundation stones one way rather than another? No very accurate generalizations can be made. But substantially, there is a rough correlation between social attitudes and metaphysical bias. Those philosophers, who in any definite age are prepared to support the status quo on the ground that the imperfections of today, because they are known, are more tolerable than the dangers of tomorrow, are likely to stress the categories of invariance. Those who are more sensitive to the remediable evils of today and are optimistic about the possibilities of human intelligence contriving techniques with which to grapple with the problems of tomorrow are apt to be experimental in their metaphysical outlook. Where conflict arises between these groups for social support, the philosophers of invariance are more likely to receive the official blessings and sugar plums than the others. Governments are always on the side of eternity. Today, however, it is not social and political allegiances which can be significantly correlated with different philosophical views. And for a simple reason. Practically all schools of philosophy in America have the same middle-class outlook upon social affairs. The significant connection must be sought elsewhere. I believe that the connection between temperament and philosophy is more fundamental and more readily ascertainable than that between class allegiance and philosophical belief. The temperament which loves peace above all other values and sees in the ordered routines of professional, social and personal life the best methods of achieving it, is likely to embrace in thought the calm options of eternity and invariance, if not the consolations of outright theology. The temperament which enjoys battle, for which variety is a genuine good, which values the perplexities that attend the pursuit of incompatible goods as the opportunities for creative action, is likely to follow the vital option of experimentalism. Of course no philosopher is either purely one thing or another in all his interests. The boldest experimentalist, Santayana somewhere suggests, had better draw the line rather narrowly in his cooking. And absolutists have been known to experiment with new arguments for self-defense. The dominant patterns, however, as James so wisely saw, will assert themselves, even if the types be different from those he classified. Since most philosophers by training, selection and the mechanisms of academic preferment have been timid, peace-above-all loving creatures, the history of philosophy, in the main, has been a history of dogmatic rationalism, mysticism and religious apologetic. The most beaten paths have been made by uni-directional tracks toward the One.

The metaphysical program of experimental naturalism recognizes, as its fundamental task, the exhaustive analysis of all the primary categories with especial reference to temporal context and experience. Here not more than a beginning has been made.

III

During the course of these years my strong social interests kept on interweaving with my technical ones. When Marx's early philosophical manuscripts were published, I took the occasion to make a systematic re-study of all his works. I was impressed by the presence in his thought of points of view— undeveloped to be sure—completely incompatible with the orthodox exegesis. After further research which took me into Germany and Russia, into the history of Marx's times, his intellectual development and the doctrines of his opponents, I became convinced that his dialectic method by which he strove to combine realism and activism, to do justice to the facts of objectivity and relativity, and to explore the logic of the process, involved a nascent experimental naturalism. This was essentially the same position which John Dewey had independently arrived at in a different idiom and developed so impressively in psychology, logic, science and esthetics.

Since many critics have insinuated that I have read Dewey into Marx, I wish to point out that nowhere and at no time have I claimed that Dewey was a Marxist or Marx the John the Baptist of pragmatism. Their social and political philosophies are quite different in spirit and emphasis. All I have asserted is that their fundamental metaphysical and logical positions are the same but developed as differently as we would expect a great social revolutionist and a great professional philosopher to develop them. From a naturalistic point of view agreement upon fundamental metaphysical doctrines does not univocally determine any *one* social doctrine, and certainly not a specific class allegiance. And as for the fundamental agreement between Marx and Dewey, I need only point here to their common left-Hegelian derivation and naturalization of the Hegelian dialectic, common criticism of atomism, sensationalism, Platonism and formalism, and a common wholehearted acceptance of the philosophical implications of Darwinism. Any philosopher who takes these three positions seriously is an experimental naturalist whether he knows it or not.

Since I have described my social philosophy elsewhere,[1] I shall not dwell upon it here except to say that I regard the social problem as the most important, and at the same time philosophically the least interesting, of all problems. It should be solved in order that mankind may devote itself to art, science and pure philosophy which can never be really autonomous disciplines in a class society. When one reflects upon the extent to which philosophy has been an apologia for some vested social right, when one recalls the undistinguished rôle philosophers played during the World War, it will be admitted that no more than any other branch of culture can it pursue its professional

[1] *Cf.* the symposium volume, *The Meaning of Marx* (Farrar and Rinehart), New York, 1934.

task independently of the economic and political miasmas bred
by capitalist society.

As to what the task of philosophy is, philosophers themselves
seem to be in quite a quandry. Judging by the amount of time
consumed in apologizing for the way in which they earn their
living and in the variety of the extra-philosophical justifications
offered in defense of their activity, one would suspect that philosophers themselves are doubtful as to whether they have
a specific subject matter. It seems to me that philosophy at its
best is not a hand-maiden to politics or theology, nor an instrument of moral edification, but a *critical activity* which aims to
clarify to ourselves what we know, what we live for and die
for, what we do and what we say. It is critically relevant to the
whole of life's activities and its exercise creates a value and adds
a dimension to experience obtainable in no other way. This is
the professional task of philosophy even though philosophers
need not be professionals. It is through philosophical activity
that mankind becomes conscious of itself—of its possibilities and
its limitations.

TOWARD RADICAL EMPIRICISM
IN ETHICS

JOHN ALLAN IRVING

My earliest interest in Philosophy was aroused by Dean G. S. Brett of the University of Toronto who combined in peerless teaching the profoundest historical knowledge and the most acute logical acumen with an extraordinary constructive imagination. To Professor E. A. Bott of the Department of Psychology and to Professor R. M. MacIver (now of Columbia) I owe an ever-deepening interest in the philosophical foundations of Psychology and of Social Science respectively. At Victoria College, one of the federated units of the University of Toronto, there was in my time a tremendous intellectual ferment, and philosophical and moral questions were constantly discussed among the undergraduates. In all this we were greatly encouraged by the teaching of Principal W. T. Brown (formerly Professor of Religion at Yale), Professor W. B. Lane, and Professor S. H. Hooke (now of the University of London). Principal Brown especially led the way as he moved about the college ceaselessly probing active minds.

A year spent in the Graduate College and several years as a member of the Faculty of Princeton University have brought me the happy privilege of personal and intellectual relations with men like Professors R. B. C. Johnson, E. G. Spaulding, Warner Fite, Robert Scoon, W. T. Stace, G. T. Whitney, T. M. Greene, Ledger Wood and Clifford Barrett of the Department of Philosophy; Professors Edwin B. Holt, H. S. Langfeld, and the late Howard C. Warren of the Department of Psychology; and Professor W. S. Carpenter of the Department of Politics.

My formal education was completed at Trinity College, University of Cambridge, where I studied Philosophy and Psychology under Professors G. E. Moore, C. D. Broad, F. C. Bartlett, the late Mr. W. E. Johnson, and Dr. Ludwig Wittgenstein.

In conclusion I wish to pay tribute to the late President John Grier Hibben, and to Professors R. B. C. Johnson (past chairman) and Robert Scoon (present chairman) of the Princeton Department of Philosophy. For the complete intellectual freedom which characterizes the philosophical Department of Princeton University is in no small measure due to the efforts and the excellent examples of these three men.

TOWARD RADICAL EMPIRICISM IN ETHICS

John Allan Irving

"It is the first step in sociological wisdom, to recognize that the major advances in civilization are processes which all but wreck the societies in which they occur:—like unto an arrow in the hand of a child. The art of free society consists first in the maintenance of the symbolic code; and secondly in fearlessness of revision, to secure that the code serves those purposes which satisfy an enlightened reason. Those societies which cannot combine reverence to their symbols with freedom of revision, must ultimately decay either from anarchy, or from the slow atrophy of a life stifled by useless shadows." (A. N. Whitehead.)

The development of pure logic and of the psychology of communication has brought to light the cardinal philosophical problem of our time, that of the meaning of meaning. The view of the problem implied in pure logic is that there are no synthetic *a priori* propositions. The propositions of logic and of mathematics are *a priori*, but only because they are analytic; the propositions of science are synthetic, but only because they are *a posteriori*. The denial of synthetic *a priori* propositions profoundly changes the status of philosophy. The view implied by the psychology of communication is that only the formal structure of experience, and never its content, can be communicated. When we deny that the immediately given in experience can be communicated we are making a profound change in the status of the theory of knowledge, and emphasizing anew the importance of the logic of relations. In this essay it is proposed to investigate the bearing of these advances on the future of

Ethics. The exposition will of necessity be dogmatic in character, for a studied eclecticism is impossible on the frontiers of philosophical discussion.

Philosophy, for those who work with the twentieth century temper, is essentially the elucidation and clarification of the *meanings* of propositions, categories, and concepts. A proposition is a symbolic representation or expression of a fact or a situation, and a fact or a situation can always be expressed in the form that *so and so is the case*. The meaning of a proposition is its verifiability and it cannot have meaning unless there is a possibility of indicating how it may be verified or refuted. We verify a proposition by exhibiting the structure of the situation to which it refers, and the process is complete when we have shown that the situation is made up of specific constituents, logically related in a specific way. In this connection it is most important to notice that we are constantly dealing with the *objects* of our thought, as well as with the *thinking*. We must examine the situation to which a proposition refers, not merely the proposition itself.

We can claim to *know* a proposition only when we can state exactly in what sense it is meaningful, and such a statement would imply that we are able to exhibit the structure of the situation to which the proposition refers. We must always seek to discover, therefore, in the search for the meaning and truth of a proposition, the data which verify the proposition, if they are the case. When we have discovered these data we must be able to express their relationship to each other by a proposition whose logical structure mirrors the structure of the situation to which it refers. This proposition points to the situation and exhibits its structure. The philosophical activity of searching for the meaning of a proposition reveals the structure of the situation which we know to be the case, and leads to a criticism and revision of our fundamental beliefs about the situation and its structure. If we cannot discover the situation that would verify a proposition, then that proposition is not one which we can truly claim to know. The philosophical elucidation of propositions is thus something more than mere examination of language, or than the laying down of rules for the combinations of symbols. Philosophy enables us both to say clearly what we really know when we declare that a proposition is true, and to distinguish those propositions which it is possible to verify, and therefore to know, from those which cannot be verified and therefore cannot be known.

Recent research in the psychology of communication has shown that all of our words and concepts have varying degrees of subjective and objective reference. On the subject of the nature of words and concepts there is a certain accord in the findings of sociologists, psychologists, and logicians, which indicates a constant drive toward extreme nominalism. Words are remotely conditioned substitutes for conditioned stimuli to action; since they have been produced by environmental pressure it follows that their *meaning* can only extend as far as their reference to atomic facts. The nature of language cannot be other than the nature of such stimuli. The true meaning of a scientific concept, as Bridgman has said, is to be found from diagnosis of what we *do* with it, not by what we *say* about it. Bridgman examines the concepts of Einstein on this radical operational basis. Logically, a concept refers to nothing more than a class of properties. What is the meaning of the concept of x? An intelligible answer can only be given when we translate the question into the form: What conditions determine x and its manifestations in the logical structure of a situation y? The only intelligible meaning of the concept x is to denote collectively the properties of the class y.

Of course people do use language in other senses than those we have just described, *e.g.*, in poetry. But language used in this way cannot communicate that which is meaningful *as knowledge*. We must distinguish between those propositions which we can verify publicly and therefore know, and those aesthetic utterances which we cannot verify and therefore cannot know.

The former propositions give us objective knowledge (verifiable belief); the latter merely induce us to take up a subjective emotional attitude toward something in our experience, the experience of others, or our external environment. These distinctions raise clearly the profound problem of the logic of language.

The origin of language is not the philosopher's concern; the uses to which language has been put in the past and is put in the present will occupy our attention exclusively here. There are two uses of language—the logical and the aesthetic. We use language *logically* when we use it to express propositions which are constructed in accordance with the rules of logical syntax and which have an unambiguous reference, true or false. We use language *aesthetically* when we use it to promote emotional attitudes. Philosophy and all the sciences except mathematics and those parts of physics and chemistry which can be expressed in mathematical or symbolic form still suffer from confusions owing to an elementary misunderstanding of these two uses of language.

Aesthetic language is that which most successfully preserves or rather reproduces the vagueness, warmth and immediacy of emotional attitudes. It is subtle and pleasure-giving according as it evokes emotional attitudes and vistas of imaginative possibilities. Logical language achieves its goal of perfect communication of the behavior and structure of the world order only insofar as it is shorn of the personal, the private, the emotive, the aesthetic. Its denotations and connotations are sealed and imprisoned in the terms which it employs. Naturally, however, in the higher types of analysis the technique of this symbolic reference must become as complex as the phenomenon itself, and as intricate and subtle as the aesthetic use of language. Indeed, it must be thus intricate to perform its task, and logical language may even take on a peculiar aesthetic beauty of its own, contributed by its very architectonic fidelity to reality—

when grammar faithfully mirrors the world architecture, point by point, structure by structure!

Logical language, then, refers to *our public world* of socially communicable meanings, in which all the concepts have a specific operational utility (they tell us how to proceed); in which every proposition can be verified by means of a *public* exhibition of the structure of the situation to which it refers; in which the thought behind the expression is guided at every stage by the brute resistance of the material. Aesthetic language refers to *my private world* of immediately perceived contents, of passionate desires, of eager wishes, in which my emotional attitudes meeting with no brute resistance may conjure up imaginative interpretations of the world. The business of the philosopher is to separate clearly these two worlds, and to elucidate the meanings of the public world, which are otherwise opaque and blurred.

What kind of knowledge does Philosophy give us? Traditionally philosophers have maintained that there are two sources of human knowledge—the *a priori* and the *a posteriori*. According to his dominant temper each philosopher has attributed greater or less constructive weight to these two factors. So that in a very real sense the history of Philosophy has been, as James saw clearly, a certain "clash of human temperaments." The *a posteriori* temper proceeds cautiously toward generalizations based on analogies from immediate experience; the *a priori* temper confidently relying on the synthetic activity of the logical reason proceeds by way of inevitable deductions from self-evident logical principles. Now it seems quite clear today that philosophical knowledge is not *in itself* derived from immediate experience. And it seems equally clear that philosophical knowledge is knowledge of self-evident logical principles.

The nature of philosophical knowledge turns therefore on the nature of self-evident logical principles. What is the nature of the *a priori*? Are there any synthetic *a priori* propositions? Kant answered this question affirmatively by taking to witness the propositions of logic, mathematics and natural science. But recent investigations into the nature of these propositions would gainsay Kant's answer in all three fields. More especially, research concerning the nature of necessary inference or formal implication seems to have demonstrated that all self-evident propositions have a very definite kind of logical structure. As Blumberg and Feigl have so clearly put it, "Logic in the wide sense is shown to be the system of conventions which determine the syntactical order required if we are to have a consistent language." Wittgenstein has proved that the propositions of logic are tautologies or identities (though not at all in Meyerson's sense). Whenever we can truly say that *p implies q*, where p and q are propositions, the truth conditions of q are included in the truth conditions of p. Since a proposition is the expression of its truth conditions it follows from this that all such propositions are really tautologies.

6.1   The propositions of logic are tautologies.
6.11   The propositions of logic therefore say nothing. (They are the analytical propositions.)
6.12   The fact that the propositions of logic are tautologies *shows* the formal—logical—properties of language, of the world.[1]

Therefore the logical reason does not synthesize and necessary inference is transformed into a type of analysis which selects one element from a complex and ignores the other elements.

These considerations suggest that the limits of human communication and of philosophical discussion are very rigidly confined. *"The limits of my language,"* says Wittgenstein, "mean the limits of my world." Metaphysicians, with the methods of mathematics and logic constantly before their eyes, have sought to unify their treatment of the world by an appeal to synthetic

[1] Wittgenstein, Ludwig: *Tractatus Logico-Philosophicus*, Kegan Paul, London, 1922; pp. 155-157.

a priori generalizations. It seems fair to state therefore that the prolonged misunderstanding of the real nature of the propositions of logic and mathematics has been the real source of those metaphysical systems which have so often led the human mind into complete darkness. In this connection even Kant has expressed himself with extreme bitterness. "Metaphysics," he writes, "has become an arena, specially destined it would seem, for those who wish to exercise themselves in mock fights . . . the method of metaphysics has hitherto consisted in groping only. . . ." And not Kant alone, but many others among the world's most famous scientists and philosophers have sought desperately to exorcise metaphysics. The discovery in our time of the nature of the *a priori* reveals clearly that we have succeeded where many others have failed. The human mind may have analytic *a priori* propositions and synthetic *a posteriori* propositions. But beyond these there is no other way—and so Philosophy stands committed to analysis and description.

What kind of knowledge does Ethics give us? Historically, ethical philosophers have mainly tried to elaborate the prescription of what *ought* to be and what *ought not* to be. They have sought to formulate the law expressing the *ought* in terms of an ultimate reference to an absolute Final End of Human Action. By the final end is meant: that of which the attainment would perfectly satisfy the nature of man as man; that which would enable him to get out of life everything of value that life can yield; that which has absolute worth in itself, and in relation to which everything else must be regarded as a means. It is not possible, Aristotle maintains at the beginning of the Nichomachean Ethics, for a man to regard his action as continually aimless, to look upon each end as a means to some other end, which in its turn is a means to something further. There must be a final end if there is to be a unity of conscious experience; if human conduct is to form an intelligible system of which a rational account may be given. And this final end, whatever be its character, must be such that in and through it a man's nature would receive its fullest expression, and through its realization attain the most complete satisfaction. In the history of Ethics attempts to determine the nature of the final end of human action have proceeded along three definite lines: (1) dialectical metaphysics (2) intuitive metaphysics (3) scientific generalization.

We have said that the meaning of a proposition is its verifiability; and that we verify a proposition by exhibiting the structure of the situation to which the proposition refers. Those who base Ethics upon dialectical metaphysics admit that their propositions cannot be empirically verified; therefore they cannot claim that their ethical systems give us verifiable, communicable knowledge. Wittgenstein's discoveries concerning the tautological character of necessary inference or formal implication suggest that the *a priori* method must be confined strictly to analysis. Moreover dialectical metaphysics cannot be logically grounded upon probable inference, for probable inference has logical validity only in the discussion of empirical questions, where the conclusions may be subjected to empirical verification.

Those who base Ethics upon intuitive metaphysics confuse "knowledge" and "immediate non-cognitive experience," and they ignore all logical factors. They attempt vainly to describe the content of experience. My experience *as it appears to me* is forever private to me; another's experience *as it appears to him* is forever private to him. The question, urged so vigorously and so emotionally by Fite in his *Moral Philosophy*, "What is it to *have* an experience?" is strictly speaking a meaningless question. Fite is really requesting us to utter the unutterable, to express the inexpressible—in logical language. His question can only be answered, as the poets from Sophocles to Eliot have always answered it, in extremely intimate and personal terms. The intuitionist writers have built for themselves a kingdom of metaphor. They have made words their vizers; logically the core of their intuition is a fluent blur. Our austere theory of meaning suggests that ethical systems based upon dialectical metaphysics and intuitive metaphysics have not succeeded in formulating any adequate technique of symbolic reference. Consequently, these systems cannot give us communicable, verifiable knowledge concerning the final end of human action.

We shall now consider briefly three attempts based upon scientific generalization to determine the final end of human action. The first and simplest scientific answer that has been proposed to the question of the final end is that it is pleasure. "The final end of human action is pleasure," say the hedonists. Is this a proposition that is truly meaningful? Is this a proposition that we can truly know? If so, where and what is the situation which would serve to verify this proposition, if it were the case? At the very beginning of the search for the situation we are confronted by the concept of pleasure. Now everyone familiar with the history of hedonistic theories knows very well that hedonists have never succeeded in giving an intelligible and exact analysis of the concept of pleasure, when that concept is erected into a final end of human action. Moreover, the hedonists have never succeeded in showing forth the situation to which their cardinal proposition refers.

An analysis of the attempts of the hedonists to determine the final end (an analysis which I cannot undertake here owing to limitations of space) would show (a) that it is impossible to give any definite meaning to the concept of pleasure and (b) that it is impossible to discover the situation which would verify the proposition, the final end of human action is pleasure, if it were the case. Since it is impossible for us to discover whether it is the case or not, the hedonistic proposition is not a proposition which we can *know*. That proposition is, strictly speaking, epistemologically meaningless, though it may have genuine emotional or affective significance. The classical hedonists erected a purely psychological concept into a final end of human action. Is it to be wondered at that a system based upon such an extraordinary feat of analogical thinking should take such fluctuating and intangible forms in the course of its historical development? Classical hedonism was very bad psychology; its chief concept, pleasure, was very blurred and opaque.

A second historic attempt to establish ethics on a sound scientific basis was made by the utilitarians in the nineteenth century. For them the proposition that the final end of human action is pleasure is replaced by the proposition: the final end of human action is the greatest happiness of the greatest number (the general happiness). Again we must ask: Has this proposition any epistemological validity? Now it would not be generally admitted that we *do* know the proposition: the final end of human action is the general happiness. Certain logical and psychological fallacies in the arguments of the utilitarians have often been indicated. Our attack on utilitarianism is at once more fundamental and less dependent upon the adoption of a particular ethical viewpoint. We maintain that the utilitarians have never succeeded in clarifying the meaning of their extraordinarily ambiguous concept, general happiness. Neither have the utilitarians ever succeeded in indicating the situation which would serve to verify the proposition: the final end of human action is the general happiness. If the concept of general happiness did really indicate a definite and unmistakable set of facts in human life the utilitarian claims might be true. For the propositions in which their claims are set forth could then be referred to the facts into which a situation divides, and then the process of elucidating the structure of a particular situation might begin. But general happiness is a holophrastic concept which has a very large subjective, emotional reference.

Has this concept any objective reference? Is it meaningful at all? If space permitted we would show that whenever, in the analysis of the cardinal utilitarian proposition, we hover on the verge of meaning, we are in the anteroom of sociology. This analysis would also show that: (a) it is impossible to give any meaning to the concept of general happiness when that concept is erected into a final end of human action; (b) it is impossible to discover the situation which would verify the proposition, the final end of human action is the general happiness, if it were the case. Since it is impossible for us to discover whether it is the case or not, the cardinal utilitarian proposition is not a proposition which we can *know*. It is, strictly speaking, meaningless, though it may have genuine emotional or affective significance. The really valuable side of the utilitarian teaching has always turned on its sociological content, however crude that may be. The entire efficacy of utilitarianism lay in its *application* of the results of whatever descriptive social science there was to the social and political problems of the nineteenth century. Considered as a system of absolute ethics, as a theory of the final end of human action, it has no epistemological validity. But, as a technique for political, social and legal reform, utilitarianism was of inestimable importance in providing emotive slogans for the struggles of European liberalism.

A third historic attempt to found Ethics upon scientific generalizations was made by Herbert Spencer and Leslie Stephen. These writers thought that the theory of evolution was the long-sought principle of explanation which would finally solve all the great problems, the so-called "deepest problems" of human life. In developing their theories they tried to combine the principles of utilitarianism with the latest generalizations of biological science. They introduced into Ethics such concepts as variation, natural selection, transmission, adaptation, organism, vitality or increase of life, organic system, organic growth, social tissue, typical society, the health of the social tissue.

By the introduction of this miscellaneous collection of biological analogies into Ethics, they hoped to show that the ethical *ought* could be resolved into factors which imply the physical *must*. But they did not realize that the ethical *ought* when thus reduced loses its moral efficacy and ceases to possess the authority with which it has been traditionally and popularly credited. The appeal to evolutionary biology was of no service either in establishing the epistemological validity of the concept of a final end of human action or in vindicating the ethical *ought.* The ethical systems of Spencer and Stephen are among the last desperate struggles of the human mind to reach the solution of the problem of the ultimate meaning of life by a frantic appeal to science. For both writers claimed that they could solve the problem of the final end of human action by conducting a strictly scientific investigation. Superficially, books which are sprinkled with allusions to the theory of evolution, the health of the social tissue, the law of natural selection, have the air of being scientific. But all these special allusions and "scientific facts" are woven into a system of Ethics only by means of the wildest feats of analogical thinking. Their propositions never remain within the realm of the empirically verifiable, and therefore they are not meaningful as *knowledge.* The basis for rejecting all such systems as those of Spencer and Stephen is therefore highly practical and methodological, as well as epistemological.

This criticism of evolutionary Ethics applies with equal force to the systems of hedonism and utilitarianism. None of these inductive systems of Ethics gives us meaningful knowledge. Hedonism and utilitarianism, if acutely analyzed, reduce on one flank to something very akin to poetry, and on the other become identified with psychology and sociology. The arguments of the writers of these three schools have a superficial plausibility because they are based upon certain vague crude analogies from biology, psychology, or sociology. But no consistent principles of symbolic reference have emerged in any of these traditional ethical discussions, and consequently the propositions set forth by these schools wither away before a sustained critical analysis.

There is no possibility of saving that gratuitous and unwarranted concept, the concept of a final end of human action, by appealing to science. The structure of the situation to which a proposition bearing the concept of a final end refers cannot be elucidated, for the simple reason that the situation cannot be discovered. The concept of a final end is meaningless; it has been for centuries the *ignis fatuus* of Ethics. Hume realized, long ago, that the ultimate ends of human action can never be accounted for by reason; and all of our researches have confirmed his position. The question of the objectivity of the final end must be dismissed to the philosophical limbo, and absolute Ethics must join the company of famous "sciences" which we have slowly and painfully realized to be an illusion. Whatever appeal the traditional absolutistic systems of Ethics may have rests ultimately upon the persuasive possibilities which are always latent in the aesthetic use of language. We shall now discuss briefly the aesthetic temper in the traditional systems of Ethics.

Among the kinds of symbolism which may be used to promote aesthetic attitudes are painting, music, sculpture, poetry, and even the dance; the language of speculative Ethics must now be included in this category. The aesthetic temper may be detected at the heart of every ethical system, including those systems which are supposed to be scientific. Systems as diverse as those of Kant, Schopenhauer, Mill, Bradley may all be taken as illustrations of our argument. Westermarck's exhaustive anthropological investigation into the nature of ethical systems amply confirms our conclusions. He maintains that ethical systems are generalizations of emotional tendencies. The authority which various ethical philosophers have assigned to intuition, reason, or conscience is the echo of the unanimous agreement of a culture at a definite period in history upon specific types of conduct.

Our view, that speculative ethical systems have no epistemological validity, in turn confirms the current anthropological attitude toward absolute Ethics, and provides at last a true Copernican revolution in Ethics. Ethical philosophers are henceforth committed to an admission of the aesthetic temper and to ethical relativity. For there will be many moral worlds—there will be moralities of race, class, and occupation. Given the cardinal assumptions and "insights" (*i.e.,* aesthetic attitudes) of the author, an ethical system should be so developed that we can in imagination envisage his personal experience of the final end of human action, his appreciation of the issues of social experience, his tragic sense of life. Such a system will have aesthetic significance insofar as its language is capable of arousing in us emotional attitudes which organize our desires and impulses into more harmonious wholes. It will have the function of a dynamic symbol, a vital lie, an *as if*. It will suggest vistas of possibilities in terms of which the significance of life and the universe at large may be shadowed forth; and it will attempt in terms of some gigantic mythology to grasp the whole of creation in an instant. Of such are the great vistas of Plato, Spinoza, and Hegel—expressions in varying artistic forms of the aesthetic significance which haunts the world. We stand transfigured underneath their vivid glow.

But in the twentieth century the aesthetic experience, magnificent and moving as it may be, is not enough. We have Socrates' passionate craving genuinely to *know*. Furthermore, the great organizing forms of aesthetic distance, in terms of which seventy generations of the men of the West have unceasingly expressed the tragic sense of life, are being maintained in the twentieth century with great and ever-increasing difficulty. The peculiar tension of our time is reflected in the cautious, insipid eclecticism of many professional ethical philosophers, as well as among the ardent moralists in literary circles. Of these latter, the works of T. S. Eliot, Ezra Pound, James Joyce, Marcel Proust, Aldous Huxley—of all the truly great and creative spirits of this age—testify universally to the aesthetic frustration of our time, to our moral agony, and some would even add to the collapse of Western culture. Amidst the many discordant voices calling for our allegience, the appeal of the Communists rings loudest. And in fairness to this call, an honest spectator cannot fail to notice that day by day the challenge of Communism mounts higher and higher in the eastern sky; that day by day the mythology of Marx and Lenin attains a greater hold over the minds of men everywhere. But Communism is a reflex of hot passions, of violent dogmas, and of paltry aesthetic attitudes; it can hardly claim the allegience of a truly disciplined logical mind.

It is the destiny of the men of the twentieth century frankly to admit ethical relativity—and having made that great renunciation to establish a scientific Ethics. The dissolution of the traditional systems constitutes a very great advance toward the construction of such a science of Ethics. For Ethics must outgrow the original formulations of Socrates, if it is to escape from the primitive discussions that have characterized it in the past, discussions in which immediate intuitions, hypostasized qualities and hasty analogies from "science" have been its only abstractions. All the concepts of traditional Ethics are too gross and too vague—such terms as *good, evil, ought, pleasure, happiness, self-realization* are all essentially private, incommunicable, aesthetic. In the past, ethical philosophers have depended too much upon the magic of words.

How must we proceed if Ethics is to be given a set of basic concepts? Clearly we must abandon the position, maintained since the time of Aristotle, that Ethics aims immediately at action rather than at knowledge. "If we had no moral sense," says C. I. Lewis, "philosophy would not give us one." Our analysis suggests that the proper method of Ethics would be to study the undeniable moral consciousness as a *fact*. And this moral consciousness cannot belong to a special realm, the realm of freedom; it must now be considered as belonging to the realm of nature. Ethics, then, must become the science of the moral consciousness. In the light of our investigations of the logic of language and the nature of communication, what will be the form of such a science? Clearly, we cannot take the moral judgments on the surface of consciousness, immediately given in introspection, as the objects of such a science. For then we should soon fall into the error of archaic Ethics—the error of classifying examples of these moral judgments according to types and of prescribing hierarchies of duties. What is the *nature* of the moral consciousness? An intelligible answer can only be given when we translate the question into the form: Under what conditions does the moral consciousness arise, and what is its *function* in the situation in which it manifests itself?

For a scientific Ethics can give us information only about the verifiable, the public, the communicable. It can give us no information about the nature of the moral consciousness except insofar as that nature is revealed in a situation which we can indicate and whose structure we can exhibit publicly. The ethical scientist must abandon the *a priori* method, the introspective technique, and the private aesthetic language of the traditional schools; not otherwise can he establish communication and formulate a system of meaningful propositions. He must speak of the moral consciousness not as *I* may know it in myself, but as *others* may know it—as a function of a very complex situation. He must ask: What are the conditions under which the moral consciousness arises and what is its function, not, what does an individual think, feel or desire when he makes a moral judgment? Ethics will then have as the proper object of its study a reality other than that to be found in the individual's states of consciousness. And since the proper study of any phenomenon is the phenomenon itself, the ethical scientist will no longer search in the starry heavens without for the deeper reasons of our moral being. He will rather investigate that narrower domain of life and society with which the moral consciousness has community of origin and of nature.

Imbued with the empirical method and anthropological interests, Westermarck, Hobhouse, Lévy-Bruhl and others have introduced the comparative method into Ethics. But the *histoires de sauvages* as carried on by these philosophers is not enough. For the answer to the question, *What is the nature of the moral consciousness?* will not have been given when we have succeeded in discovering the origin of the moral consciousness in the remote past and in tracing its development into its present form. Even if we could achieve a unilinear series with no lost links in the evolutionary chain, our problem would not have been solved. And of course it is well known that at many points the unilinear series is irretrievably broken for the data are wholly lost. Philosophers have always complained— and rightly—of the anthropological fallacy, the doctrine that when we have given a complete historical account of the genesis and development of ideas and institutions we have exhausted all the possibilities of explanation. But philosophers have not thereby been justified in substituting the metaphysical fallacy. For we can never answer a question of the form: What is so and so? in any ultimate sense. All questions about the *nature* of phenomena must be translated into the form: Under what conditions does the phenomenon arise? What is the function of this phenomenon in a complex of phenomena? The historical and comparative methods are of the greatest assistance in answering the question: Under what conditions does the moral consciousness arise? But these methods are not enough. For the historical method tells us nothing about the actual concrete situation in which the moral consciousness is now functioning. The real and pressing problem for Ethics then becomes: *What is the function of the moral consciousness in a specific social order?*

The answer to this question will require the mobilization of the data of psychology and of the social sciences on a large and unprecedented scale. Those who undertake this task will investigate the moral consciousness at all levels of development in the attempt to discover its function in a complex culture pattern. They will study all these elements and factors which control the origin and growth of moral practices and moral values. They will realize that all sociological facts are very complex; and that ethical science must include a complete analysis of the moral behavior and moral ideas of men as they actually exist and function within a concrete and complex sociological context. For moral habits and moral values do not exist in isolation; they have their place in a concatenation of social facts. We have not understood the nature of moral values and of the moral consciousness until we have discovered the place of moral values and of the moral consciousness in the larger complex of social attitudes and beliefs which lead to the traditionally standardized moral ideas and moral attitudes of a specific culture pattern. We shall still be interested in the history and comparison of the moral ideas and moral habits that are maintained in other culture patterns. But our real problem will be the elucidation of the elements and factors in terms of which the moral consciousness functions in a specific culture pattern. Such a study cannot be conducted in isolation from psychology, history, law, politics, economics and sociology. Ethics will in the future become the queen of the social sciences, for it will at last have been placed in that human context, foreseen long ago by Dewey, where it can illuminate and guide the life of man.

How can such an integrative science of Ethics assist us in the actual guidance of the moral life? Will not the interest of Ethics be entirely theoretical? In the past many philosophers have maintained that Ethics, by virtue of its prescriptions, is the eminently practical part of philosophy. This craving for salvation combined with the craving for generality has led for centuries to the eager search for that elegant pawn of Philosophy—the final end of human action. In the future philosophers will abandon the quest for elegance and will lose their contempt for the particular case. They will realize, and indeed many have realized already, that there are no "philosophical" prescriptive propositions about morality, but only moral acts. These moral acts are inspired by those personal experiences which come from the philosophical clarification of the *meaning* of the propositions of the science of Ethics—"the unexamined life is not fit for human living."

In this essay we have separated sharply the realm of the knowable from the realm of the unknowable. The unknowable, in Aristotelian phrase, belongs to perception. Questions concern-

ng it are requests not for knowledge but for aesthetic satisfac-
ion. "The solution of the problem of life," says Wittgenstein,
'is seen in the vanishing of this problem. (Is not this the reason
why men to whom after long doubting the sense of life became
lear, could not then say wherein this sense consisted?) . . .
Whereof one cannot speak, thereof one must remain silent."

PHILOSOPHY TODAY
AND TOMORROW

HORACE MEYER KALLEN

I have been with the New School for Social Research since its founding, professing philosophy and psychology. Before that I had taught the same subjects at the University of Wisconsin; and before that, taught at Harvard and Clark Universities, and English at Princeton.

Although I feel philosophy as a calling and enjoy teaching it, I have not been able to devote myself exclusively to what is euphemistically known as "scholarship" and the sheer academic life. My earliest interests were as literary as philosophical and were soon crossed by direct participation in political and economic movements of the land, especially those aiming at the protection and growth of freedom, including the labor movement, the civil liberties union and the consumers' coöperative movement. Hence I have never attained that fullness of pedagogical withdrawal which custom and prejudice ordain for the practice of philosophy in America. Unable to separate my profession from my life, I have always found myself ill at ease with the philosophy and the psychology of the schools. The first has seemed to me for the most part a ceremonial liturgy of professionals as artificial and detached from the realities of the daily life as bridge or chess or any other safe but exciting game of chance, and much of the second has seemed to me the sedulous elaboration of disregard for the living man of flesh and blood.

Although my first and most enduring interest remains aesthetics, and I have been for many years mulling over an opus to be called "Beauty and Use," need and inclination have led me into all of the ramifications of social science, from its logic and method to its most peripheral subject-matter, as my published works show: each is an attack upon a specific problem in a special field from a standpoint which might be called aesthetic pragmatism.

The influences under which this standpoint developed are too many and too varied and too mutually overlapping to be discriminated. How can anyone say who, or what, or how, or how much, in the course of half a century, has made him what he is today? Half a dozen people, however, stand out: old teachers; friends of my youth. Of the nature and extent of my debt to them, I am aware. They were paramount influences on the development of my attitude, my point of view and my method: George Santayana, William James, Edwin Holt, Canning Schiller, Barrett Wendell and Solomon Schechter. *Sicut cursores*, etc.

PHILOSOPHY TODAY AND TOMORROW

Horace Meyer Kallen

I

When I was very young the classical conception of philosophy seemed to me obvious and natural. That philosophy should consist of infallible deliverances concerning the true, the good and the beautiful seemed to me matter of course. The first philosopher I ever read was Spinoza, whose works were available in a German version in my father's house. The world predicated by the ancestral religion had, to my awakening mind, fallen in. Neither paternal authority nor young habit could sustain faith in the clearer and clearer inconsistencies within, and greater and greater conflict with the conditions of the daily life without, which we were called upon to live. The *Ethica* brought me surcease from the pang and the division of that collapse. Its amazing architecture seemed to me to set forth the very build and derivation of things as they really are, in their true linkage and go. It seemed to me infallible that knowing the architecture of the universe should be the state of all states most blessed, the perfect salvation.

Spinoza had written, of course, how his research magnificent into the improvement of the understanding was undertaken to escape life's ills and to conquer blessedness; and I had read that essay as I had read his others. But it did not come home to me. My emotions were enchanneled and my imagination entirely taken up by the stupendous totalitarian web of the *Ethica*, which linked each thing with everything else by eternal unbreakable links, logical and material at the same time. Only later, when

I was studying philosophy formally and officially, did the import of that motivation of Spinoza's dawn on me. Considering the clash and conflict of the historic systems, how each denied validity to its predecessors and contemporaries, how it refuted its rivals and claimed the crown of truth for itself alone, I realized that philosophy was not the impersonal vision of eternal being I had believed it to be. I came to see it as a man's endeavor after his personal salvation. Far from being an utterance of a revelation passively received, as Mary received the Holy Ghost, philosophy was the outcome of men's pains, hungers and frustrations actively suffered, "adversity's sweet milk," the creation of needs unserved and wishes ungratified at work upon the available materials of experience, seeking to wring from them somehow service and gratification.

Philosophy, it came to me, is in actual life a method and instrument of adjustment, a human organ in the human struggle to survive; its concepts are not actually apprehensions, its logic not really world-anatomy, its goal not genuinely insight. These may be ingredients in a philosophy, but they are assembled not for what they are, but for what they can accomplish toward a philosopher's salvation. Their function, outside of the rite and ceremony of professionals in the safe seclusion of schools, is to project an attitude toward life, the attitude of "taking things philosophically." It has its limits. "There never was yet philosopher," says Shakespeare in *Much Ado About Nothing*, "who could endure the toothache patiently, however they have writ the style of gods, and make a push at chance and sufferance." Yet philosophy consists in taking philosophically precisely such events as toothaches. Pleasure and good fortune do not require a philosophy. Living philosophy is sired by fear upon danger; and nurtured upon pain and sorrow.

So it was when primitive man began to make philosophies, so it remains today. Whether we know it or not, we live, as humans, dangerously. To our primitive contemporaries and our primitive ancestors, everything is dangerous; men to women and women to men, children to fathers, fathers to children, the dead to the living, and the natural scene with its teeming life to humankind. Civilization, which is presumed to have developed as defense against danger, only alters its locus. The safest of us lives dangerously. That our danger is not poignant and paralyzing is due to habits, which are confrontations of dangers become automatic through repetition. Habit dulls the edge of danger, transforms adventure into boredom and constitutes the substance of all the security we know. Security is but danger become habitual, danger is security unreconciled by habit. Habit makes all the difference between the two.

Yet what is this habit? On the face of it, an experience repeating itself; the past, informing the formless future with its own form, a bridge into the void whose other end we believe in but do not experience. What we experience is this end, the here and now, where we exist, and whence we direct our attention upon the past which is no more and the future which is not yet. It is these absences we reach out to and which we cannot attain so long as they remain past and future. It is these which are the referents of faith and desire, of fear and doubt and insecurity, as the present, horrible as it might feel, cannot be. And it is to these absences, therefore, the absent future and the absent past, that religion, the arts and the sciences endeavor to impart a genuine presence only to succeed in giving them a vicarious one. This vicarious presence consists in symbols; their value and meaning comes not from what they are, but from what the lapse of time fulfills them with.

II

Philosophies especially consist in elaborate architectonics of such symbols, so ordered as to banish present evil, error, and ugliness into "appearance," and to bring to hand and establish fleeting or absent good and truth and beauty as "reality." Philosophies live and work as pain-killers, as anodynes to the slings

and arrows of outrageous fortunes; the "consolations of philosophy" are ancient tradition. Of recent years, because of the
multiplication and growth of the physical and social sciences
some doubt has arisen among professional philosophers concerning philosophy's nature and rôle. It seemed to many that
squatters had preëmpted one after another of its estates, to
make of them the fields of special sciences, until nothing was
left to philosophy but the theory of method and the theory of
values, and that even these were being appropriated by logistics and sociology. Snobbery about metaphysics became fashionable. But that doubt was, and remains, a passing mood. The
lapse of time and the stretch of space continue to impose upon
the heart an insecurity no positive science can assuage; to set
before the mind an uncertainty no positive science can dispel.
The past, dead and gone beyond repair, the future, indeterminate and to come, continue to defy knowledge and to exact
faith. Philosophy is the reasoned utterance of this faith concerning the nature and intent of the unknown. At its best it is what
Plato called courage, a wisdom concerning dangers; born of
their pang; endeavoring somehow to regiment the chanceful,
the novel, the diverse and the opposed to the heart's desire and
the head's delight. This heart and this head are not, in the
first instance, the heart and head of the world, or any company
thereof. They are the heart and the head of some living man
of flesh and blood beset with inner conflict and outer assault.
His philosophy is the action and outcome of that struggle, the
lyric of his life poured out in the dialectics of language. Every
philosophy is born a lyric and the multitude die so. But of the
many voices which are raised, some are heard by other men
and awaken echoes in their souls, speaking also their interests
and enchanneling also their passions. When this happens to a
philosophic system, it is said to undergo "social selection" and
is thereby transformed from the lyric to the choral mood. The
dynamic of this change is the ruling passion of the place and
time, its prepotent hopes and dominant fears. These endow the

fundamental concepts of the system with all the authority they exercise and all the influence they wield. These establish the system's intent and shape its argument, which the professional philosophers simply repeat, elaborate, develop and refine, by means of poetic analogy and logical explication, into the verbal perspectives wherewith the fears are assuaged and the hopes gratified.

Such perspectives, I have pointed out elsewhere,[1] may express the situations in which they arise, compensate for them or serve as plans to alter them. It has come to me since that the relation between perspective and situation may also be catalytic: that is, a philosophy without undergoing any significant change itself may be the cause of great activity in other fields, as Communism is in the sciences of nature and man in Russia, and new religions are everywhere.

An expressive philosophy as a rule is a conventional and fashionable repetition, in another dimension, of the *Zeitgeist* and its traits, the substance of its atmosphere and spirit.

A compensatory philosophy—and most classical systems are compensatory—is antipathetic to the *Zeitgeist's* material ground and derealizes it without diminishing its potency, by redefining the rejected potency as "appearance" and setting up the desired but non-existent and often impossible potency as "the Real." Like the umbrella of the tightrope walker, it functions as equilibrator of life's unbalance, and works to guarantee the *status quo.* This compensating function is especially characteristic of religious philosophies.

A programmatic philosophy tends to compenetrate the perspectives in which it consists with the situation that gives them birth. It is an attitude and a plan of change somehow continuous with the situation's still germinal forces and subterranean diversifications, projecting their gradients as ideas prophetic of the shape which the future is being given.

[1] "Value and Existence in Religion, Art and Philosophy," in *Creative Intelligence,* by John Dewey and Others.

No philosophic system possesses exclusively the traits of any one type. Each has those of all, but one is dominant, the others are recessive. With the lapse of time both they and the *Zeitgeist* change within and without; they attain their fullness and they die. Many are stillborn. Most die the natural death of obsolescence. Some are fatalities of the warfare of sects and times over what shall be approved as "real" and what denounced as "unreal."

For "real" and "unreal" are designations of conventional thought, not revelations of experience. They register a consensus of the passions and perplexities of many men agreed at last that one item or event shall be "the real" and not another. "Real" and "unreal" are terms of valuation, not observation, and what shall be called so, and what not, is a consequence of chance and circumstance played upon by fear and hunger and desire. According as these are gratified or defeated we attribute "reality." In the philosophic tradition it is the pleasurable, liberating and plastic which is adjudged the real. The "reality" of metphysics is congruous with the heart's desire and conqueror over the heart's aversion; but sometimes the eulogium accrues to the painful, the obstructive and impenetrable. Since Freud became vogue, whole sections of the philosophic public have been able to approve as real only the evils of our lot, while the psychoanalytic salvation of "facing reality" consists in affirming that in human relations, selfishness and hate and horror and disease and death; that in the non-human world, the warfare of each against all with its chaos of cross-purposes, contradictions, collisions and final defeat, are "real," while their opposites are not. This *auto da fé* of confronting the avoided and accepting the rejected simply stands on its head the contrary elder philosophic illusion, which posits all reality in the world's harmony with our natures and desires, proving it, in one logically infallible system after another, One Eternal Universal Spiritual Being which guarantees Immortality and Happiness and Freedom to us and the opposite of our foes, World without End.

Both illusions are instances of the fallacy of composition which valuations are so prone to; they are world-pictures painted in passionately preferred colors, with the residue ignored, and their "facing" of reality consists only in reshaping actual experience to the perspectives of the prevailing philosophic outlook. The actual, in which our valuations of it are to be included, is neutral to the intent of those valuations. It has no foregone character or status; it lacks anything of the ready-made; it is a process where personal activities and unpersonal events compenetrate, reshape each other, endowing the past with a new meaning and determining the future to a new character. "Reality" is that in the total event which, because it helps or because it hurts, feels important to us; so that we envisage the whole event in its image. But the event itself is indifferent and, determined no more to one image than another, flows through and dissipates them all.

III

Today's philosophies prove the rule.

They set themselves off sharply from yesterdays.

Between yesterday and today broods the Great War.

During a quarter of a century, from 1890 to 1914, the ancient vendetta of religion against science was abating. The intransigence which had reawakened with the assault on Darwinism had softened down to compromise and reconciliation. The stiff dogmatism of either combatant gave way to the agnosticism of science and the fideism of religion: regarding the issues which divided them the scientist declared, "I do not know; I cannot tell"; the religionist announced, "I do not know, I can only believe." Science had so much more than vindicated itself by its consequences in the counsels and comforts of life that the religionist found he needed to adjust his scheme of salvation to scientific methods and scientific observation. He felt constrained so to reform and to reorient religion as to demonstrate that it was a necessity of life even in a world entirely scientific. He made religion Modernist by assimilating its concepts to the deliverances of the sciences. These focussed upon two themes: the stuff of existence, matter; and the order of its changes, determinism. Matter was the subject which all the sciences served as predicates; and the form of these predications was the mathematical formula: equations whose perfect balance excluded all actual variation or novelty from the "real" world. Astronomy, physics, chemistry, biology, psychology, each sought to restate its subject matter in equations. They endeavored to reduce cause and effect to quantitative identities, and to make of change the bare repetition of these identities through all eternity, with never a real difference between effect and cause. The philosophic explication of this purpose was an architectonic similar to Plato's or Aristotle's, but minus the drama, the purposefulness, and the consolation of the Greek systems; a necessary universe like Spinoza's, but with an inverse logic: instead of deriving the part from the whole, the particular from the universal and the individual from the cosmic, it built the whole of parts, setting up a static universe by compounding simples into complexes in an infinite regression wherein any whole always implied its parts, but the reverse was not true. In the course of time this employment of determinism gets to be called logical atomism, and its statement in mathematical form, logistics. It is still a ruling passion among certain professionals, but in its pre-War modes brought small comfort to the religionist.

What did bring comfort was that stream of tendency flowing from certain empirical aspects of the biological sciences conceived in the post-Darwinian manner. To philosophers sensitive to this stream the paramount data were the processes of differentiation, mutation and innovation, the actualities of struggle, fitness and survival. They indicated that effect held more than cause, that history was genuine change, that nowhere could the march of events be a mere repetition of identicals, but everywhere a new birth and a struggle for survival of novelties, with a resulting domestication of the new amid the old, and sometimes a transformation of the old by the new.

Pragmatism is the philosophic explication of these ideas in empirical and secular terms; Vitalism is their explication in terms metaphysical and religious. Vitalism sets an abyss between life and matter. Matter, it was subtly argued, is well accounted for by the physicists and chemists and mathematicians. Its existence truly is no more than a repetition of identicals changing position in space. Indeed, it is of the essence of space; and what else, hence, could characterize it save quantities and determinism? But life—life is something that grows, that is fuller and more varied with each moment; life is memory; life is at once self-conservation and reproduction, continuity and change; of the essence of time and therefore of quality and of freedom. "Scientific" materialism is thus confronted with this equally "scientific" Vitalism, while Pragmatism describes the workings of both. "Life" and its derivatives become the honorific terms they have not been since Old Testament times. The conceptions of the biological sciences are employed to vindicate the compensatory ideals of the philosophic tradition. The freedom and immortality of man, the spirituality and unity and eternity of the world are vindicated, as it were, out of the mouth of their reputed adversary. It looked as if the peace that passeth understanding was at hand.

An analogous reconciliation was apparent in public affairs. Inventions were speeding up the industrialization of the world's economy and contracting the physical distance between its parts. Travel increased, and the planned interchange of ideas and of their spokesmen became a fad. A certain assurance and goodwill was in the air. People believed that history was a progress; that this progress is a providence inherent in the nature of things, impelling their movement from simple to complex, from low to high, from unconscious to conscious, from the unmoral to perfection. They called this providence Evolution and it meant to them that all change is change for the better. One such change would be universal peace. Norman Angell produced, in his *Great Illusion*, an irrefutable argument that war could not be, because the gains of civilization made war's profits so dubious and its cost so enormous that no state could win anything by waging war against another. Events have more than vindicated Angell's exposition of the economy of modern warfare. Unfortunately, its check on the warlike passions is still to seek.

In every land, democracy was gaining; even the Tzarist beaureaucracy of Russia made some concessions to it—assembled a Duma; in Turkey the Sultan was deposed and power taken by the Young Turks; China went Republican. Democracy was being invoked by national and cultural and religious minorities, by depressed castes and trades, by ostracized classes. The woman's movement was in full swing. The "rights of man" received indefinite extension, seeming everywhere to gain authority and force. In the freer countries their claims of jurisdiction were extended from political to economic and social relations. This extension went by many names but its basic energy was the Socialist movement.

Socialism had been projected as a "scientific" gospel for industrial society. It was addressed to the servile classes, the workers and the peasants, assuring them of glorious victory in a class war which it was proved to them they were waging with their masters and exploiters. Their final supremacy was demonstrated as a foregone conclusion of the material dialectic of history, which must terminate in a dictatorship of the proletariat and be followed by a classless society. Even informed and ironic critics of the economic establishment who were not socialists were contaminated with this socialist optimism and felt, without quite admitting, that the foreordination of the classless society which Marx so triumphantly argued was inherent in the determinism of events and would be happening as water runs or grass grows. Thorstein Veblen, for example, one of the most orginative and disillusioned of American social philosophers, drew some sort of obscure consolation from the belief that the march of industrial events must necessarily culminate in a happy ending for the common man.

It was an era of good hope for peace and progress and the turn of time was apparently on hope's side.

IV

Then statesmen with a stake in the defeat of the democratic movement embroiled the world in the Great War. As that swung to its climax, one group of combatants suffused it with pat rationalizations. They justified it as a war for peace and freedom, a war to end all wars and to make the world safe for democracy. Its consequences are still in process, and among them may be counted certain transvaluations of social values consonant with those rationalizations. Such are the accelerated liberation of women, the translation of the common soldier from a person of complete unimportance except as a nuisance into an object of solicitude to every non-combatant, and a member of the kept classes; the quickened disruption of sexways and folkways; and the readjustment of the industrial order and the political tradition.

But these, liberative in their impact, were upsetting and compulsive in their quality and tempo. They were events of a crisis, not improvements of an age. Consequently, they merely defused what had been fused. They aroused, wherever they reached, feelings of insecurity and anxiety, hatred and fear. The pre-war compromises and reconciliations came to a sudden end. An epidemic of nationalism, sectarianism, racialism and xenophobia swept the western world. In the United States its stigmata were red hysteria, jingoism, fundamentalism and the Ku Klux Klan. Fideism and agnosticism went down before a recrudescent dogmatism based on fear and hate, with its inalterable doctrines, its fixed grades and ranks and classes, its determinisms and foreordinations. To feeling, the mobile, changing progressive world became once more a static one. Psychoanalysis became the rage. An extraordinary vogue accrued to Behaviorism, which interpreted men in the light of machines. Men's intelligences were defined as inalterable quantities, their stations as natural destiny, their natures as unmodifiably good or unmodifiably evil, their opinions as *a priori* righteous or *a priori* wicked. Bolshevik became a synonym for alien, stupid, envious and sinful; 100 per cent American for native, generous, wise and virtuous. "Mass" became a term to curse and bless with. Dislocated or disillusioned intellectuals, entangled by the phenomena of the War and the after-War, voiced their anxieties by inventing a crowd psychology whose fictions managed to degrade every mood and action of men in mass. Marxists, on the other hand, glorified whatever they regarded as desirable by hyphenating it with "mass."

Indeed, in the social and political arena, the issue became *Marxism contra mundum.* Its passionate affirmations generated equally passionate contradictions and refutations. In Italy it gave rise to a counter-revolution and the contrary dogma of Fascism. Wherever it seemed to challenge, to deny, to threaten, it awakened a response more dogmatic and passionate than itself. Thus, the totalitarianism of the Marxist system gave rise to counter-totalitarianisms, like 100 per cent Americanism, Fascism, Nazism, each imposing on the individual unquestioning faith and submission. The democratic ideal of "Live and let live" was *spurlos versenkt;* the old liberties of thought and speech and press and association went under the ban. The arts and the sciences, the playgrounds and the schools were to be the instruments of indoctrination in right doctrine—and woe betide the heretic!

To one field only did this sharp division fail to reach. From that day, during the Great War, when English and German and French astronomers journeyed together to Brazil and with generous rivalry coöperated to cast the sun's eclipse, and thereby put Relativity as a new and true world-picture before mankind, that free coöperation spread and germinated, undermining the established world-order and effecting a revolution stranger and more breath-taking than the Copernican, or even the Communist. The news of it brought ferment and change to every art and science, to every sect and cult. Some Communists denounced it as contrary to the material dialectics of Communist scripture; Catholics as denying God; certain scientists welcomed it as making for religion in a way the older world-views of astronomy and physics did not. In the post-War world, the concept of Relativity was the only one among those absorbing the public mind not contaminated and distorted by the War and the passions and perspectives consequent.

V

The philosophy of today is a function of those diverse confrontations of passions and events. It embraces a transvaluation of pre-War values. Works hardly known, prepared as communications but fated to remain soliloquies, are of a sudden overheard as the voice of the generation. Books stillborn, that had dropped like lead from the press, are infused with a new life. The moods of the period sweep in like tides, each flood carrying another good tiding on its philosophic crest. The seismic resurgence is of Marx; but Henry Adams, fundamentalists like T. S. Eliot, the pseudo-humanists Irving Babbitt and Paul More are heard at last. Each ancient gospel comes to the new time as a new perspective and a new meaning; each, before its mood at ebb sweeps it back, has its day as the Way and the Light.

Or again, innovations present themselves. The new data of the sciences of man and of nature are opposed or assimilated to traditional valuations with philosophies of life accordant. Thus Freud, employing the psychoanalytic material whose accumulation he himself fathered, adjudges religion to be an illusion on the way to obsolescence, culture a burden which man endures with the help of this illusion, of material opiates and of diversions and sublimations like the arts and the sciences. Every man's nature, even the savage's, is a battlefield between the components of his tripartite psyche. And who shall establish that the culture which their battle kicks up is worth the pain and the pang that are its price?

To Spengler, *per contra,* this culture is not a consequence of the struggles within men's souls and between their persons; a culture is the life of a sort of collective animal from which the men who live and move and have their being in it derive, organs of an organism, not members of an organization. All cultures are born, grow up, grow old and die, passing in a life-span of about nine hundred years, through predestinate cycles. Our generation sees the Faustian culture which bred and fed us coming to its term; in the arts, in the sciences, in religion, in industry, in human relations, the old integrity breaks down and decays. The end will be a vegetable monotony of peasant-life, soil-rooted and overridden by predacious military bands. Then, in the fullness of time a new faith will manifest itself prophetic of a new culture as incommensurable with its predecessors as they were with one another. Bergson, too, sees culture as a life, but not as a life self-sufficient and autonomous. It is a phase of the cosmic life which is the Creative Evolution, the Pure Duration, whose act brings the new out of the old and yet conserves the old by bifurcating into Time and Space, Spirit and Matter, Intuition and Intellect. The history of culture is a rhythm of alternations between these opposites. Intellect has gone to the verge, so that our age is like to collapse under the weight of its materialism and the complexity of its mechanizations and the closed societies and static religions which go therewith. But at the verge, the alternative appears. A hero, drawing his energies directly from the living God with whom he is in mystic communion, will lead mankind away from the danger into a mode of the Christian salvation. His religion is dynamic. He will affirm the Open Society of human brotherhood and universal peace and men will believe and follow him. Thus, another step will have been taken by man toward the divinity to which he is predestined. For the universe is but a machine which God has created for making Gods to be his companions.

Eddington also employs a dichotomy, but professional astronomer and mathematician as he is, he cannot quite subordinate the deliverances of science to the aspirations of religion. He comforts himself with the notion that the theory of relativity, by admitting the observer into the mathematical equation, restores Berkeleyanism with a new turn, but for the rest, he renders unto Caesar what is Caesar's and unto God what is God's. The testimony of science is to a universe running down to a dead standstill; the witness of the heart is to a God as present and as real as the armistice on an armtistice day. Whitehead, one of the fathers of logistics, deals with the data of the new physics in a more sophisticated and complex way. He turns an atom into an organism and redefines God as a "principle of concretion" which arrests the flux and reunites it to the form from which his analysis of existence has divided it.

The mathematical physicists, the while, were advancing the enterprise, which relativity and the quantum theory began, to exciting consequences. With great surprise to themselves they found that the old well-ordered universe based on the Newtonian postulates had crumbled under their mathematical hands. The "principle of uncertainty" set contingency and chance at the very springs of being. Basic concepts like cause and effect, quantity and force, lost their significance. Determinism, which is the indispensable premise of scientific discussion, ceased to be applicable exactly where it should have been most valid. Many mathematicians and physicists, among them Einstein, were disturbed by the prospect and desirous that further studies might restore determinism to its traditional prestige. But the religionists are moved happily; they have the illusion that to remove determinism is to make place for God; and indeed, the philosophers—*vide* Whitehead—employing the deliverances of the new physics as the primary colors of their world-pictures, did bring in God, though it is hardly the God of the fathers or of Bergson or of Eddington and Jeans.

But this God, who is the content of the mystical intuition in religion, who is to the religionist the subject for which the sciences of nature are predicates, who is the One deploying through their diverse multiplicity, giving them being, life and identity yet remaining beyond apprehension within any one of their patterns, this God turns out, under the depictive hand of his most skillful biographers, to be indistinguishable from the elusive Matter whose flux and drive mathematician and physicist seek to enchannel, imprison and graph. Thus all the potencies and virtues which Bergson ascribes to God, Santayana assigns to Matter, even to the point of identifying it as the content of the mystic intuition. And the inversion can be followed through the whole system of each man, Santayana's eternal essences and their static mutual implications corresponding to Bergson's space with its mathematical measurements and structures, Santayana's idea of quality to Bergson's of quantity, and so on. The more Matter and God are denuded of the defining attitudes which distinguish them, the more certainly they coalesce into that which Aristotle called ὕλη, Santayana calls matter and Bergson *Dieu*. Thought cannot reach it, nor reason account for it, but its presence is sure to every mystic experience and implied to every scientist seeking to state precisely the relation between the events which its passing gives birth to and destroys.

Under these circumstances, it is not surprising that the tradition should repeat itself in a new form, and that to many thinkers the essential philosophic enterprise should be that of logical method and form, rather than of natural substance. Although the classical hypostasis of reason has its defenders, and there are those who see the future of philosophy as a new scholasticism, a scholasticism of the sciences preparing a logistical *summa* of salvation, the direction of public discussion is toward the recognition of all the multiplying concepts of present-day physics—the electrons and protons and neutrons with

their orbits, their attractions and repulsions, additions and sub-
tractions—as inventions, as tools and schemes and stratagems
compounded upon one another, whose perceptual upshot is the
manipulation of some machine resulting in the movement of a
galvanometric needle or a thread of mercury. The significance
of the analyses and interpretations of the procedures of modern
physics by such writers as Barry, Bridgman, and especially
Clarence Ayres, and of the procedures of modern logic by Canning Schiller, is still in the making.

VI

Such, then, are the conflicts, such the issues and the solutions
of the philosophy of today. It is philosophy in America but
not American philosophy. Few of the major figures who capti-
vated the post-War heart and stirred the post-War mind are
Americans bred of the American psyche and agitated with its
agitations. We count Eddington, Whitehead, Spengler, Bergson, Marx, Freud, Veblen, Santayana, Henry Adams and John
Dewey. The most deeply stirring of these are Marx and Freud,
and the first builds his philosophy upon hunger, the second upon
sex. Spengler's *weltanschauung* frames the defeat of the Prussian caste of soldiers and landlords and constitutes their lamen-
tation; Bergson insures the compensatory ideals of philosophy
and the consolations of traditional religion against attrition from
the positive sciences, the economy of industry and the moral
defeats of the war. Eddington and Whitehead perform similar
tasks of salvage, but employ as instruments the innovations of
physics and astronomy. Of the others who may be called Americans, Santayana, Platonist without superstition and materialist
without illusion, would softly repudiate the soft impeachment;
and Veblen, philosopher of hunger without dialectics and without relativity, was in exile wherever he found himself. Hardly
less so was Yankee Henry Adams, to whom the cycles of his-

tory exemplified the law of phase in chemistry and the second law of thermodynamics pronounced the destiny of the world.

There remains John Dewey, as Yankee as Henry Adams, and never uprooted from the American scene. The foremost Pragmatist, his feeling for alternatives, his empiricism, his tentativeness and instrumentalism so diffident of dogmatisms and systems, offer little to the post-War generation demanding the indubitable certainties, the impregnable securities of a gospel of salvation. Though since the War, Dewey's interests have been chiefly enchanneled by the changing political economy, the impact of industrial and financial organizations on personal relationships, the implications of new techniques and new knowledge for the method of life, and the remaking of individuality out of the new materials in the new setting, the disturbed intellectuals would have none of him. They seek asylum from their anxiety in the aggression of Communism or in the regression of traditionalism: the foremost voices of the latter being the pseudo-humanists Babbitt and More and the pseudo-Catholic Eliot. Pragmatism continues, after the War as before, to sustain the assaults of all varieties of amateurs of philosophy, who know it hardly more than a name in a book, and to retain the disfavor of the professional practitioners.

Among the latter, signs are not lacking of a consensus toward a new orthodoxy. Although the compensatory ideals of the Genteel Tradition are still predominantly the theme of the official teaching, they are momentous to a progressively smaller public and receive at best the lip service which the vested interests of the academies impose. The new orthodoxy derives from the positive sciences, the sciences of man as well as the sciences of nature. The transformation of the psychological and sociological disciplines by the inventions and discoveries of the physiologists and neurologists goes on apace. The Pavlovian "conditioned reflex" becomes as conventional as "psychophysical parallelism" used to be, and the quantification of the psyche by statistical and other methods of measurement dominates wider and wider areas of the social sciences. The diverse enterprises of psychologists, sociologists, economists, and even historians move concentrically and convergently toward a world-view whose primary postulates are materialism and determinism. The preferred name for this view seems, however, to be naturalism, and its current focus is, of course, human relations, ethics.

Here, then, is the matrix of the philosophy of tomorrow: the confrontation, in the political economy, of pre-War individualism and liberalism with the post-War totalitarianisms and regimentations of the Marxist and Fascist cults; the confrontation, in the natural sciences, of the senior tradition of materialism and determinism with the indeterminism and configurational relationships deriving from the new physics of relativity and quanta: the impact upon the established equilibria in religion, the social sciences, and the arts of attitudes and theories deriving from these sources.

The conflicts in political economy and the disputes in the natural sciences point alike to a rethinking of the theory of relations in terms of internality and externality.

Is Heisinger's "principle of uncertainty" a final datum of observation and reasoning? How are the connections between stretches of time and points of space to be understood? In Bergson's way, with the stretches of time internally and the points of space externally related to one another, and space and time as such mutually exclusive? Or in Einstein's way, as an organic space-time? And if so, is time in fact assimilated to the externalities of point-space, or space to the internalities of time-stretches? Whether the atom shall be regarded an organism in the manner of Whitehead, an organization in the manner of the classical atomists, or something the one or the other according to circumstances will depend logically upon the answers to the prior questions.

The same dependency carries over to the field of human personality and human society. What is an individual? What is the nature of his connection with other individuals? Is he internally related to them through the social whole, as an organ of a living body is related to the others through the body? Is society prior to the individual and implied by him? Or is society an organization which implies the individual? Or do both modes of relationship hold? The issues currently so momentous in social life between free society and totalitarian state, between liberty and security, between the enslavement of its citizens to the state and the employment of the state as a tool by its citizens, will find their ultimate logic in the decision that those relations are external or internal or both or neither.

Now this decision is not a foregone conclusion. It is not indicated by "the facts." A fact is only the finish of an act, and until it is finished it keeps changing, and when it is finished it is past and dead. A decision is made, not found, and the making of a decision into a philosophy is the confluence, clash and consensus of men's passions with events and with one another. It points, as all our empirical knowledge and non-empirical speculations point, to a world of many men and many things, each different from the others, each growing different within and resisting or assimilating differentiation without. Whether existence started as One or as Many, it is now Many; and its history as evolutionary science tells it is a continuous differentiation of the One into the Many. When mankind began, the world was already an endlessly diversified manifold, and there has been no cessation of increase in the variety and number of the natures whose aggregation it is.

If the deliverances of history and of the sciences are valid, then the human passion for unity, with its compensatory aspirations after one substance, one necessity, one law, in the sciences; an eternal God and an immortal soul in religion; one church, one state and one economy in social life, is unnatural. The totalitarianism of Communists and Fascists is in effect a war upon nature, an endeavor to compel mankind to lift itself by its bootstraps. And if these compensatory aspirations, these imperial enterprises, so perennial, so fraught with hope and tragedy to the masses of mankind, are the outward manifestation of man's inward essence, the supernaturalists are right. Man himself is a being unnatural, a stranger in nature and a wanderer on earth, and his home is elsewhere. The most hopeful and most humane philosophy is, then, the supernaturalist philosophy, the philosophy of Bergson or Whitehead or Eddington, of neo-Catholics or pseudo-humanists.

But, if it should turn out that these totalitarianisms are but individuals' reactions to the diversifying individualities and pluralisms they deny, but blind endeavors of one person or group to make of others a means to their desire, but selfish Caesarisms, then the most hopeful and humane philosophy will be a philosophy of scientific humanism. Such a philosophy will be pluralist and temporalist; it will be free of invidious distinctions between "reality" and "appearance;" its morality will be "live and let live," even "live and help live;" it will acknowledge the equal claim of every event to survive and to attain excellence, and it will distinguish consequences, not set norms. The unities it validates, consequently, will be instrumental ones. They will be associative forms whose significance resides in the enhancement of life which personality by their means attains. Its attitude toward problems will be tentative and experimental; it will dispute all finalities and doubt all foregone conclusions; its rule will be nature's: *solvitur ambulando.* Above all, it will be aware that nature is as neutral to man and to human values—especially her own unity and eternity—as to all other items which compose the infinitude of her teeming overflow. It will insist that human excellence and human destiny are matters of concern to man alone. Job's utterance regarding God will be its verdict regarding human good and human fate.

I have no hope
I know that he will slay me
Nevertheless will I maintain my ways before him

. . . .

Mine integrity hold I fast and will not let it go
My heart shall not reproach me so long as I live.

THE ONTOLOGICAL
STATUS OF VALUE

K. KOFFKA

Although I come from a family of lawyers I was never attracted to the study of law, smooth as it might have made my way through life. Largely influenced by my mother's youngest brother, a biologist, I became at an early age interested in philosophy and chose this as my subject when in the fall of 1903 I matriculated at the University of Berlin, where I was born in 1886. That eventually I became a psychologist is explained by my resistance to idealistic philosophy; I was too realistically minded to be satisfied with pure abstractions.

From my early youth I was attracted by Anglo-saxon culture; I spent a year of my student life in Edinburgh, and ever after I had many English speaking friends, both British and American. Therefore when in 1924 I accepted my first invitation to this country from Cornell University I felt perfectly at home there.

The greatest event of my life as far as it can interest the reader was my coming together in 1910 with Max Wertheimer and Wolfgang Köhler at Frankfort-on-the-Main. They made me a Gestalt psychologist, and that is what I have been ever since.

THE ONTOLOGICAL STATUS OF VALUE
A DIALOGUE

K. Koffka

PERSONS:
Algernon, a Psychologist
Basil, a Scientist
Clarence, a Philosopher

Algernon: I am sorry to be late. But you seem not to have missed me. I heard your voices even before I entered the room and I see by your expressions that you must have had a heated discussion.

Basil: So we had. I really like talking to a philosopher, but each time anew I am shocked and baffled by the difference of our points of view and our fundamental assumptions. We scientists have learned to respect facts, and therefore we are striving to enlarge and refine our experience. Our work is difficult and laborious, but it is not this I am objecting to. Indeed I should be quite satisfied with my work were it not that it raised certain questions for which I can find no answers. I then turn to the philosopher and find him willing to give me an answer which, it seems to me, disregards all the achievements of science and therefore leaves me more dissatisfied than ever. A philosophy which does not recognize the primacy of experience is of no help to me. I have no sympathy with pure speculation which, as the history of philosophy should teach us, leads us nowhere.

Clarence: And where has science led us? It is responsible for the technical development which distinguishes our age from all others and which seems to progress at a continuously accelerated pace. It has, in many ways, made life easier for us, given us physical comforts and new forms of enjoyment. But what has science contributed to the essentials of life? Are we in any sense better than our ancestors, more truthful, more just, more kindly? Has all the tremendous work of science, which I admire as much as any one, brought us an inch nearer to the solution of the great problem of "What is God, what are we?" Does not science, by its very refusal to recognize this problem as a problem, show its own inadequacy and with it the inadequacy of its method, the extolling of experience? Will science never understand what was elementary to Kant, that our knowledge, even though it begins with experience, is not entirely based on or derived from experience?

Basil: No indeed, we shall not. It would be a betrayal of our heritage if we did. For us Galileo and Newton have not lived in vain. We put our trust in what we can see or hear, we are satisfied with what nature tells us in experience, and we do not possess the conceit of the philosophers who think that their own mind can reveal to them truths about the universe without experience which carried that truth.

Clarence: Why do you become so personal? I could retaliate and speak of the conceit of the scientist which seems to my mind more rampant at the present moment than the conceit of the philosopher. Science has come to be regarded as the new god. You may ask any question you like and you will hear that Science, with a capital S, gives such and such an answer; and this answer will be accepted, however silly it may be, because it is given in the name of science. However, personal recriminations will lead us nowhere. I will rather tell you where your scientific conceit prevents you from facing facts and problems. How can you, on a purely empirical basis, derive real values? What place has the Good in a purely scientific and empirical system?

Algernon: You mean this as a purely rhetorical question. But if you will bear with me, I shall try to give you some sort of an answer which may help to bridge the gulf which separates your two points of view from each other. I am not a philosopher nor a scientist, but a psychologist. But in my profession I have to deal with problems which concern you both, and to make my theories so that they do justice to both your points of view. I may have to lead you over devious routes, but if you begin to lose patience, remember that a frontal attack is not always the best way of storming a citadel.

Basil: I shall be glad to listen, although I believe your point of view will be so similar to mine that it will leave Clarence quite unaffected.

Clarence: Go on. I have often been wondering what contribution modern psychology could make to the theory of value.

Algernon: In some sense or other we all agree that we must start from experience. Let us therefore choose some characteristic value-experience, and see where it will lead us in our theorizing. I suggest as such a starting point the veneration of a disciple for his master.

Basil: From what point of view do you want this discussed, that is, which part of the experience would you call a value-experience?

Algernon: You are right, our case needs careful analysis. On the one hand we find the disciple attributing a very high value to his master; on the other hand, we have an experience, that of respecting the superior, which in itself deserves to be called valuable. But since the first is indisputable we shall begin with it. What does it mean that the disciple attributes a high value to the master?

Basil: Nothing but that the master as a stimulus arouses in the disciple certain positive emotions, or a blend of positive and negative ones, as when he is oppressed by the master.

Algernon: I don't think your case is as simple as all that. You cannot say: Attribution of value to X is identical with emotion in Y. There may be a connection between the two but you will have to explore the nature of this connection before we make any progress.

Basil: Of course I never meant anything else. I shall, as you did, call the master X and the disciple Y. Then I shall describe the behavior of Y, who attributes value to X, somewhat like this: Y has a need to love and to serve. X comes along, accepts Y's service, and thereby becomes at the same time the recipient of Y's love. Y's two strivings find their fulfilment; Y is satisfied, and he projects the satisfaction, a purely subjective state, onto X. How little this subjective feeling of Y's has to do with any "objective" value of X's is shown in all those complex cases where the same person X is found to be anything but valuable by persons other than Y.

Algernon: I must confess that I find a good many holes in the armour of your argument. Let me begin with the first: Why does Y give his love and service to X rather than to anyone else?

Basil: That is impossible to say without exact knowledge of the individual case. A simple possibility, however, is that X was the first person willing to accept Y's service. I cannot believe for a moment that, as you seem to imply, X must possess some particular characteristics in order to gain a disciple. When we see what kind of people do find followers one has to admit that the popular leader need not be a person distinguished by what *you* would call value.

Algernon: Precisely. And yet I must insist on my first question: Why does a man find disciples? All through the course of history there have been leaders who have had as many ardent followers as bitter enemies. Let us consider a single leader, then you will admit, of course, that the army of his followers would dwindle if they all had the same opinion of him as his enemies. Trite as this seems it elucidates my argument. Let us call the leader L, that is, the man as he was born, educated, etc., or in the words of Oliver Wendell Holmes: the man as God sees him, or in the terminology of many psychologists:

the man as a possible stimulus. What he is really like no one can *know*. His followers know L_f, his enemies L_e, that is, L as both of them, often on the ground of personal acquaintance-ship, think he is. It is clear that L_f is very different from L_e, and it is also clear that this difference accounts for the fact that some mén are followers of L, whereas others are not. Therefore the relation between master and disciple is not based on purely arbitrary characteristics.

Basil: Of course, if you look at it in this way, it is not. But the L_f and the L_e are all subjective and dependent on the peculiarities of the individuals. And if an individual is in the condition we have assumed for our old friend Y, his X_y will very easily have features which will elicit love and service. But X_y is a consequence of Y's desire for love and service, but not the service the result of X_y. Altogether I can only see that my cause has been strengthened, since in shifting value from X to X_y you have substituted for something objective, X, something subjective, X_y, and thereby even emphasized my contention that values are purely subjective.

Algernon: Again you seem to me to be going too fast. True enough, I have introduced a subjective factor into the value situation, which in your original account it did not contain. But this new subjectivity is not the same as your old one. You claimed values to be subjective in that they arose through purely individual peculiarities as the result of objective stimulation, the same objective stimulus arousing an experience of positive value in one group of individuals, of negative in another, and no value experience in a third. Because of diversity in the reaction to one and the same stimulus you concluded that the value experiences could not reside in the objective stimulus but existed in, and for, the individuals only. Moreover, since the individuals may have developed their peculiarities without regard to the present stimulus, the connection between stimulus and value-experience is, in principle, arbitrary, and values *a fortiori* purely relative or subjective. But the subjectivity which I introduced by connecting the value not with the stimulus X but with the phenomenal object X_y—which is a process occurring in Y and so far subjective—changes at least one of the aspects of your picture. Even you agreed that Y's admiration for X is intrinsically connected with certain properties of X_y, although you maintained that these particular properties of X_y were the effect rather than the cause of Y's admiration. You said: X_y with his admirable qualities is a result of Y's desire for love and service, and not his love and service a result of X_y. I can agree to that interpretation as being true in many cases without admitting that it is universally true. But even in those cases where I accept it, your interpretation has implications which lead far beyond what you were intent on proving. For if certain characteristics of X_y, his lovableness and his leadership, are the result of Y's desire for love and service, then the relation between my love and the quality of the object of my love, between my readiness to serve and the qualities of him I call my master are no longer arbitrary! If my desire for love creates an object for its fulfilment, this object must have lovable features. Thus, although you remain within the province of an individual subject's experience you have reached some general, objective, propositions like: only lovable objects are being loved, contemptible ones despised, holy ones worshipped.

Basil: This may be sound psychology, although I am not prepared to admit it without further consideration. But I cannot see how these propositions can be called objective when they apply so manifestly to events within individuals! All you say is that individuals are so constituted that they can love the lovable only, but it is just as possible that other individuals, perhaps the inhabitants of Mars or some other planet, are made differently so that they would love the odious, admire the contemptible, and be disgusted with the beautiful.

Algernon: I can easily tell you in what sense my propositions are not subjective, because there are different senses to your assertion. On the one hand we call a judgment subjective if, given the material of the judgment, different subjects may give different judgments. The difficulty of this definition is that it is not possible to decide whether really the same material was involved in those different judgments. When you say that the taste of tomatoes is good, and I that it is not, how can we know that we both experience the same taste? It is at least possible that if tomatoes had the same taste to me that they have to you, I might like them and vice versa. I feel convinced that the old dictum, *de gustibus non est disputandum*, becomes in a great many cases an untruth. The adage derives its plausibility from the fact that we continually fail to distinguish between the objects *per se*, O, and the objects as they are given to, or experienced by, the subjects, the O_n. By assuming in each particular case that the O_n and the O are identical we find different judgments passed upon the identical O, and therefore conclude that these judgments are subjective in the above sense. As long as the judgment is intrinsically related to its matter and not only extrinsically caused by it, the same O_n must give rise to the same judgment and this whole kind of subjectivity disappears. Subjective, however, may have another sense, in which it refers not to the dependence of the judgment upon the subject but to the dependence of the matter of the judgment upon him. In this sense, truly, my propositions are subjective, but this subjectivity, as our first argument has shown, is fully compatible with logical objectivity. Otherwise expressed, locus and occasion of the occurrence of the matter of the judgment has nothing to do with the objectivity of a judgment.

But in the second part of your argument you have said more —you have introduced the possibility of Martians who would hate the lovable and abhor the beautiful. Thereby you have tried to destroy if not the objectivity, at least the generality of my propositions. This leads me to introduce a new distinction, namely, that between judgments about occasions and judgments independent of occasions. A judgment of the first kind is: the temperature of this room is at the present moment 72 degrees. A judgment of the second kind: if one compresses a gas, its temperature rises. Therefore your argument might be expressed by saying that my propositions were judgments about occasions and not independent of occasions, the occasions being human beings.

Basil: Let me state my case more completely. I must begin with your distinction of the O and the O_n and connect it with your other distinction of judgments about occasions and such without reference to occasions. Your example of the former, the present temperature of this room, will serve my purpose very well. For we are all forced to agree to the statement although each of us only knows his own O_n. There must, then, be cases, in which the different O_n's are equal, because otherwise the judgments would not be equal. And therefore it is a question to investigate which O_n's are equal and which not, and I would say judgment is objective when all our O_n's are practically equal. I would then go on to your second class of judgments and say that your so-called judgments without reference to occasions are in reality nothing but judgments about occasions; your grammatical form of the conditional sentence, your if-so, is only a convenient form of speaking about many occasions at the same time. I deny your proposition that the law about pressure and temperature would be true if it were impossible ever to compress a gas. How should we know? The concrete occasion is our ultimate appeal and no knowledge is more secure than this ultimate appeal can make it. Therefore the alleged objectivity of your propositions about the relation of love to the lovable means nothing. Either the lovable is an O_n which is different from subject to subject or at least such that we have no evidence whatever to believe that they are equal, in that case, according to my definitions the judgments would be subjective. Or, even if I grant this possibility of obtaining evidence for the equality of all the lovablenesses-sub-n,[1] then your proposition would be a proposition about the occasion: human beings.

Algernon: I am almost sorry that I turned the argument in the direction it has now taken, for it tends to involve us in a laborious discussion of the theory of science. Thus the relation which you established between judgments about occasions and such without reference to them might be easily inverted. To come back to the temperature in this room, all you have proved with regard to its objectivity is that all persons taking a thermometer reading would give the same figure. But to call this temperature involves a highly complex system of concepts, all based on if-so statements. Without this if-so knowledge no thermometers could have been built and therefore the temperature O_n which vary from individual to individual could not have been replaced by such which for all practical purposes are equal for all subjects.

Clarence: Permit me to interrupt. After all, all scientific judgments apply to some real occasions. Therefore it seems to me simpler to eliminate the real occasions altogether by turning to judgments whose material can never be given in reality, as mathematical judgments. We should turn from *vérités de fait*—and after all all scientific propositions are such—to *vérités de raison.* Everybody agrees that, *e.g.,* no circle in the strict mathematical sense exists, and yet we can prove that such a circle is the figure which with a given length encloses the greatest area. No induction was necessary to find this proposition. No induction is capable of proving it. On the contrary, wherever in a given occasion, mass bounded by boundary of unchangeable length distributes itself in a circle, we know that it has taken up the greatest possible area. Such judgments prove that the general proposition is not the same as an abbreviated sum of

---

[1] I shall use this terminology in conformity with X_y, O_n (pronounced "X-sub-y," "O-sub-n"). Then "lovableness-sub-n," is lovableness as contained in the experience of a person, or a "circle-sub-n," a circle as it appears to one.

the particular ones, as our friend B claimed. We have knowledge of universals independent of our knowledge of particular real things.

Basil: I will use A's [1] weapons against you. Will you please tell me which circle you mean? Yours, mine, or whose? According to your own admission it must be somebody's, since you stated explicitly that a circle had no real existence.

Clarence: I thought all the time that A was helping your case far too much. I am by no means concerned with yours or mine or anybody's circle, but with the circle as such, with the "ideal object" circle, as it has been called. My circle, your circle, in short the circle-sub-n is an object of psychology, but the circle I am speaking about is the circle of mathematics, and for this circle it is quite irrelevant whether you think of it in visual terms as a black line on white, or a white line on black, or in words or concepts. Moreover, if you have a visual image of a circle it would never be a perfect circle since as an event in reality it could never have the perfection of an ideal object. All our circles-sub-n may and will be different, but the *intentional* object, the *circle*, will have the same properties. We must never confuse the psychological datum with the object that is intended by the psychological datum, a confusion which A has neglected as much as you. But I should like to know what A would say to your argument, for I have no doubt that A agrees with me about the difference between the subject-dependent circles-sub-n and the non-subjective circle.

Algernon: I agree that our mathematical propositions about circles are certainly not identical with every kind of proposition about the sub-n-circles and I further agree that mathematical propositions are examples *par excellence* of judgments without reference to occasions, or if-so judgments, and if you like *vérités de raison*. On the other hand, I see this admission in the light of a problem, not in the light of a solution. For, after all, all

[1] In the future the names of the three persons will be abbreviated in the text as A, B and C respectively.

we know directly are sub-n-objects. And even the absolute objects which we try to discover in science or to explain in mathematics are in some way sub-n-objects. This is the old idealist argument although I do not think that it proves idealism.

Clarence: Could you then say that before Lindemann's proof the squaring of the circle was still possible, or that before Descartes, the circle did not have the property of being expressed by the simple equation?

Algernon: Most certainly.

Clarence: But then you treat mathematics as though it were psychology. I never considered you such an extreme defender of psychologism. As I understand mathematics, it does not treat the circle of Archimedes or of Descartes or of Lindemann, but *the* circle.

Algernon: I am afraid, as long as I stay within the realm of mathematics I can attach to your term "the circle" only one meaning: *viz.*, the circle of the most advanced mathematician of the time. Most certainly future generations will discover properties of circles (or of other curves) entirely unknown to us. It seems to me meaningless to say that *the* mathematical circle possesses these properties now, since the discovery of these properties implies changes of the circle concepts which we cannot even divine. But in another sense I am willing to admit to you that a circle, even before any human being inhabited the earth, had all the properties which mathematics will ever discover, but then I am no longer speaking of the mathematical circle but of a real, natural occasion of circularity. Wherever distribution of matter occurred according to a minimum or maximum principle the result was (approximately) circular, just because the circle has this maximum property, although it has been proved only in the last century.

Clarence: So you are not only a "psychologist" but also a naturalist. I had put such hopes in you and now I fail to see any difference between you and B. You can defend this position on its psychological side only by neglecting again my distinction between the psychological datum and the object which it intends, toward which it points, and your position on its naturalistic side seems to lead inevitably to a denial of an essential difference between science as a system of *vérités de fait* and of mathematics as a system of *vérités de raison*.

Algernon: And this is precisely the aim of my argument, although I see the relation between science and mathematics quite differently from B who would probably agree with me in the attempt to abolish the ultimate separation of these two branches of our knowledge. But to come back to your first challenge: your distinction between the psychological datum and its intentional object has never been really clear to me. How can my psychological datum point to something else which is not also, in some way, a psychological datum? How can I derive from psychological data of circles propositions about intentional circle objects, unless the psychological data had in themselves properties which led us to state our propositions? And if they have, why do we need the intentional objects to explain our knowledge about circles?

Clarence: I shall not stress the point at the moment except by reminding you that you will have some difficulty in proving that your psychological data have the same properties as the objects toward which they point. On the face of it, it looks much more plausible to say that these properties are quite different. Evidence the fact that the O_n may all be different from each other and yet all point to an identical O. If, on the other hand, you ask me how a psychological datum can point toward something different from it, I can only answer that I do not know, and that this fact belongs among those which have to be accepted as fundamental facts, just as red has to be accepted as red and cannot be defined or explained.

However, I want to take you up on another point. You made two statements with regard to circles: you said that mathematically speaking the circle had no other properties than those that were known by the science of mathematics at a given time, but that as a physical object or occurrence the circle would have all the properties that could ever be discovered about it, and you exemplified this statement by your reference to the maximum-minimum properties of the circle. Now I happen to have read some Gestalt psychology, and I remember well that you ascribe to the circles-sub-n which occur in perception this very maximum-minimum property. As a matter of fact you teach that circles are perceived so readily, in preference to other figures, just because of this maximum-minimum property, which you sometimes call simplicity. But then you make two conflicting statements about circles. The circle-sub-n as an object of the psychologist always had this property whereas the circle-sub-n as a mathematical object did not have it before it was discovered in the last century.

Algernon: I am delighted at this argument. I believe it will help us greatly in our discussion of values. But since what you just said is but an application of my general position to a special occasion I do not see how it can embarrass me. The special occasion which you selected is that of somebody's perceiving a circle. This is in the same sense an occasion as the soap bubble taking on the shape of a sphere. But the *raison d'être* of an event is not at the same time necessarily the cause of its being known, or of its being a piece of knowledge.

Clarence: I heartily agree to this; but you with your naturalistic bias should have some difficulty with such a statement, because knowledge, cognition, must for you be just another process obeying natural laws.

Algernon: Quite, but I do not see how this is to embarrass me. Since you know so much of modern psychology, I need hardly remind you that much of the psycho-physical organization is given to us, in our consciousness, only as the finished product: we have no idea how it has come about and can make entirely false theories about its origin. This is true of practically all fundamental aspects of perception. Think of the optical illusions. Two parallel lines appear under proper conditions convergent or divergent, that is all we see; and the forces that make them so convergent or divergent have to be discovered by indirect methods.

However, if all our experience were of this kind, betraying in its finished state nothing of the forces that made it what it is, it would be vastly different from the experience we know. I suppose that one could find good examples of cases where the forces which created the product are at least partly revealed in consciousness even in the field of purely spatial non-temporal perception. But when time enters, and we experience not merely stable events, objects at rest, but a becoming, moving to and fro, hither and thither, we do at the same time experience the forces that are responsible for the change, the motion, the growth. We can make straight lines bend by introducing a new environment. Then we see not only the process of bending but also the forces in the field to which the straight lines have to yield. I need only mention briefly that this is the rule where our own egos-sub-n are concerned. I feel cold and I move to the fire. Is that all my experience tells me? Perhaps in some cases, if, for instance, I am engaged in an animated conversation. But in other situations it is not. I do not only experience the sequence of a sensation of discomfort and a locomotion toward the fire, but also a very close connection between these two events: I experience myself as going toward the fire *because* I am cold. No doubt this is the true explanation which a scientist who could not understand my language would also discover after many experiments. But if it is true, then my experience does sometimes give me direct knowledge of more than factual sequences.

Basil: You speak as though a philosopher whom you pretend to like so much had never lived. Has not David Hume once for all refuted such arguments? Has he not shown that we can have no knowledge of causality, that all we know is a succession of events? Your last argument, moreover, went, I believe inadvertently, beyond the boundaries which you had so carefully drawn. At least to me it sounded as though you claimed that events in your world, sub-n-events, contained knowledge about real events. For if the psychologists find out the causes of your approach to the fire, this fire is no more your fire, nor is this your ego-sub-A, whereas when you feel uncomfortable and attracted by the fire you are dealing with ego-sub-A and fire-sub-A. Previously you tried to convict me of the fallacy of confusing the one with the other. Are you not now doing this yourself?

Algernon: I will admit that I made the transition from the phenomenal to the real sphere without announcing it, and you are right in telling me that I should not do without justification, what I have criticized as unjustified in others. Before I defend myself, however, I will argue your first point, your appeal to Hume.

If you turn to Section VII, Part I of his *Enquiry* where he states his arguments in great detail, you will find that their plausibility derives purely from an illegitimate transition from the sub-n to the real world. What does Hume want to prove: that power cannot be an idea of consciousness. And he proves it by saying that we cannot understand the idea in our objective picture of the world.

However, I claimed that we sometimes can glean properties of the real world from properties of the phenomenal. I shall try to defend this claim now. Let us return to my example of the person shivering from cold who goes near the fire. We said that in his world his Ego-sub-n was attracted-sub-n by the fire-sub-n. Now we study the same person quite scientifically. And we reach a conclusion like this: the heat radiating from the burning logs excites warm spots on his skin, excitations are started in a number of afferent nerves toward certain nervous centers, and are switched over to other centers which in their turn are so connected with the muscles of the limbs that locomotion toward the fire ensues. This explanation seems to fit the facts; at first sight it seems in good harmony with the person's experience. The warmth of the fire, which was an attraction—object-sub-n, becomes now a stimulus which has the same result as the attraction. However, this neurological theory has no place for one item of experience, namely the experience of the connection between the attractiveness of the fire and the motion, the experience of the "because of" of the "pull toward." There is no such pull in our reflex theory. Nervous currents flow along pathways of least resistance and throw those muscles into action to which those pathways lead them. I shall not argue against this theory; I shall merely confront it with the person's experience. If it were true, the experience would lie. For it would evoke for us the illusion of an intrinsic connection where in reality there was but a factual sequence. Our experience would *not* indicate anything about the real world. Rather in view of this should we have to mistrust our experience because we do not trust a person whom we have found lying.

And this has been the attitude of the positivist, an attitude based on many cases where we had been mistaken in our implicit faith in our own experience. No science would have arisen had we not learned to be critical toward our experience, and even experience of the personal kind, such as served for our argument, has been shown up as a liar all too often to allow us to accept its words at their face value. We rationalize a good many of our actions; that is, the real origins of those actions are not what we believe them to be.

Basil: If you go as far as that, I believe I can grant you your ideas of power and so on. If they are to remain purely sub-n phenomena and not to be used for the construction of a real world I can't see that they can do any harm, and since I have to admit your criticism of Hume I am quite willing to accept them.

Algernon: Your peace proposal was premature and cannot be accepted. On the one hand you don't know what a Pandora's box you have accepted in accepting the sub-n world with all its characters. For the sub-n world is in its way also real; it occurs at a certain place and at a certain time. Therefore, if you accept all its properties you admit their reality in that sphere, although in that sphere only. And thereby you are forced into a dualism of mind rich in qualities and intrinsic relations, and matter which lacks all these finer aspects. The theologians will hail you as their brother with your distinction of brute matter and divine mind. But that was said prematurely. You interrupted me in my argument about the use of experience for the construction of the real world. I had just emphasized one aspect, certainly important and significant, namely the necessity of criticism. But I maintain that it is only one aspect. For, after all, all our data are data-sub-n; we have no other from which to build or construct. And therefore no criticism of experience can lead us to reject experience in toto for the construction of our world picture, unless we renounce such construction and maintain the position of Gorgias. Therefore we have to be critical instead of skeptical, *i.e.*, we have to examine when and how we are to employ our experience.

The simplest way is to select certain experiences and to reject all others. The ground on which such selection could be made is reliability: such experiences which never lie shall be the only ones admitted. However, in the first place it seems that such experiences do not exist. Nineteenth century science may be said to have had an unshakable trust in them, but the development of modern science which was partly ruled by the impulse to eliminate more and more experiences seems to prove that on this path we will be led into a quagmire. This is at least my interpretation of the so-called principle of indeterminacy which has given rise to so much unwarranted speculation. But since physics is not my field I return to psychology. And there I find that the type of neurological theory which I have briefly sketched is utterly insufficient, in constant conflict with facts. Therefore my suggestion is that we reëxamine our method and that we become as critical in our *rejection* of experience as we had become in our acceptance of it. If even the most analytic kind of experience may sometimes deceive us about the real world, then the fact that other types of experience have often deceived us does not warrant us to assume that they are always deceptive. We may at least try to use them always critically, always aware of the possibility that we may be deceived, just as we may be deceived by any other type of experience. When I said that the approach to the fire was to be explained as a means of transforming discomfort into comfort, I was making but a comparatively superficial use of the principle. But at least this explanation of real behavior is in conformity with the feel of experienced behavior. You want a proof of this assertion? Here it is. I simply compare my theory with the old reflex theory. Suppose it were possible to change arbitrarily the connections between centers so that now the excitation would travel most readily to centers which would move the body away from the fire. Then according to the old theory a person shivering with cold would move into a cold corner, whereas according to my theory he would move toward the grate as before. All experimental evidence which we possess is in favor of my theory. Thus according to it the person will in reality do what he feels himself wanting to do. This theory started from characteristics in the sub-n world, the attractiveness of the fire, which had not been utilized in the reflex theory, and it derives its advantage from this fact. Therefore I hope I have justified my claim that my experience does sometimes give me knowledge of more than factual sequences of events.

Clarence: I must confess that the whole discussion of movements has not interested me very much. I do not see how it is connected with our main theme, the theory of value or of mathematical truth. Moreover, since originally you intended to mention the Ego activities only briefly, you must have felt the same. Can't you now take up your thread where you dropped it and show the connection of your psychology with logic and ethics?

Algernon: That is what I want to do. I mention action only as a case where experience reveals certain intrinsic connections in reality. Probably you are right. I should not have introduced the topic for it was sure to lead to a long argument. Now I shall take up thinking which has a close relationship to logic. My question is: What is the foundation of the certainty which we ascribe to logical arguments?

Basil: I cannot give you an answer right away, but I suspect the answer will have to be purely psychological, *i.e.,* the feeling of certainty, which is after all a purely subjective feeling arises because of the way in which less familiar facts follow on more familiar facts so that the tone of familiarity, of belief, which has accrued to the former in the course of our experience, is transferred to the latter.

Clarence: Please do not confuse the issue with your unsupported faith in psychological laws. What happens is that we apprehend a logical connection, a connection which subsists independently of our apprehension, and for which the feeling of certainty is more or less irrelevant. The truth of a proposition is quite independent of our knowledge of the truth, just as your existence is quite independent of my knowledge of your existence.

Algernon: I understand your wrath. B's argument was so vague as not to be helpful. But you evaded my question as much at least as he. I did not ask what the status of a proved proposition was, but wherein our conviction of the stringency of the argument was based.

Clarence: I think Husserl has answered your question in his discussion of logical evidence. Evidence is the act of identification of what is merely intended by thought and what is given to thought. Wherever these two coincide completely, wherever the *Gegenstand* is given in the same way in which it was intended, we have evidence and as its necessary correlate truth. Evidence, then, is no feeling fortuitously attached to acts of judgment, but the very coincidence of what is given with what is intended.

Algernon: In what universe of discourse does this coincidence take place? I should be willing to discuss this theory as a psychological theory, were it not that Husserl has expressly denied that it was meant to be psychological. But perhaps if I tell you what I think about my question you can connect your and Husserl's point of view with mine. My answer is extremely simple. I say: the "feeling" of certainty is the direct result of the organization of the different objects. This organization is due to the relevant characteristics of these objects, and thus the feel of the force of an argument is the reflection in experience of the forces which bring about the organization. You remember that I laid so much stress on those cases of action in which the real causes of actions were revealed in consciousness as sub-n causes; you have not forgotten my example of the approach to the fire. Intrinsic properties of objects determine their connection.

Clarence: Very good. But how do the properties of ideal objects determine a feeling of conviction which is a psychological process? Are you not now transgressing from one universe of discourse into another?

Algernon: I thought you would know that the objects I thought of were sub-n objects, therefore certainly not ideal in the sense that they are timeless and spaceless. They are events here and now, connected with real non-sub-n events which we call brain processes. My argument means: these events have intrinsic properties, both as sub-n objects and as brain processes, which determine other objects, or other properties of themselves. And this determination is experienced in the clarity of perfect conviction.

Basil: Aren't you proving too much? So far as I can see your theory has two implications which are contrary to fact. On the one hand all thinking should be true thinking, and on the other the experience of a conviction should never lie. And you will admit that we often are thoroughly convinced of matters which we afterwards discover to be false even in the realm of mathematics.

Algernon: Of course I grant you your fact. But I do not admit that it refutes my view. Let me recall that many organizations do not betray their origin—even a new thought which has arisen on the ground of other thoughts may emerge without the experience of its whence and whither. What the layman—and certain philosophers—call intuition is such a case in hand. Such intuitions are often perfectly correct. I believe that many a mathematician has made his discovery in this way; he has seen the truth without knowing why it was the truth, *i.e.,* how it was connected with established knowledge. On the other hand such organizations, such intuitions, may be wrong. That means, they owe their emergence not exclusively to the material which appears in the organization but to other factors, alien to the proper material, as well. That is why we cannot trust these intuitions. Moreover, if an organization is produced by a number of factors, the effectiveness of some of them may be a sub-n object, may be indicated in consciousness, but not of the others. Consequently we will feel strong conviction and may yet be wrong. This, I believe, answers also your objection that my theory must exclude false thinking.

Basil: But if you grant that much, how can you know whether any one of your convictions is absolutely right?

Algernon: There is no absolute answer to this question. The only method is to make every part connection explicit, to produce every step in an argument. Not that new ideas arise in the way that we limit our progress to minute steps. That would lead nowhere. For at any moment an infinite number of steps is possible if we do not see beyond the first one. We must give all the relevant factors a chance to operate and try to prevent all the non-relevant ones from interfering. In both tasks we may fail pitiably. But we may also succeed, and the success will prove itself to be such by the fact that it will persist, that no other factor will be able to shake it. Intrinsic properties of the organization decide whether it is a true organization, *viz.,* an organization due exclusively to relevant factors. Such properties are: stability, cohesiveness, indispensability of every part, to name but three of the most obvious ones. The search for criteria of truth should be a search for such properties of organization. Of course I must add: complete truth is only possible where the number of relevant factors is relatively limited. And since reality confronts us with an indefinite number of factors, truth is only possible by limitation, which in itself is untruth. Progress of knowledge is partly a widening of these limits.

Basil: Are you not a rationalist of the old school? Have you learned nothing from modern science which has appealed to experience and found speculation to be the worst guide to truth?

Clarence: Are you not a crude naturalist who has not even understood the difference between the *vérités de faits*, the facts, the existing, and the *vérités de raison*, the ideal essences, the subsisting?

Algernon: I can answer you both at the same time. For although you accuse me of two apparently quite different sins, you share, up to a certain point, your opinions about facts. In that respect you agree better one with the other than either agrees with me. For what are these facts of yours, worshipped by B and somewhat despised by C? You seem to forget that primarily they are sub-n facts, whatever their connection with real facts may be. How does any science arise, how is any knowledge gained? Let me once more briefly refer to mathematics, in particular to geometry. For even here an extreme empiricism has been defended by such eminent mathematicians as my old and revered friend Moritz Pasch. He taught that the fundamental or "nuclear" concepts and propositions, upon which the whole structure of geometry rests, are ultimately derived from objects of our daily experience. They cannot be defined or proved, but merely pointed at. His case for empiricism was as good as any I know, but he committed the same mistake about fact and observation of which I judge you two guilty. Instead of considering sub-n objects, he was satisfied with stating the togetherness of an observer and a real object. But this is not enough. If somebody points to a straight line and says this is a straight line, then I may still get an entirely wrong idea of the straight line just as I may fail to understand a joke. Thus I might see a plain mark when shown a straight line, and have no experience of its *linear* and *straight* character. Now, the observations which form the foundation of the nuclear propositions could never be derived by me as long as I saw the object which was pointed out to me, as a mere mark, therefore, whoever first stated these propositions or used them implicitly must have seen the linear aspect. And it is the nature of this sub-n object which determines the origin and development of geometry. The error committed by empiricism is this. It confuses experience, as a sub-n datum with a non-sub-n object which has been constructed out of such experience, and then says that experience is nothing but the passive reception of this non-sub-n object. This is so abstract that you will not connect much meaning with it. I shall try to clarify my statement by one of the most fundamental concepts of geometry, the concept of *between*. If I had a straight line between the two points A and B, and C is a third point on this line, then it is evident that C lies between A and B, the "betweenness" seems a matter of very simple observation. But when I begin to look at it from the point of view of the sub-n objects the case begins to change. To call the location of C as between A and B presupposes a particular type of sub-n experience, which, because it is so very easily realized, seems to be the only possible one. But I would claim that not only would this last conclusion be wrong but also that at a more primitive stage our line with its three points would appear in a shape which would not allow of the clear between. The between, simple as it is, presupposes that in the total unit which becomes for the moment the object of our inspection, three parts are kept separate from each other and yet in a certain communication. If they were entirely separate then no relation would exist between them and no between could

arise. If entirely connected they would be too unified to lead to the between. Instead of relations between them we would experience total characters. Probably you won't believe me. Let me therefore show to you this figure which is only slightly more complicated by containing four points instead of three. It is quite easy —●————●—●————————●— to see C be-
                                          A   B C   D
tween B and D or B between A and C, or finally B and C between A and D. Notice how the aspect, the organization of the whole, changes for each of these three impressions. But now try and see simultaneously C between B and D and B between A and C and you will find it far more difficult.

Clarence: I am growing impatient. What have the psychological changes of perceptual organization to do with the fact which you, I hope, won't contest, that any of the four relations you mentioned is as good, as true as any other?

Algernon: Don't spoil my argument by your impatience. I made this little experiment, if you will honor it by that name, only to show you that not all possible between-relations are *necessarily* contained in sub-n objects at any given time. And if this is true for some, it may as well be true for any. Again you forget that the between-relationship is part and parcel of your particular intellectual equipment. But my point is that the between-relationship occurred once for the first time in this world of ours. On the ground of your between-relationship which you owe to the intellectual history of the human race you say that it existed all the time and that because of its existence you could observe it. This is, at least, Pasch's mistake. The sub-n objects had to be organized in certain ways in order to possess the between-relationship. In other words: cognition of a fact is not the passive acceptance of something which is there, but the coming into existence of something which was not there. If we agree on this we can at once accept Pasch's theory of mathematics, leaving aside the problem of the process of proof. If from a finite number of nuclear concepts and propositions a whole unlimited system of other properties may be developed, then organized wholes must have the property of being capable of forming under favorable conditions ever new organizations in accordance with their own particular properties. I am willing to accept the title of naturalist which C conferred on me, because I believe that nature is not a mass of chunks without any intrinsic connection. The organized wholes of which I said just now that they can form ever new organizations in accordance with their own properties, are not limited to the realm of sub-n events. What is true of one part of the universe, the sub-n part, may be equally true of other parts. And I am also willing to be called a rationalist for the very same reason. Less paradoxically expressed, I believe the contrast between naturalism and rationalism is artificial and unjustified. At least for the natural events which I have called the sub-n mathematical objects, it seems to me proved that they are not a mere conglomerate. And withal I can be a perfectly good empiricist, meaning by this that I must subject my organizations to constant checks, to outside pressures which may change them. Therefore I am as hostile as B to most historical systems of rationalistic philosophy, because these systems claimed a range of application which they did not have. But if we consider that the application of Euclidean geometry to the physics of the universe has been found to be false, we see how difficult it is to avoid the errors of the philosophical systems. My claim, therefore, is not that we can use any systematic character which we find in our sub-n objects to construct a picture of the universe. This to satisfy B. My claim is solely that we have to *test* the applicability of such rational features of our sub-n objects instead of rejecting them at the start. For if we find rationality in one part of the universe it seems to me to be equally false to maintain that all the rest of the universe does *not* have rationality as it is to infer that the whole universe and every one of its aspects must have it. Moreover, to maintain that rationality may be a general character of the universe, in the sense that it is not restricted to the realm of the mental, is not the same as claiming that any particular kind of rational connection which we find in our sub-n objects must have its counterpart in non-sub-n objects. Thus I hope to have reconciled C. The rationalist doctrine: *ordo et connectio idearum idem est ac ordo et connectio rerum*, is both true and false from my point of view. It is false if we mean by it that the nature of the universe can be discovered by mere speculation. It is true if we mean that the general characteristics which we discovered in our sub-n organization are also characteristics of the universe. For as I said before, if we treat our thoughts as events happening in the universe, then some parts of the universe have this characteristic of rationality, and we would need extra proof to maintain that all other parts are essentially different from them in this respect. But not only do we lack this proof, rather our knowledge of the universe points in the opposite direction. The most powerful method for dealing with the universe is mathematics. This means that nature must have certain characteristics to make it treatable by mathematical methods. It is this, I believe, Jeans means when he says God is a mathematician. In such a view the absolute cleavage between mind and matter, idea and reality, is abolished. The mind becomes part of a much larger reality, and matter finds itself endowed with characteristics which have been regarded as the privilege of mind.

Basil: I believe I see now the trend of your argument. You will proceed somewhat like this: Rationality as a subjective experience, or, as you say, a characteristic of the sub-n world, is to be used in constructing our picture of the non-sub-n world. Our subjective experience, or our sub-n world, also possesses instances of value. Therefore, value should be as little excluded from the real world as rationality. But I believe that your argument would be even more difficult to defend in the case of value than it was in the case of rationality.

Algernon: You have understood the drift of my argument, and I will admit that in the realm of value it becomes more difficult than it was in the field of cognition. But that must not

deter us from attempting to grapple with it. What I tried to
prove so far may be called the objectivity of rationality, of
necessity, of intrinsic relatedness, or whatever other name one
may choose. It is best defined by its opposition to the Humean
view which recognizes only subjective and extrinsic necessity.
Now I should prove the objectivity of value, or rather I should
explain what objectivity of value can mean. We found the objectivity of rationality in the objectivity of organization. And
we remember Keats's line, "Beauty is truth, truth beauty that
is all ye know on earth and all ye need to know." Therefore it
seems plausible to look for the objectivity of value in the objectivity of organization also.

Clarence: Do you not in this argument assume that value is
a concept with one connotation only? But the possibility exists
that different values may really be quite different. Keats speaks
of beauty, aesthetic value; but is it necessarily true that what
holds for this holds also for ethical or, if you like, religious
value?

Algernon: If value were founded in organization, then your
argument would mean that possibly organizations of essentially different types would be beautiful or ethically good,
whereas on the other hand it might also be possible that apart
from differences there might be common characteristics to
rational, aesthetic and ethical values apart from their differences. Could Keats have said: Virtue is truth, etc., with equal
right? The first problem for us, then, is whether the connection
between value and organization which I have postulated exists.
Let us go back to the propositions we established at the beginning of our discussion, *e.g.*, that only the lovable can be loved,
the noble worshipped, the beautiful admired. You remember
that these propositions referred to the lovable, noble, and beautiful as sub-n events. We must now raise the question: what is
lovable, noble, beautiful? It will help to recall our first example,
the loyalty of the disciple Y to his master X. What makes the
X_y noble? We shall compare X_y with X_z both Y and Z having

the same opportunity of observing X. We will further assume that Z far from being a disciple of X has a rather poor opinion of him. Therefore X_y is unequal to X_z, and different in a very characteristic aspect: X_y is an object of value, X_z not. Both Y and Z have, according to our hypothesis, received the same data about X, *viz.*, a, b, c, . . . n. Since, now, X_y is noble and X_z is not, the way in which these data have become organized in Y and Z must be different.

Basil: That does not follow at all. X may be fair and tall, Y might like fair and tall men, Z short and dark ones. Therefore X_y might be equal to X_z and yet be liked by Y and disliked by Z.

Algernon: That is perfectly possible, but it is not the case I am trying to discuss. Your argument would invalidate mine only if you claimed that all liking admiration, trust, were based on such fortuitous characteristics as the color of the hair or the size of stature. I was supposing that, at least for the sake of argument, we all admitted that there was such a thing, in the sub-n realm, as nobility, such that if it attached to any sub-n person in any person's experience this person would feel admiration, respect, affection for the sub-n person. And I wanted to prove that this nobility-sub-n is a characteristic of organization.

Clarence: May I anticipate in order to raise an objection: just as you tried to find properties of organization which would distinguish truth from falsehood, you will now search for similar ones to distinguish values from non-values. I may even venture a step further and predict that in the field of character and probably also of beauty you will find such a characteristic of value in the clarity, consistency and inevitability of the organization. I mean that a character would have this property if from one nucleus all his other properties would follow, so that his whole behavior would be consistent throughout. If you agree to this, what is your difference between the thoroughly

good and the thoroughly bad character, between God and
Satan?

Algernon: You have formulated what is perhaps the crucial
point in our whole discussion. Before I attempt to give you some
sort of an answer I will mention that the criterion which you
gave for value of character is by no means exhaustive, as you
will admit. You have for instance left out everything that per-
tains to "greatness." But we need not go into the study of character any further if we remember that so far our determinations
have been very incomplete. Even so your question is relevant;
there may be a great villain as well as a great and good man and
the one may be as consistent as the other. Otherwise expressed
two equally perfect organizations may have very different
values. Thus it seems as though the connection between value
and organization was not as close as I tried to make it. Nevertheless I shall make an attempt to save it. For this purpose I
shall advance two arguments which are not entirely unrelated
to each other. The first is comparatively simple. It is connected
with what was previously said about knowledge. You remember
the conclusion which I drew that perfect organization, perfect
knowledge, was possible only where the subject under investigation was limited, and that on the other hand every limitation was in itself a limitation of truth. We might argue similarly
about value. If we consider only one human person in isolation,
we limit our field of inquiry. If value belongs to the world it
will not necessarily belong to any special part however much
of the general characteristics of organization, typical of value,
it may possess. We shall have to view the individual person as
part of a larger whole. The first larger whole that would come
to mind is the group to which he belongs, or rather the many
groups of which he forms a part. Thereby the application of our
criterion becomes vastly more difficult, since the different groups
intersect and have, often enough, no clearly defined boundaries.
To escape from these difficulties one might substitute for all
these various groups, the family, the clubs and associations, the

national group, and all humanity. And then one would easily come to define as good what gives the greatest happiness to the greatest number, and a character as valuable according to the degree to which he contributes to this happiness. We are then back in a utilitarian or hedonistic ethics. I would agree to this tendency inasmuch as it claims that the individual organization alone is not sufficient. But I would emphatically disagree with the utilitarian conclusion. If the majority of mankind consisted of gangsters, would it still be good to increase the happiness of the greatest possible number? The weakness of this kind of utilitarianism derives to some extent from the fact that all humanity is not an organization to which the individual belongs with any degree of intimacy. It is a sum rather than a gestalt. When I speak of connectedness I mean real connectedness. And a concrete case will serve us better than an abstract generality.

Let us compare two thoroughly consistent characters with each other, Shylock on the one hand and Iago on the other. Both are not only consistent but also full of passion and strength, and yet of the two one only is a real villain. What is the reason of this difference in our judgment? To me it seems to be somewhat like this: for Iago there is nothing in the world more important than Iago. If he cannot get something, then nobody else must get it. The goal of his action is ultimately the full realization of what is Iago to the detriment of everything else. With Shylock it is quite different. He wants his pound of flesh not for personal motives, but in order that justice be done, and I mean by justice not the mere legal justice which consists in the carrying out of a particular contract, but the justice which makes one man as good as another and knows no distinction of race or nation. Shylock knows that if he had forfeited his own pound of flesh it would be extracted from him, and he resents this inequality not because it would injure him but because it degrades his race. Shylock's actions, then, as I understand them, are essentially different from Iago's. Unlike him he does not strive for an aggrandizement of his ego but for a better balance in the whole social structure. That his striving for justice leads him to exact an action which is at the same time an injustice, is his tragedy. But we must acknowledge the fact that in our world no complete justice is possible. Shylock's problem is insoluble and Portia's solution is as unjust as Shylock's own. Justice is balance. It is more than a metaphor that the goddess of justice holds a balance in her hand. It is a symbol, which is the expression in a new material of an essential characteristic of the objects symbolized. Injustice means loss of balance, means that small parts thrive at the expense of the whole. We might, then, try to define value of personality in terms of organization by transcending the limits of the individual person. It seems possible to define merits and faults of egoism and altruism from this point of view. But I am now concerned with wider issues. I can hear B say to himself all the time: Justice is only valuable because we like it for some utilitarian reason or other. I want to give a meaning to the statement that justice is objectively a value. What can I mean? Naturally I admit that as a rule mankind likes justice: God is just in many religions. But is this striving for justice really nothing but a striving for pleasure or utility? Not all thinkers have held that opinion: *Pereat mundus fiat justitia.* I shall then, until the contrary has been proved to me, hold to the belief that justice has been valued because it is justice and not because it is useful or pleasant. The striving for justice has led to many actions, it has produced— I admit rarely if ever without the concurrence of other factors —institutions which govern our daily lives, in short it has actually altered the real world. Don't object that the world has not become more just in the process. We might argue this point ad infinitum. But even if I grant it to you it means nothing; for at the same time the complexity of life has increased and thereby the possibility of injustice. What I am driving at is this: justice, a mere idea, has produced very material results. We cannot understand the results without taking account of the idea, and that means we cannot explain certain parts of the world at least without including value in the description of its dynamics. And then I shall ask again: Is this inclusion of value as an ontological category to be restricted to a part of reality, and if so to which?

As far as I can see our general ontological concepts, even our scientific ones, are all imbued with value. We speak of a world running *down* when we refer to the second law of thermodynamics, and we find Millikan trying to prove that the world does not only run down but at the same time runs *up*. Now this up and down means higher and lower value, and I believe some scientists will side with the defenders of the running down theory from a sort of emotional pessimism or skepticism as much as Millikan seems to defend the opposite view because of a strong theological optimism. The solution of the problem does not concern us here. No matter whether the world runs up or down it runs in a direction, and the direction of the run is a value aspect. The run down world would be an absolutely stable world, a world in which nothing more could happen, absolute balance, and yet . . . no value. The running up world might never come to an end, it can never reach stability because it would never be free of inequalities, of stresses and strains. The run down world ceases to be a gestalt, it would have attained thermodynamic equilibrium which is absolute lack of order. Running up is toward higher organization, running down toward lower; at the same time running up may never result in unchanging and unchangeable equilibrium whereas running down does. Therefore we might not be altogether right when we define perfection of organization by absolute stability and immutability. Brahma is probably not the most adequate conception of ultimate value. The same is true of personality, where mere consistency may not be the highest type of realization. *"Ich bin kein ausgeklügelt Buch . . ."* The statistically perfect organization means an end and stopping of process. But value seems to be dynamic, an aspect of a process rather than an object. This gives us another answer to the question: What is the difference between the villain and the good man? The actions of the villain, leading all to his greater satisfaction and enrichment, will stop with him. In the action system of the good man he is but a small part and therefore effects of his actions will go on.

But there arises still another difficulty in the metaphysics of value. Increase of organization of one part of the physical world occurs always at the cost of decrease of organization in other parts. That looks very much like the egotism of the villain, and if, therefore, we want to distinguish between him and the good man, or more generally between good and bad, or higher and lower organizations, we have to look for new characteristics. Possibly just this difference between the process coming to an end and the process that leads to ever new organizations is such a characteristic difference. However, I do not want to continue with this metaphysical argument. I would rather return to the epistemological aspects. My scientific creed is that the value concept has as good a claim to be used in the construction of the world picture as any other concept derived from sub-n experience. And at the same time I am convinced that all our general concepts are but dim reflections of reality. Concepts arise in thought, i.e., they are organizations of sub-n experience of a particular kind, produced under particular conditions. Compared with the original experience they are ever so much more clearly organized, but in this process of organization the original experience may have lost some of its most essential characteristics, essential as well in themselves as with regard to their epistemological applications. Humean causality and utilitarian value seem to me to illustrate my meaning equally clearly. If I am right both these concepts have lost their connection with the real experience altogether and have thereby also lost their use for an ontological theory. A scientific concept of causality need not at all be Humean. Gauss thought that the law of least action, the most general law physics knows in the realm of reversible processes, revealed the justice of God. This sounds mystic, but we can disregard the particular form of Gauss's belief and still see that his concept of causality was that of a rational causality. What is true of causality is equally true of value. Our value concepts are still very confused and yet they may have got hold of a corner of reality. Our value experience is better than our value concepts. It is one of the strongest forces of our lives. It will contain more of the real essence of that characteristic of the world which we shall, perhaps, eventually call value, but it need by no means be identical with it. I am so little of a subjectivist that I believe: value experiences themselves may, objectively, be either valuable or not.

Basil: I cannot say that I am convinced of all you said. But I have seen that my faith in experience was based on an inadequate understanding of experience. At first I thought that you were to take C's side, but then I felt deeply satisfied when I heard how much value you put on experience as you understand it. We scientists are not quite so bad as C would make us out to be. Often enough we feel dissatisfied with the world picture which we extract from our laboratories. But we mistrust our dissatisfaction. Having recognized the value of our scientific method, we are compelled by our intellectual honesty to stick to it and to be suspicious of anything that smacks of mysticism. If your ideas make it possible for us to remain loyal scientists and yet acknowledge values as realities, they will be welcomed by me.

Clarence: I can go as far in my assent as B. My situation at the beginning was different from his. Convinced as I was of the value of the scientific method, I was equally convinced of the truth of *a priori* propositions. And since science claimed as its realm the whole of existence, I needed another realm in which truth, value, and beauty, which we have omitted from our discussion, would find a place, the realm of *sub*sistence. What you are proposing is to give a place in *ex*istence to the objects which I considered as *sub*sistent, and to achieve this by

giving a different interpretation to existence from the one held
by the scientists. I do not know whether it will be possible to
make a finished picture out of your sketch, nor whether such a
finished picture would be true. But I will admit that your suggestion does not strike me any more as impossible as it did at
first, and that it has made me understand the aim of the scientist
better.

Algernon: It is good of you to grant me so much. Perhaps
you will allow me another minute to state three possible points
of view:

(1) Everything in the universe is merely contingent. If it were
so, the position which B defended would be true.

(2) The world of physics is contingent, but there are non-contingent objects in the universe. If this were true, a solution like
that defended by C would have to be found.

(3) There are non-contingent features in the world, both
physical and mental. Therefore no radical dualism either of
existence and subsistence, or of physical and mental, is necessary; and that is the possibility which I tried to defend.

VALUES AND IMPERATIVES

ALAIN LOCKE

Curriculum vitae: Born 1886, Philadelphia—Harvard A.B., 1907; graduate student Oxford 1907-10—Rhodes scholar from Pennsylvania—University of Berlin, 1910-11; Assistant Professor English and Philosophy, Howard University, 1912-16; Harvard Graduate School 1916-17—Ph.D. Harvard, 1918; Professor of Philosophy (Howard) 1918 to date. Author:—Race Contacts and Inter-racial Relations (1916); The Problem of Classification in Theory of Value (1918); The New Negro (1925); The Negro in America (1933); Frederick Douglass; a Biography of Anti-Slavery (1935).

I should like to claim as life-motto the good Greek principle,—*"Nothing in excess,"* but I have probably worn instead as the badge of circumstance,—*"All things with a reservation."* Philadelphia, with her birthright of provincialism flavored by urbanity and her petty bourgeois psyche with the Tory slant, at the start set the key of paradox; circumstance compounded it by decreeing me as a Negro a dubious and doubting sort of American and by reason of the racial inheritance making me more of a pagan than a Puritan, more of a humanist than a pragmatist.

Verily paradox has followed me the rest of my days: at Harvard, clinging to the genteel tradition of Palmer, Royce and Munsterberg, yet attracted by the disillusion of Santayana and the radical protest of James: again in 1916 I returned to work under Royce but was destined to take my doctorate in Value Theory under Perry. At Oxford, once more intrigued by the twilight of aestheticism but dimly aware of the new realism of the Austrian philosophy of value; socially Anglophile, but because of race loyalty, strenuously anti-imperialist; universalist in religion, internationalist and pacifist in world-view, but forced by a sense of simple justice to approve of the militant counter-nationalisms of Zionism, Young Turkey, Young Egypt, Young India, and with reservations even Garveyism and current-day "Nippon over Asia." Finally a cultural cosmopolitan, but perforce an advocate of cultural racialism as a defensive counter-move for the American Negro, and accordingly more of a philosophical mid-wife to a generation of younger Negro poets, writers, artists than a professional philosopher.

Small wonder, then, with this psychograph, that I project my personal history into its inevitable rationalization as cultural pluralism and value relativism, with a not too orthodox reaction to the American way of life.

VALUES AND IMPERATIVES

Alain Locke

All philosophies, it seems to me, are in ultimate derivation philosophies of life and not of abstract, disembodied "objective" reality; products of time, place and situation, and thus systems of timed history rather than timeless eternity. They need not even be so universal as to become the epitomized *rationale* of an age, but may merely be the lineaments of a personality, its temperament and dispositional attitudes projected into their systematic rationalizations. But no conception of philosophy, however relativistic, however opposed to absolutism, can afford to ignore the question of ultimates or abandon what has been so aptly though skeptically termed "the quest for certainty". To do that is not merely to abdicate traditional metaphysics with its rationalistic justification of absolutes but also to stifle embryonic axiology with its promising analysis of norms. Several sections of American thought, however, have been so anxious to repudiate intellectualism and escape the autocracy of categoricals and universals that they have been ready to risk this. Though they have at times discussed the problems of value, they have usually avoided their normative aspects, which has led them into a bloodless behaviorism as arid as the intellecualism they have abandoned or else resulted in a completely individualistic and anarchic relativism which has rightly been characterized recently as "philosophic Nihilism". In de-throning our absolutes, we must take care not to exile our imperatives, for after all, we live by them. We must realize more fully that values create these imperatives as well as the more formally super-imposed absolutes, and that norms control our behavior as well as guide our reasoning. Further, as I shall later point out, we must realize that not in every instance is this normative control effected indirectly through judgmental or evaluational processes, but often through primary mechanisms of feeling modes and dispositional attitudes. Be that as it may, it seems that we are at last coming to the realization that without some account of normative principles, some fundamental consideration of value norms and "ultimates" (using the term in a non-committal sense), no philosophical system can hope to differentiate itself from descriptive science or present a functional, interpretive version of human experience.

Man does not, cannot, live in a valueless world. Pluralism has merely given temporary surcease from what was the central problem of monism,—the analysis and justification of these "ultimates", and pragmatism has only transposed the question from the traditional one of what ends should govern life to the more provocative one of how and why activity creates them. No philosophy, short of the sheerest nominalism or the most colorlessly objective behaviorism, is so neutral that it has not some axiological implications. Positivism least of all; for in opposing the traditional values, positivism has set up countervalues bidding us find meaning in the act rather than project meaning from the plane of reason and the subjective approach; and further, as pragmatism and instrumentalism, has set up at the center of its philosophy a doctrine of truth as itself a functional value. So, by waiving the question of the validity of value ultimates as "absolutes", we do not escape the problem of their functional categorical character as imperatives of action and as norms of preference and choice.

Though this characteristically American repudiation of "ultimates" was originally made in the name of the "philosophy of common sense", common sense and the practical life confronts us with the problem all the more forcefully by displaying a chronic and almost universal fundamentalism of values in action. Of this, we must at least take stock, even if we cannot eventually justify it or approve of it. The common man, in both his individual and group behavior, perpetuates the problem in a very practical way. He sets up personal and private and group norms as standards and principles, and rightly or wrongly hypostasizes them as universals for all conditions, all times and all men. Whether then on the plane of reason or that of action, whether "above the battle" in the conflict of "isms" and the "bloodless ballet of ideas" or in the battle of partisans with their conflicting and irreconcilable ways of life, the same essential strife goes on, and goes on in the name of eternal ends and deified ultimates. Our quest for certainty, motivated from the same urge, leads to similar dilemmas. The blind practicality of the common man and the disinterested impracticality of the philosopher yield similar results and rationalizations. Moreover, such transvaluations of value as from time to time we have, lead neither to a truce of values nor to an effective devaluation; they merely resolve one dilemma and set up another. And so, the conflict of irreconcilables goes on as the devisive and competitive forces of our practical imperatives parallel the incompatibilities of our formal absolutes.

We cannot declare for value-anarchism as a wishful way out, or find a solution in that other alternative blind alley of a mere descriptive analysis of interests. That but postpones the vital problems of ends till the logically later consideration of evaluation and post-valuational rationalizations. To my thinking, the gravest problem of contemporary philosophy is how to ground some normative principle or criterion of objective validity for values without resort to dogmatism and absolutism on the intellectual plane, and without falling into their corollaries, on [1]

[1] Compare Professor Frank H. Knight's comment on Charner Perry's, —*The Arbitrary as Basis for Rational Morality*—Inter. Journal of Ethics, Vol. 53—No. 2—Jan., 1933—p. 148:—"In the present situation of the western mind, the crying need is to substantiate for social phenomena a middle ground between scientific objectivity and complete skepticism. On the one hand, as Scylla, is the absurdity of Behaviorism. . . . On the other side is the Charybdis of Nihilism, perhaps momentarily the

the plane of social behavior and action, of intolerance and mass coercion. This calls for a functional analysis of value norms and a search for normative principles in the immediate context of valuation. It raises the question whether the fundamental value modes have a way of setting up automatically or dispositionally their end-values prior to evaluative judgment. Should this be the case, there would be available a more direct approach to the problem of value ultimates, and we might discover their primary normative character to reside in their functional rôle as stereotypes of feeling-attitudes and dispositional imperatives of action-choices, with this character reenforced only secondarily by reason and judgment about them as "absolutes". We should then be nearer a practical understanding of the operative mechanisms of valuation and of the grounds for our agreements and conflicts over values.

Normally, one would expect a philosophical tradition dominated, as contemporary American thought has been, by an activist theory of knowledge, to have made a problem like this central. We might very profitably pause for a moment to take stock of the reasons why this has not been so. In the first place, in the reaction away from academic metaphysics, there has been a flight to description and analysis too analogous to science and too committed to scientific objectivism. It is impossible to reach such problems as we have before us effectively in terms of pure positivism, of the prevalent objectivism, or of the typical view that until quite recently has dominated American value theory, —the view namely that end-values exist only in so far as values are rationalized and mediated by processes of evaluation and formal value judgments. Added to this, is our characteristic preoccupation with theories of meaning limited practically to

nearer and more threatening of the two reefs. Of course, the two are related; nihilism is a natural correlate of "scientificism." . . . In any case, there is no more vital problem (pragmatically) than that of distinguishing between utterance that is true or sound and that which is effective in influencing behavior."

the field of truth and knowledge. Because of this logico-experimental slant, we again have made common cause with the current scientific attitude; making truth too exclusively a matter of the correct anticipation of experience, of the confirmation of fact.[2] Yet truth may also sometimes be the sustaining of an attitude, the satisfaction of a way of feeling, the corroboration of a value. To the poet, beauty is truth; to the religious devotee, God is truth; to the enthused moralist, what ought-to-be overtops factual reality. It is perhaps to be expected that the typical American philosophies should concentrate almost exclusively on thought-action as the sole criterion of experience, and should find analysis of the emotional aspects of human behavior uncongenial. This in itself, incidentally is a confirming example of an influential value-set, amounting in this instance to a grave cultural bias. When we add to this our American tradition of individualism, reflecting itself characteristically in the value-anarchism and *laissez faire* of which we have already spoken, it is easy to explain why American thought has moved tangent to the whole central issue of the normative aspects and problems of value.

In saying this, do we say anything more than that values are important and that American philosophy should pay more attention to axiology? Most assuredly;—we are saying that but for a certain blindness, value-theory might easily have been an American forte, and may still become so if our predominantly functionalist doctrines ever shed their arbitrary objectivism and extend themselves beyond their present concentration on theories of truth and knowledge into a balanced analysis of values generally. Ironically enough, the very type of philosophy which has insisted on truth as a value has, by rigid insistence on

[2] Compare Dewey—*The Quest of Certainty*,—p. 21:—"Are the objects of desire, effort, choice, that is to say, everything to which we attach value, real? Yes,—if they can be warranted by knowledge; if we can know objects having their value properties we are justified in thinking them real. But as objects of desire and purpose they have no sure place in Being until they are approached and validated through knowledge."

the objective criterion and the experimental-instrumental aspects of thought, disabled itself for pursuing a similarly functional interpretation of the other value modes and their normative principles.

Human behavior, it is true, is experimental, but it is also selectively preferential, and not always in terms of outer adjustments and concrete results. Value reactions guided by emotional preferences and affinities are as potent in the determination of attitudes as pragmatic consequences are in the determination of actions. In the generic and best sense of the term 'pragmatic', it is as important to take stock of the one as the other.

Fortunately, within the last few years a decided trend toward axiology and the neglected problems of value has developed, properly enough under the aegis of the *International Journal of Ethics*, promising to offset this present one-sidedness of American philosophical interests. Once contemporary American thought does turn systematically to the analysis of values, its empirical and functionalist approach will be considerably in its favor. Such a philosophic tradition and technique ought to come near to realizing the aim of Brentano, father of modern value-theory, to derive a functional theory of value from a descriptive and empirical psychology of valuation and to discover in value-experience itself the source of those normative and categorical elements construed for centuries so arbitrarily and so artificially in the realm of rational absolutes.

There is little or no hope that this can be obtained *via* a theory of value which bids us seek whatever objectivity and universality values may have outside the primary processes of valuation, whether in the confirmations of experience or the affirmations of evaluative judgments. For these positions lead only, as far as the direct apprehension of value goes, to Protagorean relativism,—each man the measure and each situation the gauge of value, and then an abysmal jump to the objective criterion of the truths of science, valid for all situations, all men and all times.

What seems most needed is some middle ground between these extremes of subjectivism and objectivism. The natural distinctions of values and their functional criteria surely lie somewhere in between the atomistic relativism of a pleasure-pain scale and the colorless, uniformitarian criterion of logic,— the latter more of a straight-jacket for value qualities than the old intellectualist trinity of Beauty, Truth and Good. Flesh and blood values may not be as universal or objective as logical truths and schematized judgments, but they are not thereby deprived of some relative objectivity and universality of their own. The basic qualities of values should never have been sought in logical classes, for they pertain to psychological categories. They are not grounded in types of realms of value, but are rooted in modes or kinds of *valuing*.

In fact, the value-mode establishes for itself, directly through feeling, a qualitative category which, as discriminated by its appropriate feeling-quality, constitutes an emotionally mediated form of experience. If this be so, the primary judgments of value are emotional judgments—(if the inveterate Austrian term *"feeling-judgments"* is not allowable philosophical English), and the initial reference for value predication is based on a form-quality revealed in feeling and efficacious in valuation through feeling. Though finally validated in different ways and by different criteria, beauty, goodness, truth (as approval or acceptance), righteousness are known in immediate recognitions of qualitative apprehension. The generic types of value are basic and fundamental feeling-modes, each with its own characteristic form criterion in value perception. For the fundamental kinds, we can refer to inveterate common-sense, which discriminates them with approximate accuracy—the moral and ethical, the aesthetic, the logical and the religious categories with their roughly descriptive predicates. For an empirical psychology of values, however, they need to be approached directly from the side of feeling and value-attitudes, and re-discriminated not in terms of formal definition but in terms of technical description of their affective-volitional dimensions and factors.

Normally a value-mode is conveyed while the value is being apprehended. Otherwise the quality of the value would be indeterminate, and this is usually contrary to fact. Though we may still be in doubt regarding its validation, its quantity, place in the value series and other specific issues of the value situation, we are usually certain of the value-mode. This is why we should think of a value-quality primarily in terms of feeling or attitude and not of predicates of judgment; why we should speak of a value-reference rather than a value claim. And if the value type is given in the immediate apprehension of the particular value, some qualitative universal is given. It supplies the clue to the functional value norm,—being felt as good, beautiful, etc.—and we have this event in mind when we say that in the feeling-reference to some value-mode, some value ultimate becomes the birthmark of the value. If values are thus normatively stamped by form-qualities of feeling in the original value experience, then the evaluative judgment merely renders explicit what was implicit in the original value sensing, at least as far as the modal quality of the value is concerned. This could only be true on one of two assumptions, *viz.*, that some abstract feeling-character functioned dispositionally as a substitute for formal judgment, or that the feeling-attitude itself moulded the value-mode and reflected sympathetically its own pattern. If the latter be the case, a value-type or category is a feeling-mode carved out dispositionally by a fundamental attitude.

Of course, this notion of a feeling-reference or form-quality constituting the essential identity and unity of a value-mode is not easily demonstrable; it may be just a hypothetical anticipation of what an experimental analysis of valuation might later establish and prove. However, the main objection to such a conception of a value form-character has been undermined, if not overthrown, by the Gestalt psychology, which has demonstrated the factual reality of a total configuration functioning in perceptual recognition, comparison and choice. There is therefore nothing scientifically impossible or bizarre in assuming a form-quality felt along with the specific value context and constituting its modal value-quality and reference. In the absence of direct evidence of this configurational element in valuation, the most corroborative circumstantial evidence is to be found in the inter-changeability or rather the convertibility of the various kinds of value. The further we investigate, the more we discover that there is no fixity of content to values, and the more we are bound, then, to infer that their identity as groups must rest on other elements. We know that a *value-genre* often evades its definition and breaks through its logical barriers to include content not usually associated with it. The awe-inspiring scene becomes *"holy,"* the logical proof, *"beautiful,"* creative expression, a "duty," and in every case the appropriate new predicates follow the attitude and the attitude cancels out the traditionally appropriate predicates. For every value coupled by judgmental predication, thousands are linked by identities of feeling-mode; for every value transformed by change of logical pre-suppositions, scores are switched by a radical transformation of the feeling-attitude. We are forced to conclude that the feeling-quality, irrespective of content, makes a value of a given kind, and that a transformation of the attitude effects a change of type in the value situation.

In this connection, a competent analyst concludes [3]: "We are compelled to recognize that in the aesthetic value situation anything animate or inanimate, natural or artificial, deed or doer, may be the object. This consideration alone makes it clear that beauty and goodness cannot always, if ever, be the same." Yet with all this qualitative distinctness, the artist may feel duty toward his calling, obligation toward his unrealized idea, because when he feels conflict and tension in that context, he occupies an entirely different attitude toward his aesthetic

[3] "Beauty and Goodness"—Herbert E. Cory—*International Journal of Ethics*, July, 1926.

material. Instead of the repose or ecstasy of contemplation or the exuberant flow of creative expression, he feels the tension and pull of an unrealized situation, and feeling obligation and conflict, senses along with that a moral quality. The changed feeling-attitude creates a new value; and the type-form of the attitude brings with it its appropriate value category. These modes co-assert their own relevant norms; each sets up a categorical imperative of its own, not of the Kantian sort with rationalized universality and objectivity, but instead the psychological urgency (shall we say, necessity?) to construe the situation as of a particular qualitative form-character. It is this that we term a functional categorical factor, since it operates in and through feeling, although it is later made explicit, analyzed and validated by evaluative processes of judgment and experiential test.

The traditional way of accounting for the various kinds of value, on the other hand, starting out as it does from the side of evaluation, leans too heavily upon logical definition. It substitutes the terminology of predicates for the real functional *differential*. A comparison, even in incomplete, suggestive outline, between a logical and a psychological classification of values will show how much more neatly a schematization of values in terms of the mechanics of value-feelings fits the facts than the rough approximations of the traditional logical classification. More than this, such a classification not only states the basis on which the primary value groups generically rest, but reveals the process out of which they genetically arise.

Taking feeling-modes as the basic factor of differentiation, the religious and ethical, moral, logical and aesthetic types of value differentiate very neatly on the basis of four fundamental feeling-modes of exaltation, tension, acceptance, and repose or equilibrium. There are sub-divisions for each value-mode determined by the usual polarity of positive and negative values, and also for each mode a less recognized but most important sub-division related to the directional drive of the value-feeling.

This latter discriminates for each type of value an 'introverted' and an 'extroverted' variety of the value, according as the feeling-reference refers the value inward toward an individualized value of the self or projects it outward toward value-sharing and the socialized plane of action. We may illustrate first in terms of the moral values. Every definition of the moral or ethical situation recognizes the characteristic element of conflict between alternatives and the correlated sense of tension. The classification we are discussing would transpose a typical pragmatic definition such as "the conflict of mentally incompatible goods defines a moral situation" into a psychological category of value grounded in the form-feeling of tension, inducing the moral attitude toward the situation irrespective of content. Where the value reference is introverted or directed inwardly toward the self, this tension expresses itself as a compulsion of inner restraint or as "conscience": where an extroverted reference directs the tension toward a compulsion outward to action, the tension becomes sensed as "duty" or obligation. Or, to illustrate again, in the mode of the religious values, we have the mechanisms of introverted exaltation determining positively the ecstasy and sense of union of the religious mystic and negatively his sense of sin and separation, with the outward or extroverted form of the religious value expressing itself in the convictions of "conversion" and salvation (active union with God) and the salvationist crusade against evil (the fear and hate of Satan).

Tabular illustration follows:

This view, if correct, leads to the conclusion that there is a form-feeling or form-quality characteristic of each fundamental value-type, and that values are discriminated in terms of such feeling factors in the primary processes of valuation. The view further regards these modalities of feeling as constituting the basic kinds of value through the creation of stereotyped and dispositional attitudes which sustain them. The substantial agreement of such a table with the traditional classification of values

MODAL QUALITY Form-Quality and Feeling-Reference	VALUE TYPE or Field	VALUE PREDICATES	VALUE POLARITY	
			Positive	Negative
EXALTATION: (Awe-Worship) a. Introverted: (Individualized): Inner Ecstasy b. Extroverted: (Socialized): Religious Zeal	*Religious*	Holy—Unholy	Holiness	Sin
		Good—Evil	Salvation	Damnation
TENSION: (Conflict-Choice) a. Inner Tension of "Conscience" b. Extrovert: Outer Tension of "Duty"	*Ethical* *Moral*	Good—Bad Right—Wrong	Conscience Right	Temptation Crime
ACCEPTANCE or AGREEMENT: (Curiosity—Intellectual Satisfaction) a. Inner Agreement in Thought	*Logical Truth*	True (Correct) and Incorrect	Consistency	Contradiction
b. Outer Agreement in Experience	*Scientific Truth*	True—False	Certainty	Error
REPOSE or EQUILIBRIUM a. Consummation in Contemplation b. Consummation in Creative Activity	*Aesthetic* *Artistic*	Beautiful—Ugly Fine— Unsatisfactory	Satisfaction Joy	Disgust Distress

merely indicates that the established scheme of value judgments has traced the basic value modes with fair correctness. However, there are differences more significant than the similarities. These differences not only make possible a more accurate classification of the types of value, but make evident a genetic pattern of values by which we may trace more accurately their interrelations, both of correlation and of opposition.

Over and above greater descriptive accuracy in value analysis, then, this view may be expected to vindicate itself most effectively in the field of the genetics and the dynamics of values. Here it is able to account for value conversions and value opposition in terms of the same factors, and thus apply a common principle of explanation to value mergings, transfers and conflicts. It is with this range of phenomena that the logical theories of value experience their greatest difficulties. We are aware of instances, for example, where a sequence of logical reasoning will take on an aesthetic character as a "beautiful proof" or a "pretty demonstration", or where a moral quality or disposition is appraised not as "good" but as "noble", or again, where a religious ritual is a mystical "reality" to the convinced believer but is only an aesthetic, symbolic show to the non-credal spectator. The logical way of explaining such instances assumes a change of the judgmental pre-suppositions mediating the values, or in other cases, puts forward the still weaker explanation of the transfer of value predicates through metaphor and analogy. But by the theory that values are constituted by the primary modal quality of the actual feeling, one does not have to go beyond that to explain the accurate appropriateness of the unusual predicates or the actuality of the attitude in the valuation. They are in direct functional relation and agreement. As a *quod erat demonstrandum*, the proof or demonstration is an enjoyed consummation of a process, and is by that very fact aesthetic in quality. Likewise, the contemplation of an ethical deed, when the tension of the act is not shared, becomes a detached appreciation, though it needs only the sharing of the tension to revert to the moral type of valuation. In fact, moral behavior, when it becomes dispositional, with the smooth feeling-curve of habit and inner equilibrium, normally takes on a quasi-aesthetic quality, as reflected in the criterion of taste and *noblesse oblige* rather than the sterner criterion of "must" and of "duty". And of course, to the disinterested spectator, the religious ritual is just like any other work of art,—an object of reposeful, equilibrated projection. Once a different form-feeling is evoked, the situation and the value type are, *ipso facto*, changed. Change the attitude, and, irrespective of content, you change the value-type; the appropriate new predicates automatically follow.

The same principles hold, moreover, in explaining the conflicts and incompatibilities of values as value-groups. Of course, there are other types of value conflicts, means-ends and value-series problems, but what concerns us at this point are those graver antinomies of values out of which our most fundamental value problems arise. One needs only to recall the endless debate over the *summum bonum* or the perennial quarrel over the respective merits of the value Trinity. How, even after lip service to the parity of Beauty, Truth and Good, we conspire for the priority of one pet favorite, which usually reflects merely our dominant value interest and our own temperamental value bias. The growth of modern relativism has at least cooled these erstwhile burning issues and tempered the traditional debate. Indeed from our point of view, we see these grand ultimates, for all their assertion of fraternal harmony, as doomed to perpetual logical opposition because their basic value attitudes are psychologically incompatible. Repose and action, integration and conflict, acceptance and projection, as attitudes, create natural antinomies, irresolvable orders of value; and the only peace a scientific view of value can sanction between them is one based not upon priority and precedence but upon parity and reciprocity.

As we dispose of this traditional value feud, we become aware of the internal value conflicts within the several value fields, those schisms within common value loyalties which are becoming all the more serious as the traditional value quarrel subsides. There is the feud between the mystic and the reformer in religion, between the speculative logician and the inductive experimentalist in the pursuit of truth, yes,—even the one, less sharp and obvious, between the aesthete and the artist. An affective theory of valuation throws these internal dilemmas into an interesting and illuminating perspective. In each of these cases, the modal value-feeling is, of course, held in common and the same ideological loyalties shared, but these sub-groups are still divided by the basic difference in their orientation toward their common values. Here we see the functional importance of that distinction in feeling-reference or feeling-direction which so closely parallels the Jungian polarity of introversion and extroversion that these terms have been adopted to describe it. These directional drives, determined emotionally in the majority of cases, deciding whether the value is focussed inwardly or outwardly, individuated or socialized, are of the utmost practical importance. For they are the root of those civil feuds within the several value provinces between the saint and the prophet, the mystic and the reformer, the speculative theorist and the practical experimentalist in the search for truth, the aesthete and dilettante versus the creative and professional artist, and finally between the self-righteous moral zealot and the moral reformer. And as each of these attitude-sets becomes dispositional and rationalized, we have the scientific clue to that pattern of value loyalties which divides humanity into psychological sub-species, each laying down rationalizations of ways of life that, empirically traced, are merely the projections of their predominant value tendencies and attitudes.

Thus our varied absolutes are revealed as largely the rationalization of our preferred values and their imperatives. Their tap-root, it seems, stems more from the will to power than from the will to know. Little can be done, it would appear, either toward their explanation or their reconciliation on the rational plane. Perhaps this is the truth that Brentano came near laying hands on when he suggested a love-hate dimensionality as fundamental to all valuation. Certainly the fundamental opposition of value-modes and the attitudes based upon them has been one of the deepest sources of human division and conflict. The rôle of feeling can never be understood nor controlled through minimizing it; to admit it is the beginning of practical wisdom in such matters. As Hartmann [4] has well observed,—"Every value, when once it has gained power over a person, has a tendency to set itself up as a sole tyrant of the whole human *ethos,* and indeed at the expense of other values, even of such as are not inherently opposed to it." We must acknowledge this, though not to despair over it, but by understanding how and why, to find principles of control from the mechanisms of valuation themselves. Without doubt many value attitudes as separate experiences are incompatible and antithetic, but all of us, as individuals, reconcile these incompatibilities in our own experience when we shift, for variety as often as for necessity, from one mode of value to the other. The effective antidote to value absolutism lies in a systematic and realistic demonstration that values are rooted in attitudes, not in reality and pertain to ourselves, not to the world. Consistent value pluralism might eventually make possible a value loyalty not necessarily founded on value bigotry, and impose a truce of imperatives, not by denying the categorical factors in valuation, which, as we have seen, are functional, but by insisting upon the reciprocity of these norms. There is not necessarily irresolvable conflict between these separate value modes if, without discounting their emotional and functional incommensurability, we realize their complementary character in human experience.

At the same time that it takes sides against the old absolutism

---

[4] Hartmann, *Ethics,* Vol. II, p. 423.

and invalidates the *summum bonum* principle, this type of value pluralism does not invite the chaos of value-anarchy or the complete *laissez faire* of extreme value individualism. It rejects equally trying to reduce value distinctions to the flat continuum of a pleasure-pain economy or to a pragmatic instrumentalism of ends-means relations. Of course, we need the colorless, common-denominator order of factual reality and objectivity (although that itself serves a primary value as a mechanism of the coordination of experience), but values simply do not reduce to it. To set values over against facts does not effectively neutralize values. Since we cannot banish our imperatives, we must find some principle of keeping them within bounds. It should be possible to maintain some norms as functional and native to the process of experience, without justifying arbitrary absolutes, and to uphold some categoricals without calling down fire from heaven. Norms of this status would be functional constants and practical sustaining imperatives of their correlated modes of experience; nothing more, but also nothing less.

Such "ends" totalize merely an aspect of human experience and stand only for a subsistent order of reality. They should not confuse themselves with that objective reality nor attempt to deny or disparage its other value aspects and the subsistent orders they reflect. This totalizing character is purely functional in valuation, and it is a mockery of fact either to raise it to the level of transcendental worship or to endow it with objective universality. This conceded, there is little sense and less need to set facts and values over against each other as antagonistic orders; rather should we think of reality as a central fact and a white light broken up by the prism of human nature into a spectrum of values. By proposing these basic value-modes as coordinate and complementary, value pluralism of this type proposes its two most important corollaries,—the principles of reciprocity and tolerance. As derivative aspects of the same basic reality, value orders cannot reasonably become competitive and rival realities. As creatures of a mode of experience, they should not construe themselves in any concrete embodiment so as to contradict or stultify the mode of which they are a particularized expression.

Should such a view become established,—and I take that to be one of the real possibilities of an empirical theory of value, we shall then have warrant for taking as the proper center of value loyalty neither the worship of definitions or formulae nor the competitive monopolizing of value claims, but the goal of maximizing the value-mode itself as an attitude and activity. The attitude will itself be construed as the value essence,— which it really is, and not as now the intellectualized *why* or the traditional and institutionalized *how* associated with the value category. In such a frame of reference, for example, romanticism and classicism could not reasonably think of themselves as monopolizing the field of art, nor Protestantism, Catholicism or even Christianity conceive themselves the only way to salvation. In such a perspective, Nordicism and other rampant racialisms might achieve historical sanity or at least prudential common-sense to halt at the natural frontiers of genuinely shared loyalties and not sow their own eventual downfall through forced loyalties and the counter-reactions which they inevitably breed. Social reciprocity for value loyalties is but a new name for the old virtue of tolerance, yet it does bring the question of tolerance down from the lofty thin air of idealism and chivalry to the plane of enlightened self-interest and the practical possibilities of effective value-sharing. As a working principle, it divorces proper value loyalty from unjustifiable value bigotry, releases a cult from blind identification with creed and dogma, and invests no value interest with monopoly or permanent priority.

However, no one can sensibly expect a sudden or complete change in our value behavior from any transformation, however radical, in our value theory. Relativism will have to slowly tame the wild force of our imperatives. There will be no sudden re-canting of chronic, traditional absolutisms, no complete under-mining of orthodoxies, no huge, overwhelming accessions of tolerance. But absolutism is doomed in the increasing variety of human experience. What over a century ago was only an inspired metaphorical flash in the solitary universal mind of a Goethe,—that phrase about civilization's being a fugue in which, voice by voice, the several nations and peoples took up and carried the interwoven theme, could in our day become a systematic phi-losophy of history like Pareto's. His historical and functional relativism of cultural values, with persistent normative con-stants ("residues") and variable and contingent specific em-bodiments ("derivatives"), is but an indication of the possibili-ties of relativism extended to historical and social thought. Cultural relativism, to my mind, is the culminating phase of relativistic philosophy, and it is bound to have a greater in-fluence than any other phase of relativism upon our conception and practise of values.

Our present way of socializing values on the basis of credal agreement, dogmatic orthodoxies, and institutionally vested in-terests is fundamentally unsound and self-contradictory. As a practise, it restricts more than it protects the values that have called institutions into being. Organized for value-sharing and value promotion, they often contradict their own primary pur-poses. One way of reform undoubtedly is to combat the monopolistic tradition of most of our institutions. This sounds Marxian, and is to an extent. But the curtailing of the struggle over the means and instrumentalities of values will not elimi-nate our quarrels and conflicts about ends, and long after the possible elimination of the profit motive, our varied imperatives will still persist. Economic classes may be absorbed, but our psychological tribes will not thereby be dissolved. So, since there may be monopolistic attitudes and policies with respect to ends and ideals just as well as monopolies of the instrumentalities of human values—(and of this fact the ideological dogmatism of contemporary communism is itself a sad example), it may be more effective to invoke a non-Marxian principle of maximizing values.

Contrary to Marxian logic, this principle is non-uniformitarian. It is the Roycean principle of "loyalty to loyalty", which though idealistic in origin and defense, was a radical break with the tradition of absolutism. It called for a revolution in the practise of partisanship in the very interests of the values professed. In its larger outlines and implications it proclaimed a relativism of values and a principle of reciprocity. Loyalty to loyalty transposed to all the fundamental value orders would then have meant, reverence for reverence, tolerance between moral systems, reciprocity in art, and had so good a metaphysician been able to conceive it, relativism in philosophy.

But if reciprocity and tolerance on the large scale are to await the incorporation of the greater community, the day of our truce of values is far off. Before any such integrations can take place, the narrowness of our provincialisms must be broken down and our sectarian fanaticisms lose some of their force and glamor. A philosophy aiding this is an ally of the larger integration of life. Of this we may be sure, such reconstruction will never bring us to a basis of complete cultural uniformity or common-mindedness about values. Whatever integrations occur, therefore, whether of thought or social system,—and undoubtedly some will and must occur,—cultural and value pluralism of some sort will still prevail. Indeed in the atmosphere induced by relativism and tolerance, such differentiation is likely to increase rather than just continue. Only it is to be hoped that it will be less arbitrary, less provincial and less divisive.

One thing is certain,—whatever change may have occurred in our thinking on the subject, we are still monists and absolutists mainly in our practise of value, individual as well as social.

But a theoretical break has come, and seems to have set in simultaneously from several quarters. Panoramically viewed, the convergence of these trends indicates a new center for the thought and insight of our present generation, and that would seem to be a philosophy and a psychology, and perhaps too, a sociology, pivoted around functionalistic relativism.

AN AMATEUR'S SEARCH
FOR SIGNIFICANCE

ARTHUR E. MORGAN

ARTHUR E. MORGAN, Hon. D.Sc., University of Colorado, 1923, Hon. D.Eng., Case School of Applied Science, 1932, born at Cincinnati, Ohio, June 20, 1878, began his search for the meaning of life under the primitive pioneering environment of the Minnesota woods. He found scientific and aesthetic interest as an amateur naturalist and geologist, knowledge in a few rare books, and practical experience as a surveyor and engineer. Largely self-educated, he later founded an engineering firm, and built more than fifty flood control projects, culminating in the Miami Conservancy District in Ohio and the Pueblo Conservancy District in Colorado. On the Miami project he directed a number of extensive engineering research projects, the results being published as the Miami Conservancy Technical Reports.

He conceived of education and self-discipline as the primary means of determining the quality and direction of human culture, and accepted in 1920 the presidency of Antioch College, Yellow Springs, Ohio, where he inaugurated a new program based upon the principle that education should concern itself with the orderly and well proportioned development of every phase of personality. The program combined practical work in arts and industries as essential educational experience, with academic study making the educative process more largely an autonomous one for the student. Education became an adventure, both in the world of ideas, and in developing skill and power in mastering actual situations. He also encouraged the development of a number of separately financed research projects in the biological and physical sciences, which are located at Antioch College.

In 1933 Mr. Morgan was appointed chairman of the Tennessee Valley Authority. The pioneering instinct of his youth, further developed in his work in education and in executive and administrative experience in organizing and carrying out engineering projects, is finding fruitful application in this significant experiment in social and economic development.

AN AMATEUR'S SEARCH
FOR SIGNIFICANCE

Arthur E. Morgan

This is an effort to state some of the elements of my conscious philosophy. It is arranged under three headings: how I endeavor to approach the truth; where, if anywhere, do human significance and value lie; and, what shall I undertake to accomplish, and by what methods.

It is not a carefully, deliberately formulated presentation, but a statement dashed off on the run. It omits much that is essential and lacks the conciseness and organization which such a statement should possess. A pertinent criticism would be that at no time during a hurried life—which a friendly tolerance might flatter by the pleasanter term of a busy life—have I found time for a closely knit and effectively organized expression of my philosophy.

How I Endeavor to Approach the Truth

The ultimate units of thought are intuitions. As I use the term here, an intuition is a belief, a conviction, an appraisal, or a sense of value, which is held, not as the direct immediate conclusion of a process of formal reasoning, but because it is self-evident. Intuitions are of many origins. Some are inborn and need no teaching. The conviction that extreme cold or extreme heat is unpleasant perhaps does not need to be learned. Of a very different kind are the mathematician's intuitions of the truth or falsity of a mathematical proposition; the marksman's intuition in shooting at a distant target; or the Brahmin's intuition that he will be reincarnated. These kinds of intuitions exist as the result of long teaching or training. An intuition is a conviction which, at the particular moment it comes to our attention, has the quality of a self-evident truth, and is not directly the result of a conscious mental process.

When I add a long column of figures, I do so because I have no intuition of the number which represents the sum, and must go through a conscious mental process to determine it. When I have added the column and have found the sum, I have confidence in its correctness, not because of any feeling that the particular number is the right one, but because I have confidence in the process by which I have arrived at it. The detailed increments of this process, such as the assumption that three and two make five, through a long process of acquaintance and use, have become intuitional.

Especially on the intellectual level, our intuitions are highly complex and varying products of a vast accumulation, of genetic inheritance, early impressions, unconscious imitation, formal teaching, indoctrination, experience, and interpretation. These intuitions are much influenced by such conditions as mental and physical health, by the prevailing public temper, and by our needs and desires. The ultimate units of thinking are these intuitions. Take a simple statement such as "I see you." Each word in this statement represents an intuitional complex of extremely involved and varied composition and background; not only varied, but varying at each moment.

Now this fact, that the ultimate units of thought are intuitions, is true of the philosopher's world as well as of any other. The systematic philosopher often assumes that by rigorous thinking expressed in words he can arrive at a dependable philosophical structure. Yet each word or other element of his thought is not an objective and definite thing but an intuition— a conviction which at the moment it is used seems self-evident. Each such unit of the philosopher's thought or intuition is the exceedingly complex result of many influences, some true and some false in their implications. Some factors making up each intuition have been consciously arrived at by efforts at rigorous thinking; other factors have crept in surreptitiously or un-noticed. The philosopher may have striven to the utmost to define each one of his terms, but the final elements in each definition are undefined intuitions or "self-evident truths," and these are complexes of the most varied origins and compositions.

A conventional systematic philosopher is like a child who undertakes to project the course of a straight line by laying square wood blocks end to end on the theory that, since they are perfect squares, if their ends are exactly and fully in contact, the border of the row of blocks must constitute a straight line. In the child's basket of blocks, however, there are very few which are perfect squares. He therefore does the best he can, and if one block is irregular in one direction, he tries to correct the error by placing against it a block which has equal and compensating lack of symmetry in the other direction. He started to produce a straight line independently of his intuitions by using blocks that in themselves have the discipline of exact and unvarying shape. Yet he finds that they do not have that quality, and so he uses his intuition in correcting the varying quality of his materials. Perhaps he would follow a more nearly straight line by trusting his intuitive judgment of straightness in the first place.

The philosopher who tries to build a rigorous system by logically relating terms or concepts to each other is trying to escape from the errors of intuition by such precise use of words or concepts. In order to give himself the satisfaction of accom-plishment he must assume a high degree of exactness in the ele-ments he uses to build his system, but since each of these ele-ments is an intuition, with infinite variations and complexities, of many of which he may be quite unaware, his intuitions are far less dependable than the child's irregular polygon building blocks; they are even worse than irregular polyhedrons with no two faces alike. They are more like a collection of wriggling and squirming worms and beetles with which he is trying to outline the course of a straight line; for intuitions are phases of life, and until the mind stops growing, they will constantly vary with health, mood and usage. His words and phrases mean one thing to the speaker or writer and something else to the listener or reader, they mean one thing today and another tomorrow. They may have one meaning when he is in vigorous health and full of courage, and something very different when he is despondent or on the defensive.

The systematic philosopher has even further difficulties. In order to avoid such imperfections in his tools he makes them limited or abstract. This effort at simplification has the result of omitting elements of reality. In order to make his terms simple enough to use, he may leave out the implications of biology or physics or of psychology. By the time his system is simplified and controlled enough to be dependable, it probably has so lost its likeness to reality that it is no longer significant as a general guide to living, though it may be tremendously significant in special aspects of living, as in the case of mathematics.

His process has even another disadvantage. In the rejection or adoption of intuitions to arrange into a system, he must select, eliminate and choose. Though he may try to let logical necessity choose for him, he cannot entirely do so. Though he aims to escape from emotional choices, yet the very sense of value which motivates and determines his selection is in itself an emotional quality. Except as it drives him, he will lack incentive to make any selection whatever. Toward one possible element of a system he may feel a glow of reality, of warmth, of validity, because of having previously come upon that element as the climax of an intensive search. So it lives and has emotional warmth and meaning for him. Some other possible element of a system may have greater intrinsic merit, yet he may pass it by because no experience has given him a sense of validity for it.

As a game for gentlemen such methods of building up philo-sophical systems may be as interesting as chess, but as significant guidance for living, I doubt whether they have been worth the ponderous volumes of paper in which they have been recorded. Not that the philosophers involved lack merit, but that their merit lies chiefly in their informal judgments, appraisals and in-sights, and not in systems achieved by formal logic.

The loss is not altogether the negative one of waste effort, for this kind of systems-building has interfered with another process which would be far more productive. I do not disapprove systems of belief as such, but rather of the way in which con-ventional philosophers sometimes try to build them. I shall describe a process which I think is more productive.

In this other process I should endeavor to become acquainted with as many types of intellectual discipline as possible, includ-ing the physical sciences, pure and applied, the general fields of mathematics, biology, psychology, sociology, philosophy, litera-ture, ethics and esthetics. I should endeavor to actually experi-ence life in many phases, getting first hand experience in the fields I have mentioned, and in many others. I should strive to avoid such experiences as probably would destroy more than they could contribute. For instance, I should not put out my eyes to get the experience of being hopelessly blind, or become a victim of narcotic drugs to experience the satisfaction and the servitude they produce. I should try to develop an inclusive discipline which would constantly endeavor to see each field of experience in the light of the others, and to endeavor to en-courage the emergence of a general intuitional view to which all these would contribute.

I should endeavor to develop power to act and to direct the course of my own life and of events, and to develop wishes, emotional appraisal of values, and a drive of life, which would not be in conflict with that discipline. I should expect a gradu-ally emerging philosophy and purpose to result, not as the con-clusion of a process of formal logic, but as the intuitive resultant or emergent of all these experiences and of the temper of mind which habitually explores them for their significance in their own field and in relation to the general view.

Several types of discipline should enter this process. There should be constant effort to increase discrimination in observation. There should be constant effort to remain sensitive to significant experience, no matter in what class it may fall, or how it may seem to fail to harmonize with other experience. There should be constant effort to be objective and disinterested (not uninterested) in observing and appraising experience, and there should be a constant aim to achieve and to maintain wholesome mental, physical, and social conditions which conduce to disinterested conclusions in accord with the nature of things.

In my opinion this somewhat informal process of providing a great range of significant disciplined experience, of letting it play freely upon the mind, and of trusting to the gradual emergence of intuitions, which are constantly subject to and disciplined by further experience, will insure the most representative and trustworthy conclusions about the nature of things. Experience alone would be barren. It must be accompanied by a craving to see significance, a craving which strives constantly to discriminate, to relate and to interpret.

I am of the opinion that this sometimes unconscious process of digesting, assimilating, appraising and synthesizing these experiences, and of bringing about the emergence of intuitive conclusions, is the soundest form for so complex an undertaking as the building of a philosophy of life. That process is biologically far older, more mature, and more complex than the processes of formal logic. True, the growth of civilization is coincident with the increase of conscious ordered thinking from premises to conclusions. That process has liberated men's minds and given vast increase of power. It should steadily increase its discipline of the intuitions, especially in limited fields such as mathematics and the physical sciences. Yet for such a varied and complex process as the building of a philosophy for living, we must for a very long time place our ultimate reliance on those unconscious mental processes which, in ways we do not understand, digest and assimilate experience and bring about the emergence of living philosophy.

One result of this process is that it tends to destroy reliance on any closed and arbitrary system of belief, and tends to prevent too great concentration of attention on limited systems of experience.

Where Do Human Significance and Value Lie?

The development of a philosophy of life is not an individual undertaking, but a social project extending through many generations. That fact I should place as one of my most important discoveries. To treat a philosophy of life as a personal and individual pursuit will so limit and distort the undertaking as to largely destroy its significance and often lead to a sense of futility.

As I compare the intelligence of even the highest mammals with that of the lowest normal men, it would seem to be futile for the mammals to try to solve many problems requiring even primitive human intelligence. The difference between primitive human intelligence and the ablest minds also is great. It may be that the solution of many problems must await a still further development of intellectual capacity.

There is another factor which limits the rate of approach of men toward the truth—it is the rate of development and mastery of the tools and data for thinking. In the field of mathematics, for instance, if Einstein had grown up among the early Romans, a lack of tools and methods of mathematics probably would have limited his mathematical comprehension to less than that of the average engineering student of today. The accumulation of the tools and data for thinking is a gradual process, but, lacking some general and permanent collapse of the race, its continuity is as inevitable as its gradualness. Just as the physical strength of men becomes less and less a limiting factor in their efforts to build great structures, so long as the development of powerful machines continues, so, just as long as improvement continues in the data and tools of thinking, the approach of men toward the truth will be less and less dependent on increase of inborn intelligence. Inborn intellectual capacity and possession of the data and tools of thinking are the two factors which, multiplied together, give a measure of intellectual power. The greater either one of them is, the less the other need be to make possible a given degree of intellectual power.

I am trying to emphasize the statement that the development of an adequate philosophy of life is not a personal undertaking, but a social project extending through many generations. In order to have a satisfactory and normal attitude toward the development of a philosophy of life, one must have a sense of continuity and of identity with other men and with the future of mankind, so that a contribution to a growing purpose will give a sense of satisfaction and of reality.

Any sense of value in the realm of outlooks and ideas can exist only as it has been gradually nurtured and developed. That is another of my most important discoveries. Unless one's sense of values has had such development, the most normal and convincing statements of value have no emotional appeal, and no sense of reality. If a normal person has no compelling sense of reality and importance in this concept of identity with the future, such a lack is not due to absence of value or reality in that concept, or generally to his lack of capacity to be profoundly impressed by it, but to lack of the nurture of a living sense of its reality and importance. The fact that a person feels no life or power in such a concept means only that he has not developed emotional responsiveness to that concept, and so has not come to have a sense for that particular value.

I see the achievement of a philosophy of life as a gradual growing process extending through many generations. I can and do make my own efforts to achieve an adequate philosophy, but I realize the preliminary and tentative character of my endeavor, and I am not dismayed if no seemingly conclusive philosophy rewards those efforts.

So little am I committed to any specific ultimate philosophy of values that I shall not here take the reader's time with a statement of my views on that subject, interesting and important as they seem to me. I do have a desire, however, to express my convictions as to the *direction* in which we must travel to achieve understanding, and I am greatly interested and concerned to make my own contribution to the increasing approach of men toward a philosophy of living. There are certain conditions of life which, I believe, are favorable to the growth of understanding of the nature of things and of the possible significance of life. I can perhaps help to bring about those favorable conditions and thereby help in the great project of the race to achieve understanding and value. So far as I know it may be possible not only for men to discover significance and value, but if these do not already exist to be discovered, then to design, synthesize and create them.

One condition essential to increase of understanding is continuity of the race. A sense of racial responsibility, especially on the part of those strains which have greatest health, intelligence and vigor, is essential. The development of genetic and eugenic understanding and a eugenic conscience is important. Physical health is important as a basis for sustained effort, and so the promotion of physical soundness and normalness deserves attention and loyalty. The same is true with reference to mental health.

The control of the physical environment, so as to reduce the element of adverse chance through catastrophes of nature, and so as to provide a wholesome and dependable environment for living, is important in setting the stage for the great quest. Fully as important is the control and development of the mental environment, so that inhibitions, vagaries, misconceptions, false beliefs, superstitions, and a host of destructive mental influences may be removed. The social environment is no less controlling. So far as the energies and resources of men are being consumed in destroying each other, and in fears, hatreds, destructive competition and in internal social friction, thwarting the fulfilment of life, progress toward the achievement of adequate purpose will be checked. International peace and social goodwill and justice are necessary conditions for releasing the creative capacities of men. At the beginning of this statement of my philosophy, I indicated my idea of the intellectual temper and habit which is most conducive to wholesome growth toward a life purpose. The promotion and achievement of such a temper are important.

Thus the pursuit of conditions most favorable for the development of a life philosophy becomes in effect a practical program for living. It may be held that there can be no better way in which to arrive at a practical program for living than to strive for those conditions which would be most favorable to the development of a life philosophy.

These brief hints indicate that, while a completely adequate and inclusive philosophy of life is beyond me, while it may be beyond all men for many generations to come, and may even be a quest which will never be completed, because greater value and significance may forever be achieved, or created and developed; yet I believe I do know the immediate road which probably must be taken and the immediate barriers which must be removed for the best approach to an adequate life philosophy, and I have intellectually and emotionally identified myself with all men and with the future in that quest. Therefore my life has a feeling of reality and importance, a feeling which has grown gradually through the years.

What Shall I Undertake to Do and by What Methods?

A sense of being a part of the race, of living and moving and having my being, not alone, but as an integral part of life, a feeling that the significance of what I do or experience is determined by its effect on my fellow men and upon the future, and a conviction that a gradual but long continuing approach to a good life may be possible for mankind,—this it is that provides my philosophical motivation. I add "philosophical" because in living from day to day I often fall short of such control, and am frequently motivated by passion, prejudice and immediate personal ends.

The general philosophical view I have outlined was arrived at by the time I was seventeen, after two or three years of most intense application to the problem of a life philosophy. All through the years since then I have taken genuine pleasure in doing things by which I identified myself with the general lot of men, present and future, in the long quest for significance and value in living. As a boy walking along country roads I would throw aside stones which made riding rough for others, although I seldom had the luxury of riding myself.

Such motives did not insure that what I did was worth while. Several of my earlier engineering projects into which I put great zeal and fervor were perhaps worse than useless. I drained quite a number of shallow or intermittent lakes in Minnesota in order to increase the nation's farm area, in accord with the prevailing craving for more land, whereas today I am of the opinion that in several cases it would have been more to the point to raise the water level and to create permanent and attractive lakes. Zeal and conscientiousness in themselves do not insure wise or productive action. If one is mistaken, the more zealous and effective he is, the greater harm he may do.

Yet a life lacking enthusiasm and drive means little. The problem of developing great interest and effectiveness, and of insuring it *against* negative and *for* positive results, forever looms large. The attitude described earlier in this account, that of endeavoring always to be sensitive and open to all new evidence, and of allowing all evidence and experience to play freely upon one's convictions, with constant practice at developing a discriminating sense of values in many and varied fields of experience, with the scientific temper in appraisal and interpretation—this attitude is the best protection I know against misdirection of enthusiasm and purposeful activity. To achieve a critical and open-minded attitude without losing decision, drive, mastery and enthusiasm in practical affairs,—that is achievement indeed. Such apparently conflicting combination of qualities should characterize the future leaders of mankind.

Whether or not I achieved the attitude in practice, my philosophical purpose was to do those things which would further the human quest for significance and value, including in proper perspective the joy of living from day to day, and also in proper perspective including myself in humanity and seeing myself as the part of humanity which I could administer most effectively and appropriately.

In pursuit of this general objective I found pleasure in any work I could do well which seemed humanly valuable. I enjoyed work as a farm hand in the wheat field, as a wood cutter in the lumber woods. Then I began to crave to make my efforts more creative and productive. A career in engineering gave satisfaction, for it helped toward that mastery of raw nature which is necessary to free men from blind chance and catastrophe. As an avocation along the way I was pleased to experiment with the improvement of a little known wild fruit as a way to contribute to general well-being.

It was my constant hope that the physical and administrative work of engineering would have by-products of another order. Though my own energies were consumed in administration, and while I lacked the technical training and intellectual insight for significant research, I did promote, organize and administer a number of projects in engineering research, the reports on which continue to rank high in their field. It was my hope also that by honestly administering public works I might change the temper of people toward public life and increase interest and confidence in straightforward public administration.

The fact that relatively few persons substantially change their views or expectations concerning life after they are thirty, and the fact that the mind of my public had but slight contact with my own mind, led me to crave kinds of endeavor that would have a still greater residue of values. I gradually came to the conclusion that the control of the physical environment, important as that may be, is yet not the crucial need of our times. I have come to feel that the spirits and motives of men, and their attitudes toward life, are the weak points in our social structure. The building of dams is an indirect and not always a very immediately effective way to change such motives and drives.

For some years I considered various other forms of endeavor, and settled upon higher education. To take a selected group of young men and women at the age when their reflective and critical faculties are awaking (I risk using the word "faculties" in this very general sense), and to present to them the general view of life I have here outlined, to develop in them a craving for emotional commitment, for critical objective judgment, for intellectual and emotional discipline, for introduction to significant fields of human knowledge and discipline, to help them to encourage the emergence of an inclusive and realistic philosophy, and at the same time to develop tempered and courageous personalities by practical contact with life—this seemed a significant undertaking.

One cannot judge closely the significance of any efforts in which there are so many variables and intangibles. Substantial satisfaction has resulted from that effort, though certain limitations which appeared have emphasized in my mind a very important principle of action. When I went to Antioch College it was with the hope of living and working there and of giving form and direction to the undertaking. This required that I should quickly find financial support which would leave my time available for that purpose. I imagined that somewhere would be a person able and glad to make such a project possible.

Though friendly and important support was given, I did not secure an adequate financial foundation, and spent nine years over the country seeking finances while others gave to the college its character and direction. As a result, the institution came to have a broader, more varied and more tolerant outlook than though it had been dominated by any one person.

Many students came in the nascent period of intellectual adolescence, ready and eager for great spiritual adventure. Sometimes that expectation was realized. Sometimes those who taught them were the matured products of the graduate schools, with the set and tempo of life to a large degree already determined. With a half conscious surprise I came to realize that no language or telepathy fully communicated to the faculty and students my intense desire for a combination of great commitment to the human adventure, disciplined by universal exposure to evidence and the correction of critical appraisal. This, of course, was largely due to my own ineffectiveness of presentation and to lack of those personal qualities which carry confidence. It was almost a discovery to realize that no matter how close they may be to each other, men know nothing of each other's thoughts, motives and aspirations except as physical arts or appearances make impressions on the physical senses, and are interpreted in the light of the personalities and former experiences of those who receive the impressions. Like so many undertakings that bear the mark of being successful, this project in education has in some respects run far ahead of reasonable expectations, with men of character and insight doing work of substantial significance, while in some respects hopes have not materialized. Some students with relatively slight encouragement seem to achieve a broad and discriminating outlook, while others seem to bear but superficial marks of the educational process.

As a result of these and many other experiences I have become greatly impressed with the importance of the *technique of effectiveness* in making one's efforts count toward his ends.

This realization of the tremendous potential importance of the science and art of leadership is another of my most important discoveries. The effectiveness of one's life depends on the clarity and thoroughness with which his ends are conceived, the suitability of his means, and lastly to the vital energy he puts into their realization. A right proportioning of these elements is of controlling importance.

The science and art of leadership can be developed until a relatively small amount of energy, wisely directed to great ends, will guide and determine the direction of vast human energies; just as the engineer, chiefly with the use of the apparently slight energy of his brain and of the nerves and muscles which move his pencil, directs and controls the expenditure of enormous amounts of energy in great construction. We must try to insure that leadership serves great and fine purpose. In my own case my shortcomings have been in lack of clarity and definition of conception and formulation of purposes, in lack of technical effectiveness in devising suitable means, in limitations of personal traits; and then in an effort to compensate for these defects by excessive output of energy.

Of the three elements of effectiveness I have mentioned, that of clear comprehension of aims is most important. An aim clearly and sanely conceived and expressed, if it has elements of vital truths, has power of reproduction somewhat like that of a living organism. A few years ago in sailing along the west coast of Greece I saw where the side of a mountain had broken off and fallen into the ocean. The splash must have been terrific, and the ripples may have traveled to the most distant shore. Yet, today, there is probably little difference in world affairs because of that great splash. Perhaps it was at about the same time a tiny dandelion seed dropped from a freight package from Europe onto the soil of America. The event was unnoticeable, but the seed had in itself the power of reproduction, and its progeny has spread across the continent. Napoleon made a great splash, but there was relatively little clarity of purpose in what he did. Spinoza in his attic was as inconspicuous as a dandelion seed, but his influence on human thought and life in the end may be greater than that of Napoleon. Human affairs are largely in chaos. All the raw materials exist, including "human nature" and capacity for intelligence, to produce a culture which would project the race far along its way. Vast energies are being spent without design and therefore largely wasted. Vast capacity for design is being consumed in abstractions of theory, undisciplined by adequate contact with reality. Great ability is unused because of the lack of a compelling sense of unity and identity with the destinies of mankind, and of a consuming desire to contribute to that destiny. In government, fairly simple-minded men equipped with valid drives, and trained in the science and art of leadership, could make great contributions. In business the purifying and selective action of these motives would be revolutionary. In philosophy a game like chess would give place to a genuine and passionate search for light. In youth there would be a jealous guarding of energies and powers to commit them to the great quest. The work of the world would be refined by the determination to live and thrive only by contributing to the real needs of men.

I see two kinds of contributions as necessary in human affairs. One is participation in the current conduct of business, government, education and society in general. The other contribution consists in achieving clear purpose and design, in the discipline of personal life and character, and in the creation and extension of a sort of brotherhood of men who will commit themselves wholeheartedly to laying the foundations for a new order. Most men should be engaged in both kinds of endeavor, but some men can serve best by committing themselves almost wholly to the letters.

I have pictured to myself a program for furthering this second purpose. It must include a clarification of personal and social aims and purposes. It must include the development and the possession by individuals of a scientific, discriminating and inclusive ethics, and wholehearted commitment to that ethics in the day-by-day conduct of life. It must achieve effectiveness through the art and science of leadership. It should, I think, include the gradual development of a society or brotherhood of men and women who will wholeheartedly and unreservedly commit themselves to such a quest, and who will discover each other, support and encourage each other, and gradually establish the conduct of life according to the design which has emerged in the common quest. There must be such continuing and growing association of men and women of like purpose to transmit aims and spirit by the contagion of personal contact, for otherwise the dilution and attrition of common life may tend to eliminate all vestiges of high aims and burning purpose. Great political leadership may stimulate a nation to a better program, but before our civilization can become stable on a higher level, such a foundation must be provided by the general occurrence through the population of character, design and commitment, and by mutual support in giving them expression.

Most of the mountains of the earth exist today because of grass and trees. But for these protective coverings the elements would have worn them away at least twenty times as fast. So most desirable human institutions exist because in the common texture of life there is the decency and loyalty to mankind to protect and sustain them. Such a program as I have outlined does not rest solely on leadership. It depends also on the effect of similar motives widely distributed, giving vitality and refinement to the common course of life.

A PROGRAM
FOR A PHILOSOPHY

ARTHUR E. MURPHY

Though a native of New York State—born at Ithaca, September 1, 1901—my early geographical background was mainly that of rural California and the San Francisco Bay region. From my undergraduate and graduate days—all spent at the University of California except for a year in Europe—I recall (of items pertinent to this volume) an earnest moral idealism—the period was that of "the social gospel" and the league of nations—a series of debates in which my preference was for the negative side of almost any question, and a growing interest in philosophy, aroused and guided by such teachers as Adams, Lovejoy, and Kemp Smith. In the eight years since that time I have learned something of my chosen subject, of human nature and of the contemporary American scene from sojourns at the University of Chicago, at Cornell and now at Brown in what is surely the most congenial of philosophical environments. I should perhaps mention also an abiding delight in motion pictures—even rather bad motion pictures—and a conviction that a sense of humor is an important adjunct to philosophic understanding.

A PROGRAM FOR A PHILOSOPHY

Arthur E. Murphy

In the spring of 1922, during my junior year at the University of California, I read for the first time Santayana's *Life of Reason*. The effect of that great book was somewhat complicated by an attack of influenza which developed just as I was completing volume one, and it is difficult to assess in retrospect the respective contributions of fever and intellectual excitement in what was for me a decisive experience. A growing but rather superficial interest in philosophy, a subject I had elected as a not too arduous preliminary to the study of law, was then transformed into the major business of life and such it has remained during the succeeding years. That so extended an investigation should have so far resulted only in a *program* for a philosophy may seem a somewhat meager result. Not only are the sources of philosophic insight in contemporary culture unusually rich and varied, but the number of available systems among which one may select or to which, by a suitable combination of familiar elements, he may add a competing system, is large. Formidable philosophies have been born, have flourished, and have died during the past twelve years, and it may seem unreasonable to stand almost empty handed in the midst of such plenty. But it has always seemed to me that philosophy is properly concerned less with the adoption and polemical defense of a set of opinions, quite probably mistaken, against certain others which could be shown to be even less plausible, than with the achieving of a certain standpoint from which the various aspects of experience could be viewed in their appropriate order and proportion, without special pleading and without distortion, and the genuine

357

insight derived from each be brought to bear on the basic problems to which that insight is relevant. Such a standpoint, adequate in scope to the complexities of the contemporary situation, I have not found in any existing philosophy, and the process by which it can be attained is not a neat and cumulative progress in the assimilation and ordering of facts. It is much more like that "Pilgrim's Progress of the Spirit" which Hegel described in his *Phenomenology*, in which the investigator is driven from narrower perspectives to more inclusive ones by the demands of a reality which shows itself at every level of experience but resists reduction to any system or formula he can fashion for it.

The philosophical exploration I undertook twelve years ago is still going on. Its rewards to date have been a realization of the meaning and relevance of dimensions of reality outside the boundaries of the culture in which, with most of my generation, I had once been content to live, together with a growing clarification of purpose and direction in the search for those principles of unity and proportion which make for wisdom in philosophy and in life. As a substitute, then, for the system which is not and, quite possibly, never shall be, I can offer only a sketch of the experiences and circumstances which have made me aware of reality in diverse and sometimes surprising places and a suggestion of the principles which I propose to follow in a continuing quest for philosophical perspective.

A. FINDING OUT ABOUT REALITY

1. *The Systems of Philosophy and Their Structure.* My introduction to philosophy and my early concern with it were "academic" in the strictest sense. Philosophy was a subject taught in universities, and a quite special subject. Its materials were (a) the systems of the great philosophers and (b) a set of unsolved problems inherited from these philosophers, together with certain characteristic contemporary solutions. The works of the philosophers proved to be an indispensable and

abiding source of knowledge. But from the first I regarded them mainly as aids in solving contemporary problems. By these I was simply fascinated. The dazzling range of the subjects discussed—"Is reality mental or material?" —"Can the object of knowledge be identified with the datum?"—combined with the ingenuity and facility with which one answer could be elaborated and others confuted, offered almost unlimited scope for an argumentative and analytic aptitude which, at that time, constituted my chief intellectual equipment. Why one should choose to defend one position rather than another remained a little obscure. The choice between monism and dualism, between idealism and realism, seemed to be dictated by considerations of preference, piety or professional bias which hardly entered into the discussion. But once a position was adopted, the means by which it could be defended, reformulated to meet objections, and brought to a recognized place among the "isms" of the period, were endless and delightful. That the result was onesided and superficial is hardly surprising. Yet there did develop out of it a conclusion about the systematic structure of philosophies which still seems to me both valid and important. This I labelled "objective relativism" and offered to the world as the latest deliverance of philosophic wisdom. In sum it amounted to this: every major philosophy has been talking about something real, but none so far has known what it was talking about. For each has treated *a* reality—mind, matter, sense-data or space-time—as though it were *the* reality, and hence has been forced to treat *other* realities as mere appearances of its own favored absolute. This distorts the world and creates artificial problems which could be adequately solved if each philosopher would admit that his "reality," though objective and genuine, is also relative, an aspect or phase of the concrete world and not its inner and exclusive being.

The thesis was first developed in criticism of opposing theories —notably those of Lovejoy and Alexander. The former, I thought, had confused an account of knowledge which was evidently valid for some situations with a theory of what knowledge as such must be; thereby rendering anomalous other ways of knowing which his own view presupposed. The latter, finding in the fashionable notion of space-time a fruitful clue to the clearing up of some epistemological mysteries, had forthwith transformed it into the very substance of events, the stuff of reality itself. And this was clearly illegitimate. As a critical weapon my theory worked well. But I soon found that other philosophies, in most respects eminently reasonable, came finally to the same sort of mistake. When Whitehead, in whose earlier works the principles of objective relativism seemed clearly implied, turned speculative metaphysician in *Process and Reality*, my disappointment was deep. Surely, so pervasive and deep-rooted an error must have its origin in something fundamental to current philosophy itself. Was it not because such "speculative deduction" was assumed to be the very essence of philosophic explanation that these wise men felt obliged to resort to it in spite of the antecedent improbability of success? Here I was confronted with a deeper question than those that I had dealt with on the controversial level. The fault I found in contemporary philosophy came not from a violation of the rules on the part of some competitors, but from the very nature of the rules which all were following. "Objective relativism," if it was to do its business, could not be one among these systems; its whole notion of the function of philosophy must be different. With this realization, my "objective relativism," occasionally mentioned as a minor variant of epistemological realism, passed beyond itself in Hegelian fashion and ceased, as an "ism," to exist.

2. *A Philosophy That Almost Happened.* What then was philosophy to be, and where, if not in speculative deduction and epistemological controversy, was reality to be discerned? To describe the world of which the objects of alternative philosophical analyses are aspects and to which they are objectively relative, I had taken over from Whitehead the term "event." But what *is* an event? That it is no mere spatio-temporal locus

for otherwise foot-loose abstractions seemed evident. It must not be any *other* reality than that which its aspects manifest in their occurrence: it must be just that manifestation itself. To show how objects of any sort are "real" would then be to show how they are *realized* here and now and how they participate in the complex but urgent actuality of contemporary nature. So far, however, this reality was only abstractly and rather technically defined. But just at this stage of reflection I went, as a young and very impressionable instructor, to Chicago, and the "philosophy of events" was soon transformed into a "philosophy of what happens," which gave promise of happening almost immediately. The nature of the transformation was twofold. In the first place I came to apprehend the *happening* of things not in its abstract definition but in its concrete embodiment. The academic philosopher is naturally suspicious of demands that he connect "philosophy" with "life" and subordinate the high aims of research to the concerns of the market-place. Here, however, I seemed to find life not as an alternative to speculation, but as its natural and appropriate completion. This actuality I had been seeking, this "event" in which reality must show itself, what was it but the fullness of contemporary life in America, in Chicago? Not here alone, of course: I claimed no geographical exclusiveness for my discovery. But here *for me*, since I too was localized and particularized by participation in it. And the philosophy that was to be my alternative to speculative deduction could now be nothing else than an attempt to render visible and articulate the incidence of all reality upon, and the possibilities of its realization in, the life of which I was a part.

I recall from that time a vivid and rather curious experience which cannot be omitted from any adequate statement of my philosophy. One October evening—I had been in the city only a month or two—I walked out along the lake shore in Grant Park and turned, just opposite the head of Van Buren Street, to take stock of the place where I had come to live. And as I looked along that magnificent skyline, it seemed to me, quite immediately and simply, that I was confronting reality itself, and that it was the very same reality for which philosophy had taught me to look—that philosophy which begins in wonder and can only be content with a world somehow wonderful enough to satisfy its need. It seemed an odd and somewhat unorthodox vision, but at least, I thought, it need not fade into the light of common day, for that light and its meaning were the substance of the vision itself.

A second influence in this period was the "contextualism" which I imbibed from my Chicago colleagues and which I still consider of basic philosophical importance. Pragmatism, as a theory of truth, had never seemed to me even plausible, and I found no reason now to alter my judgment. But while the meaning of truth is one, the contexts in which it is to be discovered and in relation to which alone specific truths are understandable are various, and without attention to such contexts no adequate theory of knowledge is possible. The *filling* of knowledge and experience, rather badly neglected in my earlier training, now seemed inexhaustibly fruitful and significant. Everywhere I found leads, suggestions, which partly verified my earlier opinions and very largely supplemented and corrected them. Why argue about "the object of knowledge," when the processes and tests of knowing *in specific situations* were so much in need of further analysis, and when so much could evidently be learned from them? What use to abstract "the world of description" from the scientific research that generates such description and, *in operation,* indicates its function? To ask in all such cases for some *other* reality for objects or ideals than that which shows itself *in* specific contexts and under conditions, was simply not to know how reality functions or where it can be found. It is not surprising that "the philosophy of what happens" seemed in those days very near an adequate expression.

3. *Beyond Relativism.* That the synthesis was premature and the reality it celebrated still far too narrowly conceived, the

logic of events was soon to demonstrate. With my first picture of Chicago I came in later years to couple another, from a day when, in great perplexity, I went back again down Van Buren Street to the lake front to try to recover from my old standpoint some part of that former experience, and to make such use of it as I could. The skyscrapers were as splendid as ever; there were even some new ones to complete the picture. Some of them I knew now from the inside, and what it was that lay behind them and made them possible. But all I could see in them was an incongruous and rather meaningless false front—like a motion picture set in Hollywood, with a pretentious perform-ance being enacted on one side and on the other nothing, or nothing that the camera and the world would care to record. The picture was flat, two-dimensional, curiously unreal. Evi-dently my approach to reality had somehow proved illusory. Later on, rereading T. S. Eliot's poems, I understood more ex-plicitly what it was that I had felt. His "unreal city" was Lon-don, but for the rest the parallel was complete enough. In exploring the spiritual resources of the contemporary world I had, like many others, found "the waste land."

The content of this discovery can be stated less metaphori-cally in terms of a distinction between two meanings of "reality" which I now found it necessary to distinguish. "Reality" stands for the ultimate objective of valid knowledge, both of facts and of values. Its locus is the environing world in which purposes are carried out and ideas verified in so far as they attain their intended fulfilment. But this world is apprehended only in terms of our adjustment to it, and in this response "reality" in a derivative sense is imputed to those ideas or preferences which at any period are accepted as ultimate on their own account and in terms of which we estimate the significance of whatever in experience lacks, in its own right, such preferential finality. In all behavior in which normative judgments are important our grasp of "reality" as conditioning environment is largely de-termined by our conception of "reality" as that which is to be accepted as ultimately authoritative in matters of belief or valuation. The critical positivist may cavil at the suggestion that such "metaphysical" considerations play any part in his own thinking, but if he is unaware of the unique status he accords to the quite special and selective principles which determine his judgment of what is to be accepted as a "fact" and what rejected as "unverifiable" and "unscientific" not only in the sciences themselves but in all questions of the estimation of evidence and the fixing of belief, then his critical acumen has not yet attained the higher wisdom of self knowledge. And my own emphasis on events, on "nature" and on the value judgments of current humanism were a patent reflection of the preoccupations of the time. The reality I had seen, and had been prepared to see, was what this standpoint, accepted on its own terms, was capable of revealing. It was this standpoint itself that I was now compelled to call in question.

The grounds of such questioning are written large in the intellectual history of the period. In the great days of a culture the standpoint it imposes on those who work within its preconceptions is the means by which experience is effectively mastered, made relevant and accessible to human purposes. The world of the 1920's had lost the sense of such mastery; the basic fact about it, for those who had worked through to its foundations, was the discrepancy between the "realities" it offered as standards for truth and goals for action and a world that failed to fit their measure or reveal its meaning in their terms. This failure to organize the complex material presented for synthesis was felt as a radical disconnection between fact and significance, between the intention of action and the objectives proposed for its consummation. The sense of the "unreality" of such a world, its inadequacy to the normative function whose authority it had assumed, was a substantial discovery.

The unreality of the philosophic enterprise under such conditions was hardly less apparent. The speculative constructions of the past were still honored in the schools as models to which a philosophy should conform, but the "isms" that echoed their pretensions were too obviously partial to carry much conviction. Each could start from an interesting set of facts, but none seemed to find a way of getting this provisional reality into connection with anything beyond itself, of using it as a standpoint for understanding the world to which it was supposed somehow to refer. No wonder that philosophy, so far as it concerned the elaboration and controversial defense of such systems, seemed hardly more than an intricate exercise in dialectic. It was meant to be more than that, but here, too, intention found no commensurate realization within the limits of its recognized preconceptions. Meanwhile the general public did not lack for philosophy of a sort. The variety of special knowledge had quite exceeded the boundaries of common sense and common intelligibility; interpreters were wanted who could make the new things plain to all and this interpretation was philosophy of a more practical sort than its "academic" counterpart. But the principles of interpretation offered were not grounded in the structure of facts that might be seen together because they belonged together; they were simply the idols of the literary market place, substituting somewhat dubiously for the benefit of a public too confused and uncertain to know the difference. How, indeed, was the difference to be known? We were all relativists together and therefore aware of the inevitable limits of *any* principles that might be employed. Why, then, be overcritical of those that happened to differ from our own? Basic principles are only preconceptions in any case, but their ultimate groundlessness need not interfere with their utility as expressions of the spirit of the times, the popularized import of the sciences, or anything else that stands in need of a generalized and somewhat imposing expression. In many quarters this conclusion was accepted as the natural outcome of relativism; it seemed to me merely a philosophic acquiescence in that disconnection between fact and meaning which registered the failure of our culture to solve its problems.

This acquiescence is easier to criticize than to correct. For how *can* a valid philosophic standpoint be distinguished from a mere bias or preconception? How can the ultimacy presupposed in the adoption of a normative standard be criticized, save from another and equally relative standpoint? Are there any rational or grounded biases? This, I believe, is the fundamental question to which contemporary philosophy must find an answer if it is to escape the impasse it has reached. And the answer must carry us beyond a merely arbitrary relativism, it must indicate a connection between the derivative ultimates of rival doctrines and the world they somehow intend to bring before us. The classical philosophers described this connection as the relation of appearance to reality and their account was right to an extent that my earlier relativism had failed adequately to acknowledge. The world as humanly apprehended is not ultimate on its own account. Its genuineness is real but provisional; it is the symbol or manifestation of a reality that can be seen through it but may also be obscured or distorted if the mediatory function of the representation is not fully grasped. For "appearance" here I would substitute "the world as interpreted from any specified standpoint" and for "reality," "the wider environment within which that standpoint is a limitation." The import for philosophy is much the same in either version. No standpoint can be taken as final on its own account. Each, when so taken, becomes a "mere" appearance; it fails in its imputed finality to convey its connection with a further reality and, lacking this connection, it cannot make good its own claim to the reality which is in fact its justification and ground. My earlier insight was true enough as far as it went. The world is to be understood only through some standpoint within itself and the lake front in Chicago is a possible station from which to view it. But the foreground may obscure the view as well as reveal it, and the first look is hardly likely to bring out the connections that place it in a wider perspective. And the philosophy which can master that wider view is not, even in Chicago, a gift; it is a long and arduous achievement.

4. *The Business of Philosophy.* Here, then, is my problem and the direction it determines for further inquiry. Philosophy is concerned with the standards men accept as ultimate for fact, truth, significance and value, and with the consequences that follow from such acceptance for the organization of experience around the dominant interests and objectives thus defined. That these standards are relative and will vary with time and circumstances is undeniable. That we shall ever be able to discover one among them which, avoiding such limitations, can serve as ground and standard for all the rest is highly unlikely. But that these standards must be accepted by philosophy as ultimate as they stand is simply false. Their validity is grounded in their representative function and this can be tested by the reality that appears in them and the reality which, seen from a different angle, must be coördinated with them in as just and discriminating an integration of experience as the resources of the time will permit. It is this examination and coördination of special insights which, at any period, constitutes the major contribution of philosophy to our understanding of the world. Instead of generalizing on what philosophy might do in this regard I shall mention what seem to me its positive current assets.

(a) It has emphasized the significance of aspects of experience which, through their disconnection with dominant and uncriticized preconceptions, had become almost inaccessible to contemporary understanding of the more sophisticated sort. The reduction of the faith and practice of the great religions to the observed or postulated events sufficient for a "scientific explanation" of the psychological abnormalities which constitute the "explicable" phenomena of mysticism is a sufficient indication of the way in which an inappropriate standpoint can trivialize the facts with which it purports to deal. In their vindication of the uniqueness of this and other dimensions of reality James and Bergson have notably broadened the horizon of accessible experience. There is more of reality to be seen as a result o their understanding of the angle from which to see it.

(b) The most pressing immediate task for American ph: losophy is the development of a coherent theory of values. Th restriction of "knowledge" to fields in which the discriminatio of values is inappropriate to the methods of investigation em ployed has left us substantially without rational guidance in thi subject. What, for example, is the appropriate relation betweer conditioning and final goods, between economic security and per sonal freedom? The answers given by our leaders are as impres sionistic, as incoherent, as the disorganization of thought in thi field would have led us to expect. What is wanted is a systemati standpoint from which the complex structure of related value: can be explored. This task falls upon philosophy not because values are more real or unreal than anything else but because the specific reality that they are is obscured by accepted notion: of "fact" and truth and the rectification of these notions, their adjustment to the objective situation to which they must relate us, is a prerequisite for progress here. Hartmann's "Ethics" is a fine indication of the fruitfulness of the application of a sound philosophy to a situation we badly need to understand.

(c) Whitehead has rightly insisted that the "Adventure of Ideas" which he has so vividly described requires for its full development some adequate awareness of the way in which our limited undertakings participate in and are sustained by the more inclusive world that underlies them. Of the genuineness of this participation I shall say something in a later section. The recognition that philosophy, after so long a period of critical negations, can recapture this sense of reality and give it effective, if still obscure, expression is itself a substantial achievement.

The furtherance of the investigation thus suggested is no slight undertaking and the philosopher engaged in it will at least not lack a feeling of responsibility to his subject and to the community to which his interpretation is directed. For my

wn guidance in further research I have set down some rules
vhich have so far proved helpful and in terms of which I intend
o proceed.

B. Some Rules for a Philosophy

1. The concern of philosophy is that reality which reveals
tself in experience. To deal with it justly a philosopher must so
)roaden and deepen his experience that he will be able to see
·eality at all the levels in which it appears and to know it when
le sees it. This is the first commandment and the hardest to
<eep. For if my own experience has taught me anything it is
:his, that the meaning of events is very frequently an unobvious
neaning: it may be missed by the clever and it will not obtrude
.tself upon the unpreceptive. Nor will any amount of logical
1cumen or technical ingenuity compensate for that spiritual ob-
:useness which, content to identify the reality of the world with
its surface, finds it in the end but a superficial reality. Santayana
has pointed out that our assurance of the external world has as
its precondition a certain animal faith, a readiness to respond to
more than given experience can infallibly guarantee. He failed
to recognize, along with this, our more than animal need for
commerce with objective spiritual reality and to honor the faith
that here, too, is the prerequisite of a rational response. Yet the
situation is in essence the same on each level. Man draws his
sustenance, both material and spiritual, from the world outside
himself. The penalty this environment exacts for failure to
respond is not "refutation" but starvation. The natural and
appropriate sequel to cultural positivism is "The Waste Land"
and "The Magic Mountain."

It follows that a philosopher is responsible in his profession
not merely for making the most of what he sees but for seeing
what is there to be seen. In any field of investigation whatever,
the conclusion reached will depend on the facts discriminated,
and this discrimination, in turn, on the perceptive capacities of
the investigator. Where value judgments are concerned this is

quite evidently true. It may be better to be a man dissatisfied than a pig satisfied, but one has to be a man to appreciate the cogency of the preference. The limitation of insight that cuts out as irrelevant or relegates to the realm of "nonsense" or "superstition" dimensions of experience from which its own preoccupation excludes it may not interfere with success in the sciences: it seems to be a positive asset in criticism of a sort. But in philosophy it amounts to sheer incompetence to deal with the subject at hand, and as such it should be recognized.

2. No claimant to the title of reality shall be accredited until it has met such tests as are appropriate to its nature and manner of manifestation; none shall be rejected because it fails to meet tests which could not have verified its claim even had that claim been valid.

It has been rightly said that philosophy is not poetry or faith, but a kind of knowledge. Like all knowledge it refers beyond itself to a reality whose nature it claims to reveal and by reference to which its claim must be tested. Truth means correspondence or conformity to fact, and however much we may value certain beliefs, we have no right to ground our assurance of their truth on any other considerations than those which tend to establish the fact to which the belief refers and by which alone it can be justified. So far the realistic theory of truth seems to me right, and even evidently right. But, as realists are fond of saying, the nature of truth is one thing, its test or criterion another. And when the realist has attempted to set down the criteria by which reality may be known, his theory has often been lamentably inadequate. Some "data" may be "sensed" and some facts perceived. It is fortunate that some features of the world are thus discernible; it would be well if there were more. But to suppose that experience has no other truth to reveal than that which thus proclaims itself, or that this rather meager equipment can serve as the measure for reality, is a grave mistake. The objectionable naïveté of naïve realism is represented not by its insistence on obvious fact but by its demand that all fact must be as obvious as that of its own infallible perceptions.

Again, some facts are discerned through the methods of the sciences, and it is reasonable to expect further progress by the use of methods so admirably adapted to the special features of reality with which it is their business to deal. To assume that what is not thus discernible is not a fact is to show but little knowledge of the development and applications of scientific method. Yet various forms of positivism, by identifying knowledge with science and science with the tested result of some special types of analysis, have thought to base a serious philosophy on just this assumption. A truer "objectivity" is that which patterns its response on the nature which the object of investigation manifests in its own context and environment; and nothing is more arbitrarily subjective than the demand that all reality shall conform to a simplified description whose success in special cases has so endeared it to its author that he has come to regard its unrestricted application as the height of philosophic wisdom.

The truth would seem to be that reality as it appears in our experience is of many aspects or dimensions, and there is *no* single criterion by which it may in all cases be recognized. The evidence for the existence of physical objects is to be discovered in physics, and by attention to the considerations which have so far directed physical research and justified its outcome. Logicians like Wittgenstein who limit their attention to the "logical picture" of the facts naturally find the belief in a causal nexus mere superstition. Poetic theologians, like Eddington in some phases of his thought, find no poetry in the equations of hydrodynamics and set down the deficiency against their claim to reality. More rarely an historian of science like Meyerson presents the structure of physics not as logic, nor as metaphysical poetry, but as physics, and we begin to understand how physical reality is discovered and under what conditions it can be known. And that is critical philosophy of the best sort.

3. No claim can be accepted for any one type or aspect of reality which is inconsistent with the legitimate claims of other or with the assumptions which practice and good judgment force upon us.

That the various aspects of the world somehow go together and that philosophers should seek out and emphasize such principles of unity and coherence as can be found is a familiar affirmation, not, as it stands, of much philosophic value. What is wanted is an idea of the *sort* of unity that will exhibit without distortion the structure of the world we know. "Reality" may be speculatively unified by the identification of the real with some aspect of the world in which a simple and striking unity does in fact exist. But the unity of reality *with appearance* then becomes a quite hopeless problem and the world we know the world in which reality should appear in *all* its aspects, is more disconnected, more confused, than ever.

In contrast with speculative idealism, a valid theory must be content with a somewhat plural and heterogeneous world. In comparison with the meticulous clarities of critical positivism, it must put up with a certain amount of confusion. For the unity it seeks is not of "reality" but of realities, each in its own kind genuine and irreducible, and the only clarity that would be relevant is that which *clarifies* a somewhat muddled and chaotic world, not the world we would have chosen for logical analysis, but that in which, with such insight as we can muster, we are compelled to live.

Yet the unifying function of reason, and of philosophy, is of central importance. Its status is rather like that of justice in Plato's ideal state, a harmony of interests, each of which best contributes to the whole by minding its own business and leaving for others the determination of that which falls outside its scope and competence. To leave open questions that *are* open, to refuse to distort life by intruding upon it the exclusiveness of one's own preoccupation, is itself a major philosophic achievement. Nor is this harmony one of mutual independence. Human

iterests are not self-contained and each in some way requires
he contribution of others for its own enhancement. To analyze
uch interdependence—as, for example, that of morality and
eligion or of science and its starting point in common sense—
vithout denying the genuine differences involved is an im-
nensely intricate and delicate task. Here are connections to be
mphasized within experience itself, and the function of philosophy is to articulate them as justly and precisely as possible.

Finally, philosophic unification is an affair of tension, contrast
nd dynamic readjustment. The structure of reality is made
known to us in an experience whose growth is radically discontinuous. A new discovery in one field, a dominant cultural
pattern in another, will bring first one aspect of its nature, then
another, into the focus of attention. The world as a whole is
hardly shaken by the episodes of its human discovery, but our
attitude toward the world is likely to be thrown completely off
its balance by such intellectual revolutions. To interpret the old
to the new, the unobvious and remote to the current fashion, the
eternal to the temporal, to discern in social change the basic
facts that underlie it, is to establish a central standpoint around
which a progressive coördination and organization of experience
becomes genuinely possible. That possibility I am now inclined
to regard as of greater importance than the unities and simplifi-
cations of much current doctrine.

4. Realty is greater than our guesses about it, and experience
must not be impoverished by the formulas through which, in
limited and human terms, it is described. And yet reality is directly present in these formulations at their best. We can participate in it, and such participation is the goal of philosophy,
and its justification.

The assurance that sustained St. Bernard and Pascal in their
search for God belongs with equal right to the philosopher: he
could not seek reality if he had not already found it. In tested
knowledge, in fully shared and realized experience, in the sustained application of a generously planned ideal, we are dealing

with facts as genuine in their own kind as anything can be. Unless reality was discoverably present here we should not know where to look for it or indeed what to look for. It is the reality *in* these facts that forces us beyond them and by that reality we are at all times constrained. My first insight in Chicago was not, then, altogether an illusion. But, like other mystical or semi-mystical experiences, it was not the end of wisdom but only the beginning. To use these beginnings for all that they are worth, and to work through them to such further truth, as is yet to be discerned—such, in substance, is my program for a philosophy.

TOWARD A NATURALISTIC
CONCEPTION OF LOGIC

ERNEST NAGEL

Born November 16th, 1901, in Nove Mesto, in what is now Czecho-Slovakia. Educated in the New York City public schools. Graduated from the College of the City of New York, 1923, with the degree of B.S.S. While teaching in the New York City high schools received an M.A. in mathematics from Columbia University 1925. Ph.D. in Philosophy 1931. Instructor in Philosophy at the College of the City of New York, 1926-30. Instructor in Philosophy at Columbia University, 1931-. Guggenheim Research Fellow in Philosophy, 1934-35. A book-editor of *The Journal of Philosophy*. Partial bibliography *Logic of Measurement: An Introduction to Logic and Scientific Method* (with M. R. Cohen): contributions to *Proceedings of the Eighth International Congress of Philosophy*, *Columbia Studies in the History of Ideas*, Vol. 3; *Journal of Philosophy*, *Erkenntnis*, *Philosophic Review*, *Symposium*, *New Republic*, *Saturday Review of Literature*.

TOWARD A NATURALISTIC
CONCEPTION OF LOGIC

Ernest Nagel

Santayana remarks in one of his books that he would be ashamed to hold views in philosophy which he did not believe in daily life, and that he would deem it dishonest and cowardly to sail under colors in an argument which were not those under which he habitually lived. The precept implied by these comments can serve as a criterion for evaluating the quality of integration which a thinker achieves in his own life; but more significantly, it helps to fix the subject matter and task of philosophy, and so to disclose the relevance of the philosophic pursuit to the society which nourishes it. It is a precept which I take for my own wholeheartedly, and one which I wish were taken as a guide in all philosophic inquiry.

Reflection has as its ultimate point of departure the qualitatively diversified world of common experience. It is a world containing joys and sorrows, brute compulsions, changing scenes, and recurrent patterns of behavior. It is this world which man tries to understand by unraveling some threads of its structure, thereby making it familiar to himself and himself more at home in it. An imaginative, liberal science will reveal to him aspects of the world he would ignore were he exclusively concerned with the tasks of everyday living. But I for one cannot give my allegiance to any system of thought which denies the obvious facts of such a more limited but nevertheless disciplined experience, or which makes unintelligible well-founded distinctions and habits of behavior. The world which philosophy tries to understand should be the world as it is found; and since what

377

is found includes the familiar things and practices of daily life, I am unable to regard any philosophy as honest or tenable which concludes them to be illusions or unreal.

The latent naturalism discoverable in the behavior and common beliefs of most men, I believe to be capable of formulation as an adequate hypothesis for a large view of the world. It is the philosophy by which I habitually live and which I consciously profess. It holds that the world consists of the coming-to-be and passing-away of substantial things, that there is a discoverable order in their rise, continuance and decay, and that nature is completely intelligible in terms of their determinate characters, so that the unknowable operation of disembodied forms is not relevant to nature's order or our knowledge of it. It regards the human scene and all things in it as possessing an ontological status neither inferior nor superior to the status of atoms, stars, or nebulae, and views the values which men cherish as an expression of the needs which the subtle organization of their bodies develop. Science and philosophy seem to me therefore both concerned exclusively with obtaining adequate knowledge of the world into which we come at birth and which we finally leave at death—the former seeking to determine systematically the precise conditions for the occurrence of specific characters of things, the latter occupying itself with the analysis and the clarification of our ideas of generic traits of existence and with tracing ideal values and logical distinctions to their natural sources.

Philosophy on this view does not legislate for the sciences and cannot prescribe the procedures they must employ nor the possible content of their theories. It is not an apologetic for religious, scientific, or social interests, nor does it stamp the seal of nature's approval upon any desires however insistent or noble. It is not a theodicy which pictures the world as devoid of the tragedies it so manifestly contains. It has nothing to say why the universe is as it is, for it cannot convert, on pain of contradiction, the pervasive traits of the world into explanations of its existence. Its task is analytical and critical. It studies the meaning and structure of statements, discovers what pervasive characters nature owns, and so determines the conditions for intelligible discourse and rational practice. The task of philosophy can be briefly defined as the analysis of categories. But this definition must be adopted with the qualification that the meaning and universality of a category must be located in and determined by the traits of subject matter, and that the validity of a categorial analysis is at all times an empirical matter. A clear recognition that all analysis and all judgments of importance are contextual, that distinctions and traits are distinctions and traits within denotatively fixed subject matter, that the extrapolation of one analysis to other situations must be attended by caution if dislocations of meaning are not to result, are important services which a thoroughgoing naturalism can render.

As I conceive it, naturalism is therefore not simply a set of fixed doctrines about the system of events which constitute nature. To profess it is to practice a method of inquiry as well as to subscribe to a metaphysics. Indeed, the term "nature" has meant many things in the history of thought, and professed naturalists have rarely agreed as to which are the generic traits of existence, or as to what are the specific set of principles descriptive of the order of birth and decay of things. In spite of variations in the content of their views, however, they seem to me to share a common method by which they support them. If there were a heaven inhabited and operated by disembodied spirits, I can fancy some of them claiming kinship with naturalism in so far as they learn from that heavenly "nature" herself the manner of her operations, and are at pains constantly to submit their principles to verification. The supposition and the fancy can easily be misleading. But they help emphasize how essential it is to a naturalist to view the world we inhabit as thoroughly intelligible, to refer the analyses he performs to their appropriate contexts, and to believe that a sound logic of inquiry is the sole guarantee against illusion. That is why naturalism is so often accepted by the laboratory scientist as a matter of course—at least in his laboratory. For like the scientist, it is more certain of the general adequacy of its self-corrective method than it is of the unalterable finality of any particular conclusion obtained through its use. And that is why I think the analysis and practice of scientific method is so essential to a thoroughgoing naturalism.

The claims of sense and of reason for an exclusive rôle in a correct logical method form one of the major themes in the history of philosophy. Facts, sensuous qualities, immediately given data as the ultimate objects and arbiters of knowledge are the stock in trade of a long line of empiricists, while the use of self-evident principles, intuitively determined canons of intelligibility, and far-reaching theoretical constructions characterize the procedure of classical rationalism.

If empiricism means that knowledge is simply a matter of immediate contact with the sensuous flux of qualities, nothing can be more absurd than that a professional thinker should profess it. Anyone who seriously holds to such an empiricism has been refuted in Greek antiquity. The immediate is often attractive, but to immerse oneself on principle in the brutely ineffable is to foreswear what is characteristically human. The evil consequences of such a myopic sensationalism for both science and morals have been frequently and conclusively portrayed by thinkers of all schools, and no one can intelligibly be an empiricist if empiricism means what they have so vividly dissected.

On the other hand, if rationalism means belief in self-evident principles, in *a priori* propositions about matters of fact, in the irrelevance of experiment to questions of truth, it is equally difficult to be a rationalist. The devastating critiques of empirical philosophers as well as the procedure of the positive sciences seem to me to make the view that the inspection of meanings alone is sufficient to determine the truth of propositions an illustration of arrogant ignorance. The consequences of such a rationalism are no less serious than those of a nominalistic sensationalism. It makes of the intellect a disembodied force fatally separated from the processes of the existing world. It shows itself to be insensitive to possibilities of behavior and structure, and often leads to fanaticism in ethics and politics. Its greatest sin is to dislocate the conclusions of an inquiry by confounding achieved knowledge of some segment of nature with necessary traits of still unknown things.

But a sound naturalism cannot regard sense and intellect as incompatible poles of human activity. And indeed in the logical methods employed in the sciences and the disciplined inquiries of daily life, no impassable gulf between sense and reason is found. Stable knowledge is there equated neither with sensation nor with an original intuition into a realm of pure meanings. On the contrary, it is acquired through the use of general ideas, suggested by traits of empirical subject matter, which are dialectically elaborated and supported by evidence secured through the senses.

A sound logical method must avoid two extremes if it is not to play into the hands of a premature dogmatism or a vicious obscurantism. It must not claim indubitability for any general proposition about matters of fact; and it must reject the view that, because the evidence for a general proposition is never complete, no distinction in the logical worth of propositions can be made. As to the first point, the history of thought reveals a flux of doctrines, and the latest theory in any science is not likely to be the last. General knowledge about matters of fact is obtained by conducting operations of sampling in a changing world. While sampling conducted according to known canons leads to knowledge on the whole stable, the propositions obtained can be asserted only as probable with some degree. Conclusions of one inquiry serve as hypotheses in another, and may require modification, although always in accordance with the character of the best available evidence. The vitality and validity of scientific method come from its essentially self-corrective nature. Indeed, the canons of inquiry are themselves forged in the process of acquiring knowledge, and serve as experimentally well-grounded principles of analysis subject to progressive supplementation. Propositions about matters of fact which are necessarily true have no footing in the logic of the sciences.

It also follows that the theories asserted in the sciences are not simply pleasing fictions or conventions which express only the esthetic and social prejudices of their originators. I think no folly is more dangerous than that practised by many philosophers who, misunderstanding the subtle techniques of contemporary sciences for making hypotheses more flexible to the demands of subject matter, preach a consolatory agnosticism in science, a spiritualistic metaphysics in philosophy, and a dubious program of action in social theory. None of the conclusions of any inquiry can be understood, none deserve our confidence, if they are asserted in independence of the procedures required to establish them; out of the context of a sound method it is silly to talk about facts. But it is one thing to say this, and a completely other thing to declare that *any* method is a sound method, that any statement is a statement of fact, and that truth is simply a matter of agreement or choice of system. For it is the structure of a subject matter which determines the relevance and truth of our discourse about it; and it is one of the tasks of philosophy to exhibit this fact. Purely dialectical considerations are therefore never sufficient to resolve problems arising from the study of nature. Insistence upon the systematic character of the natural sciences has misled many who are only dimly aware of what is involved in the brilliant analyses of Poincaré and others. By displaying the systematic connections of propositions to one another, their possible inconsistencies can be eliminated, their range of application and precise significance can be clarified, the rôle of denotative definitions can be indicated, and the material evidence can be compounded more effectively. But the character of the existential subject matter is authoritative, and is the ultimate ground for the truth of any theory. In the procedure of the sciences a rationalistic empiricism exhibits in a most perfect form the union of intellect and sense.

The doctrine that the sciences or philosophy have as their subject matter a special realm of reality, sometimes alleged to be inferior, sometimes superior to the experimental world of common-day life, does not lack supporters today. Eminent scientists rise from time to time to assure us that there is a "real" world to which we may gain entrance, via some recent theory, which is free from the precarious, qualitative traits of everyday nature. Or philosophers, not to be outdone in nonsense, declare with assurance that the sciences deal with mere abstractions existing nowhere except in the mind of the scientist, so that "reality" must be "known" in some other way—religious experience, art, or social participation.

These variations on the same theme seem to me to be the outcome of misplacing the reference of an analysis and of attempting to measure and identify all phases of nature with those discovered in a determinate context. The sciences aim to discover the conditions for the occurrence of various kinds of events. If in the process they are led to atoms and electrons whose imputed but verifiable behavior is different from the behavior of the more familiar objects of daily life, those surprising entities have no more bearing upon the "reality" of the everyday scene than does the discovery of new tribes with strange customs. The discovery of sub-microscopic entities is important for formulating a coherent account of the order to be found in some phases of nature, an importance which the discovery of new tribes may lack. But such entities are in no way relevant for disproving the existence of the characters and the behavior of familiar objects, especially if it is noted that the evidence for the former must be found in the latter. And superior reality can be attributed to such sub-microscopic entities only if generic traits of a subject matter are converted into

causative agents, and if the conditions for the occurrence of anything are arbitrarily assigned superior metaphysical ranking.

Reflective inquiry is of necessity selective of the traits which
characterize a subject matter. A situation may be studied as
the parabolic path traced out by a freely falling body; or it may
be viewed, in a context of personal and social implications, as
the fall of an aged worker from a high scaffolding. The former
analysis would be made by a physicist, the latter perhaps by a
sociologist. Each analysis isolates certain abstract features of the
total situation, and studies their interrelations within it. Neither
analysis is exhaustive of the characters of the subject matter;
but neither therefore "falsifies" it. Physics, for example, does
not study men, or animals, or flowers, or minerals as such. It
explores the relations between phases of behavior which all
these things exhibit in common, without studying all the properties which any one body exhibits. But to condemn physics because
it is abstract and selective, is to condemn all discourse and all
rational activity. It is always a delimited and selected phase of
a thing to which we address ourselves—whether it is in curiosity,
in love, or in anger. The identifiable characters which are the
guides and objects of knowledge are all discriminated and abstract—though most abstractions are more familiar, and discriminated for different purposes, than those in the theoretical
sciences. Knowing a thing is not being that thing; but the arguments leveled by both philosophers and scientists against the
thesis that the sciences give us knowledge of nature, seem to me
to contain no charge more serious than the commonplace that
discourse is not identical, as indeed it must not be, with that
about which it is made.

These latter remarks reinforce some previous ones and anticipate others. If thinking is a selective activity, every significant
idea must have reference to some context and be irrelevant to
others. It is the disregard of this elementary condition of significance which leads to the attribution of a superior reality to
atoms and electrons, or to the frequent attempts to view all of

nature as nothing but their spatio-temporal juxtaposition. A science or philosophy which professedly inquires into traits and conditioning factors common to all bodies sins against this principle when it employs such pervasive traits in order to differentiate one body from another; and it sins again when, failing in this as it must, it legislates out of reality the phases of behavior it refuses to note.

The analysis of ideas in terms of the procedures required to identify their subject matter and which define them would do much, it seems to me, to rid philosophy of many a mare's nest of problems. Ideas which are perfectly intelligible within the context in which they have an operational meaning become opaque and acquire supernatural powers when they are isolated from such contexts and viewed as substantial beings. There is only one alternative to the logical theory which finds the meanings of ideas and propositions ultimately in the characters and behaviors of natural things—the theory of clear and distinct ideas, according to which every concept must be clarified by analyzing it into a complex of indubitable simple meanings or essences. The latter has been often used as the philosophic method, and I think usually with fatal results; distinctions have been converted into contradictions, habits of thought erected into necessities of nature, discourse has been made to generate its subject matter, and analyses have been taken out of their relevant contexts.

Because I hold that nature is intelligible in terms of the relations between substantial things, and because I think that qualities like colors and sounds are objective phases of nature's behavior, I believe that a fertile field for philosophic analysis is the logic of measurement. For in the larger sense, of which numerical measurement is a special case, measurement is the procedure by which things in nature are discovered to have determinate characters, and through which terms in discourse acquire significance and relevance. I think the nature of measurement sustains the thesis that things have intelligible characters, just as they have sensible shapes and colors, in the determinate contexts wherein they are discovered to have them, but that they need not have these traits in other contexts. It is not the subjectivity of colors and shapes which is demonstrated by the fact that the same object will exhibit different colors and shapes in different lights and positions; it is their objective relativity. So also the study of measurement makes clear that the quantitative laws of the sciences have no relevance and ultimately no meaning apart from the procedures and relations between qualified things of everyday experience.

It is for such reasons that I think the analysis of categories like space and time can be most satisfactorily made by studying their operational meaning in the sciences, but through a study of their operational meaning, and not through an examination of what scientists may say about them. Such a study shows, I think, space and time to be relational characters of and ordering principles for material things, and not to be substantial themselves. But whatever be the correct analysis of space and time as scientific categories, it seems to me worth while to insist that only through studying the subject matter of the sciences can a significant categorial analysis be carried through. There is nothing so futile and depressing as the complacent and arrogant game played by many philosophers in characterizing the empirical sciences as "self-contradictory" because these latter employ categories in ways not hallowed by some tradition or some allegedly final metaphysics. In the history of philosophy, terms like space and time are not univocal, and refer frequently to different phases of natural subject matter. Philosophers in bitter dispute about the "real nature" of such matters as space, often argue at cross purposes because of the subtle differences in the reference of the terms. That is why scientific categories must be analyzed in terms of the procedures which define them.

The operational theory of meaning has, I think, some bearing on a philosophy of mathematics. Recently the thesis has been developed with great skill and patience that the propositions of mathematics are all analytical, and that the axioms are hypotheses and not fundamental intuitions or faculties of the mind. I think that the evidence for this conclusion is as complete as evidence can be. However, much more is claimed by some realistic philosophies of mathematics, namely, that pure mathematics is a branch of logic, and logic is a system of essences and necessarily true propositions which have a meaning and a being independent of the natural world.

For reasons of detail and because of the ambiguities in the notions of a pure mathematics and a pure logic, I do not think these additional claims are well-founded. In any case, if the thesis maintaining the identity of logic and mathematics is not to be a variant on classic rationalism, it must not at the same time subscribe to an ultra-platonic view of logic, and also regard mathematics to be an analytic version of the structure of natural processes such as counting. Pure mathematics, if it is to be really pure, must not be identified as contributing anything to the analysis of number, serial order, or any determinate structures of *natural subject matter*. Pure mathematics I regard as the formal study of the structure or syntax of symbolic systems, or as a general language having its own internal rules of procedure. In so far as that language is a theory *about* anything, it ceases to be pure, and becomes subject to the same criteria of validity as any of the theories of the natural sciences.

The identification of logic with mathematics seems to me possible only in so far as both disciplines are taken to have their being in the *drawing* of necessary conclusions. Indeed, from this point of view, formal logic, especially as generalized in modern symbolic systems, is a branch of the more general system of abstract mathematics. If, on the other hand, logic is viewed as the science which studies the conditions under which necessary conclusions may be drawn (as distinct from mathematics which draws them) mathematics is not a *branch* of logic but its *subject matter*.

I suspect that many of the difficulties in the philosophy of mathematics will disappear with the adoption of a procedural analysis of its central ideas. This is frankly a guess, but a guess fortified by many recent researches. With their disappearance, the obstacles which a naturalistic philosophy has always found in the so-called non-existential sciences will also vanish. The type of analysis here suggested is no panacea for mortal ills. But it is my strong conviction that such a mode of analysis is the only one which can clarify the issues of philosophy.

It is by a strange irony that those thinkers who are in the forefront in denying man to be "nothing but" the spatio-temporal juxtaposition of physico-chemical particles of matter are often the leaders in holding that all physico-chemical behavior exhibits traits sometimes supposed to especially characterize the human scene. The argument is a curious one: on the one hand, there are "emergent" qualities discoverable in the human scene which are not "reducible" to physico-chemical ones; on the other hand, these qualities must be "continuous" with the rest of nature, so that the characteristics which usually differentiate man are generic in every phase of the world. But between these apparently opposed views: that man is just what the rest of nature is in some of her aspects, and that all of nature is what man is in some of his traits, there seems to me to be no significant difference.

To a naturalistic philosophy man occupies no central position in the flux of events. He is part of the flux, and in that sense nature would not be what it is if man were not what he is. The order of the flux must clearly be favorable to man's existence if he is to exist. But this tautology cannot be interpreted to mean that the order of nature is in any way concerned with man's continued existence. There is no cosmic plan which aims at man's survival or at his achieving his ideals, for to his lot the universe is morally indifferent. All philosophies which conceive nature as concerned with human values or as developing toward some end-in-view, seem to me unregenerately romantic and immature. I find it difficult to understand conceptions of the good which assign to values an objective ontological status, independent of organic interests which generate desire; I find the notion of subsisting values without evaluating creatures as puzzling as an account of motion which specifies no framework of reference. And I suspect that theories which try to derive standards of human value or the content of human good, in any way other than through the study of man's interests and desires, are intelligible only as poetical expressions of the human need for authority and security.

This does not mean that a good or a value is to be identified with the objects of momentary desires. Desires, needs, or their objects are not primarily moral or immoral. Moral considerations arise only when, as a consequence of the structure of the human body and society, an organization of various interests is attempted. The discovery of what is good is thus as arduous a task as is the discovery of a scientific law. Goodness is not a quality belonging to things as obviously as colors do; a good life is to be identified by the comprehensiveness and accommodation of a whole process of interacting interests. The judgment that anything is a good implicitly refers to a pattern of living, and is a hypothesis which must be explored and evaluated in ways similar to those employed in the sciences.

Everyone sensitive to what are acknowledged goods of western civilization—friendship, art, and science—must be appalled by the state of contemporary society. The conditions required to cultivate these values are lacking for most people and are becoming increasingly difficult to acquire. The opportunity to enjoy the fruits of our culture is paid for with the lives and blood of one's fellow men. A naturalist will not refuse for that reason those gifts when opportunity invites, any more than he will forego the sunlight because there are dark places and hideous dungeons; for he will remember that the order of nature has not been created to minister to his ideals. Nevertheless, the price is dear and seems needlessly large. If the goodness of life lies in its integration of living interests, so that means employed enter constitutively into ends aimed at or achieved, some participation in the struggle for a better social order is an obligation upon all rational men.

A naturalist can perhaps find some consolation in the fact the brutal inequalities among men are so often man-made, and therefore perhaps adjustable. Man does not derive the measure of his existence or meaning from the atoms, stars, or nebulae, any more than they do theirs from him. The cosmic weather may swamp him, but if he wisely bases his ideals upon the capacities and limitations of his own body, life can be rich and stirring. His task is to cultivate those ideals, root out all that stands in their way, and thus literally make a portion of the universe congenial to himself. It does not seem to me absurd to think he has the power to do so; what stands in the way is often an unfree intelligence. Toward its liberation perhaps all that a professional philosopher can contribute is the loyal and passionate use of those logical methods which have in part made it free.

Logic has been variously identified as the frequently barren study of the formal rules of valid reasoning; as the examination of the operations of mind, empirical and transcendental; as the inquiry into the *a priori* bases and transcendental implications of all empirical knowledge; as the science of symbolic algebras and the conditions of their significance and application. There is a more inclusive sense of logic, however, such that some though not all of these matters fall within its purview, and yet such that it becomes more sensitive to the wealth of significant material for analysis than traditional conceptions of logic permit. This more inclusive logic studies the methods employed by men aiming at stable knowledge, assays their efficacy in achieving this aim, examines the rôle of critical thought in every department of human activity, and institutes a rigorous inquiry· into the conditions upon which the significance and effective operation of discourse rest. It is a genuine organon for achieving a rational life and society. It will discover the limitations of procedures sometimes adopted on impulse, and by acting as the searching critic of man's aspirations and customary beliefs may free him from the shackles of blind routine and force. Such a logic seems to me an essential part of an adequate naturalistic outlook. It is a conception of logic which to me is a stirring and noble one, to the service of which one can gladly devote the best of one's strength and intellectual powers.

THE PLIGHT OF PHILOSOPHY

HARRY ALLEN OVERSTREET

H. A. OVERSTREET, A.B., University of California, 1899; studied two years at Oxford, receiving the Research Degree of B.Sc. in 1901. Graduate work in the field of Aristotle and Hegel. Returned to the University of California as instructor in Philosophy in the department headed by George Holmes Howison. Advanced to associate professor and was then called to the College of the City of New York to take the headship of the department of Philosophy (including psychology). For a number of years, writings were chiefly in technical philosophical journals of America and England. In 1925, published "Influencing Human Behavior." This was followed two years later by "About Ourselves: A Psychology for Normal People." A third publication was "The Enduring Quest," a search for a philosophy of life. In response to the economic and social crisis, "We Move in New Directions" was issued in 1933. "A Guide to Civilized Leisure" appeared in the following year. Teaching experience has been in the field of collegiate education, workers' and adult education. Interests have lain chiefly along the line of the individual and social application of psychology and philosophy.

THE PLIGHT OF PHILOSOPHY

Harry Allen Overstreet

I

"He commenced dressing at top by donning his beaver hat, a very tall one, by the way, and then—still minus the trousers —he hunted up his boots." So Queequeg in *Moby Dick*. "A man like Queequeg," writes Melville, "you don't see every day, and he and his ways are well worth unusual regarding." As one looks back over the history of philosophy, and particularly as one regards philosophy in these stirring days, the Queequeg procedure seems not altogether unfamiliar. Philosophy has had a way of putting on its cosmical top hat before it has become aware that its feet need to be shod.

But then—philosophers might reply—this is precisely the sort of thing that man has always done. He studied the stars before he addressed himself to the materials of his earth; he was expert in the relationships of gods and devils before he knew how to organize his own small human affairs. True enough, the rest of us might rejoin; yet, somehow, we seem to have a right to expect more of philosophy. If not actually consummate in wisdom, it has at least been a searcher after wisdom. It is with considerable surprise, therefore, that we note that philosophy, almost without exception, has, generation after generation, failed to address itself to certain matters of immediate and quite basic human concern.

Throughout all civilized history there has been a pervasive tragedy in life—of poverty, enslavement, exploitation, social sadism. It was permissible, perhaps, for the early supernatural-isms to pass this off lightly as part of a mysterious, divine scheme of discipline and punishment. But no such deliverance from the problem involved in this tragedy has ever been permissible for philosophy. Philosophy has been supposedly a reasoning approach to reality. As "spectator of all time and all existence," it has had the task, presumably, of taking all the factors of life into account and of working out a synthesis which would be both an explanation and a solution.

But philosophy has persistently turned its attention to everything in the universe save this gross tragedy of the ages. Even in these contemporary days, when the sheer contradictions within our system of economic and social life are glaring enough to attract the most casual eye, philosophers, in large measure, have continued to put on their cosmical or their logical top halts, and, in the ardor of their supposedly "higher" pursuits, have forgotten the nether necessities.

Melville explains Queequeg. "But Queequeg, do you see, was a creature in the transition stage—neither caterpillar nor butterfly. He was just enough civilized to show off his outlandishness in the strangest possible manner. His education was not yet completed. He was an undergraduate."

II

Perhaps the collegiate implication is in some measure a clue. Philosophy, particularly in modern days, has become an essential part of the academic ritual. It has been given a favored social position. It is not altogether surprising, therefore, that it has lived within a frame of reference from which the rather crude concerns of low-bred folk have been excluded.

There are two incidents in the life of Henry George which are typical of the situation in which philosophy, in modern times, has found itself. George, after the publication of his *Progress and Poverty,* and when he was a thinker of international fame, was invited to lecture at Oxford. He started his lecture, but he was quickly interrupted by a hostile undergraduate demonstration, and because of this, he was forced to discontinue. A university was obviously no place for a man who spoke for the "lower" classes. The other incident is even more to the point. Earlier in his life, when George had become a considerable figure in California through his writings on economics and through the commendation of him by John Stuart Mill, he was invited to deliver an address on political economy at the University of California. There had been some talk of his appointment to a vacant chair of political economy at the University, and this lecture was a kind of tryout. George talked vigorously and pointedly about the causes and the cure of poverty. Incidentally, in the course of his address, he remarked that "all this array of professors, all this paraphernalia of learning, cannot educate a man. They can but help him to educate himself." He had committed two unforgivable sins: he had brought disturbing matters to the attention of students, and he had implied scorn of professoring! Needless to say, he did not become the incumbent of the vacant chair.

I refer to George, because with the exception perhaps of Veblen (who met with much the same reception in the academic world) he was well nigh the only philosopher in America who ever cared enough about the economic cruelties that darkened the land to do more about them than cover them up with a cloak of pseudo-scientific rationalization.

This is not altogether surprising. There is something about the academic life which does not harmonize with troublesome problems, and particularly with the philosophic consideration of them that goes to their very roots. The academic functionary, with his well-ordered rows of students, his roll call, his periodic quizzes, his position of secure authority among adolescents, is one who wishes things neat. He has courses to give and grades to render. He cannot admit that he is deeply puzzled about things. Above all, with adolescents in front of him, sent, for the most part, from "safe" homes, he cannot dare unsafe sentiments.

He therefore quickly adjusts himself to a situation that forbids him to stir unruly thoughts in the minds of his young people. He is not consciously dishonest; he simply learns the habit of disregarding what it is not convenient to regard in a collegiate atmosphere; and he builds around himself and his students a wall of meticulous scholarship that effectually shuts out disturbing problems.

In economic and political matters, the average undergraduate in America has, as we know, remained not only callow in his ignorance, but pathetic in his opinionated conservatism. I remember a city-wide strike of expressmen that took place in San Francisco while I was a student at the University of California. A large number of students, with sincere patriotic intent, instantly volunteered their services as strike-breakers! And for days thereafter these young men, enrolled in a public institution, openly drove express wagons in defiance of the men who were protesting against the tyranny of their employers. These college students were neither snobs nor aristocrats. They were simply woefully ignorant undergraduates, bred in an atmosphere of professorial seclusion. This seclusive procedure, of course, runs all through the school system. I have it on the authority of the National Self-Government Committee that Mr. Lyman Beecher Stowe was invited to address one of our high schools and chose for his subject the Seabury Investigation. He was courteously informed that this subject could not be discussed!

All this is of importance when we consider the plight of contemporary philosophy. Philosophy, when it is virile and original, begins always by examining the going basic assumptions of its society. Socrates did that, and earned a martyr's cup. Plato did it, and barely escaped from Syracuse with his life. Spinoza did it, and spent his life in voluntary exile. It is significant that Spinoza refused a professorship in Heidelberg. He preferred to be a free man. When, in recent decades, philosophy became part of the academic ritual, it sold its freedom for a mess of respectability. Unlike Robert Frost, it took the road more traveled, with the result that it has never, with clarity and vigor, challenged the basic assumptions of a society pervaded by the spirit of social injustice.

Novelists and poets and free-lance journalists have been they who have issued the challenge. Philosophy busied itself with other matters. There were two concerns that chiefly kept it occupied: the methods and the limits of knowledge; and the quest of Reality. In neither case did philosophy bring its conclusions conspicuously to bear upon this major issue of a prevailing social ugliness. While it studied the processes of knowing, it made practically no effort to apply these to crucial economic and social problems of the day; while it pursued its quest of Reality, it did not return from its quest with a wisdom applicable to the most pressing of our human problems. Indeed, there has been something curiously paradoxical about the quest for Reality. Among the Idealists, in particular, it has been an attempt to re-establish the dignity of human life—a dignity challenged by the materialistic results of the sciences. But while Idealism acclaimed a cosmic dignity, it proceeded quite calmly to ignore man-made indignities that cried to high heaven.

III

Nor could it be said that there was not here a rich field for philosophical activity. The science of economics, almost over night, had grown up into a commanding power. With a complete confidence and an almost equally complete lack of critical caution, it had announced its immutable "laws." It had laid down a psychological pattern of economic life. It had even reared its conclusions upon metaphysical foundations. Here, then, was a challenging situation for the philosopher—to examine these basic economic assumptions, to expose their flaws, and to proceed to stimulate reformulation. Philosophy had undertaken this task in the case of a moribund religion and had boldly inserted its logical stiletto into the dying body of supernaturalism. It had even been daring enough to take the rising young physical sciences in hand and try to steer them on their logical way. But, except for unofficial philosophers like Carlyle and Ruskin, whose criticisms were loftily excluded from academic textbooks on philosophy, it shied away from the economic system-builders, with the result that today we find ourselves in large measure the victims of economic thought grossly uncritical and almost tragically inadequate to the situation in which we find ourselves.

Meanwhile there had grown up dissenting economic views—those, for example, of Saint Simon, Fourier, Marx, Bellamy, George. The challenges these thinkers flung to the accepted systems involved matters of basic philosophic concern: the meaning of wealth; the social significance of wages, labor, capital, rent; the basis and the possibility of progress; the technique of social transformation; the goal of economic and social life. But these dissenters were permitted each to go his own way, while the main movement of philosophy was in quite another direction.

Hegel describes philosophy in terms that might well be taken as ironic: "The owl of Minerva takes its flight when the evening shadows have begun to fall." Certainly, in these matters of profound human concern, it cannot be said that the owl of Minerva was awake while it was still day.

IV

All of this gives us pause as we find ourselves, considerably bewildered, and woefully unwitting of our way, in the midst of a major depression that has played havoc with our best human values. Plato had assumed that when philosophers were kings our cities would cease from their troubles. But today philosophers are so far from being kings that they can do little more than add their voices to the general confusion, bringing neither explanation nor solution to our troubled age.

Perhaps this is inevitable. Perhaps the situation is one which could not have been foreseen. Perhaps we are at one of those stages of social mutation in which an unpredictable leap is made out of an old order into a new one. If so, philosophers, no more than bankers, business men, and economists, are to be blamed for not instantly leaping in the right direction. Nevertheless, it may quite properly be asked whether matters might not have been measurably different among our philosophers had they been differently trained.

Recently a number of leaders in the teaching profession have come to realize the inadequacy of the traditional training of teachers. They have found this training to have been of a nature which placed the prospective teacher in no intimate relation to the life of the community. It was book-training—abstract and second-hand. Teachers, trained in this tradition, went forth into the schools in pretty complete ignorance of the factors and forces that would encompass the life of their charges. They were therefore in large measure unable to be wise guardians and guides of the young. Hence these leaders have organized in New College, of Teachers College, Columbia, a new type of training which makes a radical departure from the book-dominated procedures of the past, and places prospective teachers in situations and occupations that enable them to become intelligent members of their communities.

It is a question whether a similar change must not also occur in the education of philosophers. Their education has departed curiously from the more vital and comprehensive conception of philosophy. For the most part it has been book-training. But it has been book-training of a peculiarly specialized kind. Graduate study in philosophy, in keeping with academic departmentalizing, has tended to delimit an area all its own. For the most part, little has been admitted into this area save a highly abstract type of metaphysics, epistemology, and logic.

Thus, for example, one does not find that graduate students in philosophy have occupied themselves widely and deeply with history, economics, political science, nor with the happenings in the world about them. If they have, indeed, studied history, it has been merely the history of philosophy, which itself has been a specialized abstraction from the fuller movement of human culture.

In short, philosophical education has followed the modern trend toward specialization, and a philosopher, expert in his own separate field, has, like every other specialist, grown up in ignorance of the wider sweep of human concerns.

Today, all things have "slid into confusion," and, as a consequence, in practically every area of life there is a stock-taking, a revision of attitudes and methods. It is hardly conceivable that the education of philosophers will remain unaffected. May we not expect that the education of a philosopher will be regarded as a far more difficult, far more basic and comprehensive process than has, in our recent decades, been true?

V

It is dangerous in such matters to prophesy, but it may not be presumptuous to ask ourselves what would seem to be necessary for the training of a philosopher. There has, unfortunately, been a tendency to confuse professoring in philosophy with the practicing of philosophy. Professoring, in the main, requires merely an adequate acquaintance with the technical details of philosophic systems and processes. Such an acquaintance one might call philosophic scholarship. Of philosophic scholarship there has been aplenty, for graduate schools have largely existed for the purpose of producing, not philosophers, but scholars of philosophy. Philosophic scholarship, at the most, requires an intelligent acquaintance with the philosophic process as it has taken place in others; it does not require an actual experiencing of the philosophic process in oneself. Thus in graduate schools, original observation and interpretation of first-hand materials is all too frequently discouraged. A typical doctor's thesis consists of an intricate study of someone else's philosophy. Presumably this someone else—a Plato or a Spinoza—himself approached first-hand materials with independence of observation and interpretation. The candidate for a doctorate, however, in his turn, usually confines himself to a second-hand process, seeing the materials of life not through his own, but through this other's eyes.

A parallel case would be found if candidates for the doctorate in physics were required to content themselves with commenting learnedly upon the works of the masters in their field instead of themselves making first-hand investigations. To be sure, in the sciences we expect graduate students to be thoroughly familiar with the works of the masters; but we should account it a piece of scientific scholasticism should they stop with such mere acquaintance. We expect the study of the masters to be only a preliminary and an aid to original investigation and experimentation on the part of the students themselves.

One suspects, therefore, that the first major change which must be made in the training of philosophers is to distinguish sharply between the training of philosophic scholars and the training of philosophers. There is no reason why we should not have the former. They are as necessary as dictionaries and encyclopedias. But if we wish to train philosophers, we must apparently go about the matter quite differently.

VI

One would suppose, in the first place, that to become a philosopher one would need to be possessed of a rich and wide experience. To be out of touch with the normal human processes—of work, business, social life, community interests, political policies and conflicts—would seem hardly to equip one either for wisdom or for its search. Precisely as a few pioneers in college education have seen the necessity for correlating academic work with work in the world, so a graduate school for philosophers will doubtless deem it a first essential to seek for its students rich and varied contacts with the life about them. We have had "laughing philosophers" and "weeping philosophers"; it might not be out of keeping to have working philosophers. Socrates, the marble-cutter, and Spinoza, the grinder of lenses, were doubtless in a healthier condition for observation and interpretation than are the secluded bookworms who have advanced rapidly, through high school and college, into graduate study and a doctor's degree. I remember a now-distinguished publicist's telling me that the wisest way to gain an insight into life was to become secretary to a man of affairs. Doubtless this is not always possible, but the idea underlying the suggestion is a good one. To be an intelligent commentator upon life, one must at least have been within hailing distance of its major processes.

In the second place, one would suppose that a philosopher would be widely conversant with the fine arts, inasmuch as the arts—poetry, drama, the novel, music, painting, sculpture—effect interpretative expressions of life. And if, like Plato, the philosopher can himself be poet and dramatist, or like Leonardo, be painter, all the better. One of the unfortunate by-products of our scholastic overspecialization has been a kind of desiccating of the would-be philosopher. If not precisely dry-as-dust, he has in many cases become so over-intellectualized that he has lost touch not only with the creative spontaneities, but with the fundamental urgencies of life. The arts are like rich soil into which the mind must strike its roots deeply if it is to grow in beauty and wisdom.

In the third place, a philosopher must move intimately with history. He must have a wide enough sweep of the past to give perspective to his present. Nor must his acquaintance with history be of the superficial kind that has largely been in vogue. It must be the kind of acquaintance that the anthropologists seek, the kind that becomes conversant with the cultural life of the race in all its aspects.

Such intimacy with history will move readily into an intimacy with biography. The philosopher will seek to know human beings in all their typical ambitions, needs, wisdoms, and stupidities. And from an intimacy with biography, the philosopher will pass to that kind of psychology which is interested in understanding the motives, processes, and possibilities of conscious life.

And from psychology, the philosopher will pass to the study of man active in supplying his material needs. He will not be satisfied to brush economics aside as belonging to a field not his own. He will see in the economic processes the effort of man to organize the resources of life for life's support. He will study the successes and the failures of his effort, for he will realize that the so-called higher life cannot grow save out of the soil of the physical, and that if material needs are not satisfied, other needs are supererogation. He will not exhibit the typical well-fed person's aversion to concern about bodily matters. He will be interested to note how ideals can be warped by a poorly organized economic life, and, as philosopher, he will realize that wisdom in economic life is a prerequisite to wisdom in matters other than physical.

From the economic world he will inevitably turn to intimate and intelligent contact with man's efforts to govern his social life. He will see in political life the matrix of most human values, and, like his master Plato, he will not deem it unworthy of his pursuit of philosophy to seek for creative insight into the proper ordering of the political state.

And because he lives in an age when science rapidly takes the place of superstition, and when science becomes a means of understanding and reworking the materials of existence, he will be an ardent participant in the scientific processes.

Nor will he neglect that science of the mind which devotes itself to making clear the basic processes of valid thinking. For he will realize that, for himself as well as for his fellows, thought is and must remain man's supreme instrumentality for achieving whatever he wishes to achieve.

VII

When Aristotle coined the word "metaphysics," he meant what the word literally means: *after*-physics. One might say of the genuine philosopher that his metaphysical studies should properly begin *after* all this intimate contact with the various realms of experience. Metaphysics has suffered because it has, in large measure, come *before* any adequate contact with these areas. It has been protero-physics, protero-history, protero-psychology, and the rest. It is for this reason that metaphysics, in the hands of graduate neophytes, has so largely become the abstract and rather senseless thing that is known and condemned under that name. Said Voltaire: "When he to whom one speaks does not understand, and when he who speaks does not understand himself, that is metaphysics." But that is not metaphysics in Spinoza's sense, nor in Plato's. These men pushed their way into the difficult regions of thought after much ripe thinking in the more accessible realms of life. It should be so with all philosophers. Where metaphysics is the academic logomachy of the unripe and inexperienced, it becomes the rather ridiculous affair that it so largely is. But where metaphysics is the effort of the mature intelligence to pass beyond the wisdoms of ordinary experience into regions where even the best thought falters, it becomes one of man's audacious adventures into the still-unknown.

VIII

So we may return to Queequeg and his top hat. Philosophy has to learn to begin in less exalted fashion. To be sure, there remains the problem of philosophy in academic cap and gown. Whether, in that sober and respectable garb, it can ever become an honest and fearless critic of life is a very large question. It may be that, in order to renew itself, it must take its departure from academic halls, or, if it remains there, confess that it is only philosophic scholarship. But in any event, if it is to be philosophy, and not merely a kind of meticulous logicizing about matters that scarcely matter at all, it must seek to train its adherents in some such way as has been indicated. Philosophy was once called "the guide of life." It may not be too late for it to regain that high distinction.

HISTORICAL NATURALISM

JOHN HERMAN RANDALL, Jr.

Like most New Yorkers I was born elsewhere, in Grand Rapids, Michigan, on February 14, 1899; but I arrived in New York seven years later at an earlier age than the majority of them. My father was a liberal minister, and I grew up in the atmosphere of intellectual inquiry and religious searching characteristic of pre-war America. He was by temper and training a student and philosopher, with a generous humanitarian urge, and something of a poet and a mystic. My mother was shrewd of vision and frank of tongue, with a consuming passion for fact. My youth was spent in contact with ideas and with things, and with a few close friends who shared these interests. It has always seemed natural to be questioning ideas, even those of professional questioners; but to understand is even more interesting. My college years coincided with the war, which I could not accept. I cannot, indeed, recall any experience of disillusionment or conversion; the illusions with which I started are, I suppose, still with me.

All my studies and work have been carried on in the stimulating atmosphere of Columbia, where I have learned much from association with historians and social scientists as well as philosophers. My first book was on the labor movement, which may account for a certain suspicion of political methods. I have also written *The Making of the Modern Mind*, *Our Changing Civilization*, and, in collaboration with my father, *Religion in the Modern World*. My wife, whom I married in 1922, brought me what I had hitherto lacked, a developed conscience; and she has striven manfully to temper my philosophic detachment with a modicum of missionary zeal. My two sons keep me in close touch with the youngest generation.

HISTORICAL NATURALISM

John Herman Randall, Jr.

I remember, as a college student, being asked by a friend the not unusual question, what did I intend to do? I can still recall the mood in which I realized I could not answer. Such a question had never seriously occurred to me. "Why," I replied, "I really do not know. But I think I do know clearly some of the things that must be done." This incident might be taken as a symbol of many things. It might be taken as the text of a discourse on the passing, for many of my generation, of the desire for romantic self-expression, and its replacement by the impersonality of participation in necessary work. It might be made the occasion for pointing out the compulsion in human affairs of the problems that are set before men and must be solved, whether they will or no. It is God who proposes, and though man disposes, he disposes with the tools God puts in his hands. This is true even if we prefer to view God somewhat narrowly as the forces of production. The incident might easily be pushed to a pragmatic insistence on the necessity of working in a con-- crete situation with the materials that are available, and to an end appropriate to that situation. Given a personal reference, it might well serve to illuminate the manifest shortcomings and blind spots of both the pragmatic temper and the person. Or it could be made to point to the determining character of subject-matter, forcing its facts, its structure, and its implications upon the mind in utter disregard of the preferences of the imagination.

All of these things that reply suggests. Surely they may be united in a single mind, as they are obviously entangled in the same network of idea. And as such they would reflect the several teachings to which that mind had been exposed, at the hands of those who all unwitting played the part of instrument of God in its education. Fortunately, my teachers, with one exception, are still alive. It would therefore be unfair to charge them with a more particular responsibility than they must assume through the mere fact of having been my teachers. What I have learned from them is presumably not what they intended to teach. Doubtless John Dewey did not set out to impress me with the overwhelming importance of tradition; nor did Felix Adler try to convince me, against all my natural intellectual sympathies, of the significance and perhaps necessity of that type of faith of which Communism is today the cardinal example. That such was the outcome, amongst many other things of their teaching, is due, I think, to the fact that, being great teachers, they made me see the world, in spite of myself, perhaps in spite of themselves. The man who most consciously tried to show me what is inescapably there, F. J. E. Woodbridge, I can not speak of as a teacher. I can only attempt to illustrate his teaching. In the face of what he showed me, I forget the showing, although I realize that without him to show, I should not have seen. That I may not see just what he sees is of no consequence. To him is due the fact that I can see at all.

I must renounce, however, the pleasant task of pursuing further the education that is owed to teachers. Instead, I wish to return to that early symbolic reply. "To know what must be done"—there is a whole philosophy and a method implicit in the phrase. Many of the things that when I first used it I thought I knew clearly, I have since come to doubt; and much that I see now was then undreamed of. And yet I should like to think that what I have learned and unlearned I have come upon because of adherence to that philosophy and that method. For to know what our world presents, and to know that it presents not only the possibility of thought and action, but also a possibility of thought and action in very definite and limited

channels which yet demands to be realized, still seems a fundamental wisdom. Our world may not achieve its natural end,
but if it does, it will be only because men have studied the ends
implicit in it, and have discovered the means to bring them to
pass. If this sounds a little like Aristotle, and Marx, and Dewey,
it is because it is intended to comprehend them all, and because they all saw the world. They all realized—at least that
is what they have told me—that we must begin with what we
find, and that we must find what is there in our world, not
what we might wish were there. And what we are, what we
can do, what must be done, and how we can do it, are all
things that are there to be found. What is not already there is
whether we shall do what must be done. That depends upon the
finding, upon whether we know.

We must begin with what we find. And what we find, unless our eyes are closed, is an entire culture in course of fundamental change. In that culture are many revolutionaries working for revolutions they hope will come. It would be surprising
did we not find such men. But more significant than the revolution that is to come is the revolution that is now taking place,
and that has for some time been in progress. For that revolution
is a fact, and it must be accepted as a fact. It is not something
to be fought for or against, it is something to be respected and
understood. It is not a revolution that men have worked for
or now intend; it is a revolution that men have brought about
in working for other things—the discovery of truth, the control
of nature, the making of what men want, the achievement of
power through the possession of money. That in pursuing these
ends men have created a new heaven and a new earth is perhaps surprising; that the creation should have destroyed the
old heaven and the old earth should occasion no wonder. Yet
what is least surprising has caused the most surprise, and the
incidental destruction has been harder to bear than the incidental creation. Men have been more concerned to defend what
they have destroyed than to understand what they have created.

Yet the destruction is irrevocable, while the creation is an opportunity. It is an opportunity for further creation. To God it is given to pronounce the results of his labors good, and to rest upon the seventh day, but not to man. Man is doomed to unremitting toil, and it is not human to create such good as will not demand further creation.

The fact of what man has brought about, and must bring about, need not, of course, be understood. Our culture will not cease to change because we fail to understand that change. It is not even certain that understanding would alter the main outlines of its course. What men have done sets inescapable limits upon what they can do. But men who understood would be different, and within those limits they would act differently. A revolution understood is a revolution with less wastage, a more efficient and a speedier revolution. It is a revolution in which men can make the most of the possibilities resident in what they have created, instead of leaving that realization to chance.

The acceptance of this fundamental fact of revolution in our world implies, for a philosophy resolved to know what must be done, that cultural change must be taken as a basic subject-matter. If we are to hope to understand what we find in our world, and its possibilities of thought and action, we must understand a culture in process of changing into another culture. No philosophy which leaves that fact unintelligible, whatever the illuminating insights it may develop, can be for us an adequate philosophy: it will not tell us what must be done. That this involves relegating many philosophies of today, and many philosophic activities that have awakened wide interest—like a concern with mathematical logic—to a subordinate and subsidiary position, is obvious. It is accepted with full awareness of what it involves. Such concerns are facts in our changing culture; but they are facts to be understood, not instruments of understanding. Understanding must be in terms of the problems set by cultural change itself. How is such change to be understood? What is its general pattern and method? How is

our particular changing culture to be grasped? What is the
stock of ideas and values and institutions we have inherited, at
once the material on which we must work and the tools we
must use? What are the new conditions, intellectual and practical, we have created for ourselves, within which lie our opportunities for work? What must be done? Such questions are not
so much questions we ask of our world, as questions our world
asks of us.

To answer them, it is obvious we must inquire into our world
in its temporal dimensions: we must understand our past, the
past that made us what we are and still constitutes us, the past
that is an essential part of our present world. Our culture that
is changing is itself the precipitate of a long series of changes;
and these our materials and our tools can only be understood in
terms of the past changes that forced men to create them. To
know what our ideas meant at their birth enables us to understand better what they have become; it helps us both to use
them and, perchance, to free ourselves from them. And to realize the many episodes of change that have given us our culture aids us to know what must be done in the episode that is
robbing us of it; it throws into relief the permanent elements
of change.

In some such way it would be easy to show how inquiry into
our present world leads us inevitably into our past. But the
logic of circumstance is stronger than the logic of subject-matter; and a series of happy accidents, necessitating some acquaintance with the history of ideas, was the personal introduction to
the understanding of the past. They were accidents because
they forced the development of a philosophy of social change
as the lesson of the whole sweep of Western culture, rather than
of its present crisis; but they were happy, in that to the present
they brought a knowledge which the present demands. It was
another happy and prior accident that made possible an approach
to the past at once detached and sympathetic, and quite without
emotional bias. Fate had provided a father valiant enough to

win liberation from tradition, yet wise enough to learn from it a father able both to teach and to illustrate freedom from the tyranny of attachment and the tyranny of emancipation alike His example made honest inquiry seem more natural than de fense or rebellion.

And so the philosophy of social change was developed because circumstance dictated that what must be achieved was an under standing of a whole series of changes rather than a single one— the series that is both the intellectual record of the making of our civilization, and the basic substance of that civilization it self. It was developed out of the study of the history of ideas. Doubtless this fact both colors and limits the philosophy. Though it hardly tempts one to minimize the importance of economic forces, it does make one realize that ideas as well as economic forces are continuing to have a history, and that it is an entire culture, not merely an economic system, that is in process of change.

Yet what the history of ideas has to teach about cultural change is no less important than what it leaves unsaid. It teaches men to look upon history as the continual readaptation of materials in the light of changing needs and problems—as a human achievement, within the narrow limits set by what is inescapably there, like everything human, but none the less a construction the architects of which are men. The materials they shall employ, the needs and purposes for which they shall build, are beyond their control; but the structures they erect are original, and endure beyond their builders. Sometimes, like Greek thought, they last as impressive ruins, to be looted by those who stumble upon them. Sometimes, like much of the medieval world and more of the world of the eighteenth century revolutionaries, they last as prisons, from which men struggle long to free themselves, and even in collapse their stones are obstacles. More normally in our Western tradition they have been the familiar homes from which pioneers went out to find new treasure, and to which they built additions as their wealth increased. The edifices of medieval thought have been rebuilt time and again, but their main outlines are still discernible today. We are still in a significant sense Augustinians or Aristotelians.

There is thus a genuine continuity in the materials of which a culture is built, which go on piling themselves up; there is an ever new grappling with the unforeseen ideas and conditions which have emerged because of what men have done. It is these conflicts between traditional beliefs and novel experience which drive men to construct philosophies, to fit opposing or irrelevant ideas together into some not too chaotic scheme, to adjust warring values so as to give some direction to life without excluding too much. Somehow the novel idea or condition has to be seized and worked into the accustomed pattern of living and thinking; but ideas, like conditions, have a structure and implications of their own, and when the readjustment has been made men find they have created a new pattern.

The history of ideas thus points both to a cumulative continuity in the materials of thought, in the distinctions and concepts to be used, and to a bewildering variety in its problems, in the adjustments to change that must be made. The problems which give rise to philosophies emerge when the strife of ideas and experiences forces men back to basic assumptions in any field. They have varied from age to age, and are to be understood only as expressions of fundamental conflicts within a culture, leading men on to thoroughgoing criticism. Yet the great philosophies, though they start as the battle-cries of warriors or peace-makers in the strife, have been able to raise themselves above the battle to a comprehensive vision of life. And though they speak in differing languages, they seem, to an attentive ear, to be speaking of the same universal pattern of experience. And this recurrent pattern is due not only to the fact that they once spoke a common tongue, which was Greek; not only to the fact that amidst much that is colloquial and in the latest fashion they have preserved the archaisms that point to a common source; it is due to the fact that Greeks and moderns alike have beheld the same world, and each in his own dialect is expressing the same permanences of man's experience of that world. The enemy and the fight are ever new; but fighting is not, nor are the weapons by which men can conquer.

It is well to attempt to digest this lesson before going on. The problems of one age are irrelevant to those of another. But the fact that problems must be faced does not vary. And the facing of problems illustrates a recurrent pattern. The persistence of tradition, the impingement of fresh experience, intellectual and social, upon that tradition, generating new ideas which conflict with it and yet must be understood in its terms, for there are no others—so long as our culture persists in changing, it must face such cycles. That old and new will find eager partisans to give intellectual expression to the conflict, is inevitable; just as it is inevitable that peace-makers will finally effect a settlement in which will lie the germs of new wars. For the record reveals that it is the peace-makers, those who consciously strive to blend old and new in a novel pattern, who are the creators of that which, added as a permanent deposit, is the starting-point of further change. It is the peace-makers, the adjusters, Thomas, Spinoza, Leibniz, Kant, Hegel, Marx— whose ideas make further history.

This fact has an import both practical and intellectual. It makes clear what in a changing culture must be done, though it does not dictate what we shall do. We may, if we will, bound by sentimental ties to what is old and familiar, regard the new world, so terrifying and alien, with suspicion, distrust, and fear. It is well to be critical as we mark the more than dubious value of much that is taking the place of goods once so sure. We may set our faces like adamant against what is coming, we may seek refuge in another realm, we may give way to disillusionment and despair. Or we may be so intoxicated by the promise of the new that, forgetful of the achievements of the past, we shall throw ourselves wholly into the passionate struggle for its realization. It is well to prepare ourselves for the fight that is to come, and perhaps it is well to buttress our new faith with a sophisticated and dogmatic defense, and take up the powerful weapons of intolerant zeal and emotional conviction. We may try to throw overboard blindly what need not and cannot perish, and what we shall later have to bring back again, or we may contend that with our new instruments we are for the first time able to achieve all that the old world cared for.

All these things we may do, for all these things men have done again and again. But this is not what must be done. What must be done is to face resolutely both the old world and the new, and to attempt once more the age-old task of adjustment and reconstruction: to accept the materials offered by both past and present, and out of them build still another edifice. Those materials, taken together, dictate both limitations and opportunities. Much that we cherish will of necessity be excluded, and so will much that we hope for. But to incorporate the values of the past that criticism reveals as permanent with the novel values made possible by what we are creating, is the task that must be performed. And those who do not in some fashion work upon it will not be counted among the builders of the world that is to come.

The practical import need not be pursued at this point. Let us rather allow the history of ideas to tell us of the intellectual method by which such reconstruction can be effected. It points to the inescapable persistence of that slowly mounting body of intellectual techniques and values in terms of which novel ideas must be understood and judged. We must understand what is new in terms of the ideas we already have; we have no others. We can learn from experience only if we have already learned from experience. This may be a paradox, but it is also a fact. It indicates that the concepts by which we make experience intelligible, the ultimate intellectual values we seek, the standards by which we verify, are themselves the deposit left by a long experience with the world. It is to the test of this embodied experience that we bring the fresh experience we are seeking to understand. In the testing the tests are themselves tested, and a new deposit is left. What we have learned teaches us how to ask questions, and in the asking we learn how to ask better. Without tradition, without the past, there could be no experiment, no learning from experience; without experiment, without a never-ending asking questions of the world, there could be no past, nothing but a passing present.

This fruitful and necessary interaction of tradition and experiment, of reason and experience, we have built up rather consciously into an effective intellectual tool. We call it scientific method, and the history of natural science is a cardinal illustration of the technique of cultural change, of the use of the rational lessons of clarified experience to clarify and learn from new experience. Science is at once traditional, cumulative, and rational, and critical, original, and experimental; and its method is a continued criticism of experience by reason and reason by experience. But operating at a deeper level of this same interaction than our natural science is the philosophical tradition out of which it grew and in terms of which it is itself understood and criticized. That tradition has its own carefully built-up standards of testing and criticism, and its own appeal to human experience as the setting of all man's knowledge and values. When scientific tests have left too much unexplained, when they have failed to make intelligible too large an area of experience, it has recalled them to a confrontation of experience again, and from that encounter they have emerged deepened and enlarged. It has reminded them of that universal pattern of what is, those fundamental concepts and distinctions, which, whatever the language of a particular thinker or a particular tradition, seem forced on the mind by a common world and somehow expressed; and from that rational analysis they have emerged clarified and rendered intelligible. This basic criticism of science, like science itself, is a never-ending process, a process in which an intelligible pattern of ideas and fresh contact with the world are made jointly to illuminate our knowledge of that world and its possibilities.

The appeal to experience, like the appeal to reason, on whatever level it is made, is a moment in a process of criticism. This solid fact has implications. It implies that knowledge is extended and enlarged, and its concepts and methods clarified, not through experience alone nor yet through reason, but when experience and ideas are made to confront each other. It implies that the appeal to experience, so often taken to be either the beginning or the ending of inquiry, is in fact no start and no conclusion, but an intermediate stage in a ceaseless process. It implies that philosophies of experience which start with experience as a subject-matter are in fact starting with certain ideas of experience, and that those which end with experience as a conclusion are in fact ending with a certain experience of ideas. And a whole range of philosophies, including most of those called empirical, stand condemned as inadequate, unenlightened, and blind. We must start with tradition, and we must end with tradition criticized, clarified, and enlarged.

On the level of philosophic criticism, therefore, we are forced back on the classic tradition of European thought, on that basic pattern of ideas which has persisted throughout the long search for intelligibility. The classic tradition means Greek thought, and Greek thought means Aristotle—not an Aristotle to be opposed to Plato, but the Aristotle who expressed in words that confrontation of idea and fact which Plato makes us see dramatically. There, with a clarity from which the accidents of circumstance have dropped away, and with a singular freedom from problems of adjustment and partisan loyalty, we can find the structure of the world and man's experience of it rendered in intelligible language. It is the language to which, after many a long wandering in a far country, present philosophical thought seems to be returning. It is the language in which alone, whatever the dialect, the presence of man as an intelligent and valuing being in a world that is intelligible and valuable, of human life as a natural expression of a nature that sustains and responds to its interests, can be understood. Whatever their starting-point in particular intellectual struggles—and they have been many—whatever the presuppositions that circumstance has forced upon men, those who have been honest enough to follow out the structure of the world in the light of a comprehensive view of human experience have ended by speaking in terms that can be translated into that language. It is a language that can express every human experience, knowing and acting, art and religion—a language in which we can talk equally of man and the world and God.

This is not to say that the long Odyssey of modern philosophy, from which we are today returning with many a wound and many a deep scar to the naturalism of Greek thought, has been in vain. Although without what Plato and Aristotle first said, all words would be meaningless, they did not say the final word. Emerging as they did from a single culture, they could not reflect on the conflict of cultures; creating a single science, they could not see one science leading to another. And neither the limitations nor the power of the classic tradition they created can be fully appreciated until it is seen from the perspective of all that we have since experienced and learned. Without the flesh and blood of that living experience, the classic tradition remains a rigid skeleton, sterile and dead. That struggle of two conflicting types of knowledge for man's allegiance, which became the basic intellectual issue in modern thought, in terms of which all other practical issues of adjustment have been expressed, has had many consequences. The conflict of a moral and religious tradition with new scientific concepts and techniques, of knowledge of the ends of action in morals, art, and religion, with knowledge of the structure of nature in natural science, has many sins to answer for. From the coming of Aristotelian science in the twelfth century to compete with the Augustinian tradition of Christianity, until the present-day acceptance of an enlarged and deepened scientific method as the one type of knowledge, it has dug a gulf between man and the world. It has led to philosophies which at their worst denied the reality of human life, and at their best left it irrelevant, supernatural, and unintelligible. But it did at least force men to confront the classic tradition with experience, to see it as functioning in an entire culture in rapid transition. And out of that renewed confrontation has come an Aristotelianism extended and deepened, more Aristotelian than that of Aristotle himself. No, this critical enterprise of the last hundred years has borne its own fruits.

The classic tradition insisted that the world is by nature intelligible and valuable, and that thinking and valuing are in themselves natural events. Intoxicated, however, with the discovery of the intelligibility and value of the world, it read the universe not only in terms of its own particular schemes of understanding and living, which was natural enough, and easily corrected by further experience; it read it in those purely intellectual and structural terms which are the proper objects of knowledge, and failed to take seriously its own insistence that knowledge is but one among many human activities. So long as knowledge, as with Aristotle, was so framed as to make human life intelligible, this selective emphasis was perhaps no serious danger; but with the development of a much narrower if more potent intellectual method in the seventeenth century, the exclusion became important: what could not be so known was not real. Beginning with Kant and his successors, the critical appeal to a wider experience of the world in which man lives taught first that intelligibility must be sought, not merely in one but in all the activities of human life, and then that the very search for intelligibility itself has a natural setting. Not only are poetry, self-sacrifice, and religious adoration facts to be understood; nature lends herself to lyrical expression, to moral devotion, and to idealizing worship as well as to understanding, and all these activities of men have definite implications for the character of the nature that sustains them. Nay

more: ignorance, error, and the achievement of partial interpretations are as insistent facts as truth; and all these salient
traits of human thinking are to be understood only when intelligence and beliefs are seen in their biological setting in the
behavior of living beings adjusting themselves to their environment and manipulating its materials, and in their social setting
functioning in specific ways in a cultural whole. Thus out of
this confrontation of knowledge with experience has come not
only the means of judging the success of particular schemes of
knowing, in the light of the function they were developed to
perform; there has come also an appreciation of the rôle of
knowing itself in human culture.

The present return to an enlarged and deepened Aristotelianism—or empirical naturalism, in the jargon of the day—is thus
the fruit of a process of criticism which, beginning in the attempt to put mechanical science in its setting in human experience, has ended by pointing to the setting of all science and
all knowing, of the classic tradition itself, in the manifold activities of man's group life. And thus through the discovery of
the broader biological and social context within which the search
for intelligibility finds its place, that tradition has been rendered flexible enough to deal with those problems of changing
cultures and shifting schemes of science which were originally
outside its scope. In partial independence of this philosophic
self-criticism, natural science, whose limitations a century ago
made it impossible to bring under the operation of one intellectual method the physical analysis and the non-mechanical
pursuits of men, has gradually extended its scope to embrace
human life in biology and human activities in the social sciences,
at the same time reconstructing its concepts and method to
deal with all the higher activities of mankind. Today we possess
at last a science that, insisting on the reality and importance of
all man's experiences and enterprises, has the concepts through
which it hopes to make them intelligible, and a philosophy that
can embrace in one natural world, accessible to thought in all

its parts and amenable to the operation of intelligence in all its processes, all the realities to which human experience points: symphonies as well as atoms, personality as well as reflex action, religious consecration as well as the laws of motion.

That thought and intelligence have as yet hardly made the most of their new opportunities, is a fact so obvious as to need no belaboring. That our modern naturalistic philosophies are as yet programs rather than achievements is equally patent. Yet it is also a fact with which we must begin, that they have set the general framework within which hard thinking and patient investigation may proceed. Not only has there passed the characteristic problem of nineteenth century philosophizing, born of its cultural conflicts: how can man and man's interests and values be given a cosmic significance in the face of a science undermining the traditional theological guarantee of their central place in the universe?—a problem whose passing has carried with it the solutions as well, the philosophic idealisms which placed them outside a so-called "realm of science," the evolutionary philosophies which found a new substitute religious faith within that realm, and the negative answers of nineteenth century mechanism and materialism. There has passed also that central "problem of knowledge" which persisted in modern thought so long as two different types of knowing were in conflict. Today it is no longer necessary to defend one type of knowledge against another, nor to justify any of the enterprises of the life of reason. Such enterprises have now achieved an assured and recognized status; they are once more an integral and natural part of the universe. And liberated from these traditional problems, thought can go on to explore the possibilities of human life and culture in the world it finds, to discover what must be done and how to do it, in religion, art, science, and social reconstruction. The difficulties are stupendous; but they are such as intelligence may hope to solve, not the dialectical products of contradictory assumptions, insoluble by definition.

If the world of thought we find offers once more a comprehensive nature with room for everything experience discloses, from electrons to God, and if it presents the instrument of scientific method as the tool for investigating their status, tracing their relations, and criticizing their value, what then is to be done? Intellectually, the answer seems clear: we must develop a philosophy of nature adequate to human experience, and a philosophy of scientific method adequate to the task before it. Since we are today in the midst of the most fundamental revolution in physical science since the seventeenth century, there is much present concern with the philosophy of nature. It is presumably too early to attempt to formulate the structure of nature in terms of our radically novel and still shifting physical concepts, as it is certainly premature to try to press them into a new synthesis by a *tour de force*. It is not too early, however, to try to understand the fact that such concepts do shift, and that the structure of nature is successively reformulated, nor is it ever untimely to point to facts that any theory of nature must take into account. It is clear that a theory of nature arrived at by starting from mathematical physics will be highly selective of certain aspects of the nature within which we live. It is well to ask for clarification, therefore, as to what aspects the physicists do select, and why they select them, lest we be persuaded that the nature of which they talk makes unintelligible the nature in which we live. It is well to view the formulations of physicists in the light of the function of physics, lest we assume that physics made the world rather than that the world has given birth to physics and physicists. It is well to realize that the mathematical and logical structure of events which is found conditioning the processes of nature and is perfected in imagination far beyond the limits of any observable process, is still something discriminated and found perfectible in those processes. If we forget these obvious facts, we shall find ourselves in our latest scientific philosophies falling into the traditional errors of metaphysics, identifying nature with the latest formulations of its structural aspects, and facing the insoluble problem of explaining all the rest of the experienced world that is left over.

Until very recently there was a gulf between the philosophies of nature which started from mathematical physics and those which started from the biological and social sciences, between the various logical realisms and the more empirical naturalisms. Today, however, that gulf is being rapidly bridged, and we seem to be approaching a synthesis between the structural categories of mathematical physics and the functional and temporal categories of biology and anthropology. The physicists, face to face with their new world of fields of radiant energy, have been forced by that world to develop concepts strikingly similar, on the one hand, to those of Aristotle, and on the other, to those of modern philosophies of social experience. The concepts appropriate to the functional relations of physical events within a systematic and organic structure, are no longer radically disparate to the concepts appropriate to the more complex forms of human experience. We seem to be nearing the time when a common set of categories and a common intellectual method will make both intelligible in the same terms, when both atoms and human societies will be seen as illustrations of the common structure of nature. When that time comes, we shall no longer have two philosophies of nature, based on which group of sciences is taken as furnishing the more inclusive categories and methods. We shall have rather one nature, and one scheme of understanding, within which similarities can be illustrated and distinctive differences discriminated. We have already a common emphasis on the ongoing processes of nature, on the emergence of novel ways of behaving, on the genuine creativity of the life of the universe, and on a pluralistic yet organic type of structure adequate to describe the immense variety of natural processes.

Moreover, the very fact of the reformulation of the basic principles of physics today has made it abundantly clear that principles do shift, and that the structure of nature does receive new formulation. The history of our own natural science, to say nothing of that of other systems of thought, as well as any accurate analysis of scientific procedure itself, reveals that science and knowing is a human activity, an active process of interpreting the world we live in, something men do to work out and criticize beliefs. It is highly selective of the facts from which it starts, and of the particular structural aspects of the world it is concerned to seize and express. Any systematic body of beliefs—any science—is the expression and formulation of certain natural relations in a definite language with a grammar of its own. Men can not only change their language when their interest in knowing shifts, as they did in the seventeenth century; even when it persists the same, that language has to enlarge its vocabulary and extend its grammar to express new facts and new relations, as it has done ever since. In more Aristotelian terms, when it is no longer possible to say what things are in terms of one basic principle, that principle—as Einstein has shown—must be modified or pushed back to a still more fundamental principle to enable us to say what the new things are. The history of our own science is the history of the continual criticism and modification of the basic assumptions in terms of which the structure of nature has been pieced together and expressed. Science today, moreover, involves not only assumptions of expression, of grammar, but assumptions inherent in the human systems of spatial and temporal measuring from which it derives its data, and by which it verifies its conclusions—assumptions peculiarly subject to change. Knowledge, in a word, is not an immediate seeing, is neither the intellectual apprehension or vision of rationalism, nor the sensible vision and perception of empiricism, but is mediate and functional, an active process of criticism directed toward a selected end. Such a conclusion is supported both by psychology and by the technique of scientific procedure, and is illuminated when knowledge is seen in the light of its functioning within its appropriate cultural setting.

Such an analysis of the nature and procedure of scientific inquiry, moreover, does not leave the criticism of values to the poet or the mystic. If science is an activity, a technique for the criticism of beliefs expressing the structure of the experienced world, there is no reason why it cannot work upon beliefs expressing the relations of experienced values. If science employs basic principles as instruments for organizing beliefs into an intelligible system which experience can verify, it can also employ principles for organizing the goods discovered in the world into an equally verifiable system. That scientific, moral, and religious principles of organization are all alike cumulative and traditional, that a culture operates by bringing these achieved principles of verification to bear on fresh experience, is obvious. Experimental criticism of scientific as of all values can only determine whether they result in the kind of good recognized as ultimately good. But though such ultimate values, scientific, esthetic, religious, or moral, are the premises of experiment rather than its fruit, they can be themselves modified when the organization they lend to experience leaves too much out of account. To view such principles, scientific or moral, as functional in specific ways is to provide a means of testing their validity, at the same time that they are themselves tests of the experience that comes within their scope. And thus all values are seen as amenable to the intellectual method that has proved so successful in disciplining beliefs about the physical structure of the world.

We must begin, therefore, with what we find—whether it be economic organization, moral standards, scientific beliefs and principles, or metaphysical concepts and distinctions. To this insistence our world is forever forcing us back. And since we find everywhere today both traditional beliefs, institutions, and values, and novel experience, facts, ideas, demands, and needs, we must begin with both. We can disregard either only at our peril—at the peril of an arbitrary, uncritical, and ultimately untenable choice. We cannot appeal to the immediate and uncriticized experience of the moment, in all its changing confusion; but neither can we neglect it. We can only face that experience with the full knowledge of the tests and principles and standards built up in every field through the long history of our culture, and use those tests and principles to organize the fresh experience we are creating. If we are honest, we shall find those tests deepening as they actually function in our world; if we are intelligent, we shall consciously strive to make them more adequate. But if we are wise, we shall employ our most potent instrument of criticism, the scientific technique, to discover the promise of the future and the treasure of the past, and what must be done to adjust them to each other. We must begin with what we find—so that we may find more than that with which we began.

What must be done with our several institutions should by this time be fairly clear. What has been illustrated with metaphysics and scientific method is equally applicable to all. What must be done will be done, whether or not we realize what we are doing. I would willingly illustrate it also from religion, a favorite theme. With religion too we must start with what we find. That is meager enough, God knows,—it is crude, sentimental, literal-minded, worldly, humanistic, practical, and inordinately concerned with means and instrumentalities. Yet perhaps even out of what we have we can develop a faith in a certain method and way. It is well to remember that it is all our institutions, our science and education, our art, our moral standards, our religion, our social groupings, from the family up, and not merely our political and economic organization, that must be transformed. Whether the transformation is forced upon us by our own unthinking acts, or whether intelligent criticism shall play a part, depends upon us, and our knowledge of our world.

That the economic revolution we are now involved in has

been the major determining factor in revolutionizing our
entire culture, and that the eventual reorganization of our culture will be largely dependent on the economic organization that
is worked out, is so obvious as to need no emphasis. It would be
easy to state in general terms what that economic organization
must be—so easy that the statement may well be left to others.
There are plenty of prophets today who can give us detailed
pictures if we will, and the pictures are surely plausible enough.
But economic revolutions, after all, are not produced by revolutionaries; they are produced by men working out the possibilities of the productive forces of society within the conditions
set by those forces, and it matters little whether those men
think they are communists or fascists or democrats. It is quite
possible that a political revolution will be one incident of our
economic revolution; but neither are political revolutions caused
by revolutionaries. They are caused by men too stupid or too
stubborn to develop what is implicit in technology, and they
replace those who will not with those who will. Whoever does
it, and however they achieve power, what must be done with our
economic machine will be the same; its organization will be
dictated by its inherent structure, and will be achieved only by
patient and critical inquiry into that structure. Most Americans
would prefer that the inquirers should come to power in ways
more consonant with our tradition than upheaval and dictatorship; it is surely at present premature to deny that they can.
That preference is so large a part of what we find that it may
well prove determining. It is clear likewise that both the form
and the manner of the eventual economic organization of our
society will have to grow out of the material that society offers,
not out of the material of another society half way round the
world. Respect for human personality, and devotion to the
conditions of its development, self-reliance, a widely distributed
initiative, the essence of liberty—these things are too deeply
ingrained in our life to be disregarded. Their conditions have
been revolutionized, and what they will become in our new

world is still a matter for clarification. That any American form of collectivism and economic planning must contain many elements usually called syndicalistic, is fairly certain. One may consequently vote a Marxian ticket, but unless he be blind he must realize that the programs of present-day Marxian parties have little relevance to what must and will be done, though their presence may influence its doing.

And so the philosophy of cultural change supplies an attitude, a perspective, and an intellectual method, for determining what must be done in each of the many complexly interrelated institutions of our changing culture, from metaphysics to the family, from epistemology to religion. What must be done will be clarified when that attitude and method are brought to bear upon the materials, traditional and revolutionary, of that changing culture itself. There is surely plenty to do; but the tasks can be approached with a genuine satisfaction that intelligence can once more deal, not with the inherited dialectical difficulties of a tradition grown academic, but with the insistent problems set by our own world. And it may be given to us to rise, with the great adjusters of the past, above the strife of our own intellectual adjustment to a comprehensive vision of life, and to express in our own language the universal pattern of human existence. We may start with an ideology born of the class struggle, and yet in this very human flesh we may see God.

POLITICAL MORALITY

HERBERT W. SCHNEIDER

Born, Berea, Ohio, 1892. Father, Professor of Theology at Baldwin-Wallace College. Moved to Brooklyn, N. Y., 1909, graduated from Boys High School. Entered C. C. N. Y., 1911, Columbia College, 1913. B.A. Columbia, 1915. Ph.D., Columbia, 1917. Psychological Corps of U. S. Army, 1917-1918. Assisted John Dewey in Moral and Political Philosophy and took part in organizing new curriculum in philosophy and social sciences in Columbia College (Instructor and Assistant Professor of Philosophy, 1918-1928). 1926-1927—Fellow of National Council of Social Research, study of political philosophy of Italian fascism. 1929—Appointed Professor of Religion, Columbia University. Carrying on studies in history of American religion and philosophy and in social theory.

Author: *Making the Fascist State* (Oxford, 1928). *The Puritan Mind* (Holt, 1930). (With H. L. Friess) *Religion in Various Cultures* (Holt, 1932). An editor of the *Journal of Philosophy*.

POLITICAL MORALITY

Herbert W. Schneider

Ethics is the science of human bondage, and political ethics is the inquiry into those distinctive features that characterize the bonds of citizens. In other words, the theme of this essay is to inquire what differentiates the duties and rights of citizenship from the duties and rights inherent in other forms of social bondage.

Two types of theory are both traditional and current; for want of better terms I shall call them the communal type and the contractual type. The former bases the public order on the social or general end of a community; the latter on a particular common need, namely, security. The former, when followed to its extremes, identifies the *res publica* with the moral *summum bonum;* the latter, with police power. The former sees in it the ideal or end of rational morality; the latter, a disagreeable but expedient physical force. Since the days of Hobbes our classical moralists have attempted to reconcile these two meanings of *res publica* by the doctrine of a social will or public person, embodying both physical power and moral purpose. That this conception is dubious and that it affords but a specious solution of the problem is now generally admitted. In practice, social theory has seized upon whichever horn of the dilemma has seemed for the moment expedient. In the present crisis the conflict between the rival theories is more evident than is their formal reconciliation in the theory of the public will. It may, therefore, be profitable once more to define the issues at stake and to free them, if possible, from the deliberate confusions of social idealism.

435

The contractual type is represented by the various social contract theories, which I take to be less informative for the theory of citizenship in particular than for the structure of morality in general. Morality is essentially what the social contract theories claim the state to be, namely, a formal bondage, a system of mutual agreements for a common end. It is the attempt to live by rule, by generalization. It is the willingness to be a member. It is the surrender of individuality to type, of freedom to legal formulae. When we make formal agreements, promises or contracts, we enable ourselves and others to predict our conduct. We become orderly. To live an orderly life may or may not be reasonable, but it is certainly the necessary condition of membership in any association. The principle of equity is therefore not a specifically political principle but the principle essential to all morality; it is the very essence of social bondage. Equity is merely the principle of a general rule or law applied to the members of a class indifferently. The law is no respecter of persons. My individuality or personality is irrelevant to the administration of the group interest. And my membership in any society means simply my willingness not to ask for special consideration, my agreement (or contract) to consider myself an instance of a general rule. I am, of course, an individual and not a mere case in equity, and to submit as I do to living by rule is by no means so obviously a dictate of reason as Hobbes said it was. Living by universals is at best an expedient and implies its own limitations. Equity, in other words, is not justice (except in a technical sense); it is merely the formal principle of any law or rule, be it just or unjust, wise or foolish. And the social order, if it means merely equity, or law, is necessarily not the good of any individual nor the goal of any society, but the rule of all administrative procedure.

The whole theory of the approximate physical equality of man, on which the doctrine of equity is supposed to rest, is beside the point. It is true, Hobbes asserts the doctrine of natural equality, but he immediately adds that it matters not whether men are equal, since equity demands that they be treated as if they were. The power of a state or community is, therefore, not the sum of the powers of its members as individuals, for the so-called state of nature in which each man exercises his personal physical strength as an individual is a methodological fiction to explain the surrender of approximate physical equality for group power based on the moral rule of equity. Human power is always group power, and the coercion that is traditionally said to be characteristic of political power cannot be defined simply as the sum of the powers of individual citizens or of as much of their power as they have delegated to the state.

If, as a matter of fact, power is exercised collectively,—if a man exercises control or responsibility only as a member of some association (a party, a union, a church, a corporation), the theory of the public force and of the limits of its coercive power needs considerable modification. Social power must then be conceived in terms of so-called "pressure groups," and political power in terms of the conflicts and equilibriums among these groups. The physical strength of the individual in the so-called state of nature is practically irrelevant, for man's mind or interest is here more powerful than his arms. It is curious how this individualistic theory of power has been retained by the Communists in a peculiarly naïve form. They seek the physical guarantee of freedom in the socialist state by transforming the standing army into what they call "the masses in arms." This means either the armed masses at the service of the government, in which case it does not differ from a standing army, or it means that each citizen is given arms as his possession and at his disposal, in which case the situation is identical with the so-called state of nature.

Even Hobbes, with all his emphasis on the fear of physical force as the basis of the state, recognized the moral element essential to citizenship. A citizen is not a mere subject; he is a member, acting on the principle of equity. According to

Hobbes, he who obeys the law merely because he fears the consequences of disobedience is an unjust man. For he acts not as a member of the body politic but as a man in the state of nature, that is, as an individual. His conduct is based on prudence, not on voluntary subjection to the idea of law. The idea of law or equity is part of the law of nature, antecedent to the state and basic to morality as such.

Turning from the contractual theory to the communal, we are again faced with the failure to distinguish political society from society in general. In fact, the majority of communal theories are content to take over from the contractual theories the notion that the state is essentially government by coercion, merely attempting to justify coercion as an instrument of freedom or of whatever other common good seemed to be basic. The facile way in which Rousseau turned the contractual theory into a theory of the general will is familiar, and his paradox of "being forced to be free" is the commonplace of all subsequent idealistic philosophy.

T. H. Green, still laboring with Rousseau's ideas, concludes his *Lectures on the Principles of Political Obligation* with the observation that though the ideas of moral freedom and of political coercion are antagonistic, in practice the two may be observed to go together. Harold Laski, in his *Grammar of Politics*, still laboring with T. H. Green's ideas, says: "Social good is thus such an ordering of our personality that we are driven to search for things it is worth while to obtain that, thereby, we may enrich the great fellowship we serve. . . . The will of the state seems to mean the will of government as the orders of that will are accepted by the citizen-body. Clearly, such a will, however important, has no special moral claims. It is doubtless a will to which is attached force of a peculiarly majestic kind. But the exercise of that force is always a moral issue, and the judgment passed upon it is a judgment made by each one of us. Citizenship, that is to say, means the contribution of our instructed judgment to the public good. . . .

Men build associations that, from the collective strength of the wills fused there, they may secure the chance of self-determination." (Pp. 25, 29 and 67.)

The paradox is nowhere stated more boldly than in the Marxian theory that the omnipotent state, established by the dictatorship of the proletariat as a temporary expedient during the transition from capitalist society to classless society, is necessary in order to put an end to the state entirely and to prepare men for communistic society, in which all men will habitually and spontaneously observe the "well-known principles" of social life.

Theoretically the state is here conceived as an instrument of Society or the Common Good. But all attempts to identify this single Social Order and universal Common Good have failed. "Society" is now admitted by most theorists to be merely a collective term for societies, for many associations with many particular goods. The moral status of the state thus becomes more than ever a mystery, for its social utility is generally accepted without any analysis of the social order it is supposed to serve. In fact, this absurd idolatry of the Common Good is of long standing. The odor of sanctity that still hangs over the term "society" (in the singular) is bequeathed to us from the so-called Enlightenment, when a vague humanitarian enthusiasm concealed petty bourgeois utilitarianism. "Usefulness is agreeable," says Hume in his *Enquiry*, "and engages our approbation. This is a matter of fact, confirmed by daily observation. But, *useful?* For what? For somebody's interest, surely. Whose interest then? Not our own only: For our approbation frequently extends farther. . . . We must adopt a more public affection, and allow, that the interests of society are not, even on their own account, entirely indifferent to us. Usefulness is only a tendency to a certain end; and it is a contradiction in terms, that anything pleases as means to an end, where the end itself no wise affects us. If usefulness, therefore, be a source of moral sentiment, and if this usefulness be not always considered with a reference to self; it follows, that everything, which contributes to the happiness of society, recommends itself directly to our approbation and good-will." On the basis of this sentimental enthusiasm for usefulness as such, Hume proceeds not, as he should have, to answer his question, "useful to what?" but to erect utility itself, now called general, public or social utility, into an abstract moral principle. Such praise of utility in general is easily substituted for an interest in genuine public utilities. Likewise such a meaningless use of the term "society" is easily substituted for an analysis of particular societies. For the real question is not, "Is public utility pleasurable?" but, "To whom and for what is the public useful?"

To substitute for this sentimental enthusiasm for "public affection" a utilitarian analysis of the specific values of political control is the aim of the following pages. We have seen that both the contractual and communal approaches have in reality proved to be contributions to social ethics in general but have thrown little light on the nature of the state in particular. To put the problem more technically, our aim is to distinguish between a public utility and a common good, or, using the language of the contractual theories, to distinguish political compulsion from moral obligation in general.

The financial aspect of the distinction affords a convenient starting point for an exposition of the theory of political obligation. Public goods are paid for by taxes; private goods by purchase prices. What is the difference between a tax and a price? The former is shared by all members of a community whether they share the goods or not; the latter is paid by the consumers only. The former is political distribution; the latter is business. The former goods are non-marketable. Let us, therefore, provisionally define the essence of citizenship as levying and paying taxes, and contrast it with business, which is essentially setting and paying prices. The reason for the difference is purely practical and almost too simple to be worthy of attention. In the case of public or non-marketable goods, the persons who do not choose to pay cannot readily be excluded from the enjoyment of the goods. Thus roads, in so far as they can be operated as turnpikes and toll-roads or can be paid for by gasoline taxes and automobile registration fees, are business propositions. In so far as it is impracticable to exclude those who are exempt from such taxes from using the roads, they must be paid for by the citizens generally; they then become public utilities. They are "free" in the sense that any one is free to use them and no one is free from paying for them.

The following attempt to list some of the essentially public goods, those which by their nature must be distributed by universal taxation, will further illustrate the distinction between them and goods that can be distributed privately as business commodities. (1) Police and military protection. Those who purchased private protection would (in general) find it difficult to prevent those who did not pay from being protected. Since there would be no reason for buying protection when it could be obtained free, the private protective corporation would be forced out of business. (2) Sanitation, control of contagious diseases, pests, fires, etc. These affairs need be public only in so far as the dangers are shared alike by the "just and the unjust," the diseased endangering the healthy, the fire in one house endangering others, etc. Otherwise health and fire insurance could be carried on as businesses for the exclusive benefit of those who pay the premiums. (3) Charity or relief (including education and care of children). By definition, the beneficiaries do not pay. Relief is distributed, not sold, and is hence essentially a public function from the standpoint of the beneficiaries. Philanthropists may indulge in it as they please, but relief as a good to be administered must be supported publicly. (4) Roads, parks, harbors, etc., in so far as they cannot be restricted to the use of a specified group. (5) Monetary systems, weights and measures. These must obviously be public standards. (6) Courts of law and legislation in cases where one party to the litigation is unwilling or unwitting. When both parties seek adjudication of a dispute and their dispute involves no larger "public," they may buy "justice" privately. (7) Morality, as defined above, could obviously not be bought and sold as a commodity for the exclusive benefit of the moral.

Though this is not a complete list of the *res publica*, it will serve to indicate the manner in which the public nature of a good can be determined. In the same manner the following would be determined to be private goods: (1) Commodities (by definition). Among these it might be well to mention the following, which are sometimes regarded as public merely because they are conducted (as business enterprises) by the state: postal service, transportation, power, water, adult education, insurance, etc. (2) Religion (except in so far as its "benefits" may be public).

Among the goods which may or may not be public, depending on circumstances or on further analysis, we might mention vocational guidance and training, libraries, newspapers, opportunity for art, distribution of labor and leisure, land and credit. The mention of these basic realms of social life as problematic may seem sufficient evidence to condemn this theory as futile. It is not my aim, however, to suggest a solution to these basic political problems; they will remain genuine problems regardless of social theory. My aim is rather merely to state them in such a way as to suggest new and practical procedures in attempting solutions. Therefore I shall not stop to defend my illustrations or even to claim their adequacy. My interest is more theoretical.

The above analysis seems to me to serve as a hopeful starting point for a theory of the state. It is an administrative theory of political obligation. It suggests that the element of compulsion can be located in the nature of public goods themselves, rather than in the power of the government or in the will-power of citizens. The basic power of the state is derived from the physical necessities of administering certain types of goods, not from the pooled wills or energies of the citizens. The coercion is as a rule exercised by nature, not by the government,

and every intelligent citizen understands this in the case of the
obviously public utilities. Of course there are limits to this
power. A man, though he is born into a community or state,
may desert it and take up residence elsewhere. If public utilities become too burdensome, he may resign from the public
and face nature alone or find another public. He may become
a citizen of another state or of no state, for there are still a
few odd corners left in the world for Robinson Crusoes. As has
been pointed out repeatedly, the theoretical privilege of re-
nouncing citizenship is becoming increasingly meaningless. For
a citizen is practically compelled to jump from the frying pan
into the fire. Nevertheless the ultimate measure of the power
of a state is the willingness of its citizens to die at home rather
than live abroad. Socrates was given the choice and refused
exile. Such choices are usually taken to be measures of moral
character on the part of citizens, but they are more profoundly
measures of their communities. At bottom the tendency among
modern states to breed the desire for freedom is their severest
indictment. Socrates did not seek freedom but participation.
There is a great difference between a society of liberals and a
society of freemen; the former seek freedom from each other,
the latter enjoy freedom together. The happier the society, the
less concern there is for the *res publica.*

It does not follow that the less concern there is for the *res
publica,* the happier the society. It merely follows that the fewer
freemen are needed to administer the *res publica,* the more
men can be free. The public goods are not necessarily supremely
important, nor of great dignity. Like bathrooms, they are
practical necessities but not worthy of constant attention. The
less energy is devoted to the public affairs of a community, the
more it is free to form other types of association more intrinsically interesting. The *res publica* is a soil out of which interests
and arts may grow. But, to continue the figure, if instead of
using the soil to nourish living beings, the living beings are
plowed under to fertilize the soil, the earth becomes a grave-

yard, fertile but useless. For no matter how many tombstones with their "vital" statistics we may erect in neat rows over the decaying dead, there is no genuine society among graves. And no matter how orderly human life becomes, if it produces nothing but order it is a whited sepulchre. The state, the *res publica*, therefore, is not an inclusive end of social life; it is merely its beginning.

Freedom within a community depends on the range of selection among possible goods. If the state is a *Kulturstaat*, if it administers the whole culture of the community or nation, the citizen has no choice and no freedom. He becomes then a mere member of the state or else a mere revolutionary. He has only one choice to make: to support the state or to support its overthrow. He works for the common good or for nothing. His taxes pay for everything indiscriminately. Genuine freedom is the power to decide which dues, taxes, fees and prices one wishes to pay, instead of allowing the administration to decide how the money is to be spent. Of course, such freedom involves responsibility; it is "moral freedom." It may be simpler and cheaper to throw the responsibility on the government. Freedom is only a relative good and too much of it may be too expensive. Nevertheless, this is a clear definition of real freedom. That such freedom is decreasing in economic as well as in political matters is evident. I cannot pay for my tooth-paste without at the same time paying for a part of my subway ride, my newspaper, radio program, etc. I cannot buy gasoline without investing in all kinds of businesses all over the world. Real liberty, a genuine opportunity to choose or discriminate, is becoming rare. Even rarer is the practical concern of liberals in such practical liberty.

In short, the foregoing considerations are supposed to suggest a refutation of both anarchism and totalitarianism. In any conceivable community certain goods must be distributed by political means (that is, by compulsory taxation or its equivalent). In any conceivable community, on the other hand, these public goods are not identical with the common goods, nor are the common goods necessarily public. The state has a necessary but specific and limited function. It is a particular type of moral bondage and not a disguised form of freedom. It can be distinguished by its mode of administration, rather than by its sovereign power or single end.

THE TASK OF
PRESENT-DAY METAPHYSICS

WILMON H. SHELDON

Born in Newton Highlands, Massachusetts, 1875; Harvard A.B., 1895; Ph.D., 1899. Taught philosophy at Universities of Wisconsin, Harvard, and Columbia in turn during the next four years, never ranking higher than assistant. Appointed tutor at Columbia 1903, went to Princeton as preceptor 1905 and to Dartmouth College as professor 1909; came to Yale in 1920 as professor, where he now is. Has written some 15 or 20 articles in philosophical journals, and one book, *The Strife of Systems and Productive Duality*, Harvard University Press, 1919.

THE TASK OF PRESENT-DAY META-PHYSICS

Wilmon H. Sheldon

The following paper is written for those in whom the metaphysical hope burns undimmed by current skepticism. Not attempting to justify the pursuit of metaphysics, it addresses itself to those who, like the writer, find that pursuit inevitable. But it is true that many of them feel keenly, even to the point of despair, the difficulty of the problems and the apparent lack of result which they have to face; let us therefore begin by stating how these initial setbacks are to be met.

The difficulty is undeniable; so great is it that every age rightly finds the solutions of the past insufficient, and no doubt will do so in the future. That being so, it is the task of the thinker of today, as of every day, to find a new approach; of which more anon. Enough for the present that difficulty was never a bar when there was a sufficient inward urge. It is difficult to secure a just government or a perfectly healthy body, but our constant failure in these directions does not prevent continued effort. Rather is the discouragement of the philosopher due to the apparent lack of result in the history of philosophy, where disagreement seems as great at the end as at the beginning.

But this alleged lack of result is a delusion, due to superficial study of that history; superficial not as ignorant of fine detail but as wanting in insight into the significance of the systems that have been vouchsafed to us. True, the thinkers of the past, great as well as small, tried to refute those who saw the universe in a light different from their own. It was a natural weakness;

they believed that only thus could they defend what they loved best, their own systems. Mankind must have progressed a long way in candor and tolerance before its philosophers can see and confess that other points of view than their own are correct. Perhaps to one who reads current philosophical discussion there are signs that we are beginning to acquire that candor and tolerance. But certainly the thinkers of the past, even the greatest ones, did too often claim exclusive possession of truth and wished to prove the others wrong—whence the phenomenon of mutual refutation. And no doubt in a subject so difficult mistakes are rife and refutations are needed; but to a long view they lie mostly on or near the surface of the systems. To one who genuinely studies Plato, Aristotle, Aquinas, Leibnitz, Hegel, certain precipitates of truth gradually outline themselves through the dust of combat. Some of these are common to several, some peculiar to one. What present-day idealists call the "Great Tradition" is such a common vision; hard to define clearly, never thoroughly demonstrated, reappearing as if inevitably, it puts forth a view which cannot in the main be denied. Yet on the other hand there is what we may call the lesser tradition, also common to many and dogging the footsteps of the greater, sometimes even taking the lead—to wit, the tradition of respect for the particular, as seen in much of nominalism, materialism, personalism, tychism, libertarianism, etc. Certainly an impartial contemplation finds a just claim in this equally perennial tradition; certainly we can admit exclusive truth to neither of these great trends in thought. And the like is true of other theories. To take a few instances at random—there is an insight in the scholastic substance-doctrine which the modern "functionalist" has missed, a truth in the apparently so artificial pre-established harmony, and a positive contribution in the pragmatic demand for verification. But of course the real problem is to find some key-position from which we can see how to incorporate these truths and systems into one, yet without condemning each as a false abstraction. And thus the apparent disagreements are largely supplementations which stimulate the more our quest for a combining principle.

But it is true that metaphysics is not matter for exact proof. Such proof has in fact long been an idol before which we have sacrificed many genuine insights; but there are indications that the idol is crumbling. It is perhaps the most important service of modern logic to have brought this out. Proof proceeds by appeal to some general principle, but we have no prior proof that the general principle applies to the particular case. Socrates must be mortal because all men are so and he is one of them; but how can reason justify this passage from the general to the particular? It needs another general principle to do that, which again needs another to ground its application, and so on without end. The same is true of numerical reasoning. We think to prove that 2 and 3 are 5 by deducing it from postulates, but the application of the postulates to a particular case needs a *dictum de omni* quite as in the syllogism. The proof by postulates is not what it is usually taken to be: a demonstration through principles. Of course the truth of $2 + 3 = 5$ and of the syllogism remains; but it is guaranteed by nothing else than immediate insight, so simple and clear that we can at present raise no doubt. But indubitability is never reached. Rational demonstration in the older sense is a fiction. If now we give up this idol, we admit that simplicity and clearness are matters of degree and that neither metaphysics nor anything else can be rigorously demonstrated. Also and on other grounds the certainties of physics, so long deemed absolute, have begun to weaken; the very being of rigid law is now in question. Wherefore we should not endeavor, with a Spinoza or a McTaggart, to give exact demonstration or analysis so thorough that it is not open to doubt. Indeed, the method of refined analysis now so frequent in certain quarters leads to a degree of estrangement from reality. Such analysis, in its attempt to exhaust all the possibilities, sees so much that might be the case as to prejudice its ability to estimate what is the case. With human energy limited as it is, there is always danger in carrying one method, however good in itself, so far as to crowd out others. The result is that the analytic method tends to assume that we can determine beforehand to some degree what reality ought to mean —the one thing, as this paper will later urge, that we can never do. It was the error of the Kantian subjectivism to assert that experience gives only the particular: but universal traits of the real may be found quite as well in self-repeating characters of things as in the constitution of mind. Wherefore the method of seeking exact proof with meticulous analysis seems decidedly infertile unless based on and supplemented by attention to the specific facts of the environment.

Each age, confronted by the metaphysical problem, tends to approach that problem from a more or less novel point of view. It is then the task of each age, and therefore of each thinker therein, to suggest some point of view which may lead to a fresh envisagement of reality. Pursuant to this task, the present writer offers such a perspective. As the history of thought goes on, progress is contingent upon such offerings, being indeed constituted by the successful ones. There seems to be no reason why the human intellect of today should have so degenerated as to be unable to do what its predecessors did—discover new or relatively new metaphysical principles. We should all have a try at it.

Every one of us lives in an environment whose ways he must to some extent learn, else he perishes. The reality of the environment consists in just the fact that he must learn its ways. Clearly, so far as he learns them he does not make them; and in learning them he is observant, meekly acquiescent, passive. Activity occurs in so far as he attends; there is no other activity of mind here, though of body there is plenty, in moving things about. Attention is the endeavor to be impressed by the objects in the environment. Thus reality means that to which, in the effort to live, we must pay regard, that which we must respect, that which does not depend on us but upon which we depend.

The relation between ourselves and the environment is hereby an asymmetrical one; and the asymmetry connotes reality. Reality is more than we are; more in the sense that our minds take their contents from it in so far as they know, and *eo ipso* in the sense that it has its own character, independent of our mind, in and of itself. Whether or not reality contains a reference to a perceiving mind, the content and nature of reality owe their specific character in no sense to that mind. This is the first axiom of all practical life and of all knowledge. Reality is thus a value-category, and its value lies in its transcendence and independence of mind. And that is why there can be no knowledge beforehand of the character of the real, or of any conditions to which it must conform. It must be intelligible, we say; but we do not know what intelligibility means until we know what reality is.

Now this learning of the ways of being, when carried through, is nothing more or less than metaphysics. There is no prerequisite of epistemology about it, no prior theory of the nature and limits of knowledge. We could not discuss these until we had knowledge, and to have knowledge is to have reality present to the mind. Thus metaphysics comes first, and epistemology becomes a branch of it—the branch that deals with one fact among others, the fact of knowing. But of course no analysis of knowing can discredit the fact that we have it, for the analysis rests upon that fact.

Nor can we draw a clear line of distinction between metaphysics and other domains of knowledge. Many thinkers have sharply separated metaphysics from the natural sciences, as if science gave us something sure and metaphysics did not; or as if metaphysics dealt with the presuppositions rather than the results of science. The former is, as we have seen, but a difference in degree; the latter distinction asserts a false exclusion between two things that are inseparable. The presuppositions of the sciences are found only in the results of scientific inquiry. Concepts such as cause, matter, motion, force, space, time, etc. are not presuppositions that would stand if science failed. They are justified if, and only if, scientific conclusions contain them. Their metaphysical truth is nothing apart from their scientific truth. In physics and metaphysics alike we are studying the real world—the world, that is, which we have to pay regard to, and to which in paying regard we have to accord independent being. Not, of course, that reality is confined to physical being. Materialism has never been able to reduce mind to a function of the living organism; memory of the past, foresight, comparison and other psychoses are clearly not describable in "naturalistic" terms. If psychology had as yet secured the amount of established result which some of the physical sciences have gained, it would equally be a member of the *corpus metaphysicum*. Mental facts are, as is too well known, very difficult to observe; natural selection has developed much the same sense-organs in all men, else they would have been exterminated as *homo insipiens*, while the certainties of introspection are not so requisite for bodily survival and hence have lagged far behind. Thus it has come about that men agree well about what they observe in the physical world, and so they think sure knowledge is confined to the physical. But again the difference is one of degree. There are mental facts, and no doubt some day we may know them much better than we do now. Moreover (as said above) we are today not so sure of our elementary physical facts as we were in the last century. Psychology is as essential as any other science for metaphysics, and if Ð comes to maturity later than the physical branches, we can only regret the fact and blame no one. But it may be that we already know enough about mind and the physical alike to conclude to a fairly adequate outline of reality. In any event there can be no boundary where we can definitely say: "this is physics and no part of metaphysics" or "this is metaphysics and is irrelevant to physics"—and the same holds of psychology or any other field.

There is nevertheless a certain difference of emphasis, in that metaphysics has a comparative function and "nisus toward the whole" which the special sciences do not directly exhibit. Each specialist is by training more or less cramped to the point of view of some one aspect of the real; however eminent in his own line, he cannot usually take another perspective. Someone is needed who can, however imperfectly, survey the whole; nor is it necessary to such a survey to have intimate acquaintance with each specialty. It is for the specialists to deliver their findings in such form that they can be put into some general framework; it is for the student of metaphysics to consult these findings and their deliverers to be sure that he understands them aright. But the onlooker sees the game best, and the metaphysician must fit himself as far as he can to be the onlooker.

It was said above that exact proof is not attainable, and is indeed an idol built up by bad logic: and so far it might seem that we are condemned to a theoretical skepticism. But that in turn is due to a wrong point of view; we misunderstand belief. Belief is matter of action: a point made long ago, and in modern times by Bain and others; and certainty accordingly is tested by action. Belief in the well-attested facts of our daily living— so-called common sense—is the normal case of belief. No certainty can be sounder than that which belongs to this region. Yet there is little of theoretical demonstration in our working acceptance of one another's minds, of the external being of sense objects, of the causal relation, and the predictability of events. Not one of these things has been rigorously proved; yet they are accepted with certitude. Certainty (which is in the end but certitude) is thus a practical or value-category; the point of view of logical proof and degrees of probability is not the one that gives us our best hold on the real. From the theoretical point of view the facts of common sense are more or less probable, but always doubtful; from the practical, belief is so well grounded that skepticism does not enter.

What then of the high certainty of mathematical reasoning? Is it not pure deductive cogency? Or at least is it not (as we admitted above) a case of immediate inspection so clear and simple as to be indubitable, yet of quite a distinct sort from the assurances of common sense and practice? I think the answer must be in the negative. The certainty of mathematical reasoning is not so far removed from that of common sense as is often supposed. Common sense works largely, though by no means wholly, with sense-data; and sense-data are intrinsically necessary to any but the most elementary mathematics. Where would most of our mathematical calculation be but for written symbols that all can verify by vision? Who could solve an intricate equation without the visible x's, dx's, $f(x)$'s, or the numeral characters? Who would trust anyone's mental arithmetic to multiply 453872 by 91256? The results of the thought-process have to be recorded in sense if they are to be used successfully. We trust memory for the interpretation of the written marks, and we have to see the marks in order to interpret.

Metaphysics then comes down to this: what do we find in the assured facts of daily life, the well-attested results of the sciences, well-grounded maxims of conduct and of artistic structure and religious experience that suggests a type or pattern running through all the field of the real so far as known to us? The superior dignity which the metaphysician has been wont to claim for his subject—if such dignity there be—does not lie in its independence of other subjects, but rather in its extreme dependence on them. It owes more to them than they owe to one another or to it. Its greatness lies not in exclusiveness but in inclusiveness. And that suggests another admonition for the metaphysics of today: an admonition, too, which would not always have been needed in the past. The great system-makers such as Aristotle, Aquinas, Leibniz or Hegel ranged through the whole gamut of being so far as it was known to them, applying their key-formulas to the rich specific detail of things. Thus Aquinas verifies the act-potency couple in many ways—in inorganic things, in living forms, in mind and the cognitive relation —in all the various levels of reality from the lowest with its maximum of potency and minimum of act, up to God who is pure act without potency. With profound differences from Aristotle, especially in the higher levels, he yet shows the Aristotelian spirit of interest in *both* the supreme formula and the specific detail. The two aspects of reality are for him never disconnected. So too, for another example, with Hegel. Hegel is interested not only in the dialectic as the necessary type of reality, but also in the specific ways in which the dialectic shows itself in the mechanical, the chemical, the living, in human history, the State, art, religion. These great thinkers were great because they traced the universal through the particulars; they sought no *a priori* proofs, but found the rule only in the specific instances. If they made some errors—as who could help doing? —their hearts were in the right place; they were fascinated by the wealth of actuality. Now our recent metaphysic has too often lost this connection with the rich detail of the world. It is perhaps afraid of making mistakes (as did Hegel notoriously) which will be corrected by scientists, and thus confines itself to blanket formulas which it believes are too general to be open to refutation by increasing scientific knowledge. This is, for instance, a fault of modern idealism. Deprecating the toilsome method of going through the chief known traits of the inorganic world, of plants, of animals, etc., it contents itself with the claim that there is absolute spirit which shows itself in different levels.

Of the precise relation between the levels—how one leads to another, how far each is or is not a true epitome of those below it—little information is afforded; and scarcely any new analysis is given whereby to throw fresh light on the nature of the absolute spirit. An example of this procedure is Bradley's *Appearance and Reality*. But the other schools too are sinners here. Emergent evolution is also a blanket-term; its devotees have done little to reveal the "how" of the emergence. The Bergsonian intuition too may be the only true mode of reaching knowledge: but it is much to be wished that its gifted protagonist would at least indicate some ground-plan revealed by it, that might guide our investigations or our conduct or at least our aesthetic sense. Metaphysics cannot afford to scorn the specific detail; for reality is both pattern and detailed realization, and neither has sense without the other. Why does life evolve along the two channels of plant and animal? Why should there be opposite electric charges rather than inert atoms all of the same kind? Why should there be laws, whether rigorous or statistical? It is vain to answer, as is so often done today, that these details are brute and unintelligible facts, cases of the mystery of being, and beyond the scope of understanding. Such an answer betokens a feeble and anemic condition of intellectual life; a lack of that curiosity which is the spring of all advance in knowledge. But the genuine answer can be given only to a patient scrutiny of the miscellany and confusion of nature, till a pattern appears which accounts for the actual arrangement of detail. Thus a proper metaphysic can arise only from inductive and empirical studies.

How then shall we go about the task of metaphysics? To repeat for the sake of emphasis: not by laying down at the outset some Kantian prerequisite of all experience ("experience," with its subjective flavor, is a word we should seldom use, since our concern is with the real) nor by the attempt to proceed by sure proof from some Cartesian initial certainty to a complete system. Deductive proof, we have already seen, is an idol; *a priori* knowledge is verified only *in concreto* as a pervasive form in things, a form seemingly verified everywhere. There is no deciding beforehand what conditions reality must obey. The most that can be said in this regard is that the real cannot be self-contradictory; which only means that if it is so and so we must not, having verified this fact, later deny it. For we cannot say beforehand what will contradict what; the lesson of recent studies in logic is that it is all a matter of initial postulates, none of which are either necessary in themselves or implied in the nature of fact. No, the method of metaphysics must be the empirical method—provided the term empirical is properly understood. Empirical does not mean derived wholly from pure data with no admixture of interpretation. Perhaps there are no pure data; certainly the facts which in daily life we all acknowledge are reached by inference as well as observation. Empiricism as here used means, rather, starting from facts acknowledged by all reasonably competent minds. The criterion is no *a priori* one; it is as good as, but no better than, the common-sense criterion which it includes, of reasonable competence. But it would be not only vain but needless to seek a different source of certainty.

If we were as certain of our metaphysical systems as we are of the main traits of the external world, the stars and nebulae, the plants and animals, the minds of our fellow men and the rules of good conduct—if we had indeed a reasonable certainty as strong as our everyday certainty of these—then we should have attained the metaphysician's heaven. The trouble is that our philosophers, fearing that they have fallen far below the assurances of common life, have outrageously demanded a certainty surpassing everything that men have lived by. One extreme leads to the other. But what we really want is only a system of beliefs as well grounded as our beliefs about the external world; which is to say, a reasonable certainty. Let us not then by quarreling over the shadow lose the substance. So by the empirical method in metaphysics we mean only the inductive procedure from well-attested facts acknowledged by all reasonable men; facts such as those revealed by grounded scientific inquiry, by conservative (not local or as yet questionable) taste in the beautiful and judgment approved by trial in matters of conduct. For instance: there are space, time, and body, mind fact and value; there are causal laws, and numerical calculations are trustworthy. Animals are born, move to get their food, and die; plants construct their own substance by using radiant energy; men sleep and wake, form societies, think, and die; nature is in many ways extraordinarily beautiful; man has religious experience. From such facts, which no sane mind doubts, we draw our metaphysics. If there are certain *a priori* necessities among them—and we can as little assert as deny this in advance of observation—that fact will come out as investigation proceeds. Now these facts can be viewed in this or that grouping; as in physical science, it is all a matter of getting some fertile and suggestive grouping of the facts. Taken by itself, one grouping is as true as any other; taken as suggesting some one or some few principles working throughout, one grouping may be much truer than another. It is the fertile perspective which metaphysics tries to get; the perspective, that is, which suggests, quite in the inductive manner, some large hypothesis that will throw light on the total scheme of things as far as known. Such an hypothesis, once erected, must be tested by application to details. Thus the method of metaphysics, like that of any science, is the method of hypothesis based on induction and subsequent verification in the explanation of details. There is no real difference of procedure between any science, or any trial and error grouping in a practical difficulty, and metaphysics.

And yet, in addition to this inductive survey by which the metaphysician seeks some new clue to the total scheme of things, another is needed, *viz.*, the survey of the great systems. Thus the task of metaphysics is twofold: independent inductive investigation opening out some new vista, coupled with study of the solutions proffered by the great minds of the past. Neither is of much avail without the other: the historical side is necessary for critical judgment, the inductive for advance. There is no ground for the excessive pride which deems the past outgrown and demoded; history has too often shown the failures of thinkers who worked that way. There is equally no ground for the excessive humility which regards present effort to add much to the contributions of the past as useless. It was not in such humility that the history of philosophy made itself. We have indeed far richer stores of material to draw from, in the increased knowledge of today, than were ever open to men before.

It remains only to indicate in briefest outline and without the justification which could alone render it worthy of respect, the plan of reality which the present writer would offer. Passing along the length and breadth of reality as known to us, we find a series of pairs of categories: time-space, atom-radiation, cause-chance, force-substance, life-inorganic, animal-plant, nucleus-cytoplasm, male-female, mind-body, conation-awareness, value-fact, actual-possible (act-potency), individual-universal, term-relation, and so on. All these pairs are found to be instances of one asymmetrical dyadic relation, which reveals its full meaning only in the wealth of levels in which it appears; in its independent being as the one pattern after which things are made it is nothing less than Deity—a single creative spirit. As advocating the asymmetrical dyad, this plan is not far from Aristotle and St. Thomas; in its theism, nearly Thomistic; in its theory of levels and (up to a point) the organic unity of the lower in the higher, almost Hegelian; in its defense of chance as well as causation, pluralistic. Thus it pays respect to the systems, as well as to the demand for an inductive hypothesis. Its novelty (such as it is) lies perhaps in the central notion of the asymmetrical dyad as the *fons et origo* of reality. But as this paper must be programmatic rather than systematic the matter must here be left inchoate.

TRUTH BEYOND IMAGINATION

T. V. SMITH

T. V. SMITH was born in Texas, educated at the University of Texas and at the University of Chicago. He has taught at Texas Christian University (both English Literature and Philosophy), the University of Texas, Columbia University, Syracuse University, Denver University, and Cornell University. Technically in philosophy at the University of Chicago since 1922, being professor since 1927, his interests are wider than the realm of truth, as his article here makes manifest. He has long been interested in politics, active intermittently, and is now a State Senator in Illinois from the University of Chicago district.

He is editor of The International Journal of Ethics, has been a cooperant in many books, and is the sole author of *The Democratic Way of Life, The Philosophic Way of Life, The American Philosophy of Equality, Philosophers in Hades, Beyond Conscience,* and *Creative Sceptics: In Defense of the Liberal Temper.*

TRUTH BEYOND IMAGINATION

T. V. Smith

Philosophy more than most disciplines is likely to be always repeating itself; for at any given time it is clairvoyant of all the major alternatives open to thought. Ideological changes there are and will be, but any change in these major alternatives is less likely to effect their constitution than merely their content and application. I mean to say that there will be idealists, materialists, and would-be-mediators tomorrow as well as today, here as well as elsewhere. But because this is so, I prefer to focus discussion on something else than the schools enshrining these enduring options; the ubiquitous may be let alone with the knowledge that it has always for its certain witness the fact of being taken for granted.

Inviting attention, however, is the striking difference between those who use their minds to expose or to celebrate great generalized problems and those who focus thought upon events, persons, causes. This distinction as involving the name philosophy has itself an ancient designation: it is that between history of philosophy and philosophy. I remark the distinction not with any invidious intent; but it is difficult to be entirely neutral here. Today the very term philosophy is zealously appropriated by those who can further divide a given meaning of Aristotle's or explain what Leibniz believed, without themselves having any very stout opinion on whatever point is at issue. Those, on the other hand, who speculate freely upon the turn of events and give intelligible voice to the creaking of circumstances are now inclined to be moderately disdainful of the name philosophy.

Certainly we cannot deny to the historian of general ideas the title philosopher. Indeed, I think that the chief if not the only way to assure the juices of life to the problems which are, in this sense, peculiarly philosophical is to take them over full-grown from other and earlier thinkers. They somehow lose their full-bodiedness when viewed in the interstices of things. But they come historically from back there in the domain divided between Heraclitus and Parmenides, between Plato and Democritus. What one sees in the immediate purview of experience, sprouting from the very crevices of flowing events, though possessed of interest all its own, has indeed but the semblance of a robust problem. It may be problematic enough, without a doubt; but the problematic matures into a problem only in books, where it can be emancipated from the too specific and where it can grow robust and, time and leisure favoring, even a little obese. Now I myself am not above writing such books (*i.e.*, books derived from books that have derived from other books), though the exercise never seems quite natural to me, nor does it leave any large meed of satisfaction. The point, however, that I wish to make is that what is called history of philosophy is the proper source for philosophy defined as preoccupation with problems.

But by the same token, even if for other reasons, the history of philosophy is not the best nor even a possible source for philosophy conceived as mind's best reaction to the immediate and the near-immediate. The source for that is the very complex medley itself of things, events, persons which go to make up the circumstances of the day's work and leisure or the night's play and rest. Now, it is a matter of both temperament and location, I suppose, as to which one of these possible sources makes to any given person a conclusive appeal as being his very own. Some of us are so invidiously located as regards the oases of circumstances that we have much to run away from and a long way to run. Like Love in Shakespeare's involved couplet:

We run each toward his own like schoolboys from their books,
But each from his own toward school with heavy looks.

But to run from life to books, and then from the reading of books to the writing of books about books does not, as I have said, mark my own deepest bent. There always remains as an aftertaste the suspicion that life thus lived is unduly thin. Now skimmed milk has its merits, without a doubt; but so has cream. And not the least interesting characteristic of the two is that both alike come from the same cow.

There is indeed enough continuity between preoccupation with problems and the face-on easing of difficulties to make appropriate the use of the same term—philosophy—to cover both. Meaning marks the continuity. Mind's reaction to raw circumstances and its reaction to previous delayed reactions are not unlike save in distance from, or nearness to, that which in our world contrasts with all that is mental whatever. As compensation for the "thinness" of philosophy as a reaction to a reaction, we achieve perspective: vision is, indeed, the very *quid* for thinness as the *quo*. None of us, I take it, wish to forego vision, even if we must brave the mental stratosphere to get it. While "thickness" of life has its advantages, it lacks perspective. To have the heavy substance of feeling and the light luminosity of understanding, and to have them together, is possible in only a limited degree. The best compromise possible for the soul heavy with ambition but light in capacity is to keep in touch with circumstances and trust for vision to the after-glow which a mind informed of things can shed, grieving as little as possible for the brighter lustre derived from the light of a light, *ad infinitum*. This humbler reliance will never give the peace which comes from problems treated as solutions; it will always leave one confronted with the problematic, which never moves to either a complete solution or to a well-groomed problem. But it will leave one in touch with life, and not wholly without the compensation of meanings which in a pinch may be contemplated and enjoyed as one's taunt to the too-pressing problematic.

I do not deprecate either the thick or the thin way of life as content for philosophy; but this compromise between them I wish to develop as more satisfactory to me than any so-called technical philosophy. Moreover, this compromise, I suspect, is in America more likely to be respected as philosophy tomorrow than it is today. For it represents the elevation into intellectual respectability of the novelist and the poet and the artist. It makes the *littérateur* indeed the readiest philosopher. Rewarding all skilled artisans with the coveted title, it calls them also to the supreme function of philosophy: the seeing whole of what they steadily perform.

I

This prejudice to which I incline may best be stated as the belief that for philosophy meaning is more important than truth. While Everyman looks and listens, or whether he look or listen, things are happening in his head that will reward remark by us as they reward attention from him. For the moment leaving *what is observed* to the scientist, with his wholesome respect for and practice of the logic of events, let us rise with the philosopher to the realm of imagination. Little strikes the eye or the ear of the sensitive observer which does not glance off into fantasy. If we follow the glance, we shall discover, contrary to the scientific logic of events, that what appears as the fruit of the tangent may have nothing or next to nothing to do with the source. In the graveyard, yes, consequents closely resemble antecedents; but in life anything may suggest anything: this is the dependable law underlying the easier "laws of association" of the textbooks of yesterday. Circumstances alone seem to limit the working of the more general law; mind itself appears fecund without determinable limit. Now the habitat and sum of all such tangents of fantasy is the realm of imagination. Beyond truth, it is better than truth; it is the domain of meaning, the final asylum of what in man is uniquely human.[1]

How man ever became possessed of such proliferative capacity, that is, how he ever became man, I do not profess to know. The fact remains that it is his nature when confronted by a fact (or a fiction, for that matter) to get a fancy. The variety and disorder of these fancies should not be obscured by any talk of laws in the realm of imagination. If one does not take the fact of imagination and its infinite proliferation with natural piety, he is likely to do worse; that is, he is likely to take it with supernatural piety, making thus a problem grow where only the problematic grew before. One of the elementary principles of any philosophy of tomorrow (perhaps it has come almost to characterize the philosophy of today) will be the recognition that the much vaunted principle of emergence only states a problem, which if soluble at all, cannot be solved by the mere invocation of evolution, emergent or otherwise. Better, however, than any brand of piety, natural wonder (Plato's derivation of philosophy) seems the more neatly to describe the fruitful attitude toward such facts as must be accepted even though not yet intelligible.

To dismiss the derivation of imagination as a preoccupation good only for producing greater problems than it itself (that is, as leading one back to philosophy as history of philosophy) is not, however, to obscure the fact that imagination is the only source of distinctly human value. It is because I hold it to be so

---

[1] And God saw everything that He had made and, behold, it was very bad. On the seventh day, therefore, God could not rest. In the morning and evening He busied himself with terrible and beautiful concoctions and in the twilight of the seventh day He finished that which is of more import than the beasts of the earth and the fish of the sea and the lights of the firmament. And he called it Imagination . . . for no other reason was imagination given unto us than that we might refashion the creator's wretched handiwork.—Russell Gordon Smith, *Fugitive Papers*, p. 3.

that I give preferential rating to it as that domain in which I am happy monarch of all I survey. Not that there is no value without imagination. Man has no monopoly upon value; it is surely as deep as living matter and as wide as the innumerable forms of sentiency. Plato's hypothetical oyster, full of pleasure but devoid of any consciousness of it, would have value nevertheless as its most priceless pearl, though I hold Plato right in denying to it the claim of the highest value. Pleasure (which, contrary to Plato's assumption, *is* a *kind* of consciousness) bounds the field of value; in that deeper, though non-technical sense, hedonism is the final axiology. And from that deep hedonic matrix shared alike by all that live rises the more majestic forms of the life of value. Did it rise so high as Plato's hypothetical angel, completely conscious but not pleasurably so, it would rise too high to be reckoned as among the things of value. Pleasurable consciousness (if not consciousness of pleasure) is the final description of value.

And imagination is its very seat and center. Aristotle has here, without much doubt, drawn the apotheosis of human desire. Unimpeded activity his deity represents; and since happiness is unimpeded activity, deity is completely happy. The supremely self-rewarding activity is here correctly described, but incorrectly named. For let us not too pretentiously call it, with Aristotle, Reason, nor even Thought; but let us more modestly and much more fruitfully see it as imagination at its most hedonic—day-dreaming. Aristotle's God is really doing nothing else than indulging with complete impunity in that oldest indoor sport of man—free fantasying. To think about thinking is to be emancipated from the logic of events; it is in fact to day-dream. What more than this indeed should deity be doing? It is to his everlasting sagacity that, alone and unaided, he was able to discover what is most worth while. He was as wise as man—and more fortunate; for he could without penalty live the life known of all men to be best.

This life of God, which Aristotle drew as too high for man,

is not too high to show the path of man's desire. Nor is it too high for man to practice, fugitively; had it been, Aristotle would not have created so lovely a God. It is too high for man in only one sense: the human practice of the presence of God is often interrupted by things. To imagination, or in imagination, as we have said, anything may suggest anything—and whatever can be suggested can as meaning be embraced with hedonic impunity. But it is not so in scientific thought, bounded by things, as such thought is. Our total career-line is scarred with the discipline inflicted upon imagination in the name of intellectual caution and for the sake of truth. For thought, tangentials must be ignored; thought must reckon with things. Distracted by fancy in an idle moment, thought may well be murdered by the band of ruffian things that flank it. The great scientists, then, have been those who practiced birth-control of ideas. Idle fancies may flit in the attics of scientists; but they are ignored until at last, as Darwin remarked of his sensitivity to poetry, they despair of admission and cease to knock at the door of the fore-conscious. Infinite variety in value has then given place to a narrow line of significance tinged with the royal purple but pointing like an arrow to truth—and on toward utility. It is in youth that the heaven of value-infinity lies about us. Yet, in childhood anything can really mean anything; and that meant may in turn lead to anything else—until mother calls and points to a task at hand. Now Dame Nature, that fussy mother of us all, points us to our tasks and appoints the hours of our subserviency.

But she cannot discipline us into a denial of what we would do endlessly if we could. That denial would be for man the mortal sin. Indeed, by calling us from the life of dreams where we well know the uniquely human value lies, she discovers to us a compensation: the value of discipline as furnishing us the permanent possibility of dreams. There would be reward enough in both the truth-inflicted discipline and in the free life of fancy if they could be made to rotate in some bearable fashion. But the fact of their alternation awakens in us the opportunity of shaping from our own efforts in the tough context of things the semblance of our dreams. Now and then, the medium allowing and fortune favoring, there rises from our hands a veritable eidolon of what our minds have seen. Care for these rare and precious starvelings of Fate nurses in us a solicitude, almost maternal, to leave no dream unbodied and to shed nothing from hands or loins ungirt with love. And here begins in earnest the tragic sense of life—clairvoyance of opportunity which is *there:* imaginable but unrealizable. Imagination left alone might breed endlessly of fancy and delight with little pang of sacrifice: old loveliness not so much departing as new forms of it arriving. Why grieve, when there is no loss? Dumb effort left alone might, on the other side, develop enough of utility to support life, as in lower forms, meeting new events only after they arrived and being cleanly quit of whatever was no longer present. How worry, when there's nothing to worry about? But, alas, we are men: things are fated to come to us trailing clouds of glory, and clouds of glory are doomed to be never so bright as when nestling over some lump of clay. But imagination breeds infinitely more than can ever come concretely to be: forms fired by our striving animal spirits with the thirst to become real, but unable to be quit of ideality. To be sure, anything imaginable is possible; but the number of ideal possibilities that are also probable, even with our most strenuous efforts to render them so, is pathetically small indeed. That light that ever is but never can come to be—that it is which once having illumed our eyes renders the real thereafter coarse and leaves the ideal forever weak in its splendor.

And yet we cannot deny either, without transforming what Santayana calls our "normal madness" into madness indeed. Rebuffed by the "faultiness of things," we may of course be quit of our reality-sense and live with dreams, on dreams, for dreams. But that is to be insane. The way in which much of modern philosophy skirts that willowy shore seems to me only testimonial of how hard life is underneath the efficient exterior of industrialism. For I hold with Nietzsche that over the door of every insane asylum might well be placed as motto the concentrated essence of much modern philosophy: "The ultimate test of the truth of a proposition is the unconceivableness of its negation."

II

Failing at last in our metaphysical efforts to render reasonable all that is real or real much that is reasonable, why not modestly reduce reason to plain thinking (about things), hoping thus through science and technology to transform the less into the more reasonable? Why not? The answer is simple but plain: we are men. This plain thinking about things hardly begins to skirt the body of man's capacity. Back of utility, not in it, lies truth; and back of truth lies meaning. The test of the transition from science to imagination is the renunciation of truth-motivation. Shall we, then, try again to rest in imagination, beyond truth? Now glorifying as I have the life of imagination, I am far from suggesting that all men ought to, or even can, renounce their interest in truth. It is a tragic realm without a doubt, as Santayana, Unamuno, Plato and all knowing ones discern; but human life is inured to tragedy. What I have been suggesting is, rather, that in the intellectual division of labor, philosophy may find a rich heritage in the realm of imagination, preoccupying itself with meaning, not truth. Not only may it; it already has done so.

While in general I have contrasted history of philosophy (which has deemed itself in search of truth) with what I am now assimilating to the imaginative enterprise, nevertheless, as already suggested, history of philosophy has one curious mark not ordinarily associated with seekers after truth: it specializes always in problems. Indeed, the history of philosophy may almost, if not quite, be identified with problems made more robust by would-be solutions, endlessly repeated. Now when we reach the point that problems become chronic: content to remain so, enjoying their status, attracting around them a social elite, we really find ourselves inside the field of imagination where truth is less important than meaning, whatever sporadic claims of truth may from time to time be made for the enterprise.

But I am not disposed to argue this question with any who insist that they are philosophers, that they are out after truth, and that they will keep after it until they get it. I only know that I have come myself to the view that in perhaps the most truth-devoted segment of historical philosophy, where I specifically work, *i.e.*, that of morals, truth (with the meaning found in science) is not only impossible; it is also irrelevant to the deeper spirit of the enterprise. The deepest ought of conscience cannot be shown to be true save as the claim of an Absolute with all power and the will to use it or as the claim of a purely private self with no power connotation; and these two alike belong to the realm of imagination: the former being a product of imagination, the latter the locus of imagination.

Now, my having come to such a conclusion need be of interest to no one but myself, were it not for the fact that each of us hides in himself and reveals as his philosophy some morphology of his time and place. Since we are discussing American philosophy today and tomorrow, it is convenient and fit that I should do candidly what each of us does anyhow, *i.e.*, portray the field as a projection of my own development. The validity of this does not, as I have indicated, depend upon its acknowledged narcissism; for one's career-line is itself a projection of a culture-configuration, which having had this present effect in him is sure to have future effects in and for others, through and other than through him.

In fact I have myself in person kinaesthetically spanned— as what contributor to this volume has not?—the whole history of philosophy in America. This history has had two general phases: the preoccupation with truth and the growing contentment with meaning. There perhaps awaits a third phase, to which I shall revert presently. But let us briefly detail these several phases in order. The metaphysical views of our American fathers were held by them to be true, indeed to be gospel truth; for the most sustained speculation in America has of course been theological. At the tail-end of this theological tradition I grew up, vivifying in my youthful mind its major features. Let there be no mistake about what I mean. I speak of fundamentalism in its deepest dye. That God is, that the earth is his created footstool, that the soul is a fact and is immortal, that the will is free, that Jesus was veritably Christ, that salvation, externally provided, is necessary for avoiding a hellish hell and winning a heavenly heaven—these are representative crumbs that fell to children from all tables alike in the still pioneer Texas of my day. As a child I ate these crumbs and picked the cracks in the floor for more—and for different ones. The other preoccupation was the wresting of a living from nature. Let there be no mistake here as to what I mean. I speak of a section that was not too fertile and of a day when child labor was thought to be thrice blessed, training him who gave and repaying him who took. The solid earth that we tilled, the cattle that we raised, the mules that we drove and swore at— these were not more solid facts than were the elements of religion. Propositions about these were not less subject to deceitful deviations from truth than were those about Biblical matters and moral conduct. All propositions, secular and sacred alike, were either true or false. Poetry was unknown save as maxims to enforce a moral, fine art rose to the high level represented on calendars, and fiction, though heard of and sometimes read by men behind the barn and by women in the bedroom, was in principle cried down because it was not true—and, besides, was conducive to idleness.

Now American life as a whole, conceived as devotion to religion and exploitation of science through technology, has been singularly devoted to this same objective, truth. While West

Texas was perhaps in several regards anachronistic at the beginning of the twentieth century, yet for that very reason it confronts us vividly with our true and longer past, with its popular disesteem of poetry and its almost universal moral deprecation of novels and the stage.

My own childhood deviated from this general pattern in only two regards that seem to me important in retrospect: (1) I was not as strong as a boy might be, (2) my father alternated in his reading aloud, with apparent equal enjoyment of each, between the *Bible* and *Peck's Bad Boy*. The former fact (1) necessitated on my part an imaginative escape from routine and fatigue and the latter fact (2) let me early see, in fashion not beyond my comprehension, that not all writing claimed to be equally true, that the realm of fantasy, whereunto I quickly learned every detour, had been systematically explored by those who *knew* that what they wrote was *not* so. The "different" crumbs which I sought as a child were more of the sort represented by *Peck's Bad Boy*, and later by illustrative snatches of genuine poetry and elevated prose which I progressively gleaned and memorized from grammars and other common school texts.

Though by most external influences foresworn thus to truth, I was as a child the more unyieldingly devoted by temperament to pleasures of the body and to the fantasies of the mind. My temperament won without really any inner struggle. I early discerned that the plain pleasures of food and drink and talk and sex are really what make the world of man go round. The high adventure of mind as it feels its way frictionlessly from idea to idea, unharassed by too rigorous rules of the game, became, as compensation, a close second contender for primacy in the life of value. Though this latter luxury supplemented the former pleasures, I could neither then nor can I now doubt that it is conditioned by the former and arises primarily to compensate for the poverty of the sensuous life. Hedonism, which veritably seemed foregone, rested for me as naturally upon materialism as I have later seen it to rest in and for Lucretius.

Now I do not profess, from any original point of view, to justify materialism; indeed, I acknowledge that I cannot prove that matter is the source of all, or even tell what matter is. Nor do I see how conceivably the richness of imagination could have arisen from the insentiency of such humble world-stuff. But that it has so risen and is thus conditioned I cannot doubt. Even if I had not driven mules as a boy and had not seen how cussedly curious were the ways in which mules and men elected to be good, I should have imbibed enough of the loneliness of open spaces, absorbed enough of the "down-yonderishness" of the coyote's nocturnal yowl, and felt enough the terror of the cyclone's black twisting and of the "norther's" dour thundering down the Texas plains—enough of these and such as these to make me distrust any pious person and to feel at heart that no metaphysical idealist can be emotionally an honest man. I am speaking, it will be seen, of what I feel, not of what I believe. I *believe* that idealism is one of the permanent possibilities of an intelligible statement about the world as a whole, and I believe that many a person can be happier in piety than in sophistication; but these beliefs, I candidly avow, are themselves sophisticated graftings upon the thorny seedlings that I have described.

It will hardly now require a psychoanalyst to discern that my personal identification of philosophy (my profession) with meaning, is a compensated reaction on my part against an overdose of truth. I have not been able to emancipate myself from the over-impetuosity of truth-claims without the catharsis of a complete renunciation of truth as a ubiquitous claim. But in this, too, I feel myself to be a child of America. Intolerance is laid deep in man, but involves terrible self-punishing reactions. One need only remember the pricking voices of the intolerant Saul to see that devotion to truth has its tragic side. Jesus in whose name we have carried on our major truth-quest came, he is reported as saying, not to bring peace but a sword, to set kith against kin and to sow deep the seeds of social discord.

Emerson, the best of all our American idealistic voices, has expressed the moving conviction that

> 'Tis man's perdition to be safe,
> When for the Truth he ought to die.

And over and over has echoed in our history, down to Robinson's late hero, Nightengale, the old cry

> . . . That was the curse prepared
> For me: I would not listen to my voices.

We have fought for truth, we have talked for truth, we have died for truth, we have at times almost lived for truth. If it was "revealed" truth so much the better, but secular truth is itself no mean mark and merit. How else explain the tremendous popular prestige of science—prestige alike among the humble poor who know too little of its utilities and among the rich who subsidize it but know next to nothing of its inner spirit? Science is the last refuge of truth, when, forsaken by heaven, she must be housed on earth. But even while heaven still supported her, what royal meannesses did we not commit in her name and for her sake! The history of our early religious persecutions and the story of our later strifes and lasting intolerances between scowling sectarians, though sordid from an outside point of view, is the roll of honor in the war of Truth against error. It was, of course, a war of attrition which nobody won save by subsequent amnesia. The way from such fanatical truth has lain through the elevation of meaning above truth. While Emerson, however, was still singing that "for the truth we ought to die," he was also writing down the heretical conviction that one religious way is as good as another: there is significance alike in Buddha, Mohammed, Confucius, Moses, Christ (all tolled off together, just like that). Thus Emerson the essayist. And that has been the first sign of liberalism in innumerable minds, the discovery that there is meaning and significance alike in views that, from the mere point of view of truth, contradict each other. What has been historically true in that most serious of our truth claims, religion, one now sees repeated in another sphere where for the racial truth all too many have suffered on both sides of the color line. What marks the incidence of social tolerance of the Negro in America? The discovery of significance in his spirituals, in his African and American art. Where his life and effort rise to meaningful expression, the "truth" of Nordic superiority, of Negro inferiority, ceases to send whites alone to the pharasaic altar and blacks in stupified horror to the stake. Yes, the way from fanatical truth has lain, and still does further lie, through the elevation of meaning above truth.

And for this tendency American philosophy is now going strong. The dominant characteristic today of American philosophy is not to be found in any controversy between the schools as rival claimants of truth, but in the common approach from all schools alike to the theme of this chapter: the primacy of meaning over truth in the philosophic enterprise. Dewey from the pragmatic quarters is now declaring for the primacy of meaning. Montague from the realist side is rounding out in the latest Carus lectures the contention that imagination is the philosopher's be-all and end-all. He even takes imagination so seriously as to suggest that it can substitute for the earlier Reason of idealism as the world-ground. The decline of the Absolute in idealistic quarters may be read as the negative gesture from this source to match the positive ones from other directions, or where the Absolute has not declined, the decline of idealism which espouses it answers the same roll-call. Hovering over all this commonalty of convergence is the bright genius of him who lonelily pioneered among us and mockingly left us in order to escape canonization as the very high priest of the cult of imagination now abuilding. I refer of course to George Santayana, who from childhood knew that "the works of human imagination are good, they alone are good; and the rest—the whole real world—is ashes in the mouth."

III

This, then, is, as I see it, the yesterday and the today of philosophy in America. King—Reason—is dead! Long live the king —Imagination! But how long? What of philosophy tomorrow? In my opinion, the same forces that have driven philosophy, and will probably drive it further, from reason to imagination will eventually bring us back toward if not to truth. If the way from fanatical truth has lain through meaning, may not the continued quest for meaning lead again to a more urbane truth? There are three reasons for expecting eventually a return through imagination to the quest for truth as part of the business of philosophy.

The first is the tendency of imaginative data from very excess of richness to break up into classes, which must then be distinguished and ranked. There grow up poetic truth, political truth, fictional verisimilitude, and canons of art. Emancipated from generic and earthly truth, imagination tends to develop truths of its own, which to judge between implies a general truth strangely like the best of the old one.

The second is the record of science as custodian of the old truth left on earth by philosophy. Philosophers have, of course, never forgotten truth. They thought her happier and more prosperous with science than with them, and so loved and left her there, while they devoted themselves to meanings. Scientists have meant well, and will continue to mean well, no doubt. They have meant so well that they have dismembered truth, dividing her fair body among themselves, being so intent each with his piece as never to feel the jeopardy to her fair soul. Some insensitive thus to the ravage done, have turned truth's dismembered body to utilities so brazen as themselves to usurp the mantle of truth. None are so poor as those who do not know how poor they are. But philosophers know better, and cannot remain happy over the treatment truth has got, and will get, from those who do her the more harm the less they intend her any. But other scientists, like Eddington, Jeans, Compton, rendered over-serious as trustees by sensitivity to the dismemberment practiced by their impercipient confreres, have incarnated as the soul of truth whimsical fantasies or mere grandmotherly anxieties. As it becomes clearer that the stock-in-trade of the scientists contains more mere meanings, mythologies disguised in bristling formulae as fundamental truths, than philosophers in their own modesty had supposed, sympathy aroused by the plight of truth will be transformed into a question of the justice of leaving truth longer in quarters so equivocal, even when not cramped and ungracious. Philosophy may be driven by such considerations to show again a larger solicitude for truth. But—it goes without saying—that if this be so, philosophy, fresh from a carefree vacation among easy-going meanings, will train up truth as a more urbane ward than was that austere maiden housed by her yesteryear.

The other reason for expecting this metamorphosis of philosophy in America is of a social and political nature. Philosophers long absorbed in the unheated contemplation of meanings will, as they return to earth for such humble rites as food and sex, find stranger goings-on than those just recorded of science and truth. Submerged classes awakened by sights of plenty will first pity their dire wants, then rationalize their desires as their deserts (even as you and I), and finally will hate those who have rationalized things against them. Truth will achieve new formulations, be served by new devotees, and devotion to her will now take the form of class-hate not so easily melted as our traditional sectarian bickerings.

All this will crystallize as a determination to turn right-side-up the social order that is now up-side-down. To do or to die in the name of a new truth, nobly named Class Justice, will be the ghost discovered stalking about, upon their return from the realm of imagination by philosophers who supposed that truth was being taken good care of while they pursued the richer vein of meanings. Truth will always be taken care of, for a fact; but who takes care of her is no immaterial question in a world itself at bottom material. To have escaped from Christian fanaticism through the enlargement of life by meanings would not prove compensation enough even for philosophers, if they discovered themselves set upon by a fascistic or even communistic, fanaticism less nobly named but more grimly envisaged and effectively implemented than was ever Puritan pride and harshness.

But might not the "meaning" of all this fury our voluptuary of imagination indeed enjoy as well as any other meaning? Yes, were it not for one sordid but solid fact, with the enunciation of which would fall the curtain upon our little play. That fact is this: with his body done to death, down would come his towering mind, imagination, meanings and all—leaving no sweetness and light half so potent as the natural grin of satisfaction upon the face of the fanatic who thus brought down a lofty philosophy with just one deft twist of his bayonet in the philosopher's belly.

IV

Now I am temperamentally and constitutionally opposed to having bayonets thrust into bellies; but if the two must be juxtaposed, I very much prefer, in fashion only covertly if at all Christian, to have it my bayonet which is twisted. Having lived perhaps closer to earth than have most academic philosophers, I have seen in the performance of rites humble and otherwise so much of what every philosopher is likely eventually to see that I have taken time by the forelock and have swung myself into the melee of politics. As a participant, in a small way as state senator, in the struggle for power I mean to neglect no opportunity to budge things in the direction which I prefer. But I am being too frank, for either philosophy or politics.

My turning from the academy to the arena was motivated, if I may put the best light upon the shift, by Plato's declared reason for going again and again to Syracuse: I feared if I did not do so, I should find myself at last altogether nothing but words. The conviction has grown upon me for many years, until it became at last a poignant personal problem, that I did not understand even the books I had written upon social and political philosophy. Always a dissenter, I never could get sympathetically close enough to the struggle for power underlying descriptive words to know fully what the words meant. My recent book reduces conscience to aesthesia; my felt need as an intellectual was more kinaesthesia. And politics was for me the natural activity through which to repair my greatest felt lack.

As I turned from books to men, to complete my education thus at state expense, my past life as a student and writer of books took on, in retrospect, a pattern of intelligibility clearer than it had in the living of it. A word upon the pattern as it appears to me at this juncture will close this essay by leaving me where at the writing I actually am.

Touched at birth with a philosophic turn of mind and caught in youth by a poetic fancy, my first professional love was literature, especially poetry. I was, however, quickly driven from the teaching of literature into philosophy by the discovery that the great arcs of insight from which the poet snatches only segments must be traversed by means of the system-builders. But the philosophers themselves I simply could not read without trying in my own fumbling fashion to be a philosopher.

The first book resulting from this effort, *The Democratic Way of Life*, tempered the trinity of Western social ideals—Liberty, Equality, Fraternity—to their greatest strength, and sought to re-touch them to dignity for the contemporary scene. My second, *The American Philosophy of Equality*, which I had persisted in as my own hazardous, even almost hell-bent, way of getting a doctorate, seized upon the political ideal of our historic three which seemed to me deepest, and grounded it in American history with suggestions at the end for bringing it to concreter expression here and now. My third, *The Philosophic Way of Life*, sought to turn America's greatest speculative minds—James, Royce, Santayana, Dewey—to the service of a way of life for every individual that would re-emphasize the right of each to equal independence with all.

Ignoring pedagogical and playful literary efforts, in two books immediately preceding my sprint into actual politics, I tried in *Beyond Conscience* to shame citizens from doing wrong to others merely because they feel so right in and of themselves. Conscience is itself paraded as being a power drive which drives those integrated by it toward coercion. A social order generated from conscience is but a mirage of order in a desert of disorder. Beyond the prod of moral urgencies, if anywhere, lies a tolerance which defines right in terms of what the majority can agree upon, instead of what a few can fasten upon others as already absolutely so. Meantime, and of the last importance, this book celebrates in the private life of imagination an island of refuge and safety and beauty where every disciplined man can with serenity become and remain his own blessed pope, enjoying there and thus his own tensions enough not to have to inflict them upon others as dictates of conscience.

My last book, *Creative Sceptics*, as the sub-title says, is a "defense of the liberal temper." Continuing and popularizing the argument of *Beyond Conscience*, I here acknowledge that nobody can be liberal who is not willing to meet others upon grounds not chosen by either but dictated by the distasteful fact of their differences, and on those grounds come somehow to terms. Political action, indeed all social action, must pass through the same renunciation of infallibility that every individual endures in order to grow. Doubt is inevitable, but it can be turned to creative ends if endured in the liberal spirit. Many doubters are in this book dissected to find in each and all the same moral: "He who doubts not is fossilized already." Justice Oliver Wendell Holmes is seized upon and exploited as the sceptic of our age whose doubt has most deeply grounded American democracy.

To participate in one active sector of that democracy now,

with the same solicitude in which I have watched its career heretofore—this constitutes the most potent mainspring of my conscious life. From birth I was a philosopher; I always wanted to be a statesman; at middle-age I am proud to become a politician. Democratic philosophy and practical politics meet, I fancy, in the man who can compromise an issue without compromising himself and who in a pinch can give an issue away without giving himself away.

A MEMORANDUM FOR A
SYSTEM OF PHILOSOPHY

PAUL WEISS

1901; Associate Professor, Bryn Mawr College

My early education was acquired in the New York public schools. Under the pressure of financial circumstances, I found it desirable to begin to earn my living at 16, without having completed my college preparation. For six years I read anxiously but at random, looking for answers to incoherent and partly unformulated questions regarding the nature of things, gathering finally, from a miscellany of introductions and a number of more or less classical works which I found largely beyond my grasp, that the kind of solutions I sought were provided by philosophy. I thereupon entered the evening session of City College where, under the guidance of Professor John P. Turner, I began to receive a much needed formal training. On his advice I entered the day session of the college, which is to say, I spent three exciting years studying under the inspiring, brilliant Morris R. Cohen. Upon graduating college in 1927 I went to Harvard where, having written my dissertation under Alfred North Whitehead, I took my doctorate degree in 1929. I owe to him whatever metaphysical insight or intellectual sanity I may have attained. After a year abroad I returned to teach at Harvard and a year later went to Bryn Mawr College. Until 1932, while I continued to recognize that a complete philosophical system was the *raison d'être* of an intellectual existence, I specialized in symbolic logic. Logic, I felt, had to be mastered if progress was to be made with the more important and difficult branches of philosophy. For the last three years I have been occupied with problems in ontology and epistemology and am now completing a book of which the following "memorandum" is an anticipation.

Publications:

Collected Papers of C. S. Peirce, vols. 1-6; 1931-35, edited with C. Hartshorne.

Theory of Types, *Mind,* 1928.

Relativity in Logic, *Monist,* 1928.

The Nature of Systems, *Monist,* 1929.

Entailment and the Future of Logic; *Seventh International Congress of Philosophy,* Oxford, 1930.

Two-Valued Logic—Another Approach, *Erkenntnis,* 1931.

The Logic and Metaphysics of Classes; *Monist,* 1932.

The Logical and Metaphysical Individual, *Journal of Philosophy,* 1933.

Alternative Logics, *Philosophical Review,* 1933.

Biography of C. S. Peirce, *Dictionary of American Biography.*

Metaphysics—The Domain of Ignorance; *Philosophical Review,* 1934.

Time and the Absolute, *Journal of Philosophy,* 1935.

A MEMORANDUM FOR A SYSTEM OF PHILOSOPHY

Paul Weiss

The task of philosophy does not differ today from what it has always been. It must explain, not explain away, the world we all in some sense know. A philosophy which denies the reality of macroscopic or microscopic individuals, space or time, mind or body, knowledge or being, though it be crystal clear and dialectically perfect, is a philosophy which is inadequate when it is not inconsistent, and most unsatisfactory when most plausible. A philosophy is valuable only so far as it succeeds in clarifying, in terms of a system of pervasive, inescapable, constant truths, the nature of the dynamic, resplendent, intelligible world we already partially know in common sense, art and science.

We today have recognized the inadequacies of past answers; our particular problem is not to change our questions but to get a better, though not necessarily final, system. Progress consists in the substitution of bad solutions for worse ones; not in the attainment of an absolute goal. Fortunately, we are armed in ways our predecessors were not. Firstly, we can take advantage of their folly and their wisdom, and can grow more rapidly in the direction where knowledge lies; secondly, we have a better instrument for analysis than any they possessed and can uncover truths they never could have seen; and thirdly, we can profit from the suggestions offered in disciplines which have only lately achieved self-consciousness or critical acumen, to enrich our thought with notions never before exploited.

1. We should all now know that some approaches to reality

must be avoided, centuries of genius having made their disastrous consequences strikingly clear. Yet much that passes for philosophy today is plausible only because the lessons of the past have not been studied with sufficient thoroughness. Let us hope that our successors will profit from our errors in ways that some of us have been unable or unwilling to profit from those of the past.

Five classical philosophies must be abandoned:

Atomism will not do. A theory which is compelled to say that the world of daily life is an inexplicable illusion hovering over a real world of minute, discrete, unexperienceable entities, may be useful in science and logical theory. It can never satisfy one to whom no truth is more inescapable than that he exists, together with his dog, his house and his horse, organic, complex and dynamic.

Monism will not do. A theory which is compelled to say that whatever can be grasped by the human mind is an error, wrested from the bosom of an unthinkable Absolute, must deny that the existence of multiple entities is as obtrusive or as unavoidable a truth as any logical conclusion. It successfully avoids the mistakes of extreme pluralism only by falling into others of its own.

Platonism will not do. A theory which is compelled to separate the realm of the intelligible from that of the concrete, though it does more than justice to the eternal truths of logic and mathematics, can never satisfy one to whom all aspects of experience are equally real, if not equally important.

Irrationalism will not do. A theory which is compelled to deny value or truth to discursive knowledge is forced to deny that understanding is an instrument for the achievement of wisdom. Though it pays its respects to the inarticulate richness of reality, it neglects to observe that analytic minds are also real.

Phenomenalism will not do. A theory which is compelled to deny reality to anything not constructed out of the material of sensuous experience may be successful in formulating the suppressed premisses and inferences embodied in daily discourse, but it crumbles in the face of the necessity of rejecting or accepting the concept of potentiality, which is at once empirically unverifiable and ingredient in any world in which inquiry is possible.

A satisfactory philosophy cannot be one of these five. Nor can it be one which sees no virtue in any of them, for that would mean that it would be unable to provide a place for science, metaphysics, logic, art and common sense. It cannot be an eclectic agglomeration of these discordant doctrines. It must be a new system in which their different truths all find their proper niche, supporting instead of contradicting one another.

The Aristotelian system, as supplemented and systematized by St. Thomas Aquinas, is a landmark to the wisdom of beginning philosophy with an acknowledgment of the reality of the world of daily experience. It is the first complete philosophy of the western world, balanced, persuasive and penetrating. A new science and a new religion revealed fatal (but not, I think, irremediable) faults in its structure and drove a rather precipitate age to abandon it altogether. Its basic defect was that it was not sufficiently conscious of the need to certify the truths it claimed to know. One can safely begin with an acknowledgment of the world of daily experience only if one knows the difference between truth and falsehood, insight and prejudice, and is able to discriminate the inescapable features of the world from those that are arbitrary or fictitious. The Aristotelians failed to provide a lasting philosophy largely because they failed to show why and how we know that ours is an Aristotelian world. It remained for Kant to make evident the need and value of an examination of the epistemological presuppositions of ontology. But Kant was not sufficiently conscious of the fact that such an examination is possible only so far as some ontological truths are taken for granted. The century of idealisms to which he gave impetus is a century of frantic attempts to avoid the hopeless ontology which he so naïvely assumed. The defect of the *Critique* is that it has no way of showing that the very nature of the world necessitates the acknowledgment of a Kantian epistemology. A philosophy must not only show how and why we know that which is, but how and why that which is, is a condition for what we know.

2. Logic is the instrument of analysis, *par excellence*. It is now almost a hundred years since the mathematician Boole taught philosophers how to make logic into a science, and though the subject is now encrusted in symbols and besieged by paradox, I think there can be little doubt but that it is an instrument more powerful than any ever before available. Through its use we can more successfully than heretofore avoid the traditional snares of ordinary syntax and the limitations embodied in hallowed classifications.

3. Finally, we are able to profit from the fact that science is now in the midst of a very invigorating, revolutionary, unstable period, and that the number of new fields of investigation have multiplied considerably. In its use of traditional concepts to serve its own purpose, the scientific world, for the first time since Galileo, has shown itself bolder than the philosopher has dared to be. But science cannot be accepted without criticism. Philosophy grows fat largely on the disputes and paradoxes of the lower disciplines, for it is there and then that the difficulties of wider questions are first sharpened into significance. It is in the sciences that we best see how much of that which passes for certainty is only that which has been insufficiently examined. For philosophy, modern science is an unusually powerful irritant, stimulating it to achieve new insights and to attain to new solutions.

If we take advantage of these three signal aids, we should be able to achieve a somewhat stronger and more adequate philosophy than any vouchsafed us in the past. In what follows I can give but a dark hint of what I think the framework of that philosophy to be, reserving for elsewhere the exploitation of its implications. It should be a coherent philosophy, rooted in common sense, systematically explicating the world we all know and the insights we all have. It ought to embody a methodology that preserves the virtues of both the Aristotelian and Kantian approaches by speculatively arriving at the real in terms of factors which are indispensable to any knowledge whatsoever, and speculatively inferring the conditions of knowledge from the essential characters of the real. A philosophy is adequate and internally self-substantiating only so far as the results of the speculative flights of epistemology and ontology coincide with what has been independently assumed in the other.

Knowing is a moment in the process of inquiry. If there were not something implicitly or explicitly recognized as being still beyond actual knowledge, the activity of inquiry, together with all other purposive activities, would be at an end. Deny that there is something unknown, and you must admit that everything that is, is already known, or that only what is now understood really is, alternatives which can be maintained only by rejecting all movement toward an unattained end. It is the view of one who arrogates omniscience to himself and denies the pursuit of learning to another. It is because I am aware of being ignorant that I inquire, and it is because I inquire that I know. However, I am aware of being ignorant only of that toward which inquiry is directed, and I direct my inquiry only in terms of what I already know. It is the awareness of ignorance that compels inquiry and the acquisition of knowledge; it is what we know that directs inquiry and defines what we do not know. The epistemological ultimate is the process of inquiry which is given direction by knowledge and impetus by ignorance.

Ignorance is a presupposition for the attainment of any knowledge; a final cause of that which is designed to make it vanish. It is an *a priori* condition for the possibility of knowledge. But it is not an *a priori* in the sense in which the classical rationalists understood that term, since it is not understood before, but together with other truths. Nor is it *a priori* in the sense in which Kant understood that term, since it is not a structural element of any knowledge of fact, but a correlative to such knowledge, not included or includable in what is now understood. Our knowledge that there is something of which we are ignorant begins with experience but is not derived from it. The *a priori* is not a feature of a disembodied mind, a condition which one must impose upon inchoate data to make experience possible, or a tentative hypothesis entertained in order to enable one to tread his way through the mazes of a complex world. It is an inescapable aspect of all investigation, focussed on and partially conquered by the help of knowledge which ignorance makes possible.

Supposedly cautious philosophers, such as Peirce with his "contrite fallibilism" and Dewey with his scorn for the "quest for certainty" are cautious only because they are sure that there is a domain of knowledge yet to be probed. They acknowledge the necessity and virtue of experiment and verification only because they are convinced that there are entities whose exact nature they do not yet know. The truth that they are ignorant is the one certainty they not only will not abandon, but which they use as the foundation on which everything else must rest. They are not and cannot be pure empiricists, for their very insistence on the necessity for empirical tests involves an acceptance of the reality of a realm of the unknown, a domain of ignorance, extending spatially and temporally beyond the reaches of what is now had. Such ignorance, the conquest of which is the concern of science, may be termed *extensive* ignorance.

Knowing is a discursive activity which consists in the articulation of the concrete through the use of abstractions. The knowledge that this before me is a cat involves the embodiment of an indicated "it" and a contemplated "felinity" in an adumbrated presented content so as to constitute a perceptual cat.

That perceptual cat is part of but not identical with the real cat. We do not and cannot in knowing it, become or absorb a cat. That which exists does not have a character additional to or lacking in our perception of it. It has a different status from what is known of it. We can understand the concrete cat only so far as we abstract and discriminate; yet the cat remains concrete and undiscriminated. In every act of knowing, we are *intensively* ignorant of the unarticulated concrete real which makes the articulation true and which remains forever other than that which is had in knowing it.

Supposedly skeptical and critical philosophers ground their skepticism and criticism on the certainty that knowledge is restricted in its domain. But to be skeptical and critical is to assert something about what is not yet known. Kant could be critical and skeptical only by going beyond the domain of actual knowledge to find something which he could take to be outside the possibility of human grasp. He did not deny the fact of intensive ignorance; he insisted on it and characterized it as inconquerable. Other philosophers have been less paradoxical in their characterizations of the nature of the object of intensive ignorance, but they almost all agree in taking that which is beyond empirical knowledge to be something different in nature from what is known. But we are intensively ignorant, not of some other kind of being, but of the being of what we know. That of which we are intensively ignorant is through and through knowable, differing from the known only as being differs from being known.

Just as the *acquisition* of any bit of knowledge supposes an extensive, so the *truth* of any bit of knowledge supposes an intensive ignorance. We move from epistemology to ontology by speculating on the truth of the fact that inquiry is the fundamental of epistemology. Grant no truth but that you are extensively ignorant and it follows that you are also intensively ignorant. To know that you are extensively ignorant is to know that there must be a concrete indivisible unity, "I, as extensively ignorant" which makes the proposition "I am extensively ignorant" true. You cannot be extensively ignorant unless you are a being in which such extensive ignorance is an ingredient. I as known to be extensively ignorant am a unity which is an object of intensive ignorance. But as the known differs from the intensively unknown only in mode of being, the structure of inquiry is also the structure of what inquires. The inquiring individual is one who reaches beyond himself, not only in cognition but also in fact.

It is the task of ontology to develop the implications of the truth that there are multiple beings all of whom are engaged in completing themselves. But instead of merely developing that truth in the form in which it is inferred from epistemology, it must, in self-protection, establish it and others in its own way by showing that they are material indubitables, to be denied only at the price of rejecting the world that everyone knows. One must reveal in detail what is involved in their acceptance, and demonstrate that reasoned denials of them are based on false premises or presuppose what they pretend to deny. Within the present compass, unfortunately, nothing more can be offered than a few dogmatic remarks, which merely emphasize some of the basic truths such an ontology incorporates.

I am an individual and there are no duplicates. It is nonsense to suppose that some day in some place I can meet myself coming toward me.

There are other individuals, animate and inanimate, each unduplicatable, with an inward nature that can only be lived through and flavored from within. I am not alone in the universe, nor could there ever be a universe in which there was only one individual. The existence of a multiplicity of contingent individuals is absolutely necessary.

All macroscopic individuals have aggregational as well as unit characters. They are at once summations and more than summations of their parts. A human being falls according to the laws of bodies because in falling it is only a swarm of atoms. But no group of atoms can start a war; atoms within an organism have their positions changed in unusual ways when the organism is biologically or humanly active.

Objects are spatially extended and spatially distant from one another in a contemporaneous world. It is nonsense to suppose that there are nothing but unextended spirits or that I am not in a real relation to my contemporaries.

Objects have careers, modified through the influence of others. The history of no being is encompassed in a moment. Individuals endure though they change.

Objects are temporal beings conditioned by the past and influenced by the future. The present object is a condition for what it will be at the next moment; but it is such a condition only because it is effected by the nascent future. No complete explanation of nature is possible without final causes; they make it possible for an object to survive a given moment in a definite way. If final causation be denied, and no recourse is had to a *Deus ex machina*, that abode of lost metaphysical causes, one is compelled to hold that each moment and each state stands in absolute isolation from all others, and is driven to deny the reality of both time and change.

Animate objects differ from inanimate ones in the variability they manifest in their reactions to their final causes. Mechanism is not an alternative to but an instance of teleology; the mechanical is that which is monotonous in its teleological behavior.

Life is not an elusive spirit; it is a way of being irritable, the capacity to change with new circumstances so as to remain identical. Its diverse manifestations are so many different modes in which a being reaches beyond itself in order that it may endure.

It is because to be is to transcend, that to know is to go beyond. We shall always be extensively ignorant, and science will never be at an end, precisely because we are aware of an unknown which is the incipient future as now ingredient in the present. We move from ontology to epistemology by speculating on the fact that inquiring is a mode of becoming, just as we move from epistemology to ontology by speculating on the fact that inquiry is an act of self-completion. Philosophy is an eternal circle where Kant merges into Aristotle and Aristotle gives way to Kant.

As I look about for confirmation in current American literature for the views so baldly and inadequately expressed, I find it in part in the writings of Whitehead and Dewey. Each in different ways has pressed home the observation which was so familiar to the scholastics: never derogate one truth in order better to substantiate another. There is no higher philosophic wisdom. It means that we must fight our way clear to a system which will make intelligible the fact that our universe is one where there are both qualities and quantities, animate and inanimate beings, truths and falsehoods, stability and novelty, values and activities. Until this is done, in a scheme free of mysteries and inscrutables, we live but blindly and understand only part of that which is. Our world is too miraculously concatenated for a miracle to have made it possible.

A CATHOLIC'S VIEW

MICHAEL WILLIAMS

MICHAEL WILLIAMS is the editor of The Commonweal, a weekly review which guides its policy by principles drawn from the teachings of the Catholic Church. As an author, his work has been chiefly concerned with Catholicism in its connection with various aspects and problems of contemporary life. Among his books are: "The Book of the High Romance," a "spiritual autobiography"; "Catholicism and the Modern Mind," a collection of essays and articles; "The Shadow of the Pope," a study of religious strife in American society; and "The Catholic Church in Action," an outline description of how the Church is organized, and of the functions of its chief departments. Born in Halifax, Nova Scotia, in 1877, he left school at the age of fourteen; and came to the United States in 1898, since which time he has been engaged in journalism and authorship.

A CATHOLIC'S VIEW

Michael Williams

I

I find that I have placed myself in a serious dilemma by rashly agreeing to contribute to this symposium—the dilemma of having promised to write about a view of life which I hold to be the highest and truest possible to attain—a Catholic view of life—and of now being confronted by the belated realization of my inadequacy to deal with such a theme. I console myself feebly by remembering that I at first refused to attempt the task on the unimpeachable ground that I had as little competency to discuss the technical aspects of philosophy as I had to talk about the technical mysteries of the gold standard. The editors responded by saying that what they wanted was the personal expression of a living philosophy by somebody trying to live it rather than a formal exposition by a technician. Vanity, I am afraid, and no doubt the even more serious sin of presumption, tempted me to reconsider. Mea culpa, mea culpa, mea maxima culpa! Having thus made my confession, by way of penance I must at least try to find a way out of my dilemma, although it seems unfair to inflict the results of my self-punishment upon others.

Anyhow, I may further console myself by the reflection that it would require a writer who was at once a philosopher, a theologian, a poet, an historian, a scientist, and a Saint to handle my theme adequately—and as such a paragon only appears every five or ten centuries, lesser writers must meanwhile carry on. St. Thomas Aquinas, whom not Catholics alone consider to be the greatest expositor of Catholic philosophy who has yet appeared, and who possessed most of the qualifications stated, himself condemned his whole massive body of work as worthless in comparison to the value of one flash of the apprehension of Reality granted him in ecstasy. And after that he wrote no more. However, St. Thomas himself, I think, would never have granted that what he wrote possessed no relative value. It is part and parcel of the Catholic view of life that a man's perfection in anything is unattainable in the world of space and time; yet every man's chief duty is to search after, and strive toward, the perfect. Therefore, St. Thomas' work had of course a relative though not an absolute value in aiding other minds as well as his own to attain to a Catholic view of life, which in turn leads on (if it be truly discerned and faithfully followed) to the Catholic way of life: which in turn leads on to the full possession of life itself. So highly does the Church regard the work of St. Thomas that his book lay side by side with the Gospels on the altar at the Council of Trent. Therefore, there may be some value in the hasty, superficial sketch of a journalist, treating the same subject, at no matter what distance from the plane of the high masters of the schools. Possibly it may indicate something of the truth—at least crudely point to where truth lies—even if it cannot reveal it or define it.

Such a journalist—the present writer—in attempting such a task must, however, stick closely to the terms of his editors' instructions, so far as they can be made compatible with his own limitations of knowledge and of the powers of expression. What they have asked for is "a presentation of a view of life by a modern Catholic." They are even more explicit when they say that their hope is that each contributor to the symposium will "expound his attitude and outlook in terms of his personal development and take occasion to indicate what he regards as the most pressing problems of the future." Moreover, only writers of the younger generation are to be admitted to the symposium, those "whose views are in our judgment making a difference in the intellectual climate of the country;" but for the purposes of the symposium the "younger generation is regarded as a state of mind, not a chronological age." Ah, perhaps this part of the invitation was really what was chiefly responsible for my rashness in accepting it. Irresistible was its appeal to the vanity of one who began writing his views of life more than forty years ago!

Still, putting my personal vanity to one side (with difficulty), I can agree with my editors that the exposition of a Catholic's view of life could and indeed should be included among the utterances of the younger generation. "I have come that ye may have life everlasting," said the One Who wrote nothing, save in the desert sand, but Whose life and words founded all the schools of Catholic philosophy, and, again: "Except ye become as little children ye shall not enter into the kingdom of heaven," which kingdom is precisely that everlasting life. And my own experience of Catholicism is summed up chiefly in the ever-growing apprehension of its indefectible vitality. Moreover, even for those who are farthest from acceptance of its claims, there are few social phenomena of our day more obvious— and perhaps none more worthy of being studied by thinking men—than the contemporary activity, the youthful vigor, of Catholicism, in all its phases. From the many proofs of this statement, certain ones are preëminently significant, such as, first, the renewal of the persecution of the Church; second, the revival of philosophic thought and of creative artistry among Catholics; third, the challenge of the Church to the predominant economic system of the world; finally, its coming to the rescue of mankind from the threatened slavery of men to the tyranny of impersonal forces—those of the Absolutist State more particularly, so far as exterior struggles are concerned, but essentially to save man from that universal suicide of humanity threatened by the growth of the denial of the immortal, personal soul of the individual. For man ceases to be man—

the Catholic holds—if he kills his soul, which is his link with God. For God is life.

Now, for me, life is without meaning or value unless I myself, personally, consciously as an individual, cannot only participate in its experience now, but can go on doing so for ever. Useless to talk to me about the present value of human life, or the future development of mankind, unless I—I, myself, separate and distinguished from all other units of the mass of humanity—can be assured of my present identity as myself—unique and incapable by my nature of being fused in any mass—and of my future and indestructible persistence as myself. For this is what I understand to be a Catholic view of life; anyhow, it is the only one that I can write about as an individual Catholic.

Therefore, I cannot help but conform (as best I may) to my editors' instruction to deal with my subject quite personally. I do indeed believe that what I say for myself also at least roughly represents what all Catholics believe, and, of course, what the Church justifies us in believing. Were it otherwise, of course, I would be no Catholic; at least, I would be no member of the visible Church, and to be a faithful member of that visible Church is the whole effort of my philosophy. For to balance, nay, to complement, what I have so egotistically proclaimed as my belief in myself as an individual—and the supreme value of that belief to me—I must with equal emphasis confess my belief in my participation, as one item among myriads, in a corporate—indeed a more than merely corporate fashion, in a truly organic—common life: the life of the Church, which is the body of Christ. No metaphor is this. It is the dim, stammering, utterly relative formulation of an absolute truth which words are too powerless and limited to express, but which such words as those said every day by every priest at his Mass as he mingles water and wine in the chalice before the miracle of consecration, symbolize more explicitly than any other words I know—the, *"Deus, qui humanae,"* etc.; "O God, Who in a marvelous manner didst create and ennoble human nature, and still more marvelously hast renewed it, grant that, by the mystical union of this water and wine, we may be made partakers of His divinity, Who vouchsafed to become partaker of our humanity, Jesus Christ, Thy Son, our Lord; Who liveth and reigneth with Thee in the unity of the Holy Ghost, one God, world without end."

The one (and that one myself) in and among the Many who yet are One—now and here imperfectly One, both individually and collectively: but with perfect fulfilment of that mystery of individuality-unity certain to be achieved by all who can win their way to it: such, so it seems to me, is the fundamental point from which I may best attempt to sketch my view of life.

In such a view, considering myself both individually and corporately and organically, and looking forth (from my two eyes, as from an observation tower—the windows dim and dirty, the tower itself not high, and set on no mountain top of vision but in the midst of the valley of tears, and pretty shaky, and much battered by the storms of more than half a century), but looking forth as well as I can, what is my view of life? Can the attempt to express it make any difference in the intellectual climate of our country?

Let me hope—indeed, I pray (through St. Thomas Aquinas, Lamp of Christian philosophy, and St. Francis de Sales, Patron of Catholic writers, and St. Therese of Lisieux, the miracle worker) that if not what I say, anyhow, the corporate influence of Catholicism may have some beneficent effect upon that climate. For while I doubt very much that even with the intercession of those mighty spirits what I may write will have the effect so generously attributed to it, of this I am sure, and only that assurance justifies my attempt—namely, that unless the influence of the Catholic view of life grows powerfully, nay, unless it increases even to predominance in America, the intellectual climate will become so devitalized that anything like a civilization consonant with man's true nature will be impossible of attainment.

For it seems to me that our prevailing climate has become saturated with the debilitating, illusion-breeding philosophies of the negation, even the denial, of man. The attack upon personality, based upon the loss of faith in the spiritual realities of God and the individual souls of men, have thrown multitudes of minds back exclusively upon man's instinct (spiritual in its source) to seek unity; and in place of the Christian brotherhood of mankind and the Fatherhood of God, they now place their faith and their hope in the possibilities of mass-life. Such minds dream of the attainment, in some far-off period of time, in a world mastered so far as all natural forces are concerned, by man's corporate intelligence, of some sort of universal mass-happiness, economic mass-security and plenty, national and international peace.

Well, no such Utopias interest me. None is good enough. All are too mediocre. The ideal is itself so grossly bourgeois (in the sense in which Nicholas Berdyaev uses the term) that it disgusts me. I agree with the Communist (who agrees with the Pope) that our present economic system is abominable—but the Communist conception of life as it could be lived (or as, according to that philosophy, it eventually must be lived), even granted that I were alive when it was achieved, would bore me to hell. But, anyhow, as I have already confessed, no future life, no matter how glorious or joyful or intense or beautiful, in which I cannot play a personal, conscious part, is worth while working for—*as an end in itself*.

I am perfectly willing to work for a better and healthier and happier world for people today and for posterity as well, however, and so does the Catholic Church (she has been on that job now for twenty centuries), provided the human beings for whom I work are not to be spiritually mutilated by the asphyxiation of their personal souls. Anyhow, they cannot be whole and happy and enjoy beauty and work and love—above all, they cannot enjoy love, either human or divine—if they are cripples, as they would be were their consciousness of the rights of their personalities smothered by false philosophies, which are now being implemented by tyrannical educational and political systems. Something would always be missed, by such degraded beings, in no matter what approximation of Utopia they might reach; so painfully, so continuously, at last so desperately missed that no Utopia could stand the spiritual strain. Meanwhile, however, masses of men are being polarized toward such a goal; others are being regimented into lesser but almost as objectionable experiments in mass-unity in the various Fascist, or National-Socialist schools of thought; all because Western liberalism, which has held society together perilously, is unmistakably dying, corrupted by laissez-faire economics, and by a philosophy of liberty which lacks a true major premise, since it is not based upon faith in God, from Whose existence, with all that it implies, alone can man's liberty be correctly deduced.

Is there any probability that men will turn again to a philosophy which the Catholic Church could accept; from which philosophy social systems could be developed which would be more acceptable to men both as individuals and as coöperating, unified beings, than the system which has crashed, or the Communism or the Fascisms or the absolute State dominations which are contending for power in the present chaos?

II

Before I attempt to express my guess (it can of course be no more than that) let me return to the first article of my instructions before attempting to justify it; let me go back to myself (Walt Whitman's "single, solitary person") and become sufficiently autobiographical to furnish my personal grounds for holding such a view. My editors have asked for it—for my "attitude and outlook in terms of personal development."

People write and speak about "born Catholics," and, in the sense they intend, I am one. But the expression is wholly incorrect. Nobody has ever been, or ever can be, born a Catholic. People are born into the races, and once a Chinese or a Negro, or a member of the white race, you are always one. You may be an Englishman, a Frenchman, or an American by birth; but you can change your nationality. You cannot, however, become a Catholic unless or until you are baptized, and the point is of major importance in any consideration of Catholicism, and the Catholic view of life. For in the sacrament of baptism—so Catholics hold—you are given in addition to the natural life which all enter into in their mothers' wombs, a supernatural, spiritual life; and, in addition to your racial and national status, you are given the status of incorporation into the super-racial, super-national union of men and women which in its totality is the universal Catholic Church—the Body of Christ. You may leave that Church, if you will, just as you may leave your nation, but while you are in it—and after a separation, if you return—you are a living unit in a living organism, a cell, so to speak, in a body, which lives by virtue of a life-force wholly separate and distinct from the life-force which unites the members of a race, or the less absolute life-force which holds together the members of a nation. Now, not only is the life-force which unites Catholics in the Church of its nature unique; it also—and this is the fundamental point of the Catholic view of life—is absolutely superior in the hierarchy of values to all other values. It is supreme in its claims. It is above all the (so-called) laws of nature, and the laws of man, proceeding, as also they do (the laws of nature absolutely, the laws of man relatively and imperfectly) from one common source: the will of God; but always holding the primacy which the spiritual of necessity possesses over the material, the absolute over the contingent.

I do not attempt to offer proofs for, or arguments even in support of my own acceptance of, the truth of this statement;

I simply lay it down as a personal expression of the belief held by all Catholics. As for myself, I hold that I entered into possession of my part in this spiritual life through baptism into the Catholic Church; and that I believe myself now to possess it again after an interval in my life of some twenty years during which time I was devoid of this faith.

During some forty odd years, then, after about my fifteenth year—when there occurred the break in the Faith into which I was inducted in my infancy and very sketchily educated in during my boyhood—I have lived for twenty years outside of the Catholic life, and twenty years and more within its conscious acceptance (I will not attempt to describe how imperfectly). Those years were passed in the United States, with sundry journeys, but no residence, elsewhere, to many parts of the world. None of them were spent in schools. A few were passed in various occupations, generally of a physically laborious type: errand boy, shop clerk, warehouse porter, package wrapper, berry picker, etc.; by far the most of these years, however, being passed as a newspaper reporter, magazine contributor and editor, and writer of books. Those latter tasks took me for longer or shorter periods to many parts of the country; they necessarily entailed experiences of many classes and varieties of American life. These years and all their experiences, and above all that part in them which was even more personal than the contacts established by my work, whether as a writer or otherwise—I mean my own deeper life-events, and life-probings, my love-live, my thought-life, sickness and the shadow of death, and the death of friends and loved ones—thus divided into the two parts of my Catholic and non-Catholic point of view, constitute the stuff out of which I would extract this essay.

I mention these things for the purpose of indicating the fact that this purely personal view is not wholly extracted from the pages of books. I have of course—as who has not?—read heaps of books, and what I have read is for good or evil (like all other happenings in life) part of my very soul, but I believe that other experiences, more poignantly penetrative than anything to be found in any books were also more important in giving me my view of life—my own conception of that science of the totality of all things, which is Cardinal Mercier's definition of philosophy.

At any rate, the outcome of these experiences ended my twenty years' self-exclusion from that participation in the supernatural life which I hold to be that which truly distinguishes a fully human life—an integrated human life—from all other orders of life on earth. During the interregnum, I had been deprived of that without which all other values by comparison are inferior, and hence without power to satisfy mankind's ineluctable craving for life—fulfilment through the complete development and progress of his intellectual nature. Recovering it, I knew myself again to be in possession of a view of life which showed me a way of life that led toward union with life itself. Moreover, I came to believe it to be the one and only view of life which fully corresponded to the ultimate desires not merely of myself but of all men. It was quintessentially personal and also absolutely universal. Men cannot, I hold, go further than to reach what I reached, namely, the harmony of Reason and Faith in living Catholicism. They can, indeed, and in fact must, go ever farther and farther within and upward *in* Catholicism when they reach it, for its comprehension and its apprehension will vary from the point of the slightest possible beginning of that life in any individual up to the highest incandescence of sanctity in the most perfect of all the Saints, but other than the Catholic philosophy there is none that corresponds fully to mankind's need for living truth, though all philosophies contain intimations of that truth.

Which is why the line of Catholic research into the mysteries of life and of the endless effort of Catholic thinkers to employ reason as the instrument of that research—though intuitive insight may be chiefly relied upon to illuminate the process—

goes backward from the point of the Incarnation to find and to assimilate all of truth that was known to and expounded by Jew or Greek or Hindu or Chinese from the beginning of human record or the dawn of human tradition. And it is also why Catholic philosophy today is casting about through the work of many minds to learn to examine, to test all the discoveries or the experiments of thinkers who do not consciously accept the Catholic position but who may, and often do, support or expand the grasp of that system upon the unchanging primary truths.

Putting the matter in another way, I am convinced that all the possible answers to the primary mysteries of life, when they correspond faithfully to the highest conceptions of truth held by those who give the answers, constitute all our philosophies —which in turn are what men transform collectively or individually into their social systems and social behavior. Moreover, I believe that all such answers to the everlasting questions of life can be reduced to two great classes, no matter how almost infinitely various the answers may seem to be through differences of expression, or the degrees of personal mental power in apprehension and expression, on the part of those who answer. Into one of the classes fall all the answers which begin with, and are deduced from, a belief in a supernatural spiritual Supreme Being; uncreated, self-existent, the Source, the Creative First Cause: God; secondly, all other answers, whether agnostic, pantheistic, materialistic, or atheistic, which doubt or deny the existence of a transcendental God. The first class of answers, again, can be divided into two main divisions; one, the full Catholic Faith; the other category embracing the expressions of all other forms of belief in a supernatural, transcendent Deity, ranging from those forms of Christianity closest to Catholicism, to those farthest away from it which still come within the definition of belief in a transcendent God incarnated in Jesus Christ. The answers to the question of what Catholicism is, again, may be divided into precisely the number (whatever at any time it may happen to be) of living Catholics—*so far as the expression of the answers is concerned;* but all the answers would first of all agree in saying: "Catholicism is what the Catholic Church says it is, and cannot be other than that—but this is what I understand it to be; I intend by what I say to affirm the teaching of the Church; if I am wrong, I stand ready to be corrected by the Church; which cannot be wrong."

My answer, therefore, is as follows: Catholicism is the belief that the absolute, transcendental Reality, the self-existent One Being, Who in a mystery beyond all human comprehension is three Persons, Father, Son and Holy Ghost, without division of His unity as One Being, was incarnated in the man Jesus Christ, Who established the Catholic Church, which Church constitutes the living Body of Christ on earth, which will exist until the end of time, into which Church all human beings are called to incorporate themselves; and furthermore, that the Church teaches those truths the acceptance and practice of which lead men to the fulfilment of the true purpose of human life: the eternal happiness of men in fulfilling the glory of God.

Believing this, I turn to the Church for the answers to those primary questions—Who am I? Where did I come from? Why am I here? And I understand the Church to tell me that I am the creature, the child, of God; that I came into being as the product of His will; that I am here to serve His will, with my will, which is free to serve or not to serve; and that by serving I can win complete and unending life-fulfilment in joy: if I refuse to serve Him, I self-condemn myself to endless death-in-life. And so of all other human beings.

Books without end contain the amplifications and implications of this belief; I cannot add to their number. I simply put down (however crudely and insufficiently) what I deem to be the central point of it all, and pass on to apply it, as best I may, to the contemporary American scene, in the general hope that what I say may play its part in the scheme of this symposium. For what I believe is also believed by some twenty to twenty-five millions of other Americans, and by some three hundred and fifty millions of people throughout the world. It profoundly affects whole nations, and considerable parts of all Western nations, and is gaining marked headway among Asians and Africans. It is expounded by many able philosophers; it motivates the work of an increasing number of artists; it has consequences in the arenas of politics and economics, and, in fact, of all social questions of the most profound and far-reaching kind. Therefore, no matter how fantastic or incredible it may seem to those who deny it, or combat it, as the opium of the masses, or scorn it as the absinthe of a few peculiar individuals, it cannot help but affect, in our editors' striking phrase, the intellectual climate of the country. Moreover, whether it be poison, as Lenin taught his followers to think; or the true bread and wine of humanity, as its believers hold; patently it is increasing its influence, here and throughout the world. The time when it could be regarded as the mere dwindling remnants of a dying system that once had played a great part in human affairs has passed. As I have already said, few of the social phenomena of our present epoch are more striking than the resurgence of Catholicism.

What then, holding this view of life, do I see as I turn to our contemporary American scene, in connection with (for it cannot be separated from) the world scene in general?

III

First, in spite of my conviction that Catholic Christianity, through the Catholic Church, holds and dispenses those truths which alone can provide the data of a true philosophy—which true philosophy can alone furnish the principles upon which any political or economic system tolerable to human beings may be developed, for as men think about ultimate things (and that seems to me to be philosophy), so will their institutions arise to actualize their thinking—in spite of this conviction, I say, I must record my further belief that the hold which Catholicism possesses upon mankind in general was never weaker than it is today. You may ask me how I reconcile this opinion with what I have said above concerning the contemporary resurgence of Catholicism? My answer is that the resurgence is mainly confined to an elite among Catholics, and outside of the Church is affecting only a minority of intellectuals—to use a detestable yet now indispensable term. I agree with a far more competent Catholic writer on this subject, Christopher Dawson, who in a recent essay says: "In every department of life traditional principles have been shaken and discredited, and we do not yet know what is going to take their place. There are those who hold . . . that our culture has entered the first stage of an inevitable decay, while others believe that we are only beginning to realize the possibilities of modern science and that we are about to see the rise of a new social order which will far transcend anything that the world has known. One thing is certain—the old order is dead; and with the old order has passed away that traditional acceptance of the truth of Christianity and that general acceptance of Christian moral principles, which even in the nineteenth century still retained so strong a hold on the minds of men."

So, too, it seems to me, does a man like Jacques Maritain think. In a conversation between him and Nicholas Berdyaev, the Russian Orthodox philosopher, and Carl Schmidt, the German Catholic, he is on record as anticipating that Catholicism was on its way to being expressed by intense yet small and widely diffused clusters and points, so to speak, like stars in the night of a universal eclipse of the sun. However that may turn out to be, it is scarcely to be denied that the Church has lost its hold upon the masses of men, or holds them even in countries traditionally Catholic, only in minorities. In the United States, it is a very weak minority indeed, for here, perhaps almost more than anywhere else, it not only works in an atmosphere greatly devitalized by philosophies and mores, alien to its spirit, when not wholly opposed to it, but here, too, it is

burdened with a frightful load of mediocrity and Laodicean-
ism—that spirit which is neither hot nor cold, which is a worse
enemy to Christianity than its exterior foes. Here it is difficult
to discern the presence of any considerable body of the elite, but
it is precisely here that it is most easy to mistake the situation, for a judgment here depends upon what is meant by "an
elite." Certainly, I do not mean by it merely a group of intellectuals—philosophers, artists, organizers, leaders, executives—
whether ecclesiastical or lay. Of course, the Church needs such
an elite, as she always has needed it; she needs one even more
than any other society devoted to the higher interests of this
world needs such groups—even as the mass-movements, indeed,
particularly those, require them. But the highest, most powerful,
most efficient elite of Catholicism is not necessarily to be found
among its philosophers, artists, organizers and executives—it
is constituted by the truly holy men and women of the Church.
Sometimes they are found among the intellectual elite; but
only when that is so, or when the intellectual elite ordinates
its work to the ideal of sanctity and serves the purpose of the
Church to place first things first (and holiness is above all other
human ends), only then does Catholicism flourish, only then
does it draw the multitude to follow it.

Now, in the United States, while I think it is entirely true
to say that the moral life of the mass of Catholics is good and
admirable, how far the powerful life of high sanctity is being
cultivated—the life of contemplation, of the willed endeavor to
achieve consciously the highest possible degree of self-union
with the Divine—it is impossible to know. Yet upon this all
depends. Never has Catholicism been successfully positive in
action without the presence among Catholics of those centers—
those dynamos, if one may use a mechanical figure—of spiritual
forces constituted by the souls of ascetics and mystics. Many
of them remain all their lives unknown save perhaps to a
handful of people. Others shine out like flaming lamps of light
and heat and energy. The very fact that Catholicism in general

is today so puissant would seem to be a proof that in many hidden places and in obscure individuals—many of them perhaps unlettered and totally unconcerned with "social movements" of any sort—there is pulsating the same force that created Benedictine monasticism, which civilized Europe in the Dark Ages; or Franciscanism, which transformed feudalism; or Dominicanism, which reinspired the Catholic intellect and gave us St. Thomas Aquinas. It may be so. In the United States, there has been a marked increase of the monasteries devoted to the contemplative life. The liturgical movement— so intimately connected with the mystical life of the Church— is likewise growing. Perhaps the true salt which savors and preserves the higher life of man is being scattered amongst us. It may be so.

However that may be, what there is of Catholicism in the United States, whether crescent or declining, faces a situation (or so I believe) of the uttermost gravity. In order to make the best struggle possible to help the nation win its way toward conditions of life consonant with the dignity, liberty, and independence of the individual, and also with the principle of the fullest possible coöperation of individuals for the common good of all, perforce the Church here, as elsewhere, must turn to the philosophies not explicitly Catholic, or which are opposed to her principles, not only to combat them, but, as she has done in all other ages, also to draw from them those elements of the truth, or those modes of expressing truth, which all of them contain. So, too, with the proposed systems of economics or of politics (or, perhaps, rather one should say the politics of economics, today, for the economic problem is everywhere paramount), all of which stem from the philosophies—from the thinking of men about life: their efforts to understand it, to explain it, to adjust themselves, if possible, to its antimonies and its mysteries.

If Catholicism were entirely isolated from other forces, the prospect of any improvement in our intellectual climate would be bleak indeed. But Catholicism (again I must insist upon this because of the practical importance of the fact) has many allies, even among forces which profess to fight its organized system, the Church. Those allies are those men, and the institutions formed by their thought, who know in their heart of hearts that God is, and who are determined to unite their humanity to His divinity. Their enemy, and the enemy of Catholicism, is that spirit which is revealed, but not in its complete horror of desolation and destructiveness, in words like the following quotation used as a motto on the title page of a recent book: [1]

"To penetrate to the heart of a civilization we ought to begin with a knowledge of its gods. And in the very end that is what we come back to.

"The creation of the gods is the most natural, the most secret, the slowest, the loftiest, of the works of man. It is the supreme achievement of his profound experiences. It is the mysterious fruit of minds in the mass."

All philosophies which accept that view of man as the maker of his gods are those which tend to devitalize and even to poison the intellectual climate, so that under their influence men become spiritually and mentally stupid, and are separated into an inchoate dust of degraded, disunited atoms tossed hither and yon by those purely brutal forces which racial, nationalistic, or class instincts become when torn away from the control of the higher force of brotherhood-in-the-fatherhood-of-God.

It is against that spirit which the spirit of man must contend as never before as the crisis of our age draws every human soul into the conflict. For man is not integrally man without the knowledge that the truth concerning him and the gods is precisely the opposite of the lie—or the illusion—which the words of the quotation express. Man does not create his God: God created man in His own image, and the rediscovery of that truth on the part of those who have lost it, or who have been robbed

---

[1] *The Rainbow Bridge, a Study of Paganism,* by John Strong Newberry.

of it, is the supreme task of philosophy today. The battle is already raging. There are strange shiftings and puzzling maneuvers among the fighters; but the final expression of my personal view is that around the Catholic Church the whole war must center. It must, because She was divinely established for that very purpose.